My "Everything" File®

Everything my Loved Ones Need to Know about Me

Created by

Jerrold E. Slutzky, J.D., CFP®
Attorney at Law
Slutzky Law Firm

853 Main Street, Suite A
Safety Harbor, FL 34695
(727) 475-6200 Phone
(727) 474-0157 Fax

20719 Sterlington Drive, Suite 103
Land O' Lakes, FL 34638
(813) 909-1515 Phone
(813) 949-1105 Fax

www.SlutzkyLawFirm.com

Published by Richter Publishing LLC www.richterpublishing.com

Book Cover Design: Jessie Alarcon

Editors: Katharina Jung, Monica San Nicolas, Margarita Martinez & Natalie Meyer

Cover Photo Credit: Christina Schemkes of Through the Lens Studios in Largo, Florida

Logo Design: Kim Anton of Kick Ass GraphicsTM

ISBN -10:1-945812-22-2

ISBN-13: 978-1-945812-22-4

About the Author

Jerrold E. Slutzky, J.D., CFP® is a Florida-licensed Attorney at Law and owner of The Slutzky Law Firm, which focuses primarily on **Estate Planning Services** (wills, trusts, durable powers of attorney, health care surrogate designations, living wills, probate, guardianships, etc.) and **Business Legal Services** (startups, buy-sell agreements, drafting of legal documents, contract negotiations, succession planning, and general business law, counseling, and advice).

Jerry received a Bachelor of Science Degree in Finance from the University of Illinois at Urbana-Champaign, and a Juris Doctor Degree in Law from the John Marshall Law School in Chicago, Illinois. In 1977, Jerry obtained his Illinois law license and opened his own law firm in Chicago, which focused on small business law and family financial matters such as estate, retirement, and tax planning, in addition to many other areas of the law.

In 1988, he and his family decided to move away from the Chicago winters to the Florida sunshine. He placed his Illinois law license on inactive status and pursued a career in the financial services industry in the Tampa Bay area. In that capacity, he obtained his Series 7 (General Securities), Series 63 (Uniform State Exam), Series 65

(Investment Advisor Representative), and Florida insurance licenses (Life, Variable Life, and Health). In addition, in 1999, Jerry obtained his designation as a CERTIFIED FINANCIAL PLANNER.™

Jerry continues to provide financial planning and investment advisory services to clients as a registered representative and investment advisor representative.

Although he had previously retired from the practice of law in Illinois, he yearned to be able to use all his knowledge and experience, in both legal as well as financial matters, to better serve the needs of his clients.

Inspired by his father, who retired from the practice of law at 96 years of age, Jerry passed the Florida Bar examination, obtained his Florida law license, and resumed the practice of law as a business separate and apart from his investment advisory and financial planning practice. He limits his legal practice to matters pertaining to estate planning, probate, business law, and general legal counsel and advice.

In addition, with the combination of over 40 years of experience in the legal and investment professions, he also serves on arbitration panels in adjudicating investor disputes before the Financial Industry Regulatory Authority (FINRA), the largest independent regulator for all securities firms doing business in the United States.

When not in the office or out giving educational lectures, Jerry is both an active supporter and performer of community theater in the Tampa Bay area, and can often be found performing on stage in one Broadway musical or another. It has been said that "every lawyer is a frustrated actor," and Jerry's avocation lends credence to that statement.

In addition, both Jerry and his wife, Dr. Helen Techler, an audiologist, enjoy ballroom dancing, and, as he promised Helen when he proposed to her, he looks forward to spinning her around the dance floor for the rest of their lives.

Disclaimers

Each person's goals, needs, personal circumstances, and legal situation are unique to that individual. In addition, laws, taxes, regulations, and what may be appropriate to one's unique circumstances are constantly changing and can vary significantly from person to person, day to day, and state to state.

Therefore, nothing discussed in this book is intended to be, nor shall be construed, to provide legal, tax, investment, or insurance advice. Rather, the subjects discussed in this book are intended to encourage and inspire you, the reader, to consider your own personal situation and circumstances and how the subjects discussed in the book may relate to you, to give you a basic understanding of the subjects and enable you to ask better questions when you seek the appropriate guidance and advice from your own legal, tax, insurance, and financial advisors.

Any references to websites or services mentioned throughout this questionnaire are provided for informational purposes only. **My Everything File, LLC**, and its author, **Jerrold E. Slutzky**, do not endorse, recommend, or validate the accuracy of the contents contained in said websites, and do not make any representations or warranties about said websites' safety and freedom from viruses, malware, cookies, etc.

Jerrold E. Slutzky's investment advisory and financial planning practice is an entity which is completely separate, distinct, and apart from the law practice of and legal services provided by Jerrold E. Slutzky d/b/a Slutzky Law Firm.

Any individual or organization who becomes a client of the investment advisory and financial planning practice of Jerrold E. Slutzky has not created an attorney-client relationship, and is under absolutely no obligation to use his legal services. Any individual or organization who becomes a client of the law practice of Jerrold E. Slutzky d/b/a Slutzky Law Firm has not created an investment advisory relationship, and is under absolutely no obligation to use his investment advisory and financial planning services.

An attorney-client relationship is created **ONLY** with a formal letter of engagement signed by the client and attorney and payment of the required retainer.

Credits

I would like to thank the following individuals for their review, recommendations, and content contained in some sections of this book.

Diane Daniels of MedicareNation.com regarding the section on Medicare Supplemental Policies.

Steven Adler of My Memory Lane, and Jim Webb of The Webb Works regarding the questions to ask in making one's own legacy video for future generations.

Sharon Toston of Command Your Clutter for her review and comments regarding the chapter on "Getting Organized."

Russ Haft of Mylennium.com, along with Everplans.com, regarding the chapter on digital assets, having a digital executor, and creating your own digital legacy.

Amber Laake-Copobianco of Laake Financial Services for insights regarding the section on homeowner and automobile insurance.

David Kuhnke of Prime Group Insurance for insights regarding the different types of commercial insurance available for one's business.

LifeQuest Anatomical, LLC for information regarding donating your body to science.

Everplans.com for content in the "Your Funeral" chapter regarding cremation and home burials.

Dignity Memorial for their funeral-planning materials regarding planning, bereavement, guidance, and memorial services and products.

And to all my investment and estate-planning clients, whose real-life stories have provided me with many additional need-to-know details to include in the questionnaire.

Dedication

This book is dedicated to my family, who above all, have helped to shape and guide me along my journey of life:

To my father, Irving Slutzky, who just celebrated his 100th birthday, and has always been my hero, my inspiration, and my shining role model of how a man should live his life as an excellent father, grandfather, great-grandfather, son, and brother.

To my mother, Shirley Slutzky, 96, whose loving and nurturing nature helped instill love, caring, and compassion into my soul, and whose artistic and musical talents, and hilarious sense of humor I was fortunate enough to inherit.

To my daughters, Jada and Jenna Slutzky, who, as young children, enabled me to reawaken the awe of discovery of everything in life through their eyes, and now as grown women, continue to inspire me to be the best father and grandfather I can be as I watch them pursue their own dreams.

To my first grandson, Elumin Sharman, not yet one year of age, for being the next link in our family chain, linking us from the beginning of time to the end of time. I look forward to seeing the man you will become, and intend to enjoy being a part of your journey along the way.

To my brothers, Jay Slutzky and Scott Slutzky (who was taken from us far too soon), for keeping me humble, as only big brothers can do to the "baby" of the family, and to their children and grandchildren, all loving, caring individuals.

And most of all, to my beloved wife, Helen Techler, whose love, support, encouragement, humor, and endless patience enabled me to complete this book. To quote Victor Hugo in *Les Miserables*, "To love another person is to see the face of God." Through you, my love, I have seen the face of God!

My "Everything" File®

Table of Contents

Introduction
My Own True Story

I really thought that my car would stop skidding before it hit the tree!

I was wrong!

It was an overcast day, and I was driving down I-75 from Tampa to Sarasota.

Knowing I sometimes have a bit of a lead foot, I had set my cruise control at 70 miles per hour so I wouldn't exceed the speed limit. It started to drizzle, and then started raining a bit harder, and I turned on the windshield wipers. The rain increased its intensity, and I had to turn the wipers to maximum speed.

Suddenly, the skies seemed to open, and it really started pouring—the kind of rain so heavy that you can't even see past the front of your car.

I tapped on the brake pedal to disengage the cruise control and slow down. Ironically, I had forgotten about an email I had received a couple of months earlier warning about the dangers of using cruise control in the rain. If you didn't know, you're not supposed to use your cruise control when it's raining. Please learn from my experience.

So, when I hit the brakes, I discovered that my car had already started hydroplaning, and found myself sliding sideways off the interstate at 70 miles per hour, onto the grass and toward some trees separating northbound and southbound I-75.

I generally don't use profanity, but I'll admit that a colorful word or two may have escaped my lips this one time.

The car was slowly turning out of control as it slid on the wet grass, and I saw I was sliding toward a bunch of trees at a pretty good clip, and that thankfully, if I hit one of the trees, the passenger side of my car was going to take the brunt of the collision.

I did not see my life pass in front of my eyes, so I felt reasonably sure this wasn't my time to go. I remained surprisingly calm and kept my hands on the wheel. I just had the surreal feeling of moving in slow motion as the car slid closer toward the trees. I felt the car losing momentum as I was skidding sideways and actually thought there was a chance I would come to a stop before I even reached the trees. But, just in case, I turned my head away from the probable point of impact, so I might avoid getting my face showered with glass.

The car came to a complete stop, and I thought to myself, "Whew, I did stop in time!" But when I looked toward the passenger side of the car, I did a double take when I realized the side of the car was smashed in, and when I looked up, so was the roof!

I had no recollection of the impact, but apparently, I had hit the tree sideways with enough force for the momentum to cause the car to rise up on its passenger-side wheels and smash in the roof and then plop back down to the ground! I had no memory of any crashing sound, no memory of the impact, and surprisingly, I felt no pain.

I did a rapid body check, assuming I must have hit my head and been knocked unconscious, but I felt no pain, saw no blood, and miraculously, I couldn't find any evidence of a head injury, or any other injury for that matter, other than a general tightness that felt as if I had worked out a bit too strenuously at the gym. I must have momentarily blacked out during the moment of impact.

I took a moment to give sincere thanks to the "person" upstairs who had protected me, another "thank you" to all the safety engineers who had designed a car that had spared me injuries, and yet more thanks to whoever had designed the median between the northbound and southbound lanes, which prevented me from sliding into oncoming traffic.

I was somewhat surprised that the car hadn't flipped over and that none of the air bags had deployed. As I looked at the passenger seat, I was thankful that I had had no passengers in the car with me, because I didn't believe a passenger would have survived the crash.

I looked toward the interstate and saw people running toward my car to make sure I was all right. One of them had already called 911 on his cell phone, and a state trooper and ambulance had already been dispatched. I assured them that I was fine, and they left with my thanks for their caring enough to stop to see if I was okay.

I stood in the rain, which had now slowed to a drizzle, and looked at the car. There was no question that the car was a total wreck, a fact that would be confirmed by my insurance company just a week later. I keep some large garbage bags in the car that I spread on the back seat to keep it dry when I take my dog to the beach. So, I started loading the contents of the car and trunk into the bags so nothing would get too wet or get taken away when the wrecker came to remove my car from the scene of the crash.

A state trooper came and filled out his report. I had not been drinking, and thankfully, I wasn't given a ticket. I later found out that the rain had caused a lot of accidents on I-75, and that less than a mile away, there had been one much more severe than mine and with serious injuries; I reminded myself just how lucky I had been.

The ambulance came and the crew checked me for injuries. My blood pressure was slightly elevated (big surprise!), and they wanted me to go to the hospital for observation. Knowing I felt fine, I declined (probably a foolish choice, considering the slight tightening of my back and neck muscles). But I was sure I was okay, and it turned out that I was correct, so they left. About a year later, I started having back pains and had to see a chiropractor, who attributed my pain to the accident.

Thankfully, I was able to reach one of my good friends on my cell phone, who dropped what he was doing and immediately came to get me (a true friend indeed, especially considering I was 45 minutes away).

While I was waiting for him, I took some pictures of my wrecked car on my cell phone. I knew the pictures would be a good reminder of how lucky I had been and that they would help me remember to periodically take a moment to appreciate the many blessings in my life!

Then the wrecker came, pulled my broken car out of the trees, and loaded it onto the truck's platform. The driver gave me a card indicating where the car would be stored, pending an inspection by the insurance adjuster, and drove away.

Thankfully, the state trooper stayed with me until my friend arrived to pick me up. As I waited in the back seat of the trooper's car, I counted more blessings for being able to walk away from the crash without any injury, for having good insurance (both auto and health), for not having received a ticket, for having a cell phone (and the technology that created it), and for having a friend both willing and able to drop what he was doing and pick me up.

And as the initial shock wore off, I started thinking about what might have happened had I been killed or seriously injured and hospitalized. Both of my daughters were now grown and living in Chicago and I had no relatives closer than Boca Raton, 4 hours away. I was isolated, and nobody would have even known who I was other than from the contents of my wallet.

I had followed up on an idea I had heard, which recommended adding the acronym "ICE" (In Case of Emergency) as a name or contact entry in your cell phone contact list so if you are unconscious, the police or health care providers can quickly find the name and phone number of someone to contact, rather than try to guess who they should call out of the hundred or so names probably stored on your cell phone. It's a good idea, but if a passcode is required to gain access to your contact list, it may not work. For iPhone users, I understand there is an option to add a Medical ID that is accessible without a passcode, and this allows users to enter an emergency contact as well as allergies and blood type. For Android users, several free ICE applications are available for download at the Google Play store.

Since I have a smartphone, this allows entry of a lot more information than just the phone number of someone to call. My ICE entry also has my name and address, a list of the medications I currently take, the fact that I'm not allergic to any medications, that I have asthma, the name and phone number of my primary care physician, the fact that I have a yellow Labrador retriever named Doc at my home that would need to be taken care of in my absence, and the name and phone number of a neighbor who might be able to handle that responsibility. I try to think ahead and be organized.

At the time of my accident, I had been a financial advisor in Tampa for the previous 22 years and had been an attorney for 33 years, so I knew the importance of planning for an unexpected event such as this. I knew that I had done a pretty good job at having my legal affairs in order. I had prepared my Last Will and Testament, naming my brother as my Personal Representative, as well as a Revocable Living Trust, naming him as my successor trustee. So, had I been killed, the legal documents were in place to transfer everything into my daughters' names with as little hassle as possible.

I also had prepared all the recommended "living" documents (Durable Power of Attorney, Declaration of Health Care Surrogate, Pre-Need Guardian Designation, and Living Will), which named my brother to handle my affairs if I survived the accident but was no longer capable of taking care of myself or handling my own financial, business, health-related decisions, and personal affairs.

All of my accounts and my house were either titled in the name of my trust, or had my trust named as beneficiary, which would expedite the transfer of assets to my daughters without the cost, delay, and hassle of probate.

And finally, I had a Living Will in place, directing that it was my preference that they "pull the plug" and that no heroic measures were to be taken to save my life if it appeared I was brain dead or otherwise had no chance of recovery.
I was glad I had the knowledge and experience to know what legal documents I should have in place and had actually taken the steps to prepare them. I slept well knowing my financial affairs were in order in case something like this happened.

Or at least those were my initial thoughts...for about one second. Then I thought about it all again.

My younger daughter was named as my emergency contact on my cell phone in the ICE listing. She had been living with me in Florida at the time I had drafted my estate-planning documents, but she had since moved to Chicago, which would not be much help to me in Florida in case of an emergency.

In addition, she was 19 years old at the time. While I both loved and trusted her, at that age and stage of life, I feared she was not someone with the necessary practical life experience to make rapid-fire decisions in an emergency situation, let alone make a decision whether or not to take her father off of life support. I'm sure she would have known to call my parents, my brothers, her older sister, or her mother (I trust my former wife) for guidance about what she should do, but I had never discussed any of my final wishes with her.

My brother, who was named as my attorney-in-fact under my Power of Attorney and as my successor Trustee and Personal Representative (Executor) in my Living Trust and Will, also lives in Chicago. Every year or so, I made a point of mailing him an updated list of my various bank and brokerage accounts, account numbers, phone numbers, important contacts to call, how my accounts were titled, information about my credit cards, mortgage, insurance policies, automatic payments coming out of my checking account to pay utilities, and had him as an authorized signer on my safe deposit box. I even told him where he could find my important original legal documents. With this information, he could do most of what might need to be done in my absence.

But I had never discussed other details of importance with him. He would have no idea where my important documents were located. He wouldn't know whether I had made pre-paid funeral arrangements (I hadn't); whether I have disability or long-term care insurance (I don't); that there were some items of value in my house (which one might not know had value just by looking at them); whether or not I owe money to someone (I didn't); whether or not someone owes money to me (no one does); passwords to get into important encrypted files in my computer; or the file name on my computer where the 10,000 or so family pictures are stored, along with the location of my backup disks, hard drives, and online backup storage.

The document I periodically sent him didn't provide him with the name and phone number of the other person with whom I share office space so he could notify her as to what had happened, or the landlord to whom I had to pay rent. He would have had no way of knowing who my clients were or how to let them know that something had happened to me so they could find a new financial advisor or lawyer, let alone the information that would enable him to try to sell my business to raise more money for my children.

He wouldn't know how to access my social media accounts to let my friends know something had happened to me so he could seek out whatever help and guidance they could provide to him.

He wouldn't know which bills I pay automatically out of my bank account, or how to turn off the automatic payments or renewals of subscriptions.

He wouldn't know whether I preferred to be cremated, or buried, or where I wanted my final resting place to be.

And who would take care of my dog?

So many important, but unanswered, questions!

Asking someone to undertake such a vast responsibility is a major imposition and inconvenience to someone who already has responsibilities he must fulfill to his own family and business.

My Will doesn't specify who gets all my personal belongings and artwork. And I have a lot of "stuff!" So, who gets what? Or should there just be a giant garage sale?

My mind started racing as I began to think of all the things I hadn't previously considered writing down or discussing. Someone should know the answers to these and many, many more questions in case something happens to me.

Part of my job as a financial advisor is to help my investment clients realize the importance of having their financial affairs in order, not only their investment and bank accounts, but by having sufficient life, health, auto, disability, long term care, and other types of insurance. Part of my job as an estate-planning attorney is to help my law clients realize the importance of having their legal affairs in order through the documents that need to be drafted, the proper titling of accounts with proper beneficiary designations, and ways to protect their assets and avoid the cost and inconvenience of probate when and if that is in a client's best interest. I realized that regarding my own situation, while I had done a lot toward having all my affairs in order, there was a lot more still to be done.

I started to ask my clients and friends questions, which I will now ask you: If you were killed or seriously injured in an automobile accident today, is there somebody who knows where everything you own is located, including account numbers; names and phone numbers of your important contacts; what bills need to be paid; what medications you are taking; whether or not you have allergies; the names, addresses and phone number of your doctors; where your calendar is located for upcoming appointments; passwords to your computer and websites; and more?

If you're married, you probably assume your spouse knows the answers to all these questions. But what would happen if both of you were killed in the same car crash? Who else knows the answers to these questions? And while we're considering painful hypotheticals, do you know the answers to all these questions for your own parents?

Wouldn't you want to make your representatives' or survivors' lives a bit easier by letting them know where to find the information they would need to be able to handle everything needing to be done on your behalf, with step-by-step instructions on who to call or email first, and a list of phone numbers and email addresses for individuals who need to be contacted?

Consider all the information you don't know off the top of your head and would have to look up, such as the names and phone numbers of your minister or rabbi, children, parents, and siblings. You probably know where all this information is located, but would the person handling your funeral know where to find it all? And think of the information for which you do know the general information off the top of your head, such as the bank where your safe deposit box is located, for example. But what about the more specific, necessary information, such as the box number, the bank name, address and phone number? Who else is authorized to have access to the box, and where the key is located, etc.?

My clients and friends agreed that a single file containing all this useful information would be a very powerful tool, and encouraged me to proceed with writing this book.

I have a small Lucite statue on my desk in my office. It is a depiction of a clown riding a unicycle up a ramp while juggling about 10 balls. Everyone who sees it completely identifies with that statue as a representation of what their life sometimes feels like. We all have so many things we need to deal with in our lives on a daily basis: our children, parents, jobs, health, entertainment, finances, bills, car repair, laundry, housecleaning, and so on! It is no surprise that almost nobody finds the time to create a comprehensive list of their assets, liabilities, contact names, passwords, hiding places, preferences, memories, etc. It's hard for one to remember it all, let alone tell anyone else. And considering it's all your own stuff, if you can't remember it all, how is someone else supposed to be able to figure it out?

So, with the memory of my own car crash fresh in my mind, I set out to write this book to help others tie up as many loose ends as possible and try to provide all the information someone might need to handle their affairs. Because it is such a monumental task to get the information organized and continuously updated, most people never get around to doing it. To help with this, I have broken the important information into bite-sized pieces to make it more palatable and provide a roadmap, which will hopefully make the process a bit more organized and easier to complete.

In completing the questionnaire, remember that a "no" response to a question is as valuable to your loved ones as a "yes" response. They will know you have considered each question, and they will know what details do and do not apply to you. Hopefully, these questions will jog your memory about other matters of importance that need to be discussed with the appropriate individuals.

There will probably be some follow-up activities you will find you need to do to get your affairs in order. Perhaps you will realize the need for a Will, trust, and other living directive documents. If you already have them prepared, perhaps you will recognize the need to update them, or at least let someone know where the original documents are located.

Almost every day, someone tells me, "Oh, I know I should have a Will, and I really need to get around to it someday." Please use this book as a reminder to stop thinking about it and actually do it, so you'll have one less thing to worry about when *your* car is sliding toward a tree at 70 miles per hour!

Perhaps the questions in this book will jog your memory for forgotten assets, such as retirement accounts left behind at a previous job. For example, there was a recent court case in which a man in his second marriage forgot to change the beneficiary designation on his 401(k) plan at his former place of employment from his first wife's name to the name of his second wife. The first wife wound up inheriting all the retirement plan assets. (Note: the laws in some states have been changed since then to avoid this unfortunate scenario). Still, it is a good reminder for you to periodically review the titling of your assets as well as the beneficiary and contingent beneficiary designations.

Perhaps you will discover that consolidating some of your scattered accounts into fewer accounts will simplify your life, as well as the lives of those who will be handling your affairs for you. For example, many people have a lot of small IRA accounts scattered about at various financial institutions. Why not consolidate them into a single IRA? This book will give you many suggestions like these.

And as long as we're trying to put as many of your affairs as possible in order, should you be killed or incapacitated and unable to speak for yourself, why not create a single file that also stores your important documents, shares your favorite memories, your favorite pictures and the stories behind them, your favorite songs and recipes, pearls of wisdom you have incorporated into your life, and of course, the words of love you would want to say if you knew you would never be able to speak to your loved ones again?

Personally, I consider the entire estate-planning process to be an act of love. If you have your documents prepared and a single file that contains everything your loved ones would want and need to know in order to take care of you, your business, and your family members, they will appreciate your exhaustive efforts to compile all this information for them. They will know you cared enough to make their lives easier.

Sincerely,

Jerrold E. Slutzky, J.D., CFP®

IMPORTANT: This book is not intended to provide legal, financial, or tax advice, but rather to provide you with additional considerations you may need to create a detailed list of questions to discuss with your loved ones and to alert you to issues that should be discussed with your own legal, tax, and financial advisors.

Chapter 1
Let's Get Started

In setting out to write **My "Everything" File®,** my hope was to create a resource that goes beyond the mere listing of assets and debts, places where legal documents are stored, the names of your legal, investment, banking, and accounting advisors, and other basic information someone needs to know about you. There are many other books, magazines, websites, and resources available that will provide you with handy checklists to help you compile that basic information.

My goal behind writing **My "Everything" File®** is to provide you with a single, comprehensive place to keep the details of your ever-changing life story. You have so much information buried in your brain, not only about your past history, but about your day-to-day living experiences, that unless you provide someone with a resource that contains all this information, it will be lost forever. Much of that information may be important for the person charged with your care or finalizing your affairs to know.

This book is all about you! **My "Everything" File®** is not just about your stuff! It's a storybook about all you have accomplished, experienced, life lessons you've learned from those experiences, and yes, all the stuff you've accumulated over the years, too! There is a virtual encyclopedia of information inside your brain, and it's all about you.

And while most of that information encompasses your life memories, both good and bad, a lot of that information is about important matters that concern you and your loved ones. If you are rendered incapable of sharing that important information with others due to stroke, disability, or death, someone else is going to be handed the enormous task of figuring everything out on your behalf, and it will be during a period while experiencing high stress, worry, and grief.

Forgive this stark example, but imagine you wake up one morning, have suffered a stroke, and have lost the ability to move or speak! It happens.

We all know the important things about our own lives that one should know, such as where bank accounts are located, what bills need to be paid, and whether we have prepared a Last Will and Testament, etc. But who else knows?

Think about what you do every single day. Most of it may be described as a mundane daily routine that you do without conscious thought, thanks to years of habitual repetition.

In order to prepare for completion of your own "Everything" File, I encourage you to pay attention to the details of what you do every day from the moment you wake up to the moment you go to sleep. Keep a notepad with you and, for several days, jot down details you would want someone to know about if you couldn't tell them about it.

While some, or even most, of the details of your daily routine may not be of importance, such as what soap, toothpaste, or toilet paper you prefer, or whether you have milk and cereal instead of eggs for breakfast, it may be important that a particular brand of soap gives you dry, itchy skin, that you are lactose intolerant, that you need to take an insulin shot for your diabetes before breakfast, or that you need other medications and when you need to take them.

It may not be important that you spend a few moments each morning reading your emails and friends' Facebook postings, but it should help you realize that someone needs to know how to access your emails and social media, in case there are important messages waiting for your response, or to enable them to post an entry on your behalf about what has happened to you.

It may not be important that you like to read the investment section of the newspaper over breakfast, but it may be very important if you have an investment account with open orders to buy or sell securities. Someone needs to know not only that you have an investment account or what action needs to be taken, but also who has the legal authority to manage the account on your behalf.

You reach down to pet your dog as you leave for work. Who knows which veterinarian you use and whether or not your dog is taking any medication? Jot it down. Is the dog microchipped? Do you have a preference as to who will take care of your dog while you are incapacitated? If you are single, does somebody even know you have a dog that needs to be fed?

You get in your car to drive to work. It may not be important what gasoline you use, but use that as a reminder to jot down your driver's license information, whether you owe money on the car and, if so, to whom, and your automobile insurance carrier, including policy number and your agent's name and contact information.

When you get to the office, particularly if you own your own business, it will be worthwhile to note down the vendors from whom you buy your supplies and to whom you pay rent or mortgage, insurance, etc. Who has the legal authority to continue your business operations, deposit your receipts, and pay your bills, if you aren't there to do so? I'm certain your employees would like to know that someone else has the ability and authority to write their next paycheck and that it isn't going to bounce.

The idea of this exercise is not to overwhelm you with all the details of your life, but to spend a few days focusing on the important details of your life that someone taking care of you or your affairs would need to know about.

Several years ago, I was interviewing a prospective client whose husband had died a few weeks earlier. It turned out that he had an investment account, and the market, along with his investments, were rapidly declining in value. The financial advisor on the account had no discretion to take any action, and his wife had no legal authority to give the financial advisor instructions to take any action. She couldn't get the authority to do so until being appointed as Personal Representative of his estate—which took several weeks—and by then, the account had dropped significantly in value.

How about your banking, investments, and retirement accounts? In the past, when handling an estate, I could advise a client to watch the mail for monthly statements, so we knew we wouldn't miss an important asset or bill.

But now, consider how many companies encourage you to "go green" by taking electronic delivery of your monthly statements instead of requiring them to mail paper statements of your bank accounts to you. It is a noble cause to save a few trees, but if something happened to you, how would anyone else know that your bank account, investment account, insurance policy, etc., even exist?

Many of us have a lot of bills automatically paid out of our bank account or charged to our credit cards. Somebody needs to know how to stop these payments immediately without having to wait until they are appointed your Guardian (if you are alive) or Personal Representative (if you have died).

If you've ever had to handle the estate of a loved one who has passed away or have had to take over the financial affairs and care of a loved one who has had a stroke or dementia, you'll know it is a time consuming, laborious task, having to search through their drawers and closets, files, boxes in the garage, attic, basement, and mail in the hope of finding where they banked, kept their investments accounts, with whom they had their mortgages, loans, and credit cards, figuring out what bills had to be paid, and whether or not they had insurance coverage.

And in the back of your mind, you were always wondering if you were missing something of importance.

So, consider these questions:

Does somebody know where all your important documents are located? This includes not only your estate-planning documents such as a will, trust, durable power of attorney, health care surrogate, living will, etc., but also the location of deeds to your home, insurance policies, medical records, address books, etc.

Does somebody know your medical history, what doctors you see, which medications you are taking (including dosage) and if you are allergic to any other medications?

Does somebody know where you maintain your bank and investment accounts, your account numbers, and the name, address, and phone number of your banker and investment advisor?

Does somebody know what types of insurance policies you maintain, the account numbers, where the policies are located, when the premiums are due, and the name, address, and phone number of your insurance agent?

If you have your bank account set up to automatically pay some of your bills each month, such as your utility bills, does somebody know how to access those accounts to stop the automatic outflow of money from your accounts?

Think about everything you do online. Would somebody know about all the paid websites to which you may belong? Would they know all your passwords, have access to your social media accounts, your Netflix account, and your iTunes account? What about all those frequent flyer miles and credit card points you might have accumulated?

Would somebody know about any property you own, debts you owe, how everything is titled, and whether you have named beneficiaries on those accounts?

How about storage lockers, safe deposit boxes, or hiding places? How about retirement or other employee benefit plans at your current or former places of employment? How about assets you may be holding for someone else, or assets someone may be holding for you?

The list of questions that need to be answered is very long. As I previously mentioned, over your lifetime, you have accumulated a lot of information that someone else needs to know, should something prevent you from being able to handle your own affairs.

So, where does one start? If you're like me, you have probably accumulated boxes of old bank statements, tax returns, cancelled checks, receipts, closing documents to former real estate or investment accounts, old holiday cards, and the list goes on.

Your important and not-so-important papers tend to pile up in many different places, such as the kitchen, the bedroom, the home office, your place of work, the trunk of your car, and pretty much wherever there is a place on which, or in which, to place the paper. You really do intend to deal with all it "someday!" But the piles continue to get bigger until they are so overwhelming, you simply shove them into a box or a drawer to get them out of your sight, and then the cycle starts again.

The bottom line is that, someday, someone is going to be forced to go through all those files, boxes, drawers, and cabinets. If someone else has to do it because you have been severely injured in an automobile accident, do you really want them to be forced to search for your insurance policies or other legal documents? Wouldn't it make more sense to have all the information they will need in a single convenient location, and wouldn't it make even more sense for you to have shown them, in advance, where the location is?

Nobody knows better than you what information is important for you to keep, and what can be thrown away or shredded.

By the way, I keep asking if "somebody else" knows where all this information is located. If your answer is that your spouse knows where it all is, please consider what would happen if **both** you and your spouse are injured or killed in a car crash? **Who else** knows where all this information is located? Who else has the authority to handle everything that needs to be handled on your behalf?

This book is intended to help you to eliminate most of the unnecessary piles of your paperwork, asks you a lot of important questions that you should consider and discuss with your loved ones—as well as your financial, tax, insurance, and legal advisors—and gets all your important information organized and stored in a single location so you can sleep well at night, knowing you have one less thing to worry about.

And while you're going through all those boxes, shelves, cabinets, closets, and drawers, perhaps this book will give you a gentle nudge to start purging some of stuff you've stored, but haven't used, for the past decade or so.

This is not a task that will take an evening or even a weekend to complete. It has taken you decades to accumulate the information, so dealing with all of it is a huge undertaking that will take you a fair amount of time.

I've broken the process down into small, bite-sized steps to be completed one step at a time. So, complete one small section of the project and reward yourself with a glass of wine, bowl of ice cream, or whatever you consider to be a reward. Another night, complete another small project, and take your spouse out to dinner and a movie. Reward yourself each step along the way, and before you know it, you will have tamed the chaos; you'll feel happy that you've accomplished your goal, and your loved ones will be grateful that you loved them enough to go through the process so that they won't have to do so.

But, in addition to the important, factual details contained in the workbook, I also wanted to include a fun, personal component that goes beyond the factual details someone needs to know about your life. I wanted to include some sections that allow you to talk about yourself as a person, the information someone would want to know about you, about your passions, your favorite memories, and your life experiences.

I've included questions that will encourage you to share favorite lifetime memories, recipes, songs, and pictures (and the stories behind them); lessons you've learned in life that you would like to share with future generations; and the people who have inspired you and have been a meaningful influence in your life. There is even some information about filming your own life legacy video, if you are inclined to do so.

And finally, there is a section to tell your family and friends how much they mean to you in your life; all the things you always wanted to tell them, or just want to tell them one more time.

So, the "Everything" file will help you organize and provide details in each of these major categories:

1. All about you, including information about your family, school, work, medical history, any military or public service positions you have had, your pets, and also personal stories to be shared with future generations about these topics.

2. Your financial details, including information about your assets, business, debts, taxes, insurance, sources of income, cash flow, and other financial details.

3. Where you store your tangible assets, such as a safe, safe deposit box, storage unit, hiding places, etc., as well as where you store your digital files and documents, such as on your computer, external hard drive, in the cloud, etc.

4. Your medical history and details, including information about your medical providers, prescription and non-prescription drugs you take, allergies, surgeries, and other need-to-know medical details about you.

5. Planning your funeral and related details about cremation and/or donating your body or body parts.

6. Internet and security details, including automatic payments made from your checking account or charged to your charge card; websites you commonly use, including email accounts, social media, online backup and storage, usernames, passwords; and other protective security matters affecting your online security, privacy, and presence.

7. Your life legacy, including your family history, life experiences, life lessons, words of wisdom, and other memories you want to share with future generations, and important messages to those who matter most to you.

8. Anything else you feel you need to let others know about you.

My wife, Helen, has lovingly hinted to me that nobody is going to want to fill out over 300 pages of questions. I certainly agree, which is why the questionnaire also contains a mini-version to help you decide which items apply to you, and whether you consider those items of information warrant including them in your "Everything" file.

So, whether you take the time to read the entire book or decide to jump right in and start filling out whichever sections of the "Everything" file questionnaire apply to you, please know that someone will greatly appreciate that you made the effort and took the time in providing all this information to them. Completing it is truly an act of love.

Let's get started.

Chapter 2
Getting Organized and Creating Your Own Home Filing System

The benefit of having an efficient and organized filing system at your home is reduced stress in your life. It is easier and less stressful to have an organized system to receive, sort, and if necessary, store the seemingly endless avalanche of incoming paperwork and information about all your financial matters, important documents, and everything else of importance in your life while being able to locate whatever you need, should the need to retrieve the information become necessary.

Does the following scenario sound familiar? You stop by the mailbox on the way into your home. Perhaps you walk into the kitchen, opening your mail as you walk. The obvious junk mail makes it into the trash, but you have some bills, correspondence, monthly statements, and other things you know you'll want to review before deciding whether to keep them or throw them away. So, you put all the saved items on the kitchen counter. The next day, you do the same, but the mail is opened by the front door, and the paperwork is piled up on the table near the door. Another time, the paperwork winds up in your bedroom. During the weekend, you pick up all the piles of paper in the various locations and move them all into a single "organized" pile. As the pile grows, so does the stress, knowing that each item in the pile requires your attention. All this can result in clutter that distracts you from what you need or want to do, not to mention the difficulty of immediately locating a needed document quickly!

Frequently, clients come into my office with a file box filled with paperwork, unopened envelopes containing account statements, prospectuses, correspondence, and a mountain of other documents that have become so cumbersome that the client doesn't know what needs to be kept, thrown away, or shredded. They have become so overwhelmed, they have done nothing at all.

So, the purpose of this chapter is to help you create an organized home filing system to enable you to know:

1. Whether a document needs to be kept.
2. If you need to keep it, whether you should merely scan and save it electronically, or whether you should keep and file the original document.
3. Where to file each document (should the document be filed in a filing cabinet, on your computer as a digital file, or both?), and where exactly the document or information is located so you can conveniently retrieve it should you need to do so.
4. When you can (and/or should) finally shred and dispose of the document.

While it takes some effort to set up the system in the beginning, the hours of time saved in the future when you try to find a document (in addition to the relief from the stress caused by the ever-growing mountains of paperwork) are well worthwhile.

In addition, having an organized system in place will also save your loved ones the stress of trying to figure out where everything is located should something happen to you that prevents you from taking care of your own financial affairs. They need to know the filing system exists, where it is located, and how to access the information and documents.

For your physical files, you should either show them where the physical files are located in your home or work, or clearly describe in detail where they can be found. The mother of one of my clients recently passed away. She remembered that her mother had told her that she had bought a burial insurance policy, and the policy was located "in the house." My client searched the house from top to bottom and was never able to locate the policy.

As a result, she wound up having to pay for her mother's funeral. It would have been much better for her mother to say, "The policy is in my closet, in one of the boxes on the top shelf." It would have been even better had her mother taken my client by the hand and literally shown her where it, and other important documents, were located.

For your electronic files, you should show your loved ones **where** the information is stored. Whether you store them on your computer, a backup storage drive, a CD-ROM, a thumb drive, or in a cloud-based storage vault, your loved ones need to know where the files are located and how to access them.

In addition, you also need to teach them **how** to retrieve the file. If a file name, password, and/or encryption code are required to retrieve the needed information, be sure to provide this information, too. After all, if you are unable to speak for yourself, you don't want your essential information to disappear into an electronic black hole.

Preparation of this document is a significant endeavor. But if you are thinking that this task is too enormous for **you** to complete, imagine what an even greater burden it will be to your loved ones to locate all the information, without you being able to tell them all they need to know. So, if necessary, enlist the help of the ones who will be saddled with the responsibility of handling your affairs. They will appreciate your efforts to make their lives easier should something happen to you.

As in most aspects of your life, organization requires planning to make the job easier. It will require some thought on your part to determine what type of filing system will best suit your needs. Let's break the process down into smaller, more palatable steps.

I. BEFORE YOU GET STARTED:

1. Equipment needed:

a. Filing cabinet or file boxes
b. Cross-cut shredder
c. Garbage can
d. Hanging file folders
e. File folders (I recommend tri-cut folders)
f. Scanner (if using a computer)
g. Computer and external backup drive (if desired); and
h. Fireproof lockbox, safe, and/or safety deposit box at your bank

2. How much space do you have available, and where will you store everything?

Take a few moments to look around the area where you will be doing most of your paperwork, paying bills, reviewing documents, and filing paperwork. Is there an electrical outlet nearby for a shredder and/or scanner, if you decide to buy them? Is the area well lit? When filed away, are all documents located in a place convenient to where you will file and retrieve documents? Sit at your workspace and see where you will need to reach for equipment, office supplies, and files.

If you have a work area with a desk, that's great. If not, and you must work at the kitchen table, for example, it is still possible to be organized, even if it's not as convenient as having a dedicated work space.

Very few people have an unlimited amount of storage space. So, if you have been letting paperwork pile up on a countertop, in a drawer, or on a shelf in the closet, I recommend keeping everything in a filing cabinet or individual file boxes.

I would recommend at least a two-drawer cabinet, if not a four-drawer cabinet, space permitting. A two-drawer filing cabinet can range from $50.00 to $500.00, but I have seen them for as little as $25.00 at garage sales, thrift stores such as Salvation Army, and at used furniture resales or consignment shops.

If space is too limited, consider a good-quality file box that can be kept in a convenient place, such as under a desk. If no home office or desk space is available, the file box can be kept out of view, such as on the floor of a closet. File boxes can be obtained at an office supply store for just a couple dollars for your basic cardboard banker's box or about $20.00 for a plastic one.

The goal is to make sure everything needed is stored in one location, so that when new paperwork comes in, it can immediately be filed in its designated place, rather than being thrown into one of the random piles around your house. For example, you want to open your mail right where the filing system is located.

This place should be located near a garbage can so you can immediately dispose of what you don't need now or in the foreseeable future, to a shredder so you can destroy anything you wouldn't want a thief to find in your garbage (e.g. statements with account numbers, social security numbers, etc.), and to a scanner so you can scan any non-essential paperwork to a digital file; this way you can find the information when you need it, but don't need to keep the paper version of it.

Hint: Don't scrimp on a cheap scanner that scans a single page at a time. Spend a little more and get a faster scanner with a multi-sheet feeder that will scan both sides of the paper. Nothing will sabotage your scanning (and organizing) efforts more than a slow, one-page-at-a-time scanner. Some models even have special slots to make it easier to scan photographs, bills, and business cards. You want to be able to take an entire document (e.g. a 20-page investment account statement), put it in the feeder, push the button, scan and save the entire document as a single PDF file, and then shred the paper version of it.

3. Small stuff.

Figure out a place to keep the small items that you use on a regular basis that clutter your work area, such as a stapler, tape, paperclips, pencil sharpener, Post-It notes, pens and pencils, stamps, etc. This can either be a desk drawer, a-desk organizer, or a cabinet, whatever works best for you.

4. What type of filing system will work best for you?

Everyone is different, so what filing system works best for one person will not work for another. Do you prefer to search by category (financial assets, financial liabilities, medical information, taxes, home warranties, instruction manuals, etc.), or do you prefer searching alphabetically by name or reference number? My preference is to file by category, but do whatever works best for you. This will be discussed in greater detail below.

5. How much storage space do you need?

Most of us save significantly too much paperwork, mostly because it is usually easier to throw a document in a pile or in a drawer than to risk throwing away something that we fear we may need in the future. There will be more discussion later regarding what documents you should, or need to, keep.

Determine how often you need to retrieve certain files. This will determine what information you need at your fingertips, whether you need to keep it as a physical or electronic file format, and where you want to keep it: Do you want to keep it on your desk for immediate attention, in a file box at your feet, a two-drawer or four-drawer filing cabinet near your desk, or stored as an electronic file? If you are like me, you will find that, out of all the paperwork you have saved over the decades, you probably haven't even looked at, let alone needed, over 95% of all that paperwork.

6. Determine the labeling system you will use.

It will make your life easier to retrieve needed information if all the files have easy-to-read file labels. Whether you print the labels with a pen or use label-making software on your computer, the goal is to be able to easily find the file you are seeking.

7. Consider using a combination of hanging files and file folders.

While they are a few dollars more expensive, you may want to buy colored hanging folders (including the plastic labels) and plain manila file folders. The colored hanging files enable you to separate your files by major categories, such as yellow for financial, red for medical, blue for kids and family, etc. This will enable you to immediately find the section of the files where the information you need is located, then in each hanging file category, use the manila file folders for the subcategories. For example, use one red hanging file for the medical records for each family member, and within each family member's medical records file, use a separate manila file for each doctor, dentist, prescription drugs, etc. I prefer using tri-cut folders, so you can read the contents of three files at a time.

8. Keep it simple, and your filing system will grow with you.

Start with broad categories, and you can add more specific categories or subcategories as needed. As in the example above, you may start with a single medical file containing anything having to do with your family's medical matters, which can then be expanded to include specific doctors, dentists, medical records, prescription drugs, etc. or a separate file for each of the members of your family.

II. GETTING STARTED WITH THE PHYSICAL FILING SYSTEM

1. Create a 44-file "Forever Calendar" filing system out of letter-sized hanging files.

It is quite frustrating to know there is something that needs to be done on a specified date, but you can't locate the theater tickets, birthday card you intended to send, or the medical records you are supposed to bring with you to a doctor's appointment. If you have approximately one foot of space, the "Forever Calendar" is a continuously updated system that makes it simple to locate what is needed each day.

First, create a series of 31 basic green hanging files numbered 1 through 31 for the days in a month, 12 hanging files—preferably all one color such as yellow—labeled January through December, plus 1 more hanging file labeled "Next Year."

Place all the numbered daily files first, then all the months-of-the-year files next, then the "Next Year" file. So, for example, let's assume today is January 1st. If anything requires your attention on any specific day in January, you put it in the appropriately numbered folder. So, if you want to mail out a birthday card a few days before January 18th, you put the card in the January 15th file to allow for the mailing time, or if you have a doctor's appointment on January 23rd, you put any required paperwork in the file for the 23rd. But if something is needed for April 12th or September 15th, for now, you just put it in the appropriate month's file. Or if it is next year or beyond, it gets filed in the "Next Year" folder.

Every day, you pull that day's file, retrieve whatever is in that day's file and then move the current day's folder behind the next month's folder. When you reach the last day of the month, you pull the next month's folder, remove anything that you had filed there to be done that month, and insert the documents into the appropriate folder for the appropriate date. Make it a habit to file all time-sensitive materials in the appropriate place, and be sure to pull that day's folder first thing in the day (I usually retrieve it on the night before, just in case it is a morning activity, or to avoid forgetting it in the rush of getting ready for the day). Since I use my 44-file system at the office (I don't go to the office on weekends, if possible), on Fridays, I also pull the Saturday and Sunday files to make sure I don't miss something important that may happen over the weekend.

The key to making the 44-file system work is using it consistently and habitually checking it every day as part of your daily routine. Some people prefer to do it first thing in the morning. I prefer to check the next day's file the evening before, so I can prepare for what needs to be done (e.g. what I need to wear) before going to bed, and not at the last second if I'm rushed (or groggy) in the morning.

2. Add additional hanging files for frequently needed information.

In addition to the 44 files, I also have a hanging file for anything else I use on an almost daily basis. For example, I have a file for "Unpaid Bills." Since I prefer to pay my bills once a week, rather than let them pile up on a desk and risk the potential for them getting misplaced, I put them into the "Unpaid Bills" file, and I immediately know where they are when I'm ready to pay them. I even keep my checkbook and register in the same file.

Behind my 44-file system above, I have two more hanging files: one for "Paid Bills – Non-Deductible," and one for "Paid Bills – Tax Deductible," which save me time when I need to work on my income taxes. As I pay my bills, I simply put the paid bill in the appropriate file.

At the office, I also have separate files for "Calls Out" with the information I need for calls I need to make; "Calls In" to hold notes about messages I've left for others, and waiting for them to return my calls; "Correspondence" for letters I need to read and/or reply to; "Projects" which contain my "To-Do" and "To-Buy" lists for projects around the house and office; and "Top Priority" when there is something that absolutely and positively needs to be done right away!

Use your imagination for creating whatever files or topics are most important to you.

And ever-changing technology helps. For example, the "To-Do" and "To-Buy" project lists are now stored in an application on my smartphone. So, if I find myself at the grocery store or hardware store, I have my list with me.

In the past, I had a "To Read" file, for storing articles of interest that I knew I would want to read later. It was convenient to have the file with me, and when I had some down time, such as sitting in a doctor's waiting room, I could pull out the file and have something useful to read.

But I then replaced the physical hanging "To Read" file (at least if the article wasn't a book or in a bound format), with a digital computer file. I scan the article and store it on my computer in my "To Read" file. Since I'm seldom without my laptop, the digital file is with me. As an alternative, I copy my "To Read" file to my keychain USB drive, so I can retrieve and read the article on any computer at my convenience.

As this book goes to print, while I still have the thumb drive with me, I have a duplicate file stored in the cloud so that during free moments, I can retrieve and read the articles on my smartphone, tablet, or any other media device I choose.

This has enabled me to eliminate mountains of magazines with articles I used to earmark to read someday. Did you ever notice how that free time never seems to arrive? Now, I can stand in a line at the grocery store and quickly peruse an article I previously scanned to the cloud.

Constantly evolving technology provides us with increasingly more efficient methods of accessing the information we need and eliminating the mountains of paper we don't need.

I also recommend creating an "Emergency File" in case you ever need to make a hasty exit from the house. In Florida, for example, it is recommended to keep a "Hurricane File," a sealable plastic bag that contains a copy of your home insurance policy, legal documents (e.g. Durable Power of Attorney, Health Care Directives, etc.), address book with phone numbers of emergency contacts, a copy of your health insurance card, a few blank unsigned checks, and anything else you would want with you if you had to evacuate your home at a moment's notice due to fire, flood, or other emergency. You may even want to include a flash drive with a backup of any vital personal and business computer files you would need.

III. CATEGORIES

In setting up your filing system for both a physical paper-based system as well as a digital filing system, there are six main categories I use. Consider using different colored files for each one to make them easier to find.

1. Financial (assets, liabilities, banking, credit cards, investments, annuities, etc.)
2. Insurance (life, health, auto, umbrella, long-term care, home, etc.)
3. Medical (doctor, dentist, prescriptions, vital records, etc.)
4. Household (appliance manuals, warranties, inventory, serial numbers, swatches of paint colors, etc.)
5. Personal (school, legal documents, vacation, goals.); and
6. Taxes (last year's return, deductible bills, any info that is, or may be, needed for tax preparation)

Feel free to add whatever other major categories you believe are important to you.

Each of these categories and subcategories can then be broken down further as needed or desired (and if space permits). So, for example, instruction manuals and warranties could be broken down further into household appliances (refrigerator, range, washer, dryer, dishwasher), electronics (computer, stereo equipment, cell phone), and "Home & Garden" (garage door, lawnmower, chainsaw, edger, etc.).

A computer-based or cloud-based filing system could be created, paralleling the same category breakdown you choose for your physical filing system. You may find that much, if not most, of the information you would usually file in the drawer is something you seldom need, and may find it more convenient to scan and store all that "just-in-case-I-need-it-someday" information in digital format on your computer, rather than keeping a hardcopy version of it in your file drawer.

I will discuss scanning in greater detail below.

Important: When using a digital-based filing system, be sure to back it up often! Losing all your files to computer or storage device breakdown is just as painful as losing all your paperwork to a fire.

IV. GATHER AND SORT

It's time to gather all your paperwork in one place. Decide where you will be doing all the sorting and use that as your home base. Go through every shelf in every closet in every room, every drawer in every cabinet, and don't forget to search the kitchen, laundry room, and garage. Don't forget the back pockets of the front seats and trunk of your car. If you keep additional personal records at your office or workplace, bring them home. Gather all the paperwork together and prepare to sort it all into major categories:

1. The "I Absolutely Must Keep It" pile. This is self-explanatory and will be discussed in greater detail below.
2. The "I Should Probably Keep It" pile. Include items you know you will need in the "near" future. Also include items of sentimental value you know you want to keep, such as that first "I love you, Mommy"

Valentine's Day card your daughter drew in crayon for you in pre-school (even if you are convinced, now that she is a teenager, that aliens have stolen her brain).

3. The "I Might Need It Someday (even if I haven't looked at it in the past 20 years)" pile.
4. The "I Don't Really Need It" pile.

Let's work on these 4 piles in reverse order:

1. The "I Don't Really Need It" pile

You will probably find this to be the largest pile, containing old party invitations, old monthly newsletters, playbills, expired discount coupons, advertisements, etc. This is the stuff you know you really don't need.

Look at each document. If someone went through your garbage and found it, would it have some information you would not want them to know? For example, does it contain personally identifiable information (bank or investment account numbers, social security numbers, birthdates, etc.), or other confidential information you wouldn't want to share with a thief?

If so, shred it. If not, you can throw it away. In fact, why even bother making a pile? Put it right into the trash can the moment you realize you don't need it.

You've got one pile done. Celebrate.

2. The "I Might Need It Someday" pile

This would include your bank statements, your kids' school records, old medical records, etc. If you aren't sure if you should, or just can't bring yourself to throw it away or shred it, then feel free to scan it, so you have a digital copy of it.

And then throw it away or shred it!

You've got another pile done. Do something special for yourself.

3. The "I Should Probably Keep It" pile

This pile would include instruction manuals and warranty information for appliances, furnishings, electronics, and things you have bought, recovery disks for your computer, computer software program disks, etc.

Keep the warranty information together with the instruction manual (and purchase receipt, if you have it), and write down your date of purchase on the manual along with the serial number, if any, of the item you purchased. Also write down the day the warranty expires, so you can dispose of the warranty information after the expiration date.

Keep in mind that, as a benefit of using certain credit cards for the purchase, some credit card companies will double the length of the manufacturer's warranty. Make a point of keeping the credit card receipts (so you will have proof of the purchase date) along with the warranty information.

And remember that most instruction manuals are now available online. Verify if a PDF version is available to download to your digital filing system. So, do you really need to keep the physical version of it?

Once the warranty has expired, or after you have disposed of the purchased item, throw the warranty and instruction manual away. Do the same with old computer disks and software you no longer use.

Your third pile is done. To celebrate, do something wonderful for that special person in your life.

4. The "I Absolutely Must Keep It" pile. These documents fall into several categories:

Your "Keep Forever" documents

1. Passport
2. Birth and death certificates
3. Social security cards
4. ID cards
5. Marriage license
6. Business licenses
7. Original wills, trusts, powers of attorney, health care surrogates, living wills, guardianship documents
8. Pension and retirement plan documents
9. Real estate deeds and mortgage documents
10. Vehicle titles and loan documents (shred when you replace the car, unless you need the information for business or tax purposes)
11. Diplomas and professional certifications
12. Business ownership documents (e.g. Articles of Incorporation, Certificates of Title, etc.)
13. Proof of ownership, valuation (appraisal), and purchase receipts for major purchases, such as jewelry, precious metals and coins, collectibles, antiques, artwork, etc.
14. Proof of ownership rights of intangible assets such as copyrights, patents, royalty-paying assets, etc.

Your "In Case of Emergency" Kit (consider saving a copy of these documents on an encrypted thumb drive or a secure cloud-based storage vault, too, but remember, you may not have access to a computer, smartphone, and/or electricity for an extended time period)

1. A copy of your driver's license
2. A copy of your various insurance policies (life, health, auto, home)
3. A copy of the contents of your wallets (both sides of credit cards, debit cards, driver's license, proof of insurance, etc.)
4. A digital copy of your address book
5. Emergency cash ($100, $200, $1,000. Whatever amount you feel you should have available in case of an emergency)
6. A spare key to your house and/or car
7. An "ICE" (In Case of Emergency) letter, which, if you are unconscious (or worse), will tell the reader who you are; whom to contact in an emergency with their contact information; who your doctor is; what medications you are on; any allergies you have; and any other information someone would need to know about you. It is up to you to decide just how much of information you want to provide here, considering you may have just given a stranger a key to your house and car, cash, and all the information contained in your wallet.

Your "Keep as Long as Necessary" documents

1. Tax records and supporting records and receipts (keep for seven years, then scan and shred)
2. Home purchase, sale, and capital improvement documents and receipts (keep for at least seven years after you sell the house, then scan and shred)
3. Paystubs, bank statements, and investment account statements (keep for a year). At the end of each year, I like to scan and shred the entire prior year's-worth of bank statements for each account separately
4. Medical records and bills (keep for at least a year after payment of the bill in case a dispute about payment arises)
5. Any records regarding the purchase, sale, capital improvements, and other information regarding tangible investment assets, such as real estate, precious metals, etc.

6. Any legally binding contracts regarding agreements between you, your family, and others that may require enforcement in a court of law (keep for at least 10 years after the contract ends)

Your "Update Annually" documents

1. Current Insurance Policies (also scan a copy to your "In Case of Emergency" Kit above)
2. Current year's social security statement
3. Current year's investment, bank, and retirement plan statements
4. A photocopy of both sides of everything in your wallet (e.g. driver's license, credit/debit cards, store loyalty cards, auto insurance card, membership cards, etc.)
5. A photocopy of your address book (if you use a digital or cloud-based address book, consider printing it out and saving as a PDF)
6. A list of bills you automatically pay out of your bank account or that are automatically charged to your charge card, and a list of subscriptions, software, and online websites and services you have on auto-renewal. Be sure to include information such as the name of the company, account number, phone number and/or website access (include username and password) so someone will know how to contact the company to stop the auto-pay or auto-renewal features
7. Your most recently filed income tax return

V. WHAT DOCUMENTS SHOULD YOU KEEP (AND WHERE SHOULD YOU KEEP THEM)?

There are many things that you know you should keep (such as your passport, original Last Will and Testament, insurance policies, the deed to your house, etc.), and there are many things you're not sure you need to keep (old income tax returns, paid receipts, etc.), and there is disagreement as to where you should keep them.

For vital documents, my fallback recommendation has always been to have a photocopy available to you at home and/or scanned to a secure (preferably encrypted) digital file, but keep the original document in a bank safe deposit box. Keep in mind that there are drawbacks in doing so. Your access is restricted to the bank's hours of operation. You must have the safe deposit box key. And if you are incapacitated or dead, someone else will either need to know about the safe deposit box and location and must have the key; they need to be authorized to access your box, or the bank may require a court order to give it.

As an alternative, for a relatively small sum, you may want to consider buying a home safe or lockbox. It is essential that it be fireproof and waterproof, which makes it a bit more expensive, but not so much as to make the cost prohibitive.

Now that you have your filing system set up and have sorted through, organized, and filed away all the documents you've deemed necessary to keep, we're ready to begin serious work toward creating your "Everything" file.

Chapter 3
Security Concerns, Passwords, Identity Theft, and Common Sense

It will be no surprise to anyone when I say that there are a lot of dishonest people in the world. As hard as you have worked to accumulate whatever you own, there are other people who are working just as hard to take it away from you. As I have learned over the years, honest individuals are those most prone to being the victims of dishonest individuals, because honest people assume that everyone else is equally honest, and therefore entrust others with their private information, or at least make it relatively easy to make their private information discoverable to others who may misuse it.

The opportunities to make this information available to someone who may misuse it have increased dramatically over the years. I remember when I was a child, I received my social security card on which it very clearly stated, "Not for identification purposes." Yet, over time, your social security number has become the primary identifier that you are who you say you are. It made sense for income tax purposes to be required to provide it to companies that needed to report your income, expenses, investments, insurance, credit reports, and any transactions that might impact your income tax liability. But it was, and still is, used in almost every other aspect of your life, such as your educational history, military service record, and even your medical history.

The same was true with birthdates. The people and companies asking for your birthdate were once using it to help identify who you were. But little thought was given to protecting this information from thieves. Even now, to schedule an appointment with your doctor, the person setting the appointment will often ask your birthdate before asking your name.

Nobody really thought much about it. People and companies asked for your social security number and birthdate and we willingly provided both bits of information to them. Not much thought was given to what others might be able to do with this information if it fell into the wrong hands.

I remember that many years ago, I regularly stored all my old paperwork in my garage. I had kept copies of every tax return I had filed since I was 16 years old, copies of bank and investment statements, real estate transactions, and much more. My social security number and birth date were everywhere, printed on seemingly everything.

In the house, more current records were regularly kept in drawers and home files, available for any guests or home workers to sneak a peek if they so desired.

In discussing this chapter with others, it appears that most people did the same thing. They never thought about someone going through their old stuff. They were quite casual about keeping these records stored in their garages or homes. There were a few of them who prided themselves on being good about not being "packrats," and were quite proud of throwing stuff away. But upon further questioning, they admitted that they regularly purged their homes of this information simply by throwing these old records away in their trash. They now knew that there are some dishonest people that go through others' trash in the hopes of getting this useful information from the unwary.

I would venture a guess that if you, the reader, look around your house, you will find a lot of paperwork that contains one or more of the most dangerous personal identifying numbers, which could potentially be used to steal your identity or your money and destroy your credit.

As discussed elsewhere in this book, I long ago shredded all unnecessary documents, scanned, and securely stored any information that might be of importance to me in the future. As I mentioned in my chapter on "Getting

Organized," I believe that a good starting point is investing in a good-quality cross-cut shredder to help eliminate the threat of accidentally sharing all the personal information contained in this paperwork.

The digital age in which we currently live has made it easier for us to do our banking, pay our bills, buy what we need, and have access to our important records online. It has also made it easier for thieves to steal our personal and private information, even if we are careful about designating whom we entrust with this information.

We can pay bills or make purchases by credit card, or by direct payment from our bank accounts, and we can have the choice whether or not to have the company or financial institution store our payment information online. But while this information is secure now, will some criminal mastermind figure out a way to get past the companies' safeguards?

It seems that we read about a new, massive security breach almost daily. Several million of us (including me) were affected by a security breach at Home Depot, requiring the issuance of new charge cards to all affected customers. Target was also affected by a similar breach, and we continue to read about such breaches time and time again. Major insurance companies have been hacked of both health and personal information. Even U.S. Government records have been hacked, potentially revealing the employment histories and records of several million workers.

There are a lot of brilliant criminal minds in the world. As fast as technological security advancements are made to help protect us from them, the criminals are just as rapidly discovering ways to get around these security enhancements.

As I am writing this chapter, credit cards are having chips embedded in them, presumably to provide additional security against information theft. Whether this will provide the additional security desired, we will know within a few years.

Apple, the innovative technology giant, has launched a new payment system that simply requires one to tap their smartphone against the payment device. I understand Android devices are about to do the same thing. How the payment information is conveyed securely is beyond my understanding.

Since technology changes so rapidly, for me to provide you with a list of precautions you should take to protect yourself and your important information would be a useless exercise.

However, a healthy dose of **common sense** can go a long way to protecting yourself. Don't make it easy for the thieves to get your information.

Start by identifying the information that is most useful to criminals, that which would help them to steal your identity, and gain access to your money and credit. This information should only be shared with those whom you trust completely. In my office, our standard protocol is to never provide this information in emails, unless the email is encrypted.

The information you want to protect includes your:

1. Social Security Number
2. Birthdate
3. Driver's License Number
4. Account Numbers
5. PINs (Personal Identification Numbers) and
6. Passwords

The Federal Trade Commission (FTC) has an excellent consumer information website with a lot of useful information regarding protection of your identity, and certain safeguards you can take to be more secure. The website is located at www.consumer.ftc.gov/topics/identity-theft. I don't have sufficient space here to list all the useful information contained on the website, so I encourage you to check it out on your own; it may save you significant inconvenience and financial loss in the future.

If you have already been the victim of identity theft, the FTC also maintains a secure website with useful tips on how to recover from identity theft: www.identitytheft.gov. These tips include instructions on what to do right away, such as:

1. Calling the company or companies where you know the fraud occurred, speaking to the fraud department and asking them to close or freeze the accounts, then changing logins, passwords, and PINS for your account,

2. Placing a fraud alert and getting your credit report from one of the three credit bureaus, if not all three (if you notify one, they are supposed to notify the other two for you). The FTC websites includes links to all three of the credit agencies:

    a. www.Equifax.com/CreditReportAssistance or call them at 1-888-766-0008
    b. www.Experian.com/fraudalert or call them at 1-888-397-3742
    c. www.TransUnion.com/fraud or call them at 1-800-680-7289

3. Report the identity theft to the FTC and fill out an Identity Theft Affidavit at www.identitytheft.gov or call them at 1-877-438-4338; which you should immediately print and save your FTC Identity Theft Affidavit; and

4. Take the FTC Identity Theft Affidavit along with your driver's license (or other government-issued ID with photo), proof of your address (such as a utility bill, lease, or mortgage statement), and any other proof you have of the theft; have the police file a report; and get a copy of the police report. Create your Identity Theft Report by combining the police report and FTC Identity Theft Report.

Following the steps listed above will give you the following rights. More detailed information about these rights is provided on the FTC website. You have the right to:

1. Place a 90-day initial fraud alert on your credit report
2. Place a 7-year extended fraud alert on your credit report
3. Obtain free copies of your credit report
4. Require fraudulent information to be removed (or "blocked") from your credit report
5. Dispute fraudulent or inaccurate information on your credit report
6. Stop creditors and debt collectors from reporting fraudulent accounts
7. Obtain copies of documents related to the identity theft
8. Stop a debt collector from contacting you

IMPORTANT: <u>Immediate action is essential</u> as it helps to limit your losses. For example, under most state laws, you're not responsible for any debt incurred on fraudulent new accounts opened in your name.

As for unauthorized credit card usage, under federal law, your liability is limited to $50.00. If you report the loss to the credit card company before it is used, you aren't responsible for any unauthorized charges to your account.

Your ATM or debit card can result in much higher liability to you if you don't promptly report the loss or theft of your card.

1. If you report the loss before any unauthorized charges are made, you are not liable for any losses
2. If you report the loss within two business days after learning about the loss or theft, your loss is limited to $50.00
3. Two business days after you learn of the loss or theft, but less than 60 days after your statement is sent to you, your loss is limited to $500.00; but
4. If you don't report it for more than 60 calendar days after your statement is sent to you, your loss is **potentially unlimited!**

Once you have taken the above steps to establish your Identity Theft Report, you should be sure to close any new accounts opened in your name, remove bogus charges from any of your accounts, correct your credit report, and continue monitoring your credit report periodically to watch for any additional fraudulent charges or accounts that may appear.

It may also be advisable to consider placing either a credit freeze on your account or adding an extended fraud alert on your credit. You can accomplish this by contacting all three of the credit bureaus, but unlike the creation of your Identity Theft Report, in which you need only contact one of the three credit reporting companies, the onus is on you to contact all three of them yourself.

More on Common Sense

Emails & Social Media: Think carefully about what you are saying in emails as well as what you are posting on the Internet. The 16-year-old daughter of a friend of mine was so proud when she got her driver's license, she took a picture of it and posted it on Facebook! This meant that her legal name, full address, driver's license number, and birthdate were now available to any thief and child molester who could see it.

Passwords: Who can remember them all? A common (but potentially dangerous) solution is to use the same password on all one's accounts and websites. I have well over 100 online accounts and websites I need to access, each with its own password. Some of the sites require that passwords be at least eight characters in length, and some must include a combination of uppercase and lowercase letters, numbers, and special symbols. In addition, some of my work-related websites require my password to be changed every 90 days.

One solution is to have a written list, as in the attached "Everything" file. But don't leave it in a place where it can be found by someone you don't want having access to it. You may want to leave it in your safe deposit box at the banks for your representative to be able to get in the event of your incapacity or death. But be sure to update it regularly.

Another solution is to have an encrypted file on your computer that requires a password to access. This will enable you to be able to keep it updated as needed, and be available to you to use when you can't remember your own passwords.

Possibly the best solution is to use a **password manager** that stores your passwords in an encrypted file, which is then secured by a master password. Some additionally require that a key file must be present for the password database to be unlocked, often on an external USB stick. There are far too many such services available for me to list them, and rapidly changing security protocol will render any recommendations I provide here obsolete by the time this book is published.

Remember that someone else handling your affairs will need access to all your accounts and websites to enable them to handle your affairs, so either provide them with a copy of them (and be sure they will be as careful with their protection as you would be), or let them know where the list is located, such as in your safe deposit box, and how to access it and the information contained in it, if it is digital.

Only you can determine what is best for your security comfort level, so be sure to do your own research on what password management system will work best for you.

Storage of old records

Your information may be stored in numerous locations. In my chapter on "Getting Organized," I discussed all the physical paperwork and records that are stored in boxes or file drawers in your garage, storage shed, basement, or attic. Also remember to look in your home office, kitchen, bedroom closet, shelf, or dresser drawer. And, of course, you may also store a lot of your personal information at your workplace. Finally, don't forget about your safe or lockbox.

Digital media is also quite prevalent. Over the years, data has been stored on old 5-1/4 inch or 3-1/2 inch floppy drives and zip drives. More recent storage includes the use of CD-ROM and DVDs, USB drives, and external hard drives.

Most recent additions include cloud-based storage, some of which require a subscription from you, others that do not.

And don't forget your old computers, even if they no longer work. The hard drive still contains a lot of information that should be destroyed before throwing away the old computer. This applies to your old smartphones, too.

There are programs available that help to totally destroy the data on a hard disk. I'm not sufficiently computer savvy to know which ones to use, let alone recommend. So, personally, I'm still a fan of using an old-fashioned hammer physically smashing hard drives and storage devices into little pieces, and scattering them between several different disposal locations.

Here are some more common-sense ideas for you to consider:

1. Scan and Shred

As described in greater detail in the chapter on "Getting Organized," one of the best things you can do is to eliminate as much of the paperwork you have accumulated over the years, particularly the paperwork that contains your personal information (see paragraph 2 below). Consider investing in a high speed, high-quality scanner with a multi-page feed slot, and save your piles of documents in digital format.

At the time of writing this book, I use the Fujitsu Scansnap ix500, which holds 50 pages in the feed slot, and can scan 25 double-sided color pages per minute. While at $429.95, it is pricey, but it is a true workhorse, and will pay for itself in saved time, particularly compared to one-page-at-a-time scanners. If you need to justify the expense, think of it this way: If you earn $15.00 per hour, it will pay for itself in 30 hours (i.e., one hour of scanning per day for a month).

Once you have scanned, named, and saved the document, unless it is an important document that must be saved in its paper form, you can now shred it. There are many types of shredders available that will do the job, but once again, don't buy a cheap one. Invest over $100.00 to get a cross-cut shredder that won't jam if you try to shred over 10 pages of paper at a time.

By scanning and shredding, you now have fewer documents you need to worry about getting into the hands of thieves.

2. Keep your personal information in a secure place

What is your "personal information?" Your social security number, birth date, driver's license number, passport number, account numbers, etc. All of these items can be used to steal your identity.

Whether at home or at work, there are workers or cleaning services, not to mention nosy relatives and friends, who may just take a "peek" at the papers on your desk. Don't leave your credit cards, debit cards, driver's license, passport, or any paperwork containing any of this information anywhere other than in a locked or secure place.

And for those individuals who leave credit cards in their automobile "for convenience" purposes, you are making it convenient for the thieves, too.

3. Storage devices and storage in the cloud

Just because you have eliminated the paper, you're not done. You still need to secure the digitized documents wherever you store them. Whether you store them on your computer, on an external storage device, in the cloud, or elsewhere, the devices and/or the documents containing your personal information should be encrypted and/or password protected.

4. Phone calls and emails

Unless you absolutely know and trust the person who is calling you or sending you texts or emails, do not give anyone your personal information. And don't click on suspicious links, even if you know who sent them to you. For example, you get an email from a friend, but there is no message, only a link to click. It is worth taking the time to call the person to confirm they sent it.

5. Review your credit report annually

Take advantage of the ability to review your credit report from each of the three major credit reporting agencies for any irregularities. You can obtain a report for free once a year. If anything looks suspicious, it is worth a follow-up call to the creditor named. Similarly, if you are denied credit, find out the reason and make sure it is legitimate.

6. Review your bank statements and credit card statements

Take a moment to review your bank statements and credit card bills carefully for wrong or fraudulent charges. If you don't recognize a charge, investigate it. Consider adding a monitoring feature on your bank accounts. For example, I receive an email from my bank anytime a payment goes out of my account exceeding $100.00. I caught three back-to-back eBay.com purchases allegedly made by me, which were paid through PayPal via my bank account. I succeeded in intercepting the phony charges within minutes. Of course, I changed passwords, and reported the security breach to eBay and PayPal, both of whom were very helpful in resolving the issue.

7. Secure sites

It took me a long while to become comfortable paying bills and purchasing goods online. I learned to make a point of looking for a website address beginning with **https** in the website address URL bar to make sure the site I was using was secure. This may be too technical, but "**HTTPS**" stands for **Hypertext Transfer Protocol *Secure***, and instead of acting as its own application layer protocol, it uses separate protocols called SSL (Secure Sockets Layer) and TLS (Transport Layer Security). The SSL encrypts the information that is being sent, which means that the true meaning of the data (credit card numbers, personal information, etc.) is very difficult to be cracked by anyone trying to see the information. Nowadays, most web browsers support HTTPS for more secure Internet browsing. Browsers such as Internet Explorer, Google Chrome, and Firefox will display a padlock icon to identify a secure HTTPS connection to a website.

8. Compile a list of your accounts

Maintain a record of all your credit card and debit card numbers, so you have a cross reference if an unexpected bill appears with a different account number. Call the credit card company **immediately**. Don't wait!

9. Use firewalls, anti-spyware, and anti-virus software to protect your home and work computers

Be sure to keep them up to date!

10. A final comment about common sense

As I learned in law school, "If it sounds too good to be true, it probably is!" This applies to your digital security, too. Trust your instincts. If something doesn't seem quite right, or if you find yourself pausing before clicking on a link or giving out personal information in an email or over the telephone, don't do it until you have verified you are giving it to a legitimate source.

I anticipate a time will come when, for security purposes, we will all have microchips imbedded somewhere in our body. But I am also aware that, as quickly as the security firms can create new, safer, innovative methods to keep our data secure, there are brilliant thieves developing new, creative methods to steal our information, our money, and our identities. As hard as we all work to earn our money, there are thieves working just as hard to try to take it away from us. Be careful and use common sense!

Chapter 4
The Estate-Planning Process

When we take the time to consider all the details that comprise our daily lives and think about how monumental a task it might be to put those details of our lives together in a format enabling someone to step into our shoes and handle our affairs if we become unable to do so, it is perfectly understandable why most of us never get around to it. Or perhaps it is our denial of the inevitable.

When we finally realize we need to do so, procrastination usually wins out. We rank getting our affairs in order on an even keel with getting a root canal, or cleaning the leaves out of the gutter. Cleaning out the gutters may well rank higher on our priority list, and is probably easier to accomplish, but the reason that most people procrastinate with the estate-planning process is a lack of understanding of what estate planning is, what is involved, and how to get started.

If you have life insurance, own a home, bank, or investment account in joint tenancy with your spouse, have named a beneficiary on an insurance policy, and have a file where you keep your important documents, you have already started the estate-planning process.

You may notice that I keep using the word "process." An estate "plan" is just a static snapshot of your financial assets, debts and your current state of health at the particular moment in your life when the plan is prepared. But your life is continuously evolving. People pass away, tax codes change, your financial situation changes, your health changes, and your life and the lives of your friends and family are constantly changing. People get married, have babies and grandbabies, change jobs, move to new locations, buy and sell their homes or businesses, and more.

You change insurance plans at work, doctors, banks, and medications. How about all the passwords you need to remember to have access to all your important information, websites, programs, and social media?

So, like your life, your estate plan needs to be monitored and updated periodically.

Most people think that an estate plan refers merely to the estate-planning documents a lawyer may prepare for you, such as a Last Will and Testament, Revocable Living Trust, Health Care Directives, Living Wills, and more. While these documents are an integral part of your estate plan, they are not the plan in its entirety.

I believe that an estate plan is a comprehensive review of your ever-changing life, and keeping one's health and mortality in mind, because at some point in time, it is guaranteed that someone else is going to have to have the responsibility of helping you and dealing with the details of your life, due to injury, illness, disability, stroke, dementia, or even death.

I consider that the estate-planning process includes:

1. **Preparation of your <u>estate-planning documents</u>** - Your Last Will and Testament, Revocable Living Trust, Durable Power of Attorney, Designation of Health Care Surrogate, Living Will, Pre-Need Guardian Designation, and other documents that provide the details and instructions about what you want to be done on your behalf if you are unable to handle your affairs, and name the person(s) and/or organization(s) you want to handle them for you.

2. **A review of <u>how your various assets are titled</u>** - Every asset you own should be reviewed to confirm how it is titled (e.g. is an asset owned by you solely, jointly with a spouse, in the name of your business, or in the name of your trust?). How your assets are titled (i.e., who owns the assets?) may have an impact on how your assets are administered on your behalf while you are alive and how they are distributed after your death. Ownership or title may need to be changed to better carry out what you are trying to accomplish.

3. **A review of <u>joint ownership</u> of and <u>beneficiary designations</u> on ALL your assets** - If you have named a beneficiary or own an asset in joint tenancy with right of survivorship, these designations may override conflicting directives in your will and/or trust. You and your attorney will need to clearly and correctly designate whom you want to inherit your assets upon your demise.

4. **A review of your <u>insurance coverage</u>** - A review of your various types of insurance coverage should be done with your financial and insurance professionals to confirm your loved ones are protected from potential catastrophe and will have sufficient funds available to support them should you become unable to do so. This would include reviews of:

    a. Your **life insurance** coverage, to make sure your loved ones have sufficient assets and income to support them without your paycheck (e.g. put your children through college, cover living expenses, prevent your spouse from losing the house due to an inability to pay the mortgage, provide a caregiver for your children, etc.)

    b. Your **disability** insurance coverage, to make sure your income continues if you become unable to continue working

    c. Your **long-term care** insurance coverage. At over $80,000 per year for a nursing home, one's life savings and estate can be rapidly eaten up by the costs of long-term care

    d. Various types of **business insurance** coverage, if you own a business such as: Key Person coverage, liability, business continuation, funding your business succession plan, and more

    e. Burial insurance – prepay the eventual and inevitable expense

    f. Health, automobile, homeowners, dental, vision, and many other types of insurance

5. **A review of your <u>tax situation</u>** with your CPA to consider the impact of your death or disability on your taxes and upon the taxes of the individuals who may inherit your assets.

6. **<u>Asset Protection</u>** - A discussion of methods of protecting assets from the taxes, losses, claims of judgment creditors, government agencies, and methods of paying your mortgages and other debts and obligations would be advisable.

7. **<u>Out-of-State Property</u>** - If you own real estate in more than one state, your attorney will want to take action to avoid the necessity of a second probate estate (sometimes called "ancillary administration") in order to ease the transfer title of the out-of-state asset into the name of your desired beneficiaries.

8. **<u>Business Succession Planning</u>** - If you own a business, the estate-planning process should include a discussion about your business succession plan with your attorney, CPA, insurance, and financial advisors. You have worked hard to build a business, so if it is the type of business that can be sold, you will want to have a potential buyer of your business in place, a formal written buy/sell agreement prepared to protect your loved ones should you unexpectedly die or become disabled, and have the plan properly funded so the buyer will

have sufficient funding to be able to buy your business (usually through a life and/or disability insurance policy).

9. **Consolidation and Simplification** - Do you have a hodgepodge of investment, retirement accounts, old 401(k) plans, savings, checking, and other types of accounts strewn amongst several different banking and investment companies and previous employers? While you are making the effort of going through the estate-planning process, you may want to consider consolidating your assets with fewer advisors or organizations. Consider rolling old 401(k) plans into IRAs with your financial advisors. Consider having just one banking relationship if you have two or more. Bring mutual funds held directly by the company and individual stocks and bonds in electronic format at a clearing house into your brokerage account. This will help to simplify your life by reducing the number of accounts you need to monitor, 1099 forms you need to input into your tax returns, and save your loved ones a lot of extra work in managing and finalizing your financial affairs. In addition, this may be a good time to consider scanning and/or shredding old, unnecessary account statements and documents, which will save your loved ones the hassle of having to go through mountains of unnecessary paperwork to locate the important information they need.

10. **Organization and Preparation of Your "Everything" File** - Do your loved ones know where all your important documents are located? Do they know where all your assets are located, to whom you pay your bills, and then, account numbers, names, addresses and phone numbers of your advisors and organizations to contact if you are unable to do so? Do they know what doctors you see, what medications you take and the dosages, whether you have allergies, and family medical history that may be needed in the future? Do you have automatic payments coming out of your checking account, charges automatically being charged to your credit card, automatic renewals of subscriptions and services, and how to turn them off? Does someone know how to access your online accounts and social media, along with your user names and passwords? It is important to prepare a comprehensive list of everything your named representative needs to know about you. This is the reason the **"Everything" File** was created!

11. If you are entering into a **second marriage**, especially if you have children from prior to the marriage, a discussion about whether or not you should consider a prenuptial agreement (sometimes called a premarital agreement) to protect your premarital assets for your children, or if you are already married, a discussion as to whether or not to consider a post-nuptial agreement, would be useful.

12. Planning **your funeral** in advance. You may think this is a morbid topic, but frankly, nobody is immortal. Someone is going to have to make the decisions as to whether you are to be buried or cremated, where it is to take place, whether the coffin is to be simple or ornate, whether it is to be a small, private service or a massive celebration of life. If you make all the decisions in advance, you have saved your loved ones the difficulty of making a lot of hard decisions. If you'd like, you can even make the arrangements in advance and pay for them through a pre-paid funeral plan.

The purpose of the "Everything" File is to help you to get started with the process. It will help you to collect the information your representatives and loved ones will need, and then help you to organize it, consolidate it all in one place, and establish a process to keep the information up to date.

As I will often repeat throughout this book, your thoughtfulness in having the forethought and taking the time and initiative to go through the entire estate process will be appreciated by others as a significant act of love by you.

The easiest way to begin is to understand what will happen if you do no planning at all. Let us review what will happen if you live (and are incapable of caring for yourself), and what will happen if you die.

WHAT HAPPENS IF YOU DO NOTHING?

If you live and are unable to care for yourself

If you become unable to care for yourself due to injury, disability, illness, stroke, dementia, etc., someone else is going to need to be able to care for you and handle all your financial matters.

Who is this person going to be? Hopefully, you have a spouse, parents, or children who can step in to take care of you. But without the necessary documents naming whom you prefer, granting them the written authority to act on your behalf, most doctors and hospitals will not follow their instructions about your healthcare, and banks, investment firms, and other financial institutions will not honor their instructions made on your behalf. In fact, most financial institutions will not even discuss the accounts with them if they are not co-owners of, or authorized signers on, the account with you.

In most cases, a costly and inconvenient guardianship proceeding will be required to determine who will serve as your guardian, and the guardian will serve under the supervision of the court. In other words, a judge—not you—is going to make the final decision about who will have the authority to take action on your behalf. And the judge may not name the person whom you would have preferred.

If you have no health insurance, your medical bills will need to be paid somehow. So, if you have no health insurance, your personal assets may need to be liquidated to cover your health care expenses. Consider that an emergency operation, long hospital stay, and other catastrophic medical bills are some of the most common causes of bankruptcy.

If you need to be put in a nursing home, which can cost over $80,000 per year, without some sort of long-term care insurance coverage, it doesn't take long to deplete one's life savings.

If you own a business that can be continued in your absence, someone needs to have access to your records, know what to charge, how to collect money for the business, pay the bills, order inventory (and the vendors from whom to order your inventory), and keep the business operational until you are able to return, if ever. If you are not able to return, someone needs to have the authority to determine whether to sell it on your behalf, keep it operating (if it is an ongoing business that doesn't require your personal actions to keep it running), or wind down and close the business if it cannot survive without you.

Someone will need to try to figure out everything you have, where it is located, and how to access it.

If you are married, some of the above issues may be averted, such as with some of the health issues, since medical facilities will usually follow the instructions of a spouse. Hopefully, your spouse is working and earning enough to care for herself or himself and your children while you convalesce. And hopefully, your spouse knows everything he or she will need to know regarding your financial matters, such as how to keep your business running, etc.

But will he or she have the ability to continue working while taking care of you and your children (if they are still at home or otherwise dependent on you)?

If your children are minors and their other parent is unable to care for them, once again, a judge will need to make the determination in a potentially costly Guardianship proceeding to decide who will raise the children on your behalf. And once again, the judge may not choose the person you would have preferred.

The issues mentioned above are just a few of the issues raised by doing nothing.

Maintaining adequate insurance coverage, having a list of everything someone would need to know about you, and having the appropriate estate-planning documents (such as a revocable living trust, a durable power of attorney, and a designation of a healthcare surrogate) will help to avoid many of the issues described above.

If you die

Someone will need to make all the arrangements for your burial or cremation, and will also need all the details required to carry out your wishes. Hopefully, you have told your loved ones whether you would prefer to be buried or cremated, and whether you want a plain pine box or a hermetically-sealed top-of-the-line casket. If not, someone will have to make those decisions for you.

Someone will need to take care of your minor children. If not the other parent, a potentially expensive guardianship will probably be required. As above, a judge—not you—will decide who will serve as guardian for your children. The guardian will take care of your children and manage their money for them (under court supervision), and they will then turn the money over to the child when the child turns 18 years of age. A Will can enable you to name the guardian you prefer, or you can use a revocable living trust to name a trustee to watch over your children and manage and protect the assets you have left them. These and other estate-planning documents are discussed in greater detail in another chapter.

Someone will need to find and collect all your assets, pay your bills, file your last tax return, and distribute what is left to your legal heirs at law.

Since we are discussing what happens if you have done nothing, that means you have not drafted a Last Will and Testament, so the laws of your state will dictate who will inherit your estate, and they may not be the ones whom you would have named.

If you are married, depending on the laws of your state, your surviving spouse will be entitled to inherit a large percentage of, if not your entire estate. In some states, your children will inherit nothing. If your children are minors and entitled under your state's law to inherit from you, a guardianship proceeding, as described above, will be required. As each child turns 18 years of age, he or she will receive their share of their inheritance from you. Do you want an 18-year-old to have access to your money at such a young age? What do you think would be the first thing they would buy? My vote is for a sports car.

A revocable living trust could delay the inheritance to a later time when the child may be more financially responsible and capable of handling his or her financial affairs and protect them from foolish financial mistakes they may make before they learn what it means to be a financially responsible adult. In other sections of this book, I will discuss various estate-planning documents and what they do.

Most married couples want to leave everything to each other, and then to their children. In Florida, upon your death, without any estate planning, your surviving spouse would inherit everything from you. If you wanted your children to inherit anything upon your death, it wouldn't happen in this scenario. They would eventually inherit everything from your spouse when he or she dies. But what if your surviving spouse remarries without doing any estate planning? His or her second spouse may inherit much, or all, of what you had intended to be inherited by your children.

A Last Will and Testament and/or a Revocable Living Trust can help avoid many, if not all, of these problems.

Getting creative to avoid the expense of paying an attorney to prepare estate-planning documents

I'm often confronted with ideas such as the following ways clients have tried to save money on the cost of paying an attorney to create the estate-planning documents:

1. **"I've got it covered! I own everything in joint tenancy with my spouse."**

Yes, this will help to avoid the expenses and hassles of probate, but the same problem described above with a potential second spouse remains.

If you are involved in a simultaneous death situation, such as a car crash, in which it cannot be determined which of you died first, your beneficiaries may wind up having to file two probate estates (one for you, and one for your spouse).

If you are in a second marriage and have children from a first marriage, you may have just unintentionally reduced (or eliminated) the amount those prior children would be entitled to inherit from you. Unless your surviving spouse protects your children by naming them in their own will, your children from your first marriage may get much less of an inheritance than you had intended.

2. **"I've got it covered! My children are grown. I own everything in joint tenancy with them."**

If one of your children has financial troubles, gets sued, or goes bankrupt, your assets may be fair game to a judgment creditor or bankruptcy court.

If one of your children goes through a divorce, some of the joint assets may be subject to the claims of their spouse.

You will be treated as having made a gift of part of the value of the asset. So, if you have one child as a joint tenant, one-half of the value would be treated as a gift. If you have two children as joint tenants, two-thirds of the value will be treated as having been gifted to each child (one-third to each child). If the value of the gifted amount is above the annual gift tax exclusion amount permitted in the tax code (currently $14,000 per person in 2014), you may have to file a gift tax return, if not pay a gift tax (for a very valuable gift).

Your children will lose the tax benefit of a step up in cost basis at your death. For example, if you bought some land many years ago for $50,000, and that land is worth $250,000 at your death, and then you leave the land to your child in your will or trust. If you have kept the land in your name (or in your trust), upon your death, your child will inherit the land with cost basis which "steps up" to the date-of-death value of $250,000. If your child now chooses to sell the land for $250,000, there is no taxable gain.

But if you had gifted half the land to your child while you were alive, the cost basis on your half of the land would step up to $125,000. But on the half that was gifted to your child, he or she would have to use your original cost basis of $25,000 (half of the $50,000 purchase price). This half would not step up to the date-of-death value. So, if the child decides to sell the land for the current value of $250,000, there would be no taxable gain on the half you own at death, but on the gifted half, there would be a taxable gain of $100,000 ($125,000 sale price minus $25,000 purchase price). If the long-term capital gains income tax rate is 15%, for example, this would result in a $15,000 tax on the gifted half of the property.

If your child dies before you, you may wind up inheriting the property, which would add it back into your own estate, and you would be back to where you started.

If you have several children, each with children of their own, and one of your children dies before you, would you want that child's children to take his or her share? If everything is held jointly with rights of survivorship, everything will be divided among the surviving children. The children of the deceased child will inherit nothing.

3. **"I've got it covered! I own everything in joint tenancy with my brother! He knows what to do if something happens to me."**

As with your children, you have just gifted half of everything to him. So, the same cost-basis problem may apply as described above.

If he gets sued or files for bankruptcy, the assets are at risk to the claims of creditors or the bankruptcy court.

If he gets a divorce, the spouse can try to treat half the assets as his assets.

If he dies, the assets will come right back into your estate. If you die first and then he dies, the assets will go through his estate to his heirs, who may know nothing about the assets actually being intended to be left to your loved ones. And even if they know what was intended, what if they don't care, and decide to keep it for themselves?

What if he simply decides to sell his half of the assets and keep the proceeds for himself? You have, after all, made a gift of half to him.

It is my hope that the above examples and questions will encourage you to discuss what you are trying to accomplish with an estate-planning attorney, so he or she can prepare the legal documents that will best serve your needs and protect your loved ones. A will and/or revocable living trust are two of the important documents you will want to discuss with your attorney to avoid these, and other, landmines.

4. **"I'm going to save lots of money and prepare my own Last Will and Testament. I can buy one online (or at an office supply store) for under a hundred bucks!"**

While I'm handy around the house and enjoy doing my own home repairs, I know my limitations. I can paint, wallpaper, hang a ceiling fan, lay a tile floor, and replace a light switch or even a toilet. But at a certain level of difficulty, I realize that it is more prudent (and probably less expensive) to let an electrician or plumber work on serious wiring or plumbing issues, lest I burn down my house, or find I have a swimming pool where my living room used to be.

The same logic holds true for the estate-planning process and the preparation of your important legal documents.

Many resources are available on the Internet that will help you organize your paperwork and prepare an asset list such as I have provided in this book. And most of the resources are free. But one has to decide what one's time is worth in doing all the research, compiling, and comparing all the information that is available.

But of greater concern is the risk of missing an important detail, or failing to consider something that could go wrong. These can seriously jeopardize the outcome of what you had intended. Just as you probably wouldn't drill cavities in your own teeth, it is better to have an objective person, trained with the knowledge of what needs to be done, what can go wrong, and how to protect you from those problems, to help walk you through the process.

Online or store-bought wills may be fine for a basic scenario. The reason you hire an attorney is not simply to fill in the blanks on a basic form document. You hire the attorney for the years of learning how to protect you and your loved ones, for the attorney's skills of asking probing questions to discover potential situations you may not have considered, to looking beyond the basic plan for what could go wrong; and to recommend solutions to protect your loved ones from as many potential problems as possible, before they arise.

For example, here is one of the most common and basic fact situations in preparing Wills for a husband and wife: "My wife and I want to leave everything to each other, and then to the children in equal shares." What could be easier, right? Let's look deeper.

a. Does the do-it-yourself Last Will and Testament discuss how your children are protected if your surviving spouse remarries? When you die, your spouse inherits everything. But unless there is some other provision made to protect the assets for the benefit of the children, in the event of remarriage and the subsequent death of your surviving spouse, there is a chance that his or her surviving spouse may inherit much, if not all, of what you had intended to go to your children from your first spouse.

b. The directions for your basic do-it-yourself Last Will and Testament will probably coach you to name a Personal Representative (executor). But does it recommend that you consider naming an alternate Personal Representative in case the first one is unable or unwilling to do the job, and perhaps a second alternate, too?

c. Does it discuss potentially naming a Guardian for your minor children's assets, or mention you have the ability to name one Guardian to take care of the children and another Guardian to watch over the money for them?

d. Does it ask whether you want your children to inherit everything when they turn 18 years of age or discuss whether a revocable living trust might be preferable to protect your kids from irresponsible financial decisions until later into their 20s, 30s, or 40s?

e. Does it remind you that the Will controls only assets that are titled in your name; that if you have named someone else as a beneficiary, or own the asset in joint tenancy with right of survivorship, that those assets will pass directly to the named individuals, even if you had specified in your Will that the asset was to go to someone else?

f. Does it discuss with you the costs, hassles, and time involved in putting a will through the court probate process, and recommend methods to avoid some of these types of problems?

g. Does it mention the risk of having two probate estates if you and your spouse are killed in a simultaneous death situation (e.g. car crash) in which it cannot be determined which of you died first, and discuss how you can avoid this situation?

h. If you own real estate (such as a vacation home) in another state, does it make you aware that your loved ones may incur the additional cost of a second probate estate (sometimes called "ancillary administration") in the state in which the second property is located, and that there are various methods that can avoid this problem?

i. Does it discuss how to protect assets for a special needs child, or what to do if you want to leave a larger portion of your estate to one child and less to another (or how to completely disinherit a child if you want to leave them nothing)? If you have loaned money to one child, does it ask you to consider whether the debt should be forgiven, or whether the unpaid balance of the debt should be paid out of that child's share of the estate?

The list of questions that should be considered, asked, and answered, are numerous, and vary from one person to the next.

On another note, do the instructions that come with the store-bought Will discuss the formality of the signing process required for the Will to be valid? The rules are too varied from state to state for me to go into detail in this book, which is why you need to confer with an attorney in the state in which you are domiciled. But as an example, in Florida, the testator needs to be an adult (18 years of age or older), of sound mind and memory (not mentally impaired), and not only needs to sign the Will in front of two witnesses, but the witnesses also need to sign it in front of the testator, and in front of each other. But who can serve as a witness? Can it be a relative? Can it be someone inheriting something in the Will? Who is qualified to serve as your Personal Representative (sometimes called an executor or executrix)? And does the Will need to be notarized? Knowing the right answer to these and other questions can make a significant difference in the ease and expense of how your estate must be handled after your death.

It has often been said that "we know what we know," and "we know what we don't know." But the largest category of concern is that "we don't know what we don't know," and this last category is where most of the problems arise in estate planning.

The education and training that attorneys receive, and the real-life experiences of their clients over the years, help them to foresee and protect you and your loved ones from future problems.

As a real-life example, I've recently been handing a probate matter that will illustrate the point:

Hoping to avoid paying an attorney to prepare a Will for her, a widow purchased a do-it-yourself Will kit online and prepared it herself. She had two children and five nephews. Most of what she owned named her children as joint tenants, so upon her death, all those assets passed directly to her two children, which was what she had planned. No probate was necessary to move these assets since the assets passed to her children by operation of law. Although the use of joint tenancy might have caused some problems as described earlier in this chapter, thankfully everything went as planned regarding these assets. At her death, all the joint assets passed directly to her children without any complications.

Being a loving aunt, she wanted to make a special gift of a $100,000 bank certificate of deposit she owned in her own name to her five nephews. She followed the instructions of the Do-it-Yourself-Will, and made a specific bequest that directed, "I leave my $100,000 CD, account number 12345-6789 at XYZ Bank to my five nephews in equal shares." She wrote down the names of her five nephews. So far, there was no problem. The Will went on to leave the residue of the estate, if any, to her two children in equal shares. A residue clause specified who was to receive anything else not otherwise distributed in the Will.

However, while she was still alive, the $100,000 CD matured. With interest rates being so low on short-term CDs, she decided to invest in a five-year CD in the hopes of getting a better interest rate than the shorter CDs were offering. But she also realized that if she needed access to some of the money in the CD, she would pay a penalty on the entire $100,000 CD. Due to her health concerns, the potential need to access the money was a real possibility. So rather than renew the $100,000 CD for five years, she divided the money into two $50,000 five-year CDs at the bank. This way, if she needed to break one of the CDs to get some money, the early-termination penalty would only be on $50,000 instead of $100,000.

What she hadn't considered was that the $100,000 bank CD she had specified to go to her nephews no longer existed. Remember, she identified the exact asset (including account number) that was to go to the nephews. Therefore, the way she had written her Will, the $100,000 would now go to the children under the residue clause of the Will, and not to the nephews.

Here is an example that will help you to understand the concept of how changing a few simple words could change an outcome. If you specify in your Will that you are leaving your 2009 Toyota Camry to your brother, and then trade it for a 2014 Nissan Altima, you no longer own the Camry at your death. As a result, your brother gets nothing. On the other hand, if you had specified that you were leaving <u>any</u> automobile you own at the time of your death to your brother, he would get the Altima.

As for my client's situation, a lawyer would most likely have foreseen this potential problem, and instead, might have recommended leaving a percentage of the bank account (or of the estate) or perhaps a flat dollar amount without identifying a specific account number to the nephews. (For example, the Will could have provided "I give

20% of my bank accounts at XYZ Bank, plus any accrued interest thereon, to each of my nephews who are alive on the date of my death.") This way, had she not used any of the money and accrued interest brought the value of the accounts up to $105,000, each nephew would get one-fifth of the total amount (i.e., $21,000). Or if she had made a withdrawal of $25,000, leaving just $75,000 in the accounts, each nephew would receive $15,000.

On the other hand, an attorney would foresee a potential problem with the percentage scenario above. What if one of the nephews died before her? Did she want the nephew's share to go to the nephew's children (if any)? Did she want his share to be divided between the remaining four nephews? Or did she prefer that his 20% share be added to the residue of her estate, and therefore be passed to her children?

As another alternative, she could have specified, "I give $20,000 to each of my nephews who are alive upon the date of my death." Even with this seemingly simple and clear instruction, a potential problem could arise if the estate had less than $100,000 in it, so a provision might need to be added to the bequest proportionately reducing the amount each nephew would receive, to cover this possibility.

One needs to go through a lot of what-if scenarios to make sure the assets wind up in the hands of the persons you had intended to receive them.

So, how did my case turn out? At the time of writing this chapter, the case is still pending before the probate judge. Happily, both children and all five nephews knew what the deceased had intended, and are in agreement to carry out those intentions. Even though the children may be entitled to split the $100,000, they agreed the money should be divided between the five nephews. This type of cooperation does not always happen when substantial sums of money are involved.

So, they all signed a document agreeing that it was the intent of the aunt for the money to be divided between the five nephews, even though that specific bequest had lapsed due to the original CD no longer existing. However, this agreement is not binding on the judge. It will now be up to the judge to decide whether it all goes to the two children, or whether the judge will honor the agreement between the children and nephews, providing that the money should go to the nephews only.

If the judge decides that the money is to go to the two children, they can certainly keep it for themselves. But if they prefer to honor their mother's desire to leave it to the nephews, how can they do so? They can renounce the inheritance, but this will result in the money going to their own children, not to the nephews. The only way for the nephews to get the money will be if the children decide to gift it to them.

In the hope of saving a few hundred dollars for a lawyer to prepare her Will, the decedent's unintended consequence was a lot of hassle and over $4,000 in probate fees and court costs which will reduce the inheritance of the heirs.

Ironically, a potentially easier, faster, and less expensive alternative was also available to the deceased. She could have opened five separate $20,000 CDs in her own name, naming one nephew as the TOD (Transfer on Death) beneficiary on each CD. These would have passed automatically upon her death to each of the nephews and the necessity of a probate estate could potentially have been completely avoided.

Of course, if she needed some of the money, would she take it all from one CD (meaning that nephew would get less than the others)? Or would she take it proportionately from all five CDs (meaning that she would pay an early termination penalty on the entire $100,000)?

As I said, one must continue exploring the what-if scenarios. Sometimes, there is no clear solution that satisfies everything one is trying to accomplish. But at least one can now make an informed decision as to the various outcomes and prepare for them accordingly.

The chapter on estate-planning documents will go into much more detail on how each document will help you to avoid some of the problems outlined above and more.

But as a short synopsis of some of the contents of that chapter, I'll discuss some of the pertinent forms that are involved in the estate-planning process:

A **Durable Power of Attorney** will enable your attorney-in-fact (the person you have named to act on your behalf) to continue to operate your business, manage your properties and financial affairs, and do whatever is needed to buy, sell, and otherwise deal with your assets and debts, pay your bills, deposit your checks, and almost anything else you would otherwise be able to do yourself.

A **Designation of Health Care Surrogate** (sometimes called a "Medical Power of Attorney") will enable your representative to make medical decisions on your behalf if you are unable to do so.

A **Last Will and Testament** will, upon your death, specify whom you want to serve as your Personal Representative (also known in some states as an Executor or Executrix) to collect your assets, pay your bills, and distribute whatever is left to the beneficiaries you have specified. If you have minor children, you can also name whom you would prefer to serve as their Guardian and/or the Guardian of their assets. Everything that is not titled in joint tenancy or with a named beneficiary will still be required to go through the probate process, along with the time and expense probate encompasses. The benefit of probate is that it will all be handled under the supervision of the probate court, to make sure the provisions of your Will are followed.

A **Revocable Living Trust** is one of the most powerful estate-planning documents you can have prepared. It can be used to avoid probate, as well as a second probate estate if you have out-of-state property. It can delay distribution of assets to your children beyond the age of 18 without the necessity of establishing a Guardianship. It can protect your beneficiaries from creditors through "spendthrift" provisions.

A trust is a complex, detailed document, and is therefore more expensive to have created than a simple Will. But the cost of preparation is often less expensive than the cost of probate and/or Guardianship proceedings, and sometimes is significantly less expensive.

In general, while you are in good health, a revocable living trust enables you to do anything and everything you can otherwise do with your assets while you are alive. If you become unable to handle your own affairs due to illness, injury, disability, dementia, stroke, etc., the Trust enables your successor trustee to do anything and everything you could have done on your own behalf for your own benefit. Upon your death, it becomes irrevocable and enables your successor trustee to do anything and everything that needs to be done for the benefit of the beneficiaries, without the need, time, hassle, or expense of having your estate go through probate.

Please read the chapter regarding your estate-planning documents to learn more about these and the other estate-planning documents that can be prepared for your benefit and for the benefit of your loved ones.

Chapter 5
Your Estate Plan and Estate-Planning Documents

Last Will and Testament

This document gives the probate court instructions on how your estate is to be distributed. It names whom you prefer to serve as Personal Representative (who is appointed by the court) to administer your estate (i.e., collect all your assets, pay your remaining debts, and distribute your assets in accordance with the terms of your Will.) If any beneficiaries are minors, it can also name your preference for who is to serve as Guardian for the person of the minor as well as name a Guardian of the estate of the minor. (They are often the same Guardian.)

IMPORTANT: Not all your assets will necessarily pass to the beneficiaries named in your Will. For example, If you have already named a beneficiary on an account or insurance policy, or if you own an asset in joint tenancy with someone else, that particular asset will most likely pass to that other person automatically, and the provisions of your Will may have no effect on the transfer of the asset, even if your Will names someone else who is to receive the same asset. This is the reason all assets must be carefully scrutinized as to how they are titled and whether or not they have any beneficiary designations. You want to make sure that your wishes will be carried out correctly.

Personal Representative: Often, this is one's spouse, child, good friend, or a bank or trust company named as a corporate Personal Representative. You can have co-representatives (e.g. requiring two children to serve jointly, or a spouse and trust company jointly), but your estate-planning attorney will want to talk with you about potential pitfalls of doing so. It is important that any person you name to serve as Personal Representative has the time, knowledge, and willingness to serve as your Personal Representative. It is the Personal Representative that usually hires the attorney to probate the Will, if probate is required.

NOTE: Under Florida law, most relatives and their spouses can serve as a Personal Representative, regardless of whether they reside in another state. However, if the Personal Representative is not related to you, he or she must be a Florida resident. Different states have different requirements, so if you have moved to Florida, have your Will reviewed by a Florida estate-planning attorney. If you move from Florida to another state, have it reviewed by an attorney in your new state, to make certain that state's requirements don't disqualify the Personal Representative you have designated.

In addition, consider naming at least one or two alternate individuals or a bank or trust company to serve as Personal Representatives. This will save the cost and hassle of having your Will updated if the Personal Representative you have named predeceases you or becomes unable or unwilling to serve.

Some probate judges will allow the Personal Representative to serve without having to post a bond if the Decedent's Will waives the bond requirement. Other judges refuse to allow a waiver because of concerns about protecting estate creditors and beneficiaries from misfeasance or nonfeasance.

Guardians: If you have any children or grandchildren who are minors, a Guardian should be named in your Will to care for their person and to manage their property until they attain 18 years of age in the event of the death of both parents. You may nominate joint Guardians, although complications may arise if they disagree on the handling of the child or the child's assets. You may also nominate separate Guardians for a child, that is, a "Guardian of the person" and a "Guardian of the property," especially if one proposed Guardian is better at financial matters and another proposed Guardian is a better care provider. A corporate Guardian, such as a bank or trust company, can be designated as Guardian of the property or could serve as a Co-Guardian of the property with another individual you name.

NOTE: Under Florida law, if the person you nominate as Guardian is not related to the child, he or she must be a Florida resident to be appointed.

Living Will

If you remember the unfortunate case of Terri Schiavo, a braindead woman who was kept alive during an extremely long and expensive legal battle as to whether to keep her attached to the machines that kept her alive or allow her to be removed from the machines to die, a Living Will is the appropriate document to avoid this situation.

Note: A Living Will must be signed in the presence of two witnesses. At least one of those witnesses cannot be your spouse or a blood relative. In addition, the person designated as the Health Care Surrogate cannot act as a witness to the signing of the document.

Durable Power of Attorney

This is a very powerful document which authorizes another person your "Attorney in Fact" to control your assets on your behalf and for your benefit. If you become incapacitated, this document may prevent the necessity of having someone appointed by the court to serve as Guardian to handle your personal and/or financial affairs.

IMPORTANT: The date this document becomes effective varies from state to state. Some states allow for a "springing" power of attorney, meaning that the document does not become effective (i.e. "spring into effect") until the occurrence of a particular event, which is usually a doctor's certification that you are no longer capable of handling your own financial affairs.

In other states, including Florida, the document is effective **immediately**, even if you are not incapacitated. So, the person you name must be someone whom you completely trust to act on your behalf, as that person will have access to all your assets and the legal authority to dispose of them.

Keep in mind that this is a fiduciary relationship, meaning it is a relationship of total trust, good faith, and honesty. Whomever you appoint is expected to use the power you have granted for your benefit, or to do what you would have wanted that person to do on your behalf.

Designation of Health Care Surrogate

In the event you are unable to make decisions about your medical treatment or health care, perhaps due to being incapacitated, unconscious, or disoriented, this document will designate the person who will have the legal authority to make medical decisions for you. In Florida, a doctor must declare you to be incapable of making your own medical decisions before your surrogate can make the decision on your behalf.

Declaration Designating Pre-Need Guardian

Even though a power of attorney and/or revocable living trust should help to avoid the necessity of your designated representative being required to go to court to be appointed as your own Guardian, circumstances sometimes arise requiring a court-appointed Guardian to watch over you and your assets. While it is not binding on the court, this document informs the court whom you would like to serve in this capacity for you.

The Guardian of the Estate is the representative who will watch over your assets, pay your bills, and make sure your property is properly managed. The Guardian of the Person is the representative who will be responsible for taking care of you, your health, and your personal needs. They do not have to be the same person, so if you feel one is better suited to dealing with financial issues and a different person is better suited to your personal wellbeing, it is acceptable to name different people to serve in these positions. Keep in mind, however, that they must be able to work with one another to make sure all your needs, both financial and personal, are satisfied.

Revocable Living Trust

A revocable living trust is a legal document that enables you to put money and assets into the care of a qualified person (usually yourself, while you are alive) or financial institution that will invest and distribute the money and assets according to your wishes while you are alive, and will continue to do so long after you have died. It controls how your assets and income will be managed, and under what circumstances income and/or principal can or must be distributed to you and/or anyone else you may specify. It is sometimes called "controlling your assets from the grave."

There are far too many different uses and benefits of using trusts to list here. You do not need to be wealthy to benefit from a Trust. It is something for us to discuss in detail to see whether you might benefit from creating of a Trust. For example, probably the most common use of a Trust is the ability to avoid the costs and hassles of probate, as well as to avoid the delay caused by probate in getting your assets into the hands of your loved ones. Both are valid reasons to consider a Trust.

Unlike a testamentary Trust, which is created in your Will, and does not become effective until you die and your Will is probated, a living Trust (sometimes called an *inter vivos* Trust) is created while you are alive, and can be created and used for your own benefit and/or the benefit of others while you are still alive.

A **revocable** living trust is a living trust that can be changed or revoked while you are still alive.

An **irrevocable** living trust, on the other hand, is a living trust created in such a manner that cannot be changed, even by you. Such trusts, if appropriate for you and your financial circumstances, may be used to reduce inheritance and estate taxes, help you qualify for Medicaid under limited circumstances, and sometimes is useful for asset protection purposes. Irrevocable living trusts are highly complex documents and should be prepared by experienced estate-planning attorneys.

Trusts can also be used to protect your loved ones, even from themselves, if necessary. For example, if you don't believe a child is financially responsible and might squander his or her inheritance, you can specify that only income earned by the Trust be paid to the child, but allow access to the trust assets for medical and educational purposes. It can also contain a provision known as a "spendthrift clause," which is designed to protect your beneficiaries from the claims of creditors.

Separate Writings Regarding Tangible Personal Property aka Personal Property Memorandum
This convenient document, recognized in most states, permits an individual to dispose of tangible personal property outside of the Last Will and Testament. In other words, if you want to leave a family heirloom—an antique grandfather's clock, your pocket watch, or any other item of tangible personal property to a particular person or persons—the item does not need to be specified in the Will. This document specifies who is to receive it.

However, to be effective, the Testator's Last Will and Testament must contain a statement referring to the separate writing disposing of tangible personal property.

What is particularly convenient about this document is that, unlike a Will, which needs to be signed, witnessed, notarized, and requires any changes to be made by a new Will or codicil to the existing Will, which must also be signed with the same formality as the original Will (and usually subject to an additional attorney's fee), the Separate Writing is signed and dated by the Testator only. No witnesses or notary are required. Anytime the Testator changes his or her mind, all that is required is to merely prepare a new Separate Writing document, sign and date it, and attach it to the Will. There is no other formality required for it to be effective. It can even be written on a napkin, so long as it is signed and dated.

Please note that this document may be used only for **tangible** person property. So, it cannot be used to bequeath cash, stocks, bonds, or other financial instruments (intangibles), or property used in a trade or business. Automobiles, boats, jewelry, and pretty much anything else can be disposed of in this manner.

Pre-Nuptial & Post-Nuptial Agreements
Even though these are not your typical estate-planning documents, in the context of marriage, these documents can be used to bypass statutory requirements that a surviving spouse be entitled to inherit a portion of the deceased spouse's estate.

Both the pre-nuptial and post-nuptial agreements are documents in which one or both spouses relinquish certain rights to alimony, division of assets, and inheritance rights in the event of a divorce and/or death.

They are both frequently used in second-marriage situations, especially when there are children from the first marriage. They are also often used when there is a wide disparity in the net worth of the bride and groom, to protect the wealthier spouse-to-be.

The Pre-Nuptial Agreement (also known as an Antenuptial Agreement) is signed **before** the marriage, preferably several months before the marriage, to avoid a challenge to its validity due to undue influence (e.g. the day before the marriage, the groom warns the bride, "unless you sign this, I won't marry you.")

The Post-Nuptial Agreement, on the other hand, is signed **after** the parties are married.

For example, most states frown on disinheriting a spouse, so they have "forced-share" statutes which require a surviving spouse to receive a certain percentage of the deceased spouse's estate, even if everything was left to someone else (e.g. children from a prior marriage) by naming them as beneficiary, through a trust, or owning the assets in joint tenancy with rights of survivorship. The forced-share statutes require a certain percentage (e.g., thirty percent of the estate) be given to the surviving spouse.

To be valid and enforced by the courts, there are numerous requirements, some of which are closely scrutinized, as the courts do not like to disinherit widows or widowers.

1. Both parties must **voluntarily** execute the agreement. There must be no force, threats, pressure, or coercion. And it must be in writing.

2. Both parties must provide **full disclosure** of their respective financial situations at the time the document is signed.

3. Both parties must sign the document in the presence of a notary public.

Since the courts are not particularly fond of these types of agreements, especially if the surviving spouse is relinquishing significant rights, my office policy is to require both spouses to have their own attorneys review and approve the agreements, or at least for the agreement to contain a clause acknowledging that both parties had the opportunity to have their own attorney review the agreement.

In addition, for pre-nuptial agreements, we recommend the document be negotiated, reviewed, and signed as far in advance of the wedding as possible, to avoid the undue influence or coercion challenge mentioned above. The closer to the wedding night the document is signed, the less likely it is that a judge will enforce it.

A Financial Firm's Proprietary Authorization Documents
These are not really estate-planning documents. But while the Durable Power of Attorney should be legally sufficient to authorize a bank or investment company to rely on the signature of the attorney-in-fact named and authorized in the document to disburse funds, make investments, or otherwise control the assets in the account, some banks and investment companies require their own proprietary forms be used, which I encourage clients to sign.

While some banks will honor the power of attorney as a sufficient grant of authority, some banks may require the use of their own proprietary forms to grant another person **signing authority** on an account. Some banks will require you to make the co-signer a co-owner of the account, which I discourage.

Similarly, some investment companies will honor the power of attorney, but some investment companies may require you to sign their own **limited trading authority** form, which allows your named representative to discuss the account with the financial advisor and make changes in your investments on your behalf. However, the limited trading authority form does not grant them the authority to withdraw money from the account, even for your benefit. This additional power is granted through the **full trading authority** form.

Since the whole idea of granting authority is to enable your named representative to direct your accounts on your behalf when you are incapacitated, whether the firm is right or wrong in requiring their forms to be used in addition to, or in place of, the Durable Power of Attorney is irrelevant. It makes sense to cooperate with their requirements to make sure there are no issues when the time comes for decisions regarding the accounts need to be made on your behalf.

Please note that, like the Durable Power of Attorney, the grant of authority in either a limited or full trading authorization form dies with the owner of the account. After the account owner dies, the named representative has no authority to direct any activity regarding the account.

Chapter 6
Your Digital Estate and Digital Assets

While writing this book, my family had the happy opportunity to celebrate my father's 100th birthday! About 50 family members attended the party and shared stories about this exceptional man! He was born in 1917, and one can only wonder what life was like for him, experiencing all the technological advancements that have been achieved over the past hundred years!

He was born long before the Internet; before computers, smartphones, fax machines, beepers, cable, television, air conditioning, and even before permanent press!

Until the invention of the computer about 40 years ago, pretty much everything you needed to know about someone else's assets, documents, life, or information of importance could be stored and found in a file cabinet, photo album, box in the closet, garage, attic, or storage locker. Everything had a tangible, physical form.

Books were on shelves. Photographs were in an album. Phonograph records and audio cassettes were kept near the phonograph or tape player. Family movies, and later family videos, were kept on a shelf or in a box, somewhere they could easily be found.

And important documents were in a filing cabinet, drawer, or stored with your lawyer, accountant, or elsewhere in physical form.

If you needed an address of someone to be contacted, you only had to locate the person's address book.

You might have had to search through a lot of places to find needed information, but a room-to-room search eventually revealed most of what one needed to handle the affairs of a loved one.

If the person wasn't good about saving or organizing records such as bank statements or insurance policies, you could simply wait for the mail to be delivered, and over the course of a year or less, by reviewing the incoming statements, bills, and mail, you could determine where the person banked, what accounts he or she had, what investments, annuities and insurance policies existed, and figure out what assets were owned. Similarly, you could figure out their debts, loan payments, insurance premiums, and other important bills which needed to be paid.

Now, 100 years later, most of the foregoing information is stored digitally, either on the hard drive of a computer, on some digital storage device, or stored online in the "cloud." Banks encourage their depositors to "go green" by having statements delivered digitally to their email address, rather than kill trees and send paper statements. County tax collectors now issue digital automobile Certificates of Title. Income tax returns can be filed with the Internal Revenue Service electronically. The use of paper documentation of information of importance has become less prevalent than ever before, which can cause complications if your loved ones don't know sufficient details about your financial affairs.

If your loved ones don't have actual knowledge about your assets, debts, insurance policies, or where your important documents are stored, there is a strong possibility they will <u>never</u> be able to find information about them. And even if they know where the information is located, without knowing your username and password, they might not be able to <u>access</u> it.

Some digital assets have obvious financial value, such as online bank accounts, Bitcoin or other virtual currencies, etc. But often, one neglects to include websites, domain names, online stores, and other digital accounts as assets having potential value, sometimes significant value. These assets need to be disclosed to your loved ones, and in many cases, should be included in one's Trust and/or Last Will and Testament.

Your legal documents should grant authority to your trustee (in your Trust), Personal Representative (in your Last Will & Testament), and attorney-in-fact (in your Durable Power of Attorney) to access, maintain, and legally do whatever is necessary to administer your digital assets and data.

Most states have enacted some version of the Uniform Fiduciary Access to Digital Assets Act, which gives Internet users the power to plan for the management and disposition of their digital assets. Be sure to check with your estate-planning attorney to verify whether your state has enacted it. In addition, be sure to have your attorney include language in your estate-planning documents granting your fiduciary representatives the legal authority to access your digital assets and manage them.

And watch out for the *Terms of Service Agreements* (TOS) you need to "click" before using when you access certain websites or internet content. The TOS provisions are usually contained in a pop-up box which require you to scroll to the bottom of before you can click the "I accept" box and use it. I don't believe I have met more than three people who admit to taking the time to read what they have agreed to by checking the box, but when you click it (and you won't be granted permission to use the website without clicking it), the TOS content restricts your rights to access, use, and control the content of what you have posted to, or accessed on, their site.

Different states provide different remedies and orders of priority regarding your rights to these digital assets, as to whether the Terms of Service, the Uniform Fiduciary Access to Digital Assets Act, or your own legal documents take priority in granting you the authority needed regarding these assets.

Using your email address as an example, once you have determined which grant of authority applies to your situation, each email provider usually has its own set of requirements on how your representative, assuming one has the legal authority to do so in the first place, can manage your email accounts after your death. On their website, Everplans™ lists the requirements imposed by Gmail, Yahoo, Microsoft Hotmail and Outlook, AOL, iCloud, etc., and the differences among them are quite significant.

The term *"digital assets"* encompasses a wide variety of assets we now commonly use, and the number of type of digital assets is growing as fast as the imagination of their developers can create them, especially as the power, storage, and processing speed of the devices that use them increase.

According to the digital asset management company, Everplans™ (www.everplans.com), digital property can be broken down into three main categories:

1. **Personal digital property**, which includes:
   a. Computing hardware, such as computers, external hard drives or flash drives, tablets, smartphones, digital music players, digital cameras, e-readers (such as the Amazon Kindle™), and other digital devices, including the content you have stored in the devices
   b. Online accounts, including email addresses, social media, photo and video sharing, shopping, video gaming, and online storage accounts, as well as websites and blogs you manage, including content you have written or posted to these sites
   c. Information or data that you have stored electronically, including online storage, cloud-based storage, remote storage, or physical storage devices
   d. Domain names; and
   e. Intellectual property, which includes copyrighted materials, registered trademarks, patents, and any code you may have written and own

2. **Personal digital property with monetary value**, which includes:
   a. Computing hardware
   b. Websites or blogs that generate revenue for you
   c. Art, photos, music, ebooks, intellectual property, or other digital property that generates revenue for you

d. Accounts that are used to manage money and may hold money or credits (e.g. PayPal, Bitcoin, etc.), online bank accounts, loyalty rewards programs, and other accounts with credit balances for your use; and
e. Domain names

3. **Digital business property** may include:
   a. Online accounts registered to the business
   b. Digital property owned by a business organization
   c. Online store assets, such as your own online store or other sites through which you sell things (e.g. eBay or Amazon)
   d. Mailing lists, newsletter subscription lists, email lists of your company's clients; and
   e. Any client information, including customer history

You are encouraged to make a list of all your digital assets and how to access every one of them. Without this information, access to assets and essential information may be lost forever. There is a section in the attached Questionnaire which breaks down your digital assets into the following categories:
1. Master password programs
2. Email accounts
3. Social media accounts
4. Websites, blogs, and copyrighted materials
5. Gaming, entertainment (i.e. Netflix, iTunes), subscriptions (such as magazines), family sites (e.g. ancestry.com)
6. Online storage or backup sites
7. Digital devices (e.g. computers, cell phones, tablets, etc.)
8. Financial sites (e.g. bank, insurance, investment account, 401(k), Bitcoin, etc.); and
9. Miscellaneous sites you visit (e.g. your doctor's office, monitoring your home security system, etc.)

If you haven't made an actual list yet, start doing so. If needed, every day for a month (or longer), every time you access a website you use, particularly those relating to your business or containing information you want your loved ones to know, write down the website address, your username and password, any security icons, pictures or phrases, and challenge questions.

Obviously, this is highly confidential information, which will give anyone in possession of it the ability to access your websites. So, either consider using a password manager program (and share only the access information to that account, rather than the passwords to all your sites), or make a list, such as the one contained in the "My Everything File" questionnaire.

Once you have compiled the list, you will need to decide what you want done with these digital assets. Different assets may need to be handled differently from one another:
1. Archive and save the assets
2. Delete or erase the assets
3. Freeze the assets
4. Transfer assets to family members, friends, or business colleagues
5. If assets have monetary value, you will need to decide whether to shut down the site (such as an online store), transfer revenue-generating assets to someone else (e.g. websites you manage), and whether credits, points, or cash values should be redeemed

You may also want to consider naming a Digital Executor to handle your wishes regarding your digital assets. This is not currently a legally binding or enforceable designation, such as the Executor of your Last Will and Testament, but it is a useful method of carrying out your preferences regarding assets which are usually not part of your Trust or probate estate.

The Everplans™ website also mentions something almost nobody ever thinks about, namely identifying potential "skeletons" in your closet." This is information or paraphernalia you wouldn't want anybody else to know about, both digital and nondigital, such as websites you would be embarrassed for your loved ones to discover. You can name someone whom you trust **implicitly** to serve as a "**Cleaner**," who would have the authority to delete your browser history and cookies on your computers, locate and delete offending files on your computer and external backups, drives, and other storage media, delete emails and social media postings (or entire accounts), delete pictures and texts on your smartphone, dating or adult websites, digital help or support sites for abuse, addiction, etc., and potentially offensive tapes, DVDs, magazines, photographs, toys, weapons, diaries, narcotics, criminal record, secret society membership, and anything else you want to permanently dispose of when you are gone.

Since this book is not intended to be comprehensive resource regarding digital assets, I have included only the most basic of information. For additional information, check out these sites which discuss digital assets, your digital estate plan, and your digital legacy at greater length. Providers of these sites state that they maintain secure digital storage of your important documents and information.

Disclaimer: As stated elsewhere in this book, as a senior citizen, I don't completely trust the safety and security of anything that is stored on the Internet, but I confess this to be a personal bias. Hopefully, providers of these sites are correct regarding the security of your information stored there, but please do your own due diligence regarding storage of confidential digital data.

Everplans™ www.everplans.com
This website provides digital asset management and document storage, much of which is discussed in this book and questionnaire. Their website contains a wealth of information about digital assets and their use and management when you are gone.

Mylennium Digital Executor Services www.mylennium.com
Their website has a very user-friendly online Digital Estate Assessment Questionnaire, which helps you to identify which types of digital assets you use and what may be needed to create your own digital estate plan. This digital estate plan includes:

1. Personal and business email addresses
2. Digital devices you use
3. Devices on which you store documents, photos, and videos
4. Websites on which you store documents, photos, music, and videos
5. Social media websites
6. Online genealogy websites
7. Digital legacy websites to store digital assets
8. Personal or business blogs
9. Electronic address books
10. Subscription-based sites for online services or products
11. Online banking, gambling, crowdfunding, gaming, and virtual currency websites
12. Professional or business sites you own, sell products, or manage for others
13. Domain accounts you use
14. Backup, storage, websites; and
15. Much, much more

There are numerous other websites and software applications relating to Digital Asset Management (DAM), so I encourage all readers to learn as much as they can regarding this ever-expanding field, as it has a significant effect on our assets and our use of those assets, as well as how our loved ones will be able to use those assets.

Chapter 7
Your Assets

What is an asset? For the purposes of this book, I am **not** referring to a person's inner strengths, qualities, talents, or other attributes that make him or her such a wonderful person to know personally or in business, although such a person may very well be considered a valued and essential employee of a company for purposes of "key person" insurance described in the insurance chapter of this book.

In this book, an asset is deemed to be an item you own, either having economic value or being capable of producing economic value. It can be tangible (something you can touch, like an automobile or diamond ring) or intangible (something you cannot touch, such as patents, trademarks, and goodwill). It can also be something having sentimental value (such as your grandparents' wedding picture).

1. **You need to identify <u>what</u> you own that may have value**

The purpose of identifying assets in your "Everything" file is to make sure your loved ones know it is an item that has monetary or sentimental value.

Most assets are easy to identify, such as real estate, automobiles, jewelry, and bank accounts.

But what about other types of assets that might not have obvious value?

For example, I have a collection of lawyer and judge figurines and artwork. Most of them are cute little statues I bought at an art fair or in a store for under $50.00 each, and probably wouldn't fetch more than a few dollars at a garage sale. But a few pieces are figurines by Royal Doulton and Lladro and have a value more than $1,000.00. To the uneducated eye, a person trying to liquidate an estate might not know that some of the pieces have value, and could wind up selling them at a garage sale for a fraction of their value. It is important that particular items of value like these be identified, so they can found by your loved ones.

Perhaps you have some collections of your own such as some relatively valuable coins or stamps haphazardly kept in a jar or a desk drawer? How about valuable jewelry mixed in with costume jewelry? Maybe some antiques or vintage items that the uneducated might perceive as "old stuff" to be donated to charity?

Have you invented something? Written a book? Are you a plaintiff in a lawsuit? Does someone owe you money? Without identifying them, who else would know about these assets?

2. **You need to identify <u>where</u> your valuables are located and <u>who to contact</u> to get them**

In the questionnaire I have provided, the questions may seem endless, but each question is meant to spark your memory as to a potential asset you might have otherwise forgotten to include in the list. Every "yes" answer lets your representatives know the asset exists. Every "No" answer saves them time by letting them know it is unnecessary to search for an asset that does not exist.

Similarly, you may have bank accounts, investment accounts, retirement plans, insurance policies, and other monetary assets. But someone needs to know the institutions at which they are located, account numbers, contact information for a representative of the institution, and more. Today, companies encourage you to be "green" (i.e., being kind to the environment by saving a few trees and getting your statements sent to you electronically instead of printing them out on paper and mailing them to you).

Going "green" may be an admirable goal, but without paper statements, how would anyone else know you have these accounts unless you tell someone? Perhaps an end-of-year or tax informational form would give them a clue, but those forms and statements may not be sent out for several months, if at all. If your representatives need money to take care of you now, you may not have the luxury of hoping your representatives find out about the account.

Think about other places where you may have assets of value. What about at your place of work? While most of my non-financial assets are kept at home, all the computer equipment, filing cabinets, and more are at my office belong to me (not to mention the extremely valuable business information stored in my office computer—dutifully backed up offsite on a regular daily basis, of course). Do you keep things of interest (including important documents) in a desk drawer, filing cabinet, or office safe? Do you keep important information on your office computer? Would your representatives know whom to contact and how to contact them to get access to these assets, documents, and information? Would they know what belongs to you (as opposed to assets belonging to the business you work for) and how to retrieve your important information from your business computer?

Is someone holding onto anything of value to you or your loved ones? If so, you want to identify the asset, who is holding it for you, why (e.g. is the asset meant to be collateral for a loan), and how to contact the person.

Does anyone owe you money? If so, what is the amount and circumstance of the debt? Is there a promissory note or other evidence of the debt, and where is the documentation located? If not, what are the terms of the debt?

Are you involved in a lawsuit in which you are seeking damages from someone else? Your representative will need to know the details, case name and number, and know how to contact the attorney who is representing you.

Do you have a safe deposit box at a bank? Your representative needs to know the location and telephone number to the bank branch, and needs to have the legal authority to get access to it. This is where I recommend you keep the all-inclusive copy of the "Everything" file. Assuming you fully trust your representative (why would you name this person as your representative if you don't fully trust him?), you may want to provide him with a key and have him as an authorized signatory on the box.

Do you store anything in a storage facility? Your representative will need to know where it is located, whom to contact, along with their contact information, how much you are paying, where the rental agreement is located, and who has a key (or knows the combination) to the lock on the door. After a certain period of time, if the rent isn't paid, storage facility owners may have the right to dispose of all the valuables you have stored there.

Some people have hiding places. In administering estates over the years, I have discovered valuable stock certificates taped behind drawers, under carpets, and mixed in with unrelated files in a drawer. I have found jewelry and cash in an oatmeal box in the pantry, in a feminine hygiene product box under a bathroom sink, and in a hollowed-out book on a bookshelf. Some people still bury cans filled with cash and other valuables in their backyard.

I had one particularly interesting estate in which a retired schoolteacher passed away. She was an avid reader with wall-to-wall bookcases overflowing with books in her apartment. The children were sure she owned nothing of value, and that she was living on her social security, so they called a local charity to pick up all the books and bookcases, so that the apartment could be turned back to the landlord.

Over their objections, I reminded them that, as Personal Representatives of the estate, they had an obligation to search for assets, which turned out to be a good thing. While none of the books were collectible or had any particular monetary value, we discovered a $10, $20, $50, or $100 bill on page 77 of every single book in the apartment! All in all, the discovery totaled $35,000.00!

Do you have a hiding place? Since you haven't told anyone about it (why would you? After all, it IS a hiding place!), rather than risk the hidden assets being lost forever, at least indicate where the hiding place is located on the copy of your "Everything" file that will be kept in your safe deposit box or other secure location.

Look around your house (including your closets, garage, attic, and basement), your workplace, your storage unit, and any other place you may have assets having economic or sentimental value. Your representative will need to know what the asset is, where it is located, who needs to be contacted to gain access to the asset, and how to retrieve, sell, or dispose of the asset.

Unclaimed Property

Don't forget about assets that are missing. This is a redundant statement, as they are missing, because you have already forgotten about them.

Unclaimed property (sometimes referred to as abandoned property) refers to accounts in financial institutions and companies that have had no activity generated or contact with the owner for one year or a longer period. Common types of unclaimed property include:

- Bank accounts and safe deposit box contents
- Stocks, mutual funds, bonds, and dividends
- Uncashed checks and wages, traveler's checks
- Insurance policies, annuities, CDs, trust funds & distributions
- Utility deposits, escrow accounts
- Customer overpayments, unredeemed money orders or gift certificates, etc.

Each state has enacted an unclaimed property statute that protects these assets from reverting back to the company if you have lost contact with them. The companies are required to turn these assets over to a state official who will make a diligent effort to find you or your heirs. The states hold the lost assets until you are located, and will return them to you at no cost, or for a nominal handling fee for filing a claim form and verification of your identity. Since it is impossible to store and maintain all the contents of safe deposit boxes that are turned over to the state, most states hold auctions and hold the proceeds from the sale for the owner. Some states sell stocks and bonds and return the proceeds to the owner in the same manner.

Occasionally, you may receive a letter from a company that says something like "We have located assets that may belong to you, and for a fee of 30% (or some other percentage) of whatever we recover for you, we will help you retrieve it." The assets they have "found" are usually the types of assets that have been turned-over to the state. You don't need the company to retrieve the asset for you, let alone pay them a third of its value.

A friend of mine received such a letter, so I contacted the Florida Bureau of Unclaimed Property on her behalf and discovered that 30 years earlier, when she was a teenager and had worked for Busch Gardens one summer, she had been awarded one share of Anheuser-Busch stock (Budweiser). She knew nothing about it (or had forgotten about it). Over the 30 years, there had been a stock split or two, as well as reinvested quarterly dividends, bringing the current value to over $2,000.00. It cost her nothing to file a claim, and she was able to retrieve the money without having to pay the company sending out the letters. She didn't need them to file the claim.

As an experiment, I made a similar search under my own name and discovered a $190.00 security deposit I had given to Tampa Electric when I first moved to Florida 25 years earlier. I had completely forgotten about it and had no trouble getting it back from the state.

There are several ways to search for such assets, and I encourage you to do so, as you may be pleasantly surprised. You can check on the website for the National Association of Unclaimed Property Administrators (NAUPA) at www.naupa.org. While NAUPA is the association of all the states' unclaimed property programs, each state maintains its own database.

Or, if you prefer, you can simply do an Internet search for the name of the state in which you live or lived in the past, click "unclaimed property" and you should be able to locate the state's site. An owner, and often an heir, can make a claim. Links to all the states' unclaimed property websites, as well as several Canadian provinces, are provided at the end of this chapter.

Probably the easiest way to search most of the states at once is to use www.MissingMoney.com, which is officially endorsed by NAUPA and the participating states. The site will help you to search for your family's missing, lost, and unclaimed property, money, or other assets. They are continuously adding more states, so you may need to use any missing state's own website. A complete listing of each state's links is provided at the end of this chapter for your convenience.

While writing this book, as an experiment, I typed in my wife's name on www.MissingMoney.com, and while her name was not associated with any unclaimed assets, it did reveal that two of her brothers had unclaimed assets, one being an unclaimed asset from a department store (it was less than $100), and the other finding more had been turned over by the Hewlett-Packard Company.

3. You need to identify where the proof of ownership of the asset is located

Some assets have proof of ownership. For example, your representative may need the deed to your home, title to your car or boat, stock or bond certificates, insurance policies, etc. Your representative needs to know where these documents are located. In many cases, it may be more difficult, and sometimes more expensive, to transfer ownership of these assets without having proof of ownership.

In the case of stocks and bonds, most people keep them in book-entry form at a brokerage firm. If there is a stock split, the new shares will automatically appear in one's brokerage account. But not too many years ago, this wasn't the case. People would keep their stock or bond certificates at home, in a lockbox at home, in their bank safe deposit vault, or in one client's case, taped behind a painting on the wall. If your representative needs to sell the stock or bond on your behalf, he will need to be able to deliver the certificate to the brokerage firm selling the security. If the certificate cannot be located, a lost certificate affidavit will need to be completed, and a surety bond will need to be obtained at an additional expense to your estate.

Up until recently, if you were holding a stock certificate, and the company had a stock split, or the company merged into another company, you would receive additional stock certificates. Today, if one already had the stock certificate that had not been deposited into their investment account, stock splits and reinvested dividends might be held at an electronic clearing house, transfer agent or registrar, such as Computershare, Ltd, BNY Mellon, or EquiServe. Often, ownership of these additional shares are overlooked, because your representative might not realize or understand there are shares in addition to the certificates found.

A few years ago, I had a 95-year-old widower client who kept all his stock certificates in his safe deposit box at the bank. He liked getting and depositing his dividend checks, although there were so many stocks, he frequently got confused as to which dividends were paid and when, and often forgot to deposit the checks. I recommended that he consider putting all his stocks into a brokerage account, which could hold the stocks and receive all the dividends, and that he have an estate-planning attorney establish a revocable living trust in order to avoid the costs of probate. Based on the amount of his stock and bond holdings, probate would have cost his heirs over $20,000, so the $1,500 spent on the trust was a worthwhile expenditure. We retitled his stock account into the name of the trust, and when he passed away, all the account assets were easily distributed to the beneficiaries of the trust.

However, the client failed to, or didn't realize he should, tell the attorney that many of his stocks had multiple stock splits and mergers. All the additional shares that would have previously been sent to him were now held in electronic book-entry form by the company or clearing house. Most likely, the client didn't realize or understand the electronic shares also needed to be changed into the name of the trust. As a result, these electronic shares remained in his name individually and had to go through probate at a cost of over $15,000 to the beneficiaries of his Last Will and Testament. All this could have been avoided had the electronic shares been changed into the name of the trust, which would have cost nothing to accomplish. Luckily, the beneficiaries of his Will were the same as the beneficiaries named in his trust; otherwise, someone else might have inherited all these assets.

This scenario is one reason I always recommend that clients deposit any physical stock and bond certificates into their brokerage accounts. Any stock splits, dividends, and interest payments are paid into the account, so one doesn't need to worry about misplacing a certificate, having it stolen or destroyed in a fire, and dividends from all stocks and mutual funds can be retained in the account, reinvested (if permitted), or paid out directly to the client's bank account or mailed in a single, combined check to the client. Everything is conveniently held in a single place for your representative to handle on your behalf.

In addition, if a client has several accounts scattered about amongst several brokerage firms, banks, and mutual fund companies, it is a major inconvenience for his or her representative to locate them all, and go through the hassle of consolidating them (when possible) into just one or two financial institutions for ease of administering the assets. Therefore, I recommend that clients take the initiative to do the work needed to consolidate the various accounts into one or two financial institutions to make it easier on their Personal Representatives and loved ones, and reduce the possibility of an asset being overlooked.

The same analysis applies to mutual funds held directly at the mutual fund company and annuities held directly at the insurance company.

4. You need to identify how the asset is titled, and whether the asset has a named beneficiary

Determining how the asset is titled (i.e., how it is owned) and whether or not there is a named beneficiary is extremely important.

Sole ownership

If you own an asset in your name only, it is clear. It belongs to you, and you can do with it as you please while you are alive.

If you are alive but no longer able to handle your own affairs, your representative operating under your power of attorney or guardianship should be able to handle the asset on your behalf. (I say "should" be able to deal with it, because some financial institutions may not honor a Power of Attorney, even though many state laws require them to do so. So, with banks, I recommend having the person(s) you have designated as your "Attorney in Fact" under your Power of Attorney be an authorized signer on your account(s), so long as you trust the person so designated).

Upon your death, the asset will most likely need to go through probate before it can be sold or delivered to whom you have designated to receive the asset in your Will (if you have one), or through the intestacy statutes of your state (if you do not have a Will).

TOD Accounts, POD Accounts, and Beneficiary Designations:

As with sole ownership, you are still the owner of an asset held in a Transfer on Death or Pay on Death account, and you can do with it as you please while you are alive.

If you are alive but no longer able to handle your own affairs, as with sole ownership, your representative operating under your power of attorney or guardianship should be able to handle the asset on your behalf.

Upon your death, the beneficiary or beneficiaries designated on these types of assets will automatically receive the assets without the necessity of the asset passing through probate. The asset is said to have passed to them "by operation of law."

It is important to periodically review your beneficiary designations to make sure they are up to date and accurately reflect whom you want to receive the assets. There was an unfortunate case which illustrates the point: A man was in his second marriage, and had been happily married to his second wife for over 20 years when he passed away. The bulk of his assets were in a retirement account at his former place of employment where he had worked his entire career, which spanned both marriages. When he started working there (during his first marriage), he dutifully named his wife (now his ex-wife) as beneficiary but forgot to change the beneficiary designation when they got divorced. Upon his death, the court upheld that his first wife, not his current wife of 20 years, was entitled to receive the entire retirement account!

Note: To avoid this horrific result, many states now have laws that, upon divorce, deem the first spouse to have predeceased the owner of the asset. This would have enabled his second spouse to inherit the retirement account, but probate may have been required for her to get it. Sometimes these laws limit to certain types of assets (e.g. retirement accounts), but not to other types of assets (e.g. insurance policies).

A similar problem may occur due to the death or birth of a loved one. If you name someone as beneficiary, that person will automatically inherit the asset upon your death without probate. But if the beneficiary dies and you don't name a new beneficiary, the asset will go through a probate estate and will pass to whomever you have named in your Will (if you have one), or under the intestacy laws of your state (if you don't).

Also, consider the birth of a child. As an example, assume you have named your spouse as beneficiary of a life insurance policy, and your two children as contingent beneficiaries (the two children inherit the proceeds only if your spouse predeceases you). A third child is now born to you, and your spouse passes away. If you did not change the contingent beneficiary designation to include the after-born child, he or she may receive nothing. (Note: some states have statutes that may protect these "pretermitted" children, but it is easier and better to simply review your beneficiary designations when a new child is born).

Similarly, assume that you have three children named as beneficiaries, and each of them has children of their own. If one of your children predeceases you, is it your intention that the other two children inherit the asset? Or did you want the children of the predeceased child to take the share to which he or she would have been entitled? The beneficiary designation must be clear as to your intentions.

Doesn't it make sense to periodically review whom you have named as beneficiary on your various assets? I always recommend a review of all beneficiary designations every year, but at a minimum, upon the occurrence of major life events such as the birth or death of a loved one, marriage, divorce, change of home, change of jobs, and retirement.

Ownership in a Trust

If you own an asset in the name of a revocable living trust, you are probably named as the initial trustee, and as with sole ownership, you can do with the asset as you please.

If you are alive are but no longer able to handle your own affairs, your successor trustee will be able to handle the asset on your behalf.

Upon your death, the asset will bypass probate and the terms of the trust will dictate who is entitled to receive the asset. An asset properly titled in the name of your trust will control who receives the asset, because the asset will not go through probate. The terms of your Will control only assets that go through probate, so, if someone else is named in your Last Will and Testament to receive the asset, that beneficiary will not receive it; the beneficiary of the trust will prevail.

If you choose to create a Trust (often in the hope of avoiding the expense and delay of probate), it is important to change the title and ownership of the asset into the name of your Trust. This is called "funding" the Trust. If you fail to do so, the asset may wind up in the hands of someone you didn't intend to receive the asset, and the time, effort, and money, expended in having an attorney create a Trust for you will be wasted. For example, if you wanted your 1000 shares of a particular stock to be held in trust for a favorite nephew to be delivered to him when he turns 30 years of age, but you forgot to change title in the stock to the name of your Trust, the stock will pass through probate to whomever is entitled to receive your assets under the terms of your Will (if you have one) or under your state's laws of intestacy (if you don't).

Joint Ownership

There are three different types of joint ownership, each with potentially different consequences:

Joint Tenancy with Rights of Survivorship (JTWROS)

The asset is owned by you and someone else in equal shares. While you are alive, each of the joint tenants has a right to do with the assets as they please, which in some cases, may enable one joint tenant to take all the assets, even without the consent of the other. In other cases, the signature of both joint tenants may be required before the asset may be sold, or proceeds taken out of a joint account. You will want to verify which situation applies to any assets you own in this form of joint ownership.

Upon death, by operation of law, the surviving owners become the equal owners of the asset, without the need of passing through probate. For example, if you own a bank account as joint tenants with rights of survivorship with your spouse and your three children, all five of you are equal owners. If your spouse dies, it is now owned by your and your three children. If a child then dies, it is owned by you and the two remaining children. If it was your intention that the children of the child who died inherit that child's interest, you have just made an error that may lose them their ownership.

Often, rather than pay an attorney to write a Will, and in the hopes of avoiding probate, individuals will put their individually-owned home, bank account, or other asset in JTWROS with a child. In many circumstances, this will work out fine. The parent dies, and the child inherits the asset.

But when the child is added to ownership in this manner, there are many potential unforeseen and unintended consequences.

1. You have made a gift to the child. If you add one joint tenant, you have gifted half of the value. If you add two joint tenants, you have gifted one-third of the value to each of the two joint tenants. If the value of the gift exceeds $14,000 (as of 2014) to each joint tenant, you must file a federal gift tax return, even though a gift tax may not be owed. This amount varies from year to year, so be careful.

2. You may lose the benefit of a stepped-up cost basis in the property. For example, if you bought your house 30 years ago for $50,000 and it is now worth $500,000, when you die, the cost basis is reset to the date-of-death value (i.e., it "steps up") to $500,000. If the house is now sold for $500,000, there is no taxable gain. But if you put the property into joint tenancy with a child, that child takes your original cost basis, namely one-half of your $50,000 investment or $25,000. Upon your death, your half steps up to $250,000 (half of the $500,000 date-of-death value). But your child's cost basis remains at $25,000. So, for that half, the difference between the $250,000 selling price and the $25,000 cost basis results in a taxable gain of $225,000. If long-term capital gain tax rates are at 15%, there will be a $33,750 tax due. This tax and probate could have been easily avoided

through other means, such as through the use of a Revocable Living Trust, or transfer-on-death designation, if appropriate. Even probate may have been less costly than this tax, depending on the size of the probate estate.

3. By making this gift, you have made your child a co-owner of the property. So, if he or she goes through a divorce, bankruptcy, loses a lawsuit, or such, your asset may be at risk to the ex-spouse, the trustee in bankruptcy, or judgment creditor.

4. If the joint tenant dies before you, the asset comes right back into your estate, exactly what you were trying to avoid by adding the joint tenant to the title of the asset.

5. If it was your intention for the property to go to your child, and then to his children, but not to that "no-good spouse whom you never liked," you may not like the result. When you die, the child will properly become the sole owner of the property. When he dies, his spouse will probably inherit the property. Perhaps the children will inherit the property when she dies. Perhaps not. If she chooses to remarry and then dies, her second spouse may inherit the property and the children inherit nothing!

6. The child could clean out the bank account or force a sale of the asset. The child is a co-owner of the property and can therefore claim the asset.

These are just some examples of the potential unintended consequences of adding someone as joint owner to your assets. Be careful.

Tenants by the Entireties

This is similar to Joint Tenants with Rights of Survivorship (JTWROS), but is limited to ownership between a husband and wife.

It provides a few extra protections not provided by JTWROS. A Tenancy by the Entirety treats both spouses as a single legal entity, so that property owned this way may be exempt from judgments obtained against one spouse for that spouse's sole debts. Thus, property cannot be seized from the innocent spouse who is not legally responsible for them. For example, only a creditor of both the husband and wife can try to claim the asset. If the debt is the obligation of just the wife or the husband, but not both, the creditor will not be able to seize the asset. While most customarily used with real estate holdings, many states and/or financial institutions will recognize this form of ownership on investment and bank accounts. It is worthwhile to ask your investment advisor or banker whether or not this form of ownership is available to you and your spouse, as opposed to owning an account as joint tenants with rights of survivorship.

There are additional differences between JTWROS and Tenancy by the Entirety that are beyond the scope of this book. Most of these differences make ownership as Tenants by the Entireties advantageous to a husband and wife, but there are some disadvantages. For example, one spouse cannot convey his or her ownership share of real estate to another; both spouses must sign the deed for it to be effective. So, be sure to discuss the differences, and how they may impact your ownership of joint assets, with your estate-planning attorney.

Tenants in Common

This is simply a form of ownership of an asset by more than one individual. There is no automatic right of survivorship, and the shares do not need to be owned equally as they do in JTWROS or Tenancy by the Entireties above.

Each co-owner owns their respective proportion of the asset, so if one co-owner dies, that person's share goes to his or her heirs.

As with any form of co-ownership, there are numerous advantages and disadvantages, and it is important to understand the different consequences of owning the asset in one form of ownership versus another.

An example will highlight one of the differences regarding inheritance:

Let us assume you own a bank account with your two children as co-owners. Also assume that each child has two children of their own.

If the bank account is owned as Joint Tenants with Rights of Survivorship, upon your death, the assets in the account will automatically, without the need for probate, become the assets of the two surviving children. If they don't change anything, upon the death of the first child, the remaining child will automatically inherit the entire account. In other words, the last person standing gets everything. The first child's children will inherit nothing, because it all passed to the surviving child.

On the other hand, if the account is owned as Tenants in Common with your two children, upon your death, your one-third ownership will pass through the heirs you have designated in your Will (having to go through probate), if you have a Will, and if you have no Will, then by your state's intestacy laws (still having to go through probate). Your children still own their respective one-third interests, and upon their death, once again, their share of the account will have to go through probate to go to their heirs. If one of their heirs is a minor, a Guardianship may be required until the child turns 18 years of age.

There can also be significant tax consequences in the form of co-ownership you choose, which is beyond the scope of this book. So, be certain to discuss ownership of all your assets with your estate-planning attorney.

Ownership in an LLC or Corporation

Sometimes, for liability, tax purposes, or privacy reasons, you may choose to title the asset in the name of a corporation, limited liability company (LLC), or another entity name.

It is important to remember that the asset itself is no longer owned by you. It is owned by the corporation, LLC, or other entity. You may be the owner of the shares of the corporation or LLC, but not the asset itself.

So, when filling out the asset portion of the questionnaire, be sure to list the asset correctly. For example, if you have bought an investment piece of real estate individually, list it as such in the real estate section of the questionnaire. But if you bought it in the name of an Limited Liability Company (LLC), list your ownership of the LLC, and indicate what the LLC owns (e.g. I own "100 shares [or perhaps 100% of the shares of XYZ, LLC, a Florida Limited Liability Company, which is the owner of 12345 Blackacre Avenue, Anytown, FL 12345).

As you can see, as I have discussed at greater length in other sections of this book, the estate-planning process requires a careful coordination of your various legal documents, proper titling of your assets, and the proper use of beneficiary designations, to make sure your assets will be received by the people you intended to receive them, and not by those whom you did not intend to receive them. One must always be aware of the unintended consequences of failing to consider all the what-if scenarios.

Categories of Assets

This list of assets is not meant as an all-inclusive list of every type of asset you may own or that should be included in your "Everything" file. But it is a good starting point. Add any additional categories that are appropriate to you.

Remember, the "Everything" file is not only a resource for what you own, but also to enable your representatives to be able to find it, know how to gain access to it, and know what to do with it for your benefit and for the benefit of your loved ones.

So, for each asset, including other assets you may have remembered while going through the categories I've included, you will want your representative to know:

1. The asset exists
2. Where it is located (or how it can be found)
3. Approximate value (remember to include items of sentimental value)
4. Who needs to be contacted and what needs to be done (e.g. passwords, combinations to locks, etc.) in order for the representative to be able to claim it
5. How it is titled (and with whom, if not just you)
6. Whether the asset is encumbered by a debt or mortgage and the payment details
7. Whether there is insurance on the asset; and
8. Who, if anyone, is named as beneficiary of the asset
9. You may even want to add some personal, special notes or other details you'd like to let your loved ones know about it, such as how you acquired it, what made it so special to you (if applicable), and any other story behind it. To them, it may just be your "stuff." To you, it may be the source of a happy memory. Share the memory and make someone smile.

Here are some of the asset categories to include in your own "Everything" file:

Real estate (Your home, vacation home, investment properties, vacant land, farmland, timberland, time shares, mobile homes, leaseholds, etc.)
Accounts (Bank savings, checking, & CDs, investment accounts, etc.)
Accounts you hold for others (Educational 529 plans, Uniform Transfer to Minor Accounts (UTMA), etc.)
Vehicles (Cars, motorcycles, vans, trucks, boats, jet skis, skimobiles, tractors, etc.)
Permanent insurance with cash value (Whole life, universal life, variable life, etc.)
Annuities (Fixed, variable, indexed, immediate, etc.)
Retirement plans (IRA, SEP-IRA, Simple IRA, Profit Sharing, Money Purchase Plan, 401(k) plan, 403(b) plan, 457(b) plan, etc.)
Other employee benefit plans (Deferred Compensation, Stock Option, Cafeteria Plans, etc.)
Business ownership (sole proprietorship, partnership, LLC, corporation, etc.)
Contracts in which you are entitled to receive something or a service of value
Inheritances or gifts you are expecting or may be entitled to receive
Jewelry, antiques, artwork, collections, etc. (Does someone know their value?)
Patents, trademarks, copyrights, royalties
Digital or online assets (iTunes, Shutterfly, online storage vaults, Bitcoin accounts, etc.)
Lawsuits in which you are Plaintiff (you are suing someone else)
Judgments you have against others
Loans / debts that are owed to you
Hiding places (hidden jewelry, cash or other valuables, something buried in the ground, etc.)
Things of value which someone else would not realize have value
Musical instruments, camera equipment, hobby gear, exercise equipment
Tools, hardware
Computers, tablets, electronics, cellular phone
Appliances
Furnishings
Books, music, record albums, CDs, DVDs, etc.
Frequent-flyer miles and credit card reward points

Ownership of websites and online domains
Assets in your home
Assets at your place of business
Assets in storage units, a bank safe deposit box, home safe or lockbox
Assets held as collateral for a loan (e.g. at a pawn shop, to a private lender, etc.)
Loans and mortgages owed to you
Assets being held by someone for your benefit
Money or other assets lent to others (and is there any written evidence of it?)
Pensions (do payments continue past your death?)
Clothing being stored for you, such as furs in cold storage, or valuable clothing at a dry cleaner
Litigation claims against others, whether currently pending (write down the name and contact information of your lawyer, and what the case is about), or that you are planning on pursuing (there are statutes of limitations that will limit the amount of time you or your Personal Representative can legally file the claim or lawsuit)

Making a Home Video Inventory

As long as you have committed to create a list of assets for your "Everything" file, why not take it to a higher level and create a home inventory? This will not only be a useful tool for helping you to remember what you own to create a list of your valuable assets for the "Everything" file, but if you ever have to file an insurance claim due to your home being destroyed in a fire or storm or being robbed, it will also give you an important visual reminder of everything you own, even the not-so-valuable items. All those not-so-valuable items can add up to a significant sum of money.

Many people know they should take pictures of valuable items around the house (just in case), but few ever do so. Better than pictures would be a video inventory of absolutely everything in your home, including the closets, cabinets, drawers, shelves, garage, attic, etc. With a video inventory, not only will you be able to document absolutely everything that is contained in your home; you can narrate additional useful information about what the camera is recording, what the item is, an approximate date and price of purchase, the manufacturer and serial number, the approximate value, etc. This information will help complete your insurance claim form and document what you owned, particularly when used in conjunction with the receipts and invoices you will have (hopefully) digitally stored as recommended in the chapter on getting organized.

Pretty much everything you own in your home has value, and most items around your house, especially the "non-essential" items, will most likely be forgotten once you can no longer look in your drawers and closet to remind you they exist.

To illustrate my point, go into your bedroom with a pen and a pad of paper. Sit down on your bed, and without looking around, start writing down the contents in the room: the furnishings, lighting fixtures, television, telephone, clock radio, etc., and then list the contents of your drawers, cabinets, and closet. How many shirts, pairs of pants, suits, dresses, skirts, sweaters, shorts, pairs of underwear, shoes, etc., do you own?

While used clothing may not be worth much for resale purposes, you have spent a lot of money on all those assets. If you have spent a little extra amount for replacement cost coverage on your homeowner's policy (as discussed in the insurance chapter), you should be able to recover a significantly greater amount if you can detail the contents of your house, especially with visual evidence of what you owned, than by relying on your memory and guessing what was formerly in your room.

Since I would like to help turn what might otherwise be a tedious project into a potentially fun one, if you'd like, in addition to providing the factual details above, consider narrating the story about the item you are looking at in the camera, how you acquired it, and why it was important enough to you to have chosen to keep it, or perhaps the story behind some of the pictures hanging on your wall. They may be happy reminders of family vacations, a special moment in your life, or a special remembrance of something your 50-year old daughter made for you when she was a child. You know the stories behind your stuff, but does anyone else?

We tend to put things on shelves, and then after a while, not even notice them any more when we walk into the room. This is a good exercise to relive a pleasant memory for yourself, and perhaps for future generations. It will take some additional time to make the video, but you may get some joy out of it, too.

It may also encourage you to purge some of the excess stuff you have accumulated over the years. (I'm sure my wife, whom I lovingly refer to as a "minimalist," will appreciate my adding this paragraph, as I'm as guilty of accumulating as much stuff as anyone else, maybe more so.)

Steps to Follow in Creating Your Home Video Inventory

1. Before you get started, remember that you are going to be making a video of pretty much everything. So if you have something in a drawer that you don't want someone to see, or the contents of your drawers or closets are in such disarray you would be humiliated if someone viewed the video, consider organizing them before you start the video process. You may want to use this step as the initial purge of the stuff you no longer need or want.

2. This project is going to take several hours, if not an entire day, so be sure you have enough video tape or digital storage to record it all. This process also tends to jog one's memory as to things that need to be repaired or purchased, projects that need to be done, or people that need to be called for one reason or another, so have a pad of paper and pen nearby, so you can make notes of things that come to mind as you are making the video.

3. Unless there is no other alternative, this is not a do-it-alone project. Have someone who will help you. It is quite difficult and distracting to hold a video camera steady while going through drawers and closets. It's much easier for someone else to be moving things around as you narrate and video what you are seeing.

4. For items of higher value, such as electronics, make a point of getting a video of the manufacturer's name, model, and if possible, the serial number, which may involve turning the equipment around while the video is running. If available, you may want to have the receipt or other purchase documentation available, and zoom in on the receipt showing the date, place of purchase, and purchase price.

5. Buy a newspaper with the date you will be making the video. Focus the camera on the front page of the newspaper and zoom in on the date as you dictate the date out loud. This will establish the date the video is being made for purposes of identifying what you own in the house as of that particular date. A more recent tape will certainly be more meaningful than one taken a decade ago, which is why this is a project you should update ever year, if possible, but every few years, at a minimum.

6. Systematically, with the video equipment running, go through the entire house room by room, documenting everything in each room, narrating everything you see, as discussed above. Remember to have your helper open every drawer and move the contents of the drawer around as you narrate what is in each drawer. Do the same thing for the contents of every closet, in every cabinet, and on every shelf. If storage containers or boxes are used to store items, do the same for the contents of each container or box. In your bedroom closet, while it is not necessary to pull every shirt or dress off the rack, at a minimum, literally count each category out loud, while the video is running—Dresses: 1, 2, 3, ... 16, 17. Suits: 1, 2, 3, 7, 8. For items of higher value, make a point of zooming in on the item. For example, you may have 50 pairs of shoes and purses, and it would be fine to count them out loud. But if certain pairs are a particularly expensive brand, it will be worth the few extra seconds to zoom in on those particular shoes and identify them.

7. Don't forget the kitchen and bathrooms, the garage, the attic, patio and any outdoor storage shed you use. Video the contents of your car(s) while you're at it.

8. Do the same thing at your workplace if you own anything of value there. If you have purchased some of the items, such as a desk chair, filing cabinet, computer or electronics that you keep at the office, be sure to identify the items that belong to you, as opposed to belonging to the company, in case a disagreement arises at a later time when you are not capable of confirming what is yours. If you rent a storage locker, again, video all the contents.

9. Make several copies of the video and be sure at least one of the copies is kept away from your home or office, perhaps in your safe deposit box. If possible, store them with copies of your receipts or other documentation of ownership. A friend of mine proudly told me she had gone the effort of making a video inventory. When I asked her where it was stored, she said it was still in the video camera. When I asked her where the video camera was stored, she said it was in her closet at her home. When I asked her what would happen to it if the house burned down, she opened her mouth, but said nothing. However, the very next day, she made a point of moving a copy of the video to her safe deposit box at the bank.

10. With your big-ticket items (furnishings, appliances, electronics, etc.), you may want to simultaneously create a written list of all the items, including copies of the receipts, if available. Going forward, as you acquire new items, you can update the list, and get into the habit of keeping the receipts with the list. As you dispose of old items, you can remove them from the list and dispose of the receipts and documentation.

11. Be sure to update your video inventory every year or so, to keep it up to date. This is important for insurance claim purposes in the event of theft or a fire. Be sure to store the video away from your home, preferably in a safe deposit box, so it won't be destroyed along with your other assets if your house burns down.

Home Inventory Checklist
Air conditioner window units and portable heaters
Appliances
Artwork
Attic furniture and contents
Automobile repair and maintenance equipment
Basement furniture and contents
Bathroom(s) furniture
Beds & Bedding
Bedroom furniture and contents (master and all additional bedrooms)
Bikes
Books
Cabinets
Camera and video equipment
Carpets and rugs
Ceiling fans
Chairs
China
Christmas (and other holiday) decorations
Clothing
Collections
Computers, computer accessories, and tablets
Couches and recliners

Craft materials
Crystal and glassware
Curtains and draperies
Decorative items
Dehumidifier
Dining room furniture and contents
Dishes and utensils
DVD player
Electronics
Exercise Equipment
Family room furniture and contents
Fireplace equipment
Fixtures
Food in pantry, refrigerator, and freezer
Freezer
Furniture
Game systems (such as Wii, PlayStation, Xbox, etc.)
Garage furniture and contents
Garden equipment
Golf clubs
Grill
Hobby items
Home office
Ironing equipment
Items in storage (within your home)
Jewelry
Kitchen appliances, furniture, and contents
Ladders
Lamps
Laundry room furniture, appliances and contents
Lawn furniture
Lawn games
Lawnmower, edger, blower, pressure washer, etc.
Living room furniture and contents
Musical instruments
Piano, organ, and harp
Pots, pans, and other kitchen equipment
Plants and landscaping
Refrigerator
Sewing machine
Shelving
Silverware and cutlery
Sporting goods
Stereo
Stove and oven
Tables and chairs
Table linens
Telephones, answering machines, smartphones
Television, DVD, VCR, DVR, and other television equipment
Tools & power tools
Toys and games

Video equipment
Washer and dryer

Unclaimed Property Websites (State, U.S. Territories, & Canadian Provinces)

NAUPA Website	**https://www.unclaimed.org/**
State or U.S. Territory	
Alabama	http://www.moneyquestalabama.com/
Alaska	http://treasury.dor.alaska.gov/Unclaimed-Property.aspx
Arizona	http://www.azunclaimed.gov/
Arkansas	http://auditor.ar.gov/
California	http://www.sco.ca.gov/upd_msg.html
Colorado	http://www.colorado.gov/treasury/gcp/index.html
Connecticut	http://www.ctbiglist.com/
Delaware	http://revenue.delaware.gov/unclaimedproperty.shtml
District of Columbia	http://cfo.dc.gov/service/unclaimed-property
Florida	https://www.fltreasurehunt.org/
Georgia	https://dor.georgia.gov/unclaimed-property-program
Guam	http://doa.guam.gov/
Hawaii	https://www.ehawaii.gov/lilo/app
Idaho	https://www.yourmoney.idaho.gov/
Illinois	https://icash.illinoistreasurer.gov/
Indiana	https://indianaunclaimed.gov/apps/ag/ucp/index.html
Iowa	https://greatiowatreasurehunt.gov/
Kansas	https://kansascash.com/prodweb/up/ownr_1.php
Kentucky	http://treasury.ky.gov/Pages/index.aspx
Louisiana	http://www.treasury.state.la.us/default.aspx
Maine	http://www.maine.gov/treasurer/unclaimed_property/
Maryland	https://interactive.marylandtaxes.com/individuals/unclaim/default.aspx
Massachusetts	http://www.mass.gov/treasury/unclaimed-prop/
Michigan	http://www.michigan.gov/treasury/0,1607,7-121-44435---,00.html
Minnesota	http://mn.gov/commerce/consumers/your-money/find-missing-money/
Mississippi	http://www.treasurerlynnfitch.com/unclaimedproperty/Pages/default.aspx
Missouri	http://www.treasurerlynnfitch.com/unclaimedproperty/Pages/default.aspx
Montana	http://revenue.mt.gov/home/businesses/unclaimed_property
Nebraska	https://treasurer.nebraska.gov/
Nevada	http://www.nevadatreasurer.gov/Unclaimed_Property/UP_Home/
New Hampshire	http://www.nh.gov/treasury/unclaimed-property/index.htm
New Jersey	http://www.unclaimedproperty.nj.gov/
New Mexico	http://www.tax.newmexico.gov/Individuals/search-unclaimed-property.aspx
New York	http://www.osc.state.ny.us/ouf/
North Carolina	https://www.nctreasurer.com/Claim-Your-Cash/Claim-Your-NC_Cash/Pages/default.aspx
North Dakota	https://land.nd.gov/UnclaimedProperty/
Ohio	http://www.com.state.oh.us/unfd/
Oklahoma	https://www.ok.gov/treasurer/
Oregon	http://www.oregon.gov/dsl/up/pages/index.aspx
Pennsylvania	http://www.patreasury.gov/
Puerto Rico	http://www.ocif.gobierno.pr/UnclaimedProperty.htm
Rhode Island	http://www.treasury.ri.gov/treasury-divisions/unclaimed-property/
South Carolina	http://treasurer.sc.gov/

South Dakota	https://southdakota.findyourunclaimedproperty.com/
Tennessee	http://treasury.tn.gov/unclaim/index.html
Texas	https://mycpa.cpa.state.tx.us/up/Search.jsp
Utah	http://new.mycash.utah.gov/
Vermont	http://new.mycash.utah.gov/
Virgin Islands	http://ltg.gov.vi/
Virginia	https://www.vamoneysearch.org/
Washington	http://ucp.dor.wa.gov/
West Virginia	http://www.wvtreasury.com/
Wisconsin	https://www.revenue.wi.gov/ucp/index.html
Wyoming	https://treasurer.state.wy.us/upsearch.asp

Chapter 8
Your Debts and Liabilities

Just as you have accumulated many different types of assets during your lifetime, it is also possible to accumulate many types of debt and bills. Having someone else take over the obligation of paying your bills and debt obligations on your behalf can be an onerous task, particularly if he or she has no clue what debts need to be paid and when.

Before the digital age, it was easy to find out what bills needed to be paid. The person you had designated to be responsible for the task would simply have your bills (and other mail) forwarded to his or her address, and within several months, they would have a good idea what your current obligations were. They could notify the utility, credit card, and other companies to change the address on the accounts to their address, and could therefore conveniently continue paying your bills on your own behalf.

But while the U.S. Postal Service still allows mail forwarding, there is a limit to how long you can continue having mailed forwarded. In certain circumstances, a fee may be assessed by them for forwarding the mail. And certain types of mail (e.g. certain government mailings) cannot be forwarded at all.

As in my discussion in the chapter about assets, many companies encourage you to "go green," and rather than have them mail a monthly bill to you, they now send you a digital bill via email. That may be convenient for you, but if someone else needs to pay your bills for you, if they don't know the bill is being transmitted to you in this manner, how will that person know the bill even exists, let alone that it needs to be paid?

An even greater convenience to you is the ability to have your bills paid automatically from your bank checking account. You may authorize your utility, credit card companies, and other service providers, to automatically debit your checking account for the amount due to them. The auto-pay service most banks provide is an excellent method to remain current in paying your obligations and avoiding those nasty late charges and interest on what might otherwise be past due bills.

Similarly, many subscriptions and services can be set to automatically renew and charged to your credit card or debited from your checking account.

But if you become incapacitated or die, who knows that you have authorized these automatic payments and renewals to take place? And more importantly, who knows how to turn them off? Your designated representative needs to know about all auto-pay and auto-renew services being used, and know how to stop the payments from coming out of your account. This means that your representative will need to know the account information, your log-in username, and your password, to be able to turn off the payments and renewals.

And your representative also needs to know which auto-pay services should **not** be terminated! For example, if you are incapacitated, you are not going to want to stop automatic payments of your life insurance and health insurance coverage, lest you lose your coverage. Similarly, you want your mortgage and utility bills to continue being paid.

Some types of bills and debts need rapid handling to avoid high interest, penalties, and potential foreclosure or repossession, so the sooner your representative knows about them, the better.

For example, upon your death, social security payments, pension payments, and other payments being made to you, need to be terminated immediately. Any payments to which you are not entitled after your death, if paid to you (or directly deposited into your bank account), need to be returned to the sender, or they become a debt of the estate.

Not remaining current with payment of your secured debt items may result in adverse actions. For example, your mortgage lender may foreclose on your property if you (or your representative) don't remain current on your payments. Your automobile, jewelry, and other large-ticket items may be repossessed if the monthly payments aren't kept current. If the automobile, for example, is then sold by the lender for less than the remaining balance owed, you or your estate may become liable for the deficiency still owed.

Speaking of large-ticket items such as furniture, jewelry, or major construction work done on your house, as an incentive to you to buy their product or service, the vendors often charge no interest if the bill is paid within a particular time period (e.g. six months, a year, etc.). But if the entire balance isn't paid by the end of that term, all the unpaid accumulated interest (often at a high interest rate) gets added back in, and the entire debt becomes due. Your representative needs to know about this type of purchase and the debt payment obligations.

Where are the documents?

Just as important as knowing where you store the documents proving your ownership of assets, such as deeds, certificates of title to your vehicles, etc., it is also important for your named representative to know where you store the documents regarding your debts and contractual obligations.

Examples include mortgages on any real estate you own, car loans, leases (both personal and business), contractual obligations, etc.

And don't forget about litigation paperwork if you are the defendant in a lawsuit. Your representative must know about pending litigation, so your representative knows he or she needs to notify your lawyer about your infirmity or death.

Secured debt

In order to reduce the risk of loss to lenders associated with a loan, the debt is secured by collateral, which the lender is allowed to claim to satisfy or reduce the amount of your obligation, should you fail to pay off the debt in full.

The most common examples are a mortgage note secured by your house. If you fail to make your payments in a timely fashion, the mortgage company can initiate a foreclosure action to seize the house, sell it, and use the proceeds to pay back the debt. If the sales price is not enough to pay off the balance in full (plus accrued interest, attorney's fees, and court costs), you or your estate may become subject for the deficiency on the unpaid balance.

Similarly, an automobile loan is secured by the vehicle. If you fail to make your payments in a timely fashion, the lender can repossess the vehicle, sell it, and use the proceeds to pay back the debt. Again, if the sales price is insufficient to pay off the balance in full, you or your estate may become subject for the deficiency balance.

On occasion, the lender may "forgive" a deficiency balance. But under current federal income tax laws, forgiveness of a debt may result in you or your estate becoming liable for payment of income taxes on the forgiven debt. Due to the financial crisis in 2007 resulting in many houses being sold for less than the debt owed on them, if the house was your primary residence from 2007 through 2014 (subject to certain limitations and regulations), forgiveness of a deficiency balance on a mortgage did not create a taxable situation.

At the time this chapter is being written, it is unclear whether this waiver of taxability of debt forgiveness on a personal residence will be continued beyond 2014. This waiver applied only to debt on a personal residence, as defined in the Mortgage Forgiveness Debt Relief Act of 2007 (H.R. 3648).

But whether or not the temporary waiver is extended beyond 2014, for any other forgiven debts, the taxability of the forgiven amount may still create a taxable obligation, adding an additional, seemingly cruel, consequence. You have already lost the house or other asset, and will still be required to pay income taxes on the forgiven amount of the loan.

Unsecured debt

This term applies to most other types of debt. There is no security interest or collateral reducing the risk to the lender. As a consequence, the interest rate you pay on the debt obligation is a higher rate than the secured debt.

Typical unsecured debts include:
Credit cards
Student loans
Leases (apartment, store, automobile, etc.)
Business debt
Tax obligations
Personal loans
Child support and alimony
Judgments entered against you
Debts on which you are a co-signer or guarantor
And much, much more

Dischargeable and non-dischargeable debts

While a discussion of the bankruptcy code is far outside the scope of this book, a brief discussion of which debts can, and which debts cannot, be discharged in a bankruptcy is appropriate, as your representative will need to know the consequences of the types of bills he or she may need to pay on your behalf.

While most debts are dischargeable (and therefore non-collectable by the creditors), your secured debts are still subject to the lender's security interest. Therefore, while they will need the bankruptcy court's approval, your mortgage lender can still foreclose on your house, and your car lender can still repossess your car. You may be able to reaffirm the debt, and therefore keep your house and/or car, but it is also subject to the court's approval.

Certain types of obligations are not dischargeable in bankruptcy. These include:
Certain tax obligations
Certain types of student loans; and
Alimony and child support obligations

A conversation with a bankruptcy attorney is recommended if you or your representative (on your behalf) are considering filing for bankruptcy relief.

Co-signers and Guarantors

In addition to your own debts and obligations, your representative needs to know about any debts or obligations of others for whom you have either guaranteed payment or have co-signed on the obligations.

If your daughter needed a car but didn't qualify for a loan without you signing as a guarantor, if she fails to make the payments, it becomes your obligation. Your representative needs to know about these types of obligations.

Similarly, if you own a business as a corporation or limited liability company, in order to help protect your personal assets from the claims of creditors if the business should fail, many vendors will require you to sign as a personal guarantor of the obligation. These vendors are not limited to the corporate assets to satisfy their claims; they can pursue your personal assets.

And when you and your spouse buy a house or automobile together, and you then divorce, even if one of you is awarded the house and the car, the other is still obligated on the loans. You may no longer be the owner of the asset, but you are still obligated on the loan if your spouse fails to make payments. The only way to completely absolve yourself of potential liability is to require the spouse receiving the assets to refinance the house or car in his or her name only, and get your name off the obligation.

Filial Laws

Most people understand that parents are responsible for supporting their children. Beyond co-signing a debt obligation for a child, a parent can be held liable for the "necessaries" of a child (e.g. housing, food, health care expenses, etc.). So in some states, if your child is under 18 years of age and requires hospitalization, you may be responsible for the health care bill.

But in addition, in certain states, and under certain conditions, adult children can become legally responsible for supporting their **parents**. These are called filial laws, and at the time of writing this chapter, approximately half of the states have adopted them in one form or another. Usually, your parent must be indigent and receiving some sort of governmental assistance, or help to pay for a nursing home or hospital bill, before you can be held responsible for the debt.

If you or your parents are living in a state where filial laws exist, you will want to make sure your representative knows about this potential debt obligation.

Priority of Claims in Probate

We have discussed above what happens to your debts if you are unable to pay them while you are alive. Secured creditors can foreclose on your house, repossess your car, and/or sue you for any deficiency. Unsecured creditors can sue you, and try to collect the debt from you.

But what happens when you die? Do your heirs and surviving family members become responsible for your debts?

The laws are too varied among the states, so it is important to have this discussion with an attorney in the state in which you reside. Unless your heir(s) have co-signed or guaranteed your obligation, they have no obligation to pay your debts and obligations. Basically, your debts die with you, which is not to say they don't need to be paid. Your debts are paid out of the non-exempt assets in your estate.

The probate court will appoint a Personal Representative to administer your estate. If you have a Last Will and Testament, you may have specified whom you want to serve in that capacity, which will usually be honored by the court. If you don't have a Will, the Personal Representative will usually be a close family member.

The Personal Representative is charged with the duties of collecting the assets of your estate, paying your debts, and then distributing what is left to your heirs. But what happens if there aren't sufficient assets to pay off all the debts?

Different rules apply in different states, so be sure to confer with an estate-planning attorney in the state in which you reside. But basically, each state sets the order in which claims must be paid, with certain types of claims having a higher priority to payment than others.

For example, in Florida Statute 733.707, obligations are paid in the following order:

Class 1: Administrative costs and fees for the personal representative, estate attorney, and court costs get paid first

Class 2: Reasonable funeral, internment, and grave expenses up to $6,000.00 are paid

Class 3: Debts and taxes with preference under federal law, which include reimbursement of Medicaid and public assistance payments

Class 4: Reasonable and necessary medical and hospital expenses of the last 60 days of the decedent's final illness

Class 5: Family allowance to support surviving spouse and dependents during estate administration, up to a maximum of $18,000.00

Class 6: Court-ordered child support arrearage

Class 7: Debts acquired after death by continuing decedent's business

Class 8: All other claims, including any judgments against the decedent and any overage on Class 3 and Class 4 items

Why is the order of priority important? In Florida, if a Personal Representative pays creditors of a lower Class and then does not have sufficient assets to pay the creditors of a higher priority Class, then the Personal Representative will be **personally responsible** to satisfy in full the higher priority creditor! Therefore, a Personal Representative should not pay **any** creditors without first consulting the estate attorney handling the probate administration.

All the debts of the estate need to be satisfied (some can be compromised as to amount) before distribution can be made to the heirs. If there are insufficient liquid assets, other types of assets may need to be sold to satisfy the claims of creditors.

If you live in a community property state, the laws can be even trickier, and consulting with an attorney well versed in the estate planning and/or probate laws of that state is strongly advised.

Payment of Periodic and Occasional Bills

Most bills are paid **monthly**. The most common monthly bills include rent, mortgage, utility bills (electric, gas, water, sewer, scavenger, telephone, cable, internet, etc.), credit cards, student loans, child support and/or alimony payments.

Some bills are paid **quarterly**, such as income tax and business tax obligations.

Some bills are paid **semi-annually**, such as automobile insurance premiums.

And some bills are paid **annually**, such as life insurance premiums, real estate tax bills, and income taxes.

So, it is important to provide your representative with detailed information on your debts and customary obligations. This will help to avoid having late charges or interest assessed against you by credit card companies, your utilities being shut off, your car being repossessed, your insurance lapsing, or a home mortgage foreclosure action being filed by your bank.

Go through your check register or bank statements to start compiling the list of all the bills you pay. You'll be amazed by how many bills there are, and by the ones you may have forgotten to include in your list.

Chapter 9
Insurance

From both a financial planning and estate-planning standpoint, insurance is one of the most powerful tools for creating, preserving, protecting, and transferring wealth. An important part of having an estate plan is protecting one's estate from losses that can wipe out one's hard-earned wealth. Nothing can deplete an estate faster than a life catastrophe without the proper and sufficient insurance coverage.

However, the topic of insurance is one that will often cause one's eyes to glaze over. Insurance agents sometimes half-jokingly refer to the "insurance shuffle," referring to the backwards dance-like steps someone makes after inquiring what they do for a living and discovers that they sell insurance.

Insurance, like taxes and death, is one of those subjects nobody wants to think about, let alone talk about. It seems to be a complete waste of money as you pay premium after premium on your house, car, health, life, and more, sometimes for decades at a time, without ever filing a claim. It feels as though one is getting nothing in return for all the money being "wasted." At least, until something happens and a claim needs to be filed.

My personal insurance representative's tagline is, "You don't need insurance ... until you need it!" She knows everyone knows the obvious, but unspoken, "And when you do need it, you will be very thankful you had the foresight to have gotten it!"

Consider a widow with young children, whose husband was critically injured in a fire in their home, required emergency surgery, and sadly, did not survive. A property and casualty insurance policy will cover the cost of repairs to the house. A health insurance policy will cover the medical bills.

Having sufficient life insurance proceeds will provide financial stability by providing the widow with enough money to keep the house, pay the mortgage and bills, feed her family, and even provide money for the future educational needs of the children. Most of all, it will provide her with peace of mind, allowing her to decide if she wants to work while the kids are growing up. Without the insurance, she may be forced into taking a job to keep food on the table.

If the husband owned a business, along with a buy-sell agreement with a willing purchaser, a life insurance policy on the husband's life could provide the buyer with the funds needed to buy the husband's business, protect the husband's widow from the stress of trying to sell a business she may have no interest in owning or operating, and provide her with a sum of money to provide for herself and her children.

On the other hand, if his widow would prefer to remain the owner of the company, but lacks the knowledge, skill, or time to do so, a key-person life insurance policy will provide the funds needed to cover the salary of someone hired to continue to operate the business.

Say the husband hadn't died, but rather was disabled or seriously injured in the fire. A disability insurance policy would provide an income during his recovery, and an income continuation or business expense policy would cover lost income and/or the costs incurred in continuing business operations

If the husband needed to go into a nursing home or rehabilitation facility, long-term care insurance would cover the cost for several years.

Let us review some of the powerful ways that insurance can be used to create, preserve, protect, and transfer wealth.

Insurance is a tool that can be used to <u>create</u> wealth

Certain types of life insurance policies enable you to invest your money on a tax-deferred (and sometimes tax-free) basis to grow your assets and provide a future income to yourself and loved ones.

When you invest in a bank account, stocks, mutual funds, etc., all the interest, dividends, and realized capital gains are taxable to you when you file your annual income tax return, even if you don't take any of the money paid out and reinvest all of it. In an insurance or annuity product, all the interest, dividends, and realized capital gains continue to grow on a tax-deferred basis, enabling the investment to grow at a faster rate.

Certain policies will even allow you to borrow funds from your own policy on a tax-free basis should another opportunity come along requiring investment capital.

In addition, insurance creates wealth by enabling you to **leverage** your premium dollars to provide for your goals.

At the time of writing this book, I am 65 years of age. If I am in better-than-average health for the next 10 years, I can get $100,000 worth of term life insurance for an annual premium of about $1,500.00 per year. So, if I should die this year, my $1,500.00 will provide a death benefit of $100,000 to my beneficiaries. The tradeoff is, of course, if I live, neither I, nor my beneficiaries, will get the $1,500.00 I paid for the insurance each year.

Obtaining insurance at younger ages provide even greater leverage: If I was 50 years of age, I could get $300,000 for the same premium (or $100,000 coverage for about one-third of the cost). If I was 40, I could get $600,000 for the same premium (or $100,000 coverage for about one-sixth of the cost).

Other types of insurance policies allow you to build up cash reserves in a tax-advantaged manner, and may allow you to borrow funds from your own policy, should the need arise.

So, for a relatively small premium, a significant sum can be available to provide for your loved ones' future needs, provide capital to enable someone to purchase your business for cash, and provide a significant inheritance to your beneficiaries, often free from federal income taxes.

Insurance is a tool that can be used to <u>preserve</u> wealth

Insurance protects one from being wiped out in the event of a catastrophe by spreading the risk amongst thousands of people. Without health insurance, emergency medical care can range from tens of thousands to hundreds of thousands of dollars, which is why unanticipated medical expenses are probably the leading cause of bankruptcy in the United States. Without homeowner's insurance, would you be able to replace your house if it burned down? Without liability coverage on your automobile insurance policy, if you cause an automobile accident, you could be sued for hundreds of thousands of dollars.

When my daughter was 16 years old, while driving her car, she was temporarily blinded by the sun and rear ended another car. Since she was under 18, her car was registered in my name. And since she was the driver, and I was the owner, we were both named in the lawsuit. And even though there wasn't significant damage to the other car, the driver of the other car was injured sufficiently to result in a $55,000 settlement. Our insurance automobile insurance policy paid all of it, as well as the legal fees for our defense attorneys.

The very same year, while driving in the rain, I hydroplaned into a tree, totaling my car (the same accident that was my inspiration for writing this book). Within a few days, my insurance company paid me the $16,000 value of the car. It also covered the year's worth of treatments by a chiropractor to cure my injured back, an injury that didn't appear until weeks later. I was fortunate to have been in my car alone, as the passenger side of the car took the brunt of the collision. Had a passenger been in the car with me, I don't know if he or she would have survived. But my liability insurance would have covered my potential liability to my passenger, too. And if the claim exceeded my policy limits, an umbrella policy, which adds additional coverage limits over the basic limits, would have covered most, if not all, of the excess liability.

The total of the claims covered by my insurance that year exceeded $80,000.00, preserving that money for my future use. So, if I had previously been complaining about wasting my money on insurance premiums for so many years without a claim, this was certainly one year I didn't complain at all.

Insurance is a tool that can be used to protect wealth

In most states, the value of annuities and the cash value in life insurance policies are often protected from the claims of creditors in the event of a lawsuit. Sizeable amounts of assets can be invested in annuities and insurance policies, but this protection varies from state to state, so be certain to ask your financial advisor, insurance agent, and estate-planning attorney about the protection your state provides you.

Insurance is a tool that can be used to transfer wealth

In general, life insurance passes to your beneficiaries free from federal income taxes and, for most people, free from federal estate taxes (but check with your estate-planning attorney regarding inheritance laws in the state in which you reside). It is a fast, convenient, and relatively inexpensive way to provide a particular sum of money to your loved ones upon your death. Please note that life insurance may be added back into your estate to calculate federal estate taxes and state inheritance taxes, so if life insurance brings your total net worth above the amount that would result in federal estate or state inheritance taxes, advanced estate planning with an attorney will be advisable.

I will discuss some of the uses of life insurance below, but also want to discuss many other forms of insurance one may want to consider to protect their assets, preserve their estates, and meet other important objectives. After all, a catastrophe involving your property, business, health, as well as your life, can cause financial devastation on the assets you have for your future needs, and on the wealth you had hoped to pass onto your loved ones.

This chapter is not intended to be an all-inclusive treatise on insurance. The laws of each state are too varied, and how your needs and objectives may be served by the various types of insurance available are far too varied to discuss here. This chapter is merely meant to be an introduction to the subject of insurance in order to pique your interest, consider coverage you may not have known was available or suitable for your circumstances, and to encourage you to be sure to speak with your financial advisor, insurance agent, and/or estate-planning attorney regarding the use of various types of insurance as tools to achieve some of your estate planning and financial planning goals.

Many of the most common types of insurance are provided as benefits by many employers to their employees, sometimes at no cost to the employee, but more often at a lower rate than might otherwise be available to the employee if he or she obtained the insurance individually.

The most common types of insurance offered through employers are life, health, disability, and dental coverage.

For example, many employers will provide $50,000 in life insurance at no cost to the employee, although the employee can often pay to increase the coverage, if desired, often to as many as 5 times the employee's annual salary.

A benefit of an employer-sponsored life insurance plan may enable an employee, who might otherwise not be insurable due to medical circumstances (e.g. cancer, heart attack, etc.), to be covered by a group plan.

This is usually a **term life insurance** policy, which means the employee is insured only for the term of the policy, usually one year at a time. If the employee separates from the company (i.e., quits or is terminated), the policy may lapse, although the employee may be allowed to maintain the coverage, albeit at substantially higher rates.

Since the cost of term insurance increases every year, as the employee gets older, the cost continues to rise. In one's 60s and older, the annual increase in premium starts to rise dramatically.

For this reason, you may want to discuss the matter with your life insurance agent to see whether a level premium term policy would work for you, either in place of, or as a supplement to, the life insurance coverage offered through your employer. A level premium term policy enables you to lock in a fixed annual premium for a set number of years during which the protection is needed. For example, when my children were young, I took out a 20-year level term premium on my life, which gave me peace of mind, knowing I had provided them with enough financial security to protect them through the age of college. Note: At the end of the 20 years the coverage lapsed unless I was willing to continue the policy at a significantly higher annual premium. After all, I was now 20 years older than when I initially took out the policy. Accordingly, I was now a much higher risk to a life insurance company.

Life Insurance
Quite simply, a life insurance policy pays out a sum of money either on the death of the insured person or after a set period. As described above, it can be used in a multitude of ways, but most commonly it is to provide a source of financial stability for your family upon your death.

Second-to-Die Insurance
Generally, second-to-die insurance is used for estate planning. It is a type of cost-effective life insurance on two people that provides benefits to the heirs only after both spouses die. This differs from regular life insurance in that the surviving partner doesn't receive any benefits after their spouse dies.

People who take out this type of insurance are thinking of their heirs, not themselves. For example, it could be designed to pay estate taxes or support any surviving children. It is also called dual-life insurance and survivorship insurance.

These policies cover two or more people for less money than two individual policies would cost. For even more cost flexibility, you can choose to have a joint policy issued as term coverage, or you can choose the protection and cash value accrual of a permanent policy.

Annuities
An annuity is offered through insurance companies as a financial product designed to accept and grow funds from an individual, usually on a tax-deferred basis, and then, upon annuitization, pay out a stream of payments to the individual at a later point in time. The period of time when an annuity is being funded and before payouts begin is referred to as the accumulation phase. Once payments commence, the contract is in the annuitization phase.

In practical terms, an annuity is a type of insurance product which provides the opposite type of protection provided by life insurance. Life insurance is to protect your loved ones if you die too soon. Annuities provide you with an income stream, usually for the balance of your life, to protect you from living too long.

Accidental Death & Dismemberment (AD&D) Insurance
As the name suggests, accidental death and dismemberment (AD&D) insurance is a policy that pays benefits to the beneficiary if the cause of death is an accident, and is considered a supplement to life insurance and disability insurance.

In the event of an accidental death, this insurance will pay benefits in addition to any life insurance but only up to a set amount total, regardless of any other insurance held by the same insurer, held by the client. This is called double indemnity coverage and is often available even when accidental death insurance is merely an add-on to a regular life insurance plan. Some of the covered accidents include traffic accidents, falls, heavy equipment accidents, and drowning. Accidental deaths are the fifth leading cause of death in the United States.

Accidental death insurance is not an investment vehicle and thus, clients are paying only for sustained protection. Most policies must be renewed periodically.

The "dismemberment" portion of the name refers to benefit payments made for the loss of limbs, fingers, toes, sight, and permanent paralysis, and is generally calculated as a percentage of the "face amount" of the policy, depending on the seriousness of the injury. For example, the accidental death portion of the policy will pay 100% of the face amount for an accidental death. Different percentages of the face amount will be paid if you lose a thumb and finger on the same hand, more if you lose a hand, foot, or sight in one eye, and 100% if you lose two or more limbs, or sight in both eyes.

Some policies will pay double the face amount (i.e. **double indemnity**) for injuries or deaths due to accidents under certain circumstances, such as riding as a paying customer on a plane, bus, etc.

Compare that to life insurance, which pays money to your beneficiary if you die from ***any*** cause—such as accident, illness or old age—except for suicide during the first one or two years of the policy, depending on the state and the terms of the policy.

Long-Term-Care Insurance (LTC)

The U.S. Department of Health and Human Services estimates that approximately 70% of Americans will need long-term care during their lifetimes. In addition, 69% of Americans older than 90 years of age will have some form of disability, which often results in the need for long-term care.

Consider that, in 2013, the median annual cost of a private room in a nursing home was $83,950, or $230 per day. A private one-bedroom unit in an assisted living facility has a median cost of $3,450 a month, or $41,000 annually. The cost of both types of care have been rising at the rate of approximately 4.5% per year. Compare these amounts with your life savings, retirement accounts, and other assets, and ask yourself if you will have enough money to pay $40,000-$85,000 per year. If you are married, multiply the number by two. How long will your money last?

While long-term care coverage can cost several thousand dollars a year, compared to the above costs of a nursing home or assisted living facility, the expense of the insurance may be well justified for you. This is a matter to discuss in detail with your insurance and/or financial advisor.

As with life insurance, the longer you wait to obtain the coverage, the more expensive the premiums will be. For this reason, many people purchase this coverage before they retire from their job, usually in their 60s. If you wait until you are 80 years of age or in poor health, you will probably be ineligible for coverage.

Many people incorrectly believe long-term care insurance covers just nursing home care. This is inaccurate, as it can pay for a wide variety of nursing and rehabilitative services at home and away from home, for people with a chronic illness or disability, or people who need less intensive help, as with bathing, eating, or dressing.

People often think that Medicare will cover long-term care expenses, which is incorrect. Medicare will pay for the first 100 days of nursing home care, but only if you are getting skilled care, and if you go into the nursing home immediately after a hospital stay of at least three days. Both are required. Medicare may also cover limited home visits for skilled care and some hospice services for the terminally ill, but that's pretty much all that is covered.

On the other hand, Medicaid, which is provided at the state level, can pay for long-term care, but only if you are destitute. Do you want to spend all your money on your care before qualifying for Medicaid? Note: There are methods of "Medicaid planning" some elder law attorneys can discuss with you, which may help to preserve some assets for your beneficiaries, but this type of planning is quite specialized and can be expensive to implement.

I consider a discussion of long-term care and life insurance coverage to be such an important topic and integral part of the estate-planning process that I require my clients to sign a statement acknowledging that they understand the importance of discussing both types of coverage with their insurance and/or financial advisors, and if they already have either or both types of coverage, to reconfirm that the amount of coverage they own is sufficient for their current and future needs, and the needs and protection of their loved ones.

Health Insurance

Health insurance is a type of insurance coverage that pays for medical and surgical expenses incurred by the insured. Health insurance can reimburse the insured for expenses incurred from illness or injury, or pay the care provider directly. Prescription drug plans are a form of insurance offered through some health insurance plans. There is often a deductible amount and/or a co-pay, which must be satisfied by the patient before the insurance company is required to pay anything. Since insurance is meant to share the risk between the patient insured and the insurance company, requiring the patient to pay a portion of the medical bills helps to prevent the patient from seeking unnecessary (and sometimes expensive) medical treatment for minor illnesses or injuries.

Disability Insurance

Disability insurance is an insurance plan that provides for periodic payments of benefits when a disabled insured is unable to work. The insurance product is designed to replace anywhere from 45 to 65% of your gross income on a tax-free basis should illness keep you from earning an income in your occupation.

There are two types of disability insurance:

1. **Short-Term Disability** policies (STD), which have a waiting period of 0-14 days before payments begin, and usually limit the protection period to no longer than two years.

2. **Long-Term Disability** policies (LTD), which have a longer waiting period (e.g. several weeks to several months) before payments begin, with a maximum benefit period ranging from a few years to the rest of the insured's life.

Medicare & Medicare Supplemental Insurance

Medicare is a U.S. federal government health insurance program that provides health care for the aged, defined as 65 years of age or older. It also covers certain disabled persons under 65. The program is administered through the U.S. Social Security administration, and reimburses hospitals and physicians for medical care provided to qualified people. The basic Medicare plan will pay most medical expenses, but is subject to certain deductibles for health care, hospitalization, surgery, drugs, and more, which must be paid by the patient.

Therefore, supplemental plans are offered through select private insurance companies to cover most, if not all, of the deductibles.

Homeowner's Insurance – Property, Liability, and Casualty

Be certain that you understand what is, and equally important, what is not, covered by your insurance policy. Assuming you are covered for anything and everything that can happen can be an extremely expensive mistake.

What happens in case of a fire, flood, earthquake, or a sewer backing up?

What happens if someone hurts themselves inside your house?

What happens if a worker you have hired falls off your roof?

What happens if you are robbed?

Does your homeowner's insurance cover you when you are out of the house, say, on vacation?

What else does it cover?

Is all your jewelry covered? Most policies limit coverage to a certain dollar limit unless you increase the coverage through purchase of a "rider," which provides a formal modification to the terms in the policy. This also applies to other types of valuables, such as collections, artwork, antiques, etc. What about your computer and other electronics?

Don't forget about replacement-cost coverage. Most policies will pay you a depreciated value due to the age of the item. So, that big screen television that cost you $1,200 5 years ago, and would cost the same to replace today, may have a depreciated value of just $300. Ask your agent about replacement-cost coverage, which is usually just a nominal additional amount when compared to the difference between buying a new replacement for whatever has been stolen or damaged, compared to the depreciated value.

Personal property coverage – jewelry, artwork, computers, and electronics.

Here's a "fun" assignment: Take out a sheet of paper. Assume that your house has just burned to the ground. Start listing everything you own that was in the house. Include the obvious, such as kitchen appliances, bedroom set, dining room, dishes and glassware, bowls, pots and pans, silverware, good china and crystal, etc. Now, think about every picture hanging on the wall, all the contents of your shelves and drawers, all the boxes of stuff in your closets, how many suits, pants, shirts, etc. (for the guys), or dresses, slacks, blouses, etc. (for the ladies). What about underwear? I bet you'd be surprised by how much of everything you have. Now, try to put a value on all it. It is quite a hefty amount, isn't it?

For this reason, I recommend taking a video inventory of the contents of your house (or paying a service to do it for you). I believe the above exercise will reinforce the concept that one is unable to remember all the contents of one's home order to file a claim. Having a video inventory of every room, closet, drawer, shelf, etc., while you are dictating aloud what the camera is capturing will help jog your memory, and may be useful evidence establishing what you had in your home on the particular date of the video. Remember to chronicle the date of taking the video (e.g. video the front page of the local newspaper, zooming on the date), try to get as many serial numbers as possible for high-expense items (see chapter on getting organized), and keep it in a different location, lest it be destroyed in a fire – safe deposit box. Don't forget to include the garage, attic, basement, shed, the trunk of your car, outside storage unit, and things kept at your place of employment.

Some people just take pictures, which is better than nothing, but I prefer a video for the accompanying narrative describing the contents of the house, and counting the number of dresses, pants, and yes, even socks and underwear.

Ask your insurance agent what type of proof the insurance company will want if you need to file a claim. What will they require and what will suffice to satisfy them? Receipts of purchase? Pictures? Videos? A written list of assets?

Condominium Insurance

If you own a condominium, as opposed to a house, your condominium association's insurance does not cover the contents of the unit you own. The insurance that is included in your monthly assessment generally covers the structural elements of the building (roof, floors, walls, etc.) and common elements of the building (e.g. hallway, parking garage, etc.). It does <u>not</u> cover your own valuables, furnishings, or other contents of your unit. Similarly, if there is a fire or other catastrophe, while the insurance may cover the installation of the structural components of new walls, it may not cover the cost of decorating them with new paint, retiling the bathroom, or replacement of other improvements (e.g. upgraded kitchen cabinets) you have made within your unit.

You should have your own policy to cover your valuables and other contents of your unit, as well as for liability if someone hurts themselves inside your unit.

Renter's Insurance

As with condominium insurance above, if you are a tenant, whether it is a house, condo, apartment, or other rental unit, your landlord's homeowner's insurance does not cover your own contents or valuables inside your rental unit. If a thief breaks into your unit and steals your valuables, while the landlord's insurance may cover the cost of replacing a broken lot, renter's insurance is needed to replace your own stolen valuables and protect you if someone hurts themselves while inside your unit. The cost of this coverage, unless you have significant valuables, is rather nominal in cost. And as above, do not forget to obtain replacement cost coverage.

Prepaid Funeral/Burial/Cremation Insurance

The typical funeral can cost between $7,000 and $10,000, including the services at a funeral home, casket, burial in a cemetery, and installation of a headstone. There are plenty of additional expenses that can be incurred, depending on the desires of the decedent and his or her survivors. This type of insurance covers the cost, determined in advance by the insured, to be paid for **funeral** services and merchandise costs.

Similarly, National Cremation & Burial Society, Neptune Society, and other organizations, offer pre-paid cremation services.

By making all your arrangements (and paying for them in advance), you save your grieving family the hassles and pressures of making numerous decisions on many of the difficult details regarding your funeral, as well as having to come up with the funds to pay for it.

Automobile Insurance (including uninsured and under-insured motorist coverage)

As a condition of having a driver's license, most, if not all, states require drivers to purchase a minimum amount of liability insurance coverage, which pays for injuries and property damage that you cause to others in an accident. It does not cover your own injuries or property damage. Sadly, the mandatory requirement is often a very low amount, such as $10,000.00.

I recently had a new probate matter referred to me in which the father of two young children was killed by a drunk driver who had no insurance (and no other assets to pursue). Before he died, he was flown by medevac (air ambulance transport) helicopter to a nearby hospital at a staggering cost of $42,000.

The deceased father had the state-mandated minimum liability policies ($10,000) on both of his vehicles, which enabled the attorney handling the wrongful death claim to "stack" the policies, qualifying for double coverage, or $20,000 under the uninsured motorist coverage on his policies. The father had no life insurance coverage.

So, $20,000 less a fee to the attorney (30% of the proceeds, which is $6,000) left 14,000. Subtracting the funeral expenses of $6,000 left $8,000. Subtract probate expenses and the potential need of Guardianship for the minor children, and not much remained for two children.

Having no insurance coverage, of course, is inexcusable. Having just the mandatory minimum coverage to have the legal right to drive isn't much better.

Having sufficient coverage (including uninsured and under-insured coverage) is essential to protect not only the cost of your own medical bills, repairs to your automobile, and liability for others' medical and automobile repairs, but also a sufficient amount to protect and provide for your loved ones and protect your hard-earned assets.

If the drunk driver in the above scenario had had bank or investment accounts, owned a business or non-homestead protected assets, he could have potentially lost all those assets due to his actions.

While I have absolutely no sympathy for the drunk driver (or for any drunk or otherwise impaired driver), my heart goes out to the family of all the victims of his action: the deceased father, both children, and the families who will need to raise the children without sufficient financial resources needed to give them a good life.

And the $42,000 medevac helicopter bill gets paid by Medicaid, or more accurately, by everybody else's tax dollars.

Various automobile insurance coverages often included in a comprehensive coverage policy include:
Liability
Personal Injury Protection (PIP) & Medical Coverage
Collision and Comprehensive (optional)
Uninsured/Underinsured Motorist
Emergency Road Service Coverage
Towing and Labor Coverage (optional)
Gap Insurance; and
Rental Reimbursement Coverage (Optional)

And whatever you do, don't forget to obtain adequate uninsured/underinsured coverage!

Umbrella Policy
An umbrella insurance policy is extra liability insurance coverage that goes beyond the limits of the insured's home, auto, or watercraft insurance. It provides an additional layer of security to those who are at risk for being sued for damages to other people's property or injuries caused to others in an accident.

Business Insurance Policies
As for types of business insurance, the types of coverages available are as numerous and varied in what they cover as the number and variety of businesses.

Since this chapter is not meant to be a treatise on all the types of insurance policies that are available—which are numerous!—a short list of coverages you may want to discuss with your commercial/business insurance agent include:

Property Insurance
Property insurance pays for losses and damages to real or personal property. For example, a property insurance policy would cover fire damage to your office space.

You can purchase additional coverages for business property, including:

- **Boiler and Machinery Insurance**, sometimes referred to as "equipment breakdown" or "mechanical breakdown coverage," provides coverage for the accidental breakdown of boilers, machinery, and equipment. This type of coverage usually will reimburse you for property damage and business interruption losses (e.g. fire damage to computers).

- **Debris Removal Insurance** covers the cost of removing debris after a fire, flood, windstorm, etc. For example, a fire burns your building to the ground. Before you can start rebuilding, the remains of the old building must be removed. Your property insurance will cover the costs of rebuilding, but not the cost of removing the debris.

- **Builder's Risk Insurance** covers buildings while they are being constructed. For example, a builder's risk policy would cover losses if a windstorm takes down your partially-constructed condominium complex.
- **Glass Insurance** covers broken store windows and plate glass windows.
- **Inland Marine Insurance** covers property in transit and other people's property on your premises. For example, this insurance would cover fire damage to customers' clothing from a fire at your dry-cleaning business.
- **Business Interruption Insurance** covers lost income and expenses resulting from property damage or loss. For example, if a fire forces you to close your doors for two months, this insurance would reimburse you for salaries, taxes, rents, and net profits that would have been earned during the two-month period.
- **Ordinance or Law Insurance** covers the costs associated with having to demolish and rebuild to code when your building has been partially destroyed (usually 50%). For example, your three-story building is 100 years old. A flood destroys the basement and first two stories. Because more than 50% of your building has to be rebuilt, a local ordinance requires that the building be completely demolished and rebuilt according to current building codes. Property insurance covers only the replacement value, not the upgrade.
- **Tenant's Insurance.** Commercial leases often require tenants to carry a certain amount of insurance. A renter's commercial policy covers damages to improvements you make to your rental space and damages to the building caused by the negligence of your employees.
- **Crime Insurance** covers property crimes such as theft, burglary, and robbery of money, securities, stock, and fixtures from employees and outsiders.
- **Fidelity Bonds.** A bond company covers losses due to a bonded employee's theft of business property and money.

Liability & Products Liability Insurance covers injuries that you cause to third parties. If someone sues you for personal injuries or property damage, the cost of defending and resolving the suit will be covered by your liability insurance policy. A general liability policy will cover you for common risks, including customer injuries on your premises.

Errors and Omissions ("E & O") Insurance covers inadvertent mistakes or failures that cause injury to a third party. The act must be one of inadvertent error, and not merely poor judgment or an intentional act. For example, an E & O policy will cover damages arising from an insurance agent failing to file policy applications, or a notary forgetting to fill out notarizations properly.

Malpractice Insurance, or professional liability insurance, pays for losses resulting from injuries to third parties when a professional's conduct falls below the profession's standard of care. For example, if a doctor makes a mistake that other doctors of his specialty would not have made, his patient might sue him. A malpractice policy will pay his defense costs and any judgment or settlement. Malpractice insurance is available for doctors, dentists, layers, accountants, real estate agents, architects, and other professionals.

Commercial Automobile Insurance cover the cars, vans, trucks, and trailers used in your business. The coverage will reimburse you if your vehicles are damaged, stolen, or if the driver injures a person or property.

Directors' and Officers' Liability Insurance is generally purchased by corporations and nonprofit organizations to cover the costs of lawsuits against directors and officers.

Workers' Compensation Insurance covers your business for an employee's on-the-job injuries. Businesses with employees are required by various state laws to carry some type of workers' compensation insurance. In most cases, workers' compensation laws prohibit the employee from bringing a negligence lawsuit against an employer for work-related injuries.

Cyber liability/data breach insurance is designed to cover consumers of technology services or products. More specifically, the policies are intended to cover a variety of both liability and property losses that may result when a business engages in various electronic activities, such as selling on the Internet or collecting data within its internal electronic network.

Most notably, but not exclusively, cyber and privacy policies cover a business' liability for a data breach in which the firm's customers' personal information, such as social security or credit card numbers, is exposed or stolen by a hacker or other criminal who has gained access to the firm's electronic network. The policies cover a variety of expenses associated with data breaches, including: notification costs, credit monitoring, costs to defend claims by state regulators, fines and penalties, and loss resulting from identity theft.

In addition, the policies cover liability arising from website media content, as well as property exposures from: (a) business interruption, (b) data loss/destruction, (c) computer fraud, (d) funds transfer loss, and cyber extortion and ransomware.

Key Person Insurance is life insurance on the key person in a business. In a small business, this is usually the owner, the founders, or perhaps a key employee or two. These are the people who are crucial to a business; the ones whose absence would sink the company. You definitely need to consider key person insurance on those people.

Succession Planning for small, family-owned companies, often means training the next generation to take over the business. A larger business might groom mid-level employees to one day take over higher-level positions. In a partnership, one method of succession planning has each partner purchase a life insurance policy that names the other partner as the beneficiary. That way, if a partner dies at a time when the surviving partner otherwise wouldn't have enough cash to buy the deceased partner's ownership share, the life insurance proceeds will make that purchase possible. This type of succession plan is called a cross-purchase agreement and allows the surviving partner to continue operating the business.

Chapter 10
Your Funeral

As one of the two well-known certainties in life (the other being taxes), death is the inevitable final curtain call to every person's life. From the time you take your first breath, you are on the path to taking your final breath.

While you may believe it to be a morbid and uncomfortable topic of conversation, someone is going to have the unpleasant task and be required to bear the responsibility of planning for the disposition of your earthly remains, as well as being required to make a surprisingly large number of decisions on your behalf. If you don't take the initiative to make all the plans in advance, or at least let your preferences be known, all these hard decisions will have to be made by your loved ones at the time of their greatest grief and stress. Or worse, if there are no loved ones to make the decisions, they will be made on your behalf by government bureaucrats.

I recently lost a long-time client of over 20 years. He had no wife, no children, and he had lost his only sister. His only remaining family members were his two nephews. I found out about his passing through a frantic call from one of his nephews, "Do you know if Uncle John had made any arrangements regarding his funeral, and whether he owned a cemetery plot?"

Neither of them lived nearby, so they found out about his passing through a call from an observant neighbor who had noticed he didn't take his two dogs for their customary morning walk. Since he lived alone and in a rural area, one wonders how long it might have been before someone discovered his body.

The nearest nephew, who lived several hours away, made the drive to my client's home and was immediately thrown into the high-stress position of having to arrange for the body to be taken to a funeral home, frantically searching through boxes and drawers of paperwork to see whether or not there was a burial policy or other pre-planned funeral arrangements, and then having to make numerous rapid-fire decisions on behalf of the deceased and the family.

Who are the first people that need to be notified? Who else should be contacted? Should something be posted on his Facebook page or other social media?

What did he want to be done regarding the disposition of his remains? Did he want his usable organs to be donated for others to use? If so, did he want to donate all them, or just some of them, such as his heart, liver, kidney, cornea, skin and more? Or did he want his body donated to science, and if so, where was the paperwork with the arrangements?

Did he want to be buried or cremated? If buried, where did he want his final resting place to be? Which cemetery? Did he own a cemetery plot, and if so, where was the deed located? Did he own a burial policy, and if so, where was the policy? Did he want a memorial service? Did he want an expensive funeral with a top-end, satin-lined casket with platinum handles, an open-casket viewing, a big ceremony with a choir, and a celebration-of-life party? Or did he want a plain pine box and a small private ceremony? Or something in between? What apparel should he wear?

What was the budget for the funeral, and where would the money come from to pay for it?

Was he entitled to a military honor guard? Did he want a religious ceremony performed by clergy?

Who should be asked to speak at the memorial service, if anyone?

Who were to be the pallbearers?

Were there to be flowers, or would he have preferred donations to be made to a charity, and if so, which one?

What music, if any, should be played? What scriptures, poems, or life stories should be told? And who would be the ones to read them or tell the stories?

If he was to be cremated, did he want his ashes kept by a family member, scattered on the ocean, or kept in a vault somewhere?

Who would write the obituary, and what should it say? And how about the eulogy?

There are so many decisions to be made, and somebody has to make them. Why not take the pressure off of your loved ones and make them yourself?

There is a section in the "Everything" file section of this book that asks these ,and many more, important questions regarding your final wishes and arrangements.

While you're at it, if you have some favorite family photographs or videos, why not put together a video montage of them? Think of it as a video replay of your happiest moments in life to share with others.

How about writing your own eulogy in your own words? You can pick someone to read it for you, or better yet, how about recording an audio or video of yourself saying your farewells that can be played at your funeral? You may consider it to be strange, morbid, or even in bad taste, but who can tell your life story, and talk about what you felt was important in your life, better than you?

I hope you will discover, as I did in writing my own eulogy, that in looking back over all that you have experienced over the years, you have had a pretty fabulous life!

As an example, mine would be a video, recorded now, and hopefully updated every five years or so, and would say something along the lines of what follows below. Since my hobby consists of performing in local productions of Broadway musicals, which I have done for almost 40 years, most of the people who attend my funeral will know that theater was an important and wonderful part of my life. My final message would contain, a lot of theater references. And please note that, despite the serious content in this book, I love to make people laugh, and have done so my entire life, with my wacky, and sometimes irreverent, since of humor. I may as well continue doing so in my final message to them ... my eulogy. I want their final memory of me to be one filled with laughter!

But that's just me. Make yours as solemn and reverent as you want your own final message to be.

Here is my own eulogy, at least as of the moment of publishing this book (subject to modification in future years due to new life experiences):

> "Hello to all my good friends and family! If you're seeing this video, I guess the curtain has gone down on my last performance, hopefully to thunderous applause and a standing ovation!
>
> At the time of recording this video, it is 2017 and I'm 65 years of age. Hopefully, by the time you are seeing this, a lot more years have gone by since recording it, and I officially qualify as an "old geezer"!
>
> But if not, that's okay. Like everyone else, I've had my shares of peaks and valleys in life, but happily, I've had many more ups than downs! So over all, I've had a **WONDERFUL** life!
>
> I had two fabulous parents, Irving & Shirley! They taught me to live my life as a positive, optimistic, enthusiastic, caring person, with compassion and empathy for others in need, and an appreciation for the arts, all the wonders of the world that surround us, and all the blessings I have been given.

I've had a varied and wondrous life. I've been a son, grandson, brother, father, grandfather, and stepfather. I was a Cub Scout, Boy Scout, explorer, and sergeant in the Air National Guard. I played trombone from fifth grade through college and played in the pit orchestra for numerous Broadway musicals. I was drum major of the University of Illinois Marching Illini and the 566th Air Force Band. I've snow-skied the slopes of most of the western states, Canada, Austria, and Switzerland. I've visited many countries, including Israel, England, Germany, Austria, Spain, and have been on numerous cruises to the Caribbean and around the world. I've sung at a governor's inauguration, and at more karaoke events than I'd care to remember. I've danced West Coast swing, East Coast swing, salsa, tango, cha cha, waltz, fox trot, and more. I've done country dancing and line dancing, worked out with weights, and spent thousands of hours on the elliptical trainer. I've been a lawyer, arbitrator, mediator, financial advisor, certified financial planner, but still mowed my own lawn, shoveled my own snow (when I lived in Chicago), and loved to do projects around the house. Every day was an adventure.

As many of you know, musical theater has always been a passion of mine, and if you appreciate that warm and wonderful feeling of stepping out of a freezing-cold office into the hot Florida sunshine, that's the feeling I always experienced when I stepped onto stage and the spotlight hit me as I began to sing a song! I've performed in over 50 productions of Broadway musicals, written dozens of funny music parodies, had the privilege of sharing the stage with many fabulously talented performers, danced a lot of fun choreography, made audiences laugh and cry (my favorite was to make them roar with laughter), and I got to kiss lot of girls (Hey, it was written in the script!) Oh, and there was that one show in which I even kissed a guy ("La Cage aux Folles")! In one show, I even got a pie thrown in my face ("Mack & Mabel")!

After so many years of looking, I finally found the love of my life, Helen, who brought love, joy, elegance, beauty, and class into my life! I love her children, Tamara and Tony, and her entire family who embraced me as one of their own! And I have to give a special "Thank you" to her sweet and beautiful daughter, Tamara, and to Match.com for helping me to find my sweet, beautiful, and exceptional lady!

Helen, I loved that you would laugh at my wacky antics and shared my sometimes-juvenile sense of humor. I loved your intelligence, sweet disposition, work ethic, and extremely wide variety of talents! I made a point of trying to do something to enhance every day of your life, to keep you laughing, and promised to continue spinning you around the dance floor to the end of our days together. I hope I have lived up to all the promises I ever made to you!

The final lyrics of the Broadway musical, "Les Miserables" are, "To love another person is to see the face of God!" Through you, my beloved Helen, I have had the privilege of seeing the face of God! You are my real-life angel and I will love you to the end of time!

To my amazing daughters, Jada and Jenna, you gave my life meaning! I thank your mother for bringing me such wondrous miracles! From the instant I first held you in my arms, each of you have brought joy into my life! Watching you grow from being infants totally dependent on me, to toddlers absorbing all you could learn, to Daddy's girls, having me wrapped around your little fingers, (including the countless, but wonderful, hours spent taking Jada to her horseback riding lessons and Jenna to her gymnastics), to growing into young ladies experimenting with and discovering your own thoughts and opinions, and laying the groundwork for the rest of your lives, and finally, becoming the mature women you have each become, each of you pursuing your own dreams and living your lives on your own terms. I am so proud of you both! As my final words of fatherly advice, please make a point of doing the things you love to do. Enjoy every day of your lives, and live each day with humor and passion. Thank you for being my sweet girls! I love you both to infinity and beyond! And yes, you both make me KVELL! (That's Yiddish for "burst with pride!")

To all my friends and family, thank you for taking some time out of your busy lives to honor me with your presence here today! To those who could not attend, I understand, and love you anyway! Thank you all for being a joyous part of my life and for allowing me to be a part of your lives, too. Our journey together was a continuous laugh-fest! I've had the privilege of seeing some of you grow up, seeing some of you get married, seeing some of you have children of your own, and watching those children grow up. I've had the privilege of performing on stage with you, working with you, dining, laughing, and crying with you, singing with you, and dancing with you. I loved every minute of being with you and spending time with you! Thank you all for helping me to have such an exceptional life!

If I have ever done or said anything to hurt or offend any of you, I sincerely apologize and ask your forgiveness. And if you've ever said or done anything that hurt my feelings, whether intentional or not, I forgive you.

I have a few final requests: If you are here with someone you care about, please take their hand, look them in the eyes, and tell them how much they mean to you ... right now! If you're angry with someone, forgive them. If you've fallen out of touch with someone, reach out to them. And please, try to do a random act of kindness for a stranger.

I don't know if there is an afterlife, but if so, I look forward to seeing you all again ... but hopefully, that won't be for a <u>very</u> long time! (wink)

My favorite of all lines, spoken by my favorite of all characters, in my favorite of all shows, a role I performed in 4 different productions, has also been my life motto, and I tried to live these words. It is a line spoken by Harold Hill in "The Music Man:"

"Pile up enough tomorrows, and you'll find you've collected nothing but a lot of empty yesterdays! I don't know about you, but I'd like to make TODAY a day worth remembering!"

To you, my friends and family: Please make today ... and **every** day for the rest of your lives ... a day worth remembering! Thank you all for coming today and thank you for being a part of my life."

Note: All the above would take less than 8 minutes to record.

Please be sure to keep your final message positive and loving. This is not the place or time to be mean, vindictive, or say something you've "always wanted to say to that 'no good son of a #$%#.'" In some states, words "spoken" after death can still be the basis for a defamation lawsuit. Keep it pleasant, positive, and uplifting, so people will remember your last words as a happy final remembrance.

And don't forget, regardless of whether you have written it down or recorded it as an audio or video, be sure to let someone know that it exists, and where you have it stored, so the person charged with the responsibility of reading or playing it will know where to find it.

Your funeral is your final opportunity to create a special memory of yourself, what was meaningful to you, what best expresses your life experience, education, passions, and loves! You can be modest and have someone else do and say what they think you would have wanted, or you can take the initiative and write down exactly what you want to be said and done.

Speaking in theatrical parlance, this is your final show, and if you want, you can write the script, select the music and costumes, choose the cast members, and pick the props and setting. You are the producer, and most importantly, you are the STAR!

By providing the information needed to prepare for your funeral, you are providing the director (a chosen loved one or the funeral director) with the details to make for a special remembrance and memorial on your behalf.

I remember attending a funeral for a much-loved theater friend. She had been a dance teacher and choreographer in the area for decades, so after her funeral, there was a "Celebration of Life" event. There were at least 500 people in attendance; all seats were filled. In her honor, there were videos and numerous pictures of her, shows she had choreographed, and her family. Several dances were performed by former students in her honor, funny and loving songs were sung from shows she had choreographed, and loving stories were told. It was a full-blown theatrical event.

Everyone left with big smiles on their faces, appreciative tears in their eyes, and hugs for one another, celebrating her life and her contributions to our theater community.

I joked with a friend about the number of people in attendance, "At my funeral, I'd be lucky to fill the front row of pews." He smirked and quipped back, "Well, if you have an open bar, I'll be there!" And I thought, "I like that idea!"

I don't want a sad and somber final event for myself. I want a Celebration of Life! I want everyone to celebrate what a great life I've had, filled with a loving family, wonderful friends, and a multitude of special, memorable experiences. I want everyone to be laughing, dancing, and remembering special moments we shared together. And I want them to all leave with smiles on their faces, inspired to appreciate their remaining days on earth.

Oh, and yes, there WILL be an open bar!

But that's my final production. You design your own. If you want a quiet, private ceremony for your immediate family, that's your privilege. It's your show.

If you want to be cremated and have your ashes scattered over the sea, made a part of a barrier reef, or even compressed into a diamond ring (yes, I discovered organizations that actually do all these!), it's your show.

Or if you prefer to be buried in your 1968 Pontiac GTO convertible, holding your prized baseball bat autographed by Babe Ruth, wearing a gold sequin tuxedo, and carried to your final resting place in a carriage drawn by six snow-white horses, with baton twirlers and a marching band playing "The Stars and Stripes Forever" leading the way, and a 21-gun salute and fireworks, go for it! It's your show, limited only by your imagination (and bank account)!

There are organizations, such as Dignity Memorial® (www.DignityMemorial.com, Phone number: 1-800-DIGNITY), which will help you with such planning. In their materials they say that they work with more than 1,800 funeral, cremation, and cemetery service providers, helping to honor and preserve a life's story, and providing an interesting array of planning, bereavement, guidance, and memorial services and products.

Take some time to write down what you want, and save your loved ones the stress of having to guess what you would have wanted. They will appreciate it. And be sure to discuss your preferences with them, and show them where your preferences are written down, so they know what they are and where to find them.

Information Needed in Preparing for the Funeral

For the Death Certificate and placement of the notice/obituary, provide

1. Your name and address
2. Your date of birth
3. Your social security number
4. Armed services number, if applicable
5. Mother's full name (including maiden name) and birthplace
6. Father's full name and birthplace
7. Your place of birth
8. Education
9. Work history
10. Church affiliation
11. Organizations or memberships

12. Special achievements; and
13. Names of surviving relatives and the cities in which they live. Include parents, spouse, siblings, children grandchildren, grandparents, etc.

Questions they will need answered

1. Who are the first people who need to be contacted, along with their contact information?
2. Do you prefer to be buried, cremated, have your body donated to science, or other disposition?
3. Do you have a preference as to the funeral home, mortuary, or other funeral provider?
4. Do you have a pre-paid burial or funeral plan, and if so, where are the documents?
5. Do you already own a cemetery plot or interment vault, and if so, where is it located? Where is the deed, and what is the cemetery section name, block, and plot number? If not, do you have a preference as to a memorial park or cemetery?
6. Place of worship preferred, if any?
7. For burial, do you prefer a mausoleum, ground burial, or cremation?
8. For cremation, do you prefer your remains be buried, scattered (and where), given to whom?
9. Casket preferences: Hardwood, metal, cremation container, or other (specify)?
10. Were you in the military, and if so, do you want military honors?
11. Do you prefer a funeral or memorial service, Celebration of Life, Life Appreciation Ceremony, or a combination?
12. Do you prefer a funeral service for the community, a graveside service, or both?
13. Is there to be a reception or gathering after the funeral, and if so, do you have a preference as to where it is held?
14. Are out-of-town family members to be reimbursed for their travel expenses?
15. Financially, do you have a price preference as to how much you want to be spent for the entire funeral (bare-bones minimum, moderate, extravagant with all the bells and whistles)?
16. Do you want perpetual care for your gravesite?

For your service

1. Do you have a religious preference?
2. Do you have a preferred clergyman or other person to serve as celebrant?
3. Are there organizations you want invited (military, fraternal lodge, fraternity, etc.)?
4. Is there to be a wake or rosary service, and if so, where?
5. Is there to be a viewing, and if so, is it to be public or private? Open casket or not?
6. What clothing do you prefer to wear?
7. Do you want a flag draped or folded, and if so, to whom shall it be presented?
8. Is your wedding band (if any) to stay on, and if not, to whom should it be given?
9. Do you want your eyeglasses to stay on, and if not, to whom should they be given?
10. Is there a special remembrance you would like buried with you (some article of significance to you)?
11. Do you have a floral preference (type and color preferred)? Or would you prefer memorial donations be made, and if so, to what charitable organization?
12. Do you have a music preference, and if so, what musical selections, soloist, organist, etc.?
13. Do you have any special religious passages you would like read, and if so, by whom?
14. Who would you like to give the eulogy? Are there any special stories or memories you would like him or her to include in the eulogy?
15. Who would you like to serve as pallbearers? (Name six to eight, and include their telephone numbers and/or email addresses so they can be notified of the funeral date, time, and place).
16. Provide a photograph for cosmetic purposes.
17. Provide a collection of photographs, meaningful objects, and special notes, letters and cards to display.
18. Who is to be invited (and is there anyone who you specifically do NOT want to be invited)?
19. Are children to be allowed to attend?
20. Is there to be a guest register for guests to sign?

21. Is there to be a photographer?
22. Who should serve as a "gatekeeper" (a person to protect your surviving spouse or loved one from uncomfortable situations that sometimes arise, such as someone asking for possessions that belonged to the deceased or asking prying or stupid questions)?

Announcements and/or Program

1. Which publications/newspapers should be notified (local newspapers, religious affiliations, alumni and fraternal organizations, etc.);
2. Social media (Facebook, LinkedIn, etc.);
3. Do you want an obituary, and if so, who (if not you) will write it? Be aware, publishing an obituary can be expensive, so an online obituary can be used, or some will include the information in a program at the memorial or funeral service.
4. For the announcement and/or obituary, include:
    a. Spouse information and date of marriage (if deceased, include place and date of death)
    b. Mother and father's names
    c. Family to be listed (spouse, children, brothers, sisters, etc.). Include names and relationship
    d. Birthplace
    e. Schools attended and educational highlights
    f. Work or professional history
    g. Affiliations you wish to mention (religious, charitable, social, civic, fraternal, lodge, etc.)
    h. Special achievements, awards, offices held, and other memories you wish to mention
    i. Hobbies and activities
    j. Favorite charities; and
    k. Your favorite photograph of yourself

Miscellaneous legacy information (more about this is contained the chapter about Your Family Legacy). **Write down information and memories about:**

1. Your family history
2. Your early childhood and upbringing
3. Your adolescent and early adulthood years
4. Your educational and work history
5. Your proudest family moments
6. Your favorite memories
7. Your favorite inspirational and meaningful quotes
8. Your heroes and inspirational individuals, and how they inspired you
9. Your proudest career and civic accomplishments and involvements
10. Your special achievements, awards, offices held
11. Life lessons learned that you want to share with others
12. How would you like others to remember you
13. Special thoughts you would like to share with your family

Alternative Methods of Disposition of your Remains

Alternative methods of disposition of your remains beyond the customary burial are discussed below. In doing research for this book, I have found some websites and organizations that provide useful information. In mentioning them, I am not endorsing or recommending any of these organizations, services, or websites. They are merely provided here as a starting reference point to help you perform your own research and due diligence in determining what is appropriate for you.

Whole Body Donation
You may want to consider willing your body to science or education. By supporting medical research, you may be contributing to medical advancements that may have a significant impact on the lives of future generations, perhaps even your own descendants.

Donations of your body to a medical school or other educational facility will enable future doctors to learn anatomy, identify medical conditions, learn surgical and curative techniques, and give them the education needed to treat and cure others.

Donations of your body to science may help in the creation or improvement of medical instruments or devices.

One such organization of interest that I discovered in my research is LifeQuest Anatomical, LLC (www.lifequest-anatomical.com, 866-799-2300), which describes itself as a medical research and education "whole body to science" tissue bank, which "assists your family in making your final wishes happen with dignity and sensitivity." LifeQuest performs no medical research itself. Rather, it recovers, processes, and stores the body until it is determined what tissue and specimens can be provided to well-known and respected companies and institutions across the country. They also distribute tissues for surgical education, providing hands-on surgical training for doctors around the world.

Their services abide by the Uniform Anatomical Gift Act (UAGA) and the U.S. Code of Federal Regulations Title 45, Part 46, which protects donor confidentiality. They further require researchers and educators interested in obtaining human tissue from LifeQuest to complete a stringent application and agreement.

There is no cost to you or your family. LifeQuest arranges for the transportation of the body to their facility, the filing of required permits, cremation of the remains, and the cost of mailing the cremated remains back to the family, if desired.

It is not necessary to register to donate ahead of time, but doing so provides the greatest benefit to the surviving family needing to handle the death arrangements.

Cremation
In doing my research for this book, I discovered a company known as Everplans (www.everplans.com), which provides resources which are similar to the ones contained in this book, namely to provide guides, resources and an online platform to help you create a plan that contains everything your loved ones will need if something happens to you, as well as allowing you to share the plan with your family so they know what you want.

Here is what they say about cremation on their website:

"When a body is cremated, the remains are burned to ash (sometimes called 'cremains' or 'cremated remains') and may be buried in the earth, interred in a columbarium niche, kept by the family in an urn, or scattered."

Having a Funeral or Memorial Service Before or After a Cremation
Many people incorrectly believe that choosing cremation means that a traditional funeral cannot be held. In fact, choosing cremation in no way interferes with having a "traditional" funeral, and many cremations commonly take place after a traditional funeral has been held. Alternatively, you can choose to have a direct cremation followed by a memorial service at a later date.

Cremation Products

The products you will need to purchase for the cremation depend on your personal preferences, the type of service you want to have, and what you want to do with the cremated remains. For the most part, however, you will likely need:

- Cremation casket

- Urn

If you will be having a funeral before the cremation, you may want to purchase a casket or rent a casket. Would you like to purchase a casket that can be used for the funeral and the cremation, or would you like to rent a casket from the funeral home for the service and use an alternative container for the cremation?

- If you will be burying the cremated remains in a cemetery, you may also need a burial vault or grave liner, depending on the cemetery's rules. What are the cemetery's requirements regarding outer burial containers?
- Does the funeral home offer burial vaults or grave liners that meet both the cemetery's requirements as well as your own preferences, including affordable pricing?
- What are the cemetery's requirements regarding headstones and grave markers?
- Does the cemetery only work with specific vendors, or can you purchase a headstone or grave marker from a vendor of your choosing?

Handling the Remains

Cremated remains are usually buried in a cemetery (either in a plot in the ground or interred in a columbarium), kept in an urn or other container by family members, or scattered. There are also a number of unconventional things one may do with cremated remains, such as turn them into jewelry, incorporate them into an artificial underwater reef, make them into fireworks, or shoot them into space, among other options.

Cost of Cremation

The cost of cremation generally includes:

- Any products you'll be purchasing, including a cremation casket, an urn to hold the remains, a burial vault or grave liner (if the remains will be buried in a plot at a cemetery), and a headstone or grave marker (if the remains will be buried in a plot or interred in a columbarium at a cemetery)
- Any services from the funeral home you'll be purchasing, such as transportation of the body, the cost of the cremation, and the use of funeral home staff and equipment for the service, among other services
- Cemetery costs, including a plot or a space in a columbarium, fees for opening and closing the grave, "endowment care" fees, and headstone installation fees, among others

How to Plan a Cremation

A funeral home can help you coordinate a cremation. In some cases—mostly depending on whether or not you want to have a funeral service before the cremation—you may be able to work with a crematory directly. In addition, certain states have laws about who may coordinate a cremation, and in some states a funeral director at a funeral home must legally handle the arrangements. It's best to reach out to your local crematories and talk to them about the laws and regulations in your state.

Home Burial

Quoting from the Everplans website (www.everplans.com), "if you live in a rural area you may be allowed to bury a body on your own property. For many families, home burial is a more intimate, economical, environmentally friendly, and personal method of burial."

Features of Home Burial May Include

- Preparing the body for burial, such as washing and clothing the body
- Transporting the body to the burial site, including acquiring the necessary body transport permits
- Preparing the burial site, including digging and perhaps lining the grave; and
- Burying the body in the ground, including placing the body in the grave and filling the grave

Home Burial Products: In the case of home burial, many of the products needed for a conventional burial are not required. This may include a casket, an outer burial container, or a headstone. However, if you are planning a home burial and you would like to use any of these products, you can.

Legal Requirements for Home Burial: Depending on the state in which you're planning on having the home burial, the laws and rules may vary. Home burial is prohibited in California, Indiana, and Washington, and all other states have regulations around home burial. For you to qualify for burial on your own land, you may need to obtain permits from local government (county or town clerk) or follow local regulations on the location of the site, the depth of the grave, and other issues. For the most part, however, so long as you own the land you should have no trouble obtaining the necessary permits. You can be in touch with local authorities to register any necessary permits, licenses, or paperwork.

As a final comment, funerals are one of the most expensive purchases many consumers will ever make, often exceeding $10,000. For detailed resources that will help you make these important decisions, visit the Federal Trade Commission's website (https://www.consumer.ftc.gov/articles/0070-shopping-funeral-services), where you can also download their extremely useful and free publication, **"Funerals: A Consumer Guide"** (https://www.consumer.ftc.gov/articles/pdf-0056-funerals.pdf). You may call them toll-free at 1-877-382-4357.

Chapter 11
A Checklist for Your Survivors:
Tasks that need to be done after the death of a loved one

This chapter is addressed to survivors who will have the responsibility of handling the final affairs of one who has passed on.

No one likes to think about death, and yet we will all have to face it sooner or later. There are so many things to be done at a stressful time when survivors want time to grieve and heal. So, this checklist is meant as a resource to assist you during a time that can seem overwhelming.

For surviving spouses, at the end of this chapter is a supplemental checklist which focuses more specifically on additional matters a surviving spouse may need to do and consider.

This checklist is not meant to be an exhaustive list of everything that must be done, but merely a guide to help you along the path of things to be done and prioritize them as to when they need to be done. If you discover issues that need to be handled that are not addressed in this guide, feel free to contact your attorney for additional guidance.

Be sure to ask questions of the deceased's close friends and relatives to ensure that you are fully informed of the deceased's assets, debts, pending lawsuits, and any other pending matters that may need your attention.

A Few General Comments

1. Each estate is unique. Your own legal, accounting, and financial planning professionals should guide you through the overall process.
2. If there is a Trust and you are named Trustee or Successor Trustee, the estate-planning documents will most likely give you immediate access to funds possibly needed for funeral and other expenses related to the death of an individual.
3. If there is no Trust, but there is a Last Will and Testament (Will) naming you as executor (also called a Personal Representative), you will have to wait for court appointment for access to the deceased's assets, but you should be able to get permission to retrieve the deceased's original Will from his/her safe deposit box for filing with the Clerk of the Court.
4. Under Florida law, the Will must be filed with the Clerk of the Court of the county in which the deceased was residing within 10 days of the date of death.
5. Keep in mind, criminals are out there, watching for opportunities to steal assets from unsuspecting individuals. Unfortunately, "obituary robberies," in which families' houses are robbed while attending a funeral, are a growing concern. Don't provide full names or hometowns of relatives in the obituary. And have someone stay at your home during the funeral, or at least park some cars in the driveway to make it look like someone is home.

Within the First 24 hours

Take your time. Recognize that you are going through a grieving process. Do not be rushed into any decisions. At the immediate time of death, there is nothing that needs to happen from a legal standpoint. You can spend your time dealing with the doctors, funeral homes, and immediate family members. Get yourself through this time and process. In the meanwhile:

1. Locate any estate-planning documents (Will, Trust, etc.) and review them for possible instructions about disposal of the body, use of vital organs, and funeral arrangements.

2. Ensure that proper funeral arrangements have been made. Locate any papers relating to prearranged and/or prepaid funeral plans or pre-purchased burial plots. Review papers for possible instructions about the deceased's wishes regarding disposal of the body, organ donations, and funeral or cremation preferences.

3. If there are any pets requiring care, be sure to feed them, and arrange for a temporary, if not permanent, home for them.

4. Determine whether any of the deceased's property needs to be safeguarded, such as a motor vehicle, vacant house, etc.

5. If the house is vacant, change the locks immediately. Often, neighbors, cleaning companies, and others have copies of spare keys. You don't want them having access to the house. If there is a security system, activate it and make sure the security code is changed. Make sure all windows, sliding doors, and other entry points are locked and secure.

6. With another trusted person for verification as a witness, search every room for cash, jewelry, collectibles, firearms, and anything else that could be easily pocketed by people who will be coming into the house. Catalog the items with descriptions and photographs, and store them in a safe place.

7. Catalog and remove checkbooks, statements, tax returns, documents, and letters that may contain account numbers, social security numbers, passwords, or other personal information that could be used for identity theft purposes. Don't forget to search wallets, purses, briefcases, and desk and kitchen drawers.

8. Catalog and remove electronic storage devices including computers, laptops, tablets, smartphones, external hard drives, thumb or flash drives, and backup CD-ROMs and DVDs, which may contain information that can be used to access online accounts.

9. Notify the deceased's employer (if employed), or if the deceased was a business owner, make provision for short-term continuation of business.

10. If the deceased was a tenant, notify the landlord, and find out the terms of the lease as to when rent is due and how much is being paid.

11. If the deceased has served in the U.S. Military, check the website www.USMilitary.about.com and search for information on Military Honors available at burial, such as a U.S. flag and Military Representative.

12. Cancel newspaper delivery subscriptions to the deceased's house/apartment. A pile of uncollected newspapers is a signal to thieves that nobody is home. Similarly, take care of garbage and recycling, arrange for lawn care or snow removal, and install timers on interior lights.

13. If you know that the deceased was an active trader of stocks, and if you know the investment advisor, or if the deceased used an online stock-trading account, you may want to contact them to make sure any open limit orders to buy or sell stocks are cancelled (Note: They may not follow your instructions until they have confirmed the death, and that you have the legal authority to give them instructions (e.g. as Trustee or Personal Representative).

14. Go through the mail to see if there is anything requiring immediate attention. If you have the legal authority to do so, pay any bills that may be delinquent or due within a few days (e.g. mortgage or car payments).

15. If you have access to the deceased's Facebook, LinkedIn, Twitter, or other social media, website, and/or email services, consider posting an announcement of the deceased's passing. And you may want to provide your own contact information for funeral information. You probably don't want to post the actual funeral details, as this lets potential burglars know when the home may be unattended, while others are attending the funeral.

16. Write and arrange to publish the deceased's obituary, and determine who will write and deliver the eulogy, if any.

17. Notify the local police department if the home is vacant, to make sure they monitor the property. Provide the authorities with needed contact information.

18. If the decedent was single and didn't have joint credit cards accounts with someone else, notify the major credit reporting bureaus of the deceased's passing, and request that the credit report be flagged with the note: "Deceased. Do not issue credit." If you can, obtain a copy of the deceased's credit report, so you will have a list of all the accounts needing to be paid and/or closed.

19. Start and maintain a log, and keep notes of conversations you have with companies, banks, insurance companies, credit card companies, social security, VA, etc., noting the date, with whom you spoke, and their phone number, as well as a summary of your conversation with them.

20. Also, keep accurate records of the time you spend and expenses you incur in administering the estate, as you may be entitled to payment for services rendered, and reimbursement for your expenses from the estate.

Within the First Week

During the first week, there are some top-priority matters that need to be handled—Mark them off as you complete them:

1. Check with the deceased's banks to see if they have any safe deposit boxes.

2. Locate the original Last Will and Testament and/or Trust, and take the time to read it. Consult with a Florida attorney to determine what actions must be taken. Check for an established Trust document. Locate the deceased's letter of instruction, if any.

3. File the original will with the Clerk of the Circuit Court in the County of his/her domicile (legal residence). Florida requires this to be done within 10 days of the date of death.

4. Locate important records and documents, such as vehicle titles, deeds, life insurance policies, driver's license, social security card, passport, birth certificate, divorce decree, legal separation agreements, marriage license, military separation papers, citizenship, and retirement documents.

5. Start a file in which to accumulate statements for any assets, such as bank and investment accounts, annuities, mutual funds, individual stocks and bond reports, employee benefit statements. Also include tax returns for the past three years.

6. Start another file in which to accumulate bills and expenses needing to be paid, and from which you can create a comprehensive list of creditors.

7. Start a notebook, maintaining a detailed list of all **expenses** relating to the final care and/or death of the deceased. You will probably be able to obtain reimbursement for these expenses from the deceased's estate or Trust, and some of these expenses will be deductible to the deceased's estate for estate tax or income tax purposes.

8. In the same notebook, start maintaining a log of the date and amount of **time** you spend carrying out your duties as an executor, Personal Representative and/or trustee, as you may be entitled to compensation reimbursing you for the time you expend in carrying out these duties.

9. Contact the deceased's financial planner, CPA, and estate-planning attorney. They each need to be informed about the deceased's passing, and each will have a role in helping you to do everything necessary to wind up the deceased's final affairs. The attorney will prepare any documents necessary to confirm the authority of the successor Trustee of the Trust, if any. This will give the Trustee access to assets within the Trust to cover costs of the funeral and/or other related expenses.

10. If you have access to the deceased's bank accounts (and the legal authority to do so), stop automatic payments coming out of the deceased's bank account to pay for non-essentials, if any. Similarly, if you have access to the deceased's credit cards, stop automatic payments being charged to the credit card, if any.

11. Request a minimum of ten (10) death certificates from the funeral home. To claim the proceeds of most life insurance policies, investment and bank accounts, and related assets, an original death certificate is usually required to be submitted along with the claim form. You can also visit the U.S. Vital Statistics website, which provides a listing for every state's Department of Vital Statistics from which you can order extra death certificates. The website can be accessed online at http://www.cdc.gov/nchs/howto/w2w/w2welcom.htm.

12. Contact all applicable insurance companies (auto, life, health). You will need the following information for each insurance policy: the policy number and/or social security number of the deceased, the full name of the deceased, the date and cause of death, a certified copy of the death certificate.

13. If the decedent is a tenant, track down and contact the landlord to discuss what needs to be done to remove everything from the apartment, and when, and discuss payment of rent in the interim. If the decedent owned a business, the same conversation needs to take place with the landlord of the business premises.

14. If the decedent owned his or her home, notify the mortgage company of the death and make arrangements for payment of the mortgage. If you know the house will probably be sold by the estate or the beneficiaries, and you don't want the hassle of trying to sell everything in the house, you may want to contact a professional estate sale company, which can help organize, value, and sell the furnishings of the house that the decedent's beneficiaries don't want to keep for themselves. Your estate-planning attorney probably has the name of several such companies that can help you with this task. But remember to talk to your attorney first, to verify whether you have the legal authority to sell the assets.

15. If the deceased was over 70 ½ years of age and had an IRA account, and if the death occurred close to the end of the year, quickly verify with his/her financial advisor that he/she has taken the Required Minimum Distribution (RMD) for the year of death. There is a 50% tax penalty for not taking this mandatory distribution prior to the end of each calendar year.

16. If you know that the deceased actively traded stocks online or through a financial advisor, be sure to notify the appropriate brokerage company of the death so they can cancel any outstanding limit orders. Please be patient if they are unwilling to discuss the account with you or follow your instructions until they have received a copy of the death certificate. Even then, they may not follow your instructions until you have provided them with proof of your legal authority to give them instructions on the investment account.

17. Contact the U.S. Post Office to make necessary changes in delivery of mail, if any.

18. Turn off any bills set for auto-pay from the deceased's checking account and turn off any auto-renew accounts (usually automatically charged to the decedent's credit card).

19. Stop home delivery of newspapers, if any.

Within the Second Week

The deceased's financial planner and/or insurance agent, if any, will often help you with some of the following activities:

1. Make an appointment with an attorney to discuss the estate.

2. Contact the insurance agent or agency handling each life insurance policy and request death benefit claim forms. If the deceased had a financial planner, they will often do this for you. Note that most insurers will usually cut a check relatively quickly following the death of a loved one.

(If you know the deceased had a life insurance policy but you cannot find it, contact the American Council of Life Insurers, Information and Reference Service, 1001 Penn Avenue NW, Washington DC 20004. Phone: (800) 942-4242, website: www.acli.com, which offers guidance in tracing missing policies.)

NOTE: *Do* ***not*** *feel compelled to invest insurance proceeds immediately. Most insurance companies will let you keep the proceeds from a life insurance policy in an interest-bearing cash account until you have a plan for using or investing them.*

3. Notify all other insurance carriers (i.e., health, long-term care, umbrella, disability, accidental death, travel, vehicle, homeowners or renter's insurance).

4. Put together a list of all the beneficiaries of the insurance policies with their age, relationship to the deceased, and their current address and phone number.

5. Contact the deceased's current and previous employer(s) to find out whether or not there are any retirement plans or group life insurance policies or other survivor benefits available to the survivor(s) and request the necessary claim forms.

NOTE: Many companies make every attempt to help the families of their employees after a death. They may cut you a check right away for wages owed, vacation pay, sick pay, and life insurance benefits. If the death was the result of an accident on company time, there may also be accidental death and dismemberment benefits.

6. If the deceased was receiving worker's compensation, unemployment compensation benefits, public assistance or other benefits, notify the appropriate state agency to stop the benefits.

7. Gather all the deceased's bills and expenses that are coming due, bank and brokerage statements, and last year's tax return. Determine if any bills must be paid immediately. Contact creditors who are demanding immediate payment and notify such creditors of the death.

8. Locate and organize notes regarding assets and liabilities, such as promissory notes, loans, business interests, patents, and royalties.

9. Check with banks and credit card companies to see if there was additional life insurance connected with the deceased's loans and accounts (e.g. mortgage insurance on the deceased's home).

10. Notify all credit card companies of the death.

11. Cancel any credit cards on which the deceased was the only signer.

12. Obtain bills for last illness from hospital, hospice, and other medical providers.

13. Contact all financial institutions that hold any assets of the deceased. Tell them you need the values of every asset in each account as of the deceased's date of death. Ask them to send you a copy of this information. Note the name, phone number, and address of the individual assisting you.

14. Locate and secure any items mentioned in a governing document, Will or Trust, or documents of title.

15. Do a careful search of the deceased's home for other important documents and potential hiding places. Literally look behind every picture, under and behind drawers and dressers, fan through the pages of books on shelves (a popular place to hide currency), inside toilet tanks, under carpets, and don't forget behind air vents, up in the attic, in the garage, basement, and storage lockers. Do a similar search of the deceased's vehicle(s). Other potential hiding places include:

    - Under refrigerators, freezers, and washing machines
    - Inside boxes of cereal, rice, or oatmeal in pantry, and jars or Ziploc bags in freezer
    - Inside coffee or flour canisters or other pantry items

- Fake electrical outlets or "dummy" PVC piping attached to real pipes
- Inside an old sock in a dresser
- Inside pill bottles in a medicine chest
- Pockets of clothing
- Hollowed-out books

16. Contact the Veterans Administration for applicable benefits for the deceased and/or surviving spouse and dependent children. You will need the following information: certified copy of the death certificate, copy of your marriage certificate (spouses only), copies of the birth certificate for dependent children. Their phone number is 1-800-827-1000. Their website is www.va.gov.

17. If the deceased was retired from the military, contact the Defense Finance and Accounting Service (Cleveland, OH) Casualty Assistance Line to report the death and check for survivor annuity (SBP, RSFPP). You will need the following information: a certified copy of the death certificate, a copy of your marriage certificate (spouses only), and copies of the birth certificate for dependent children.

18. Contact Social Security to check on any available survivor benefits. You will need the following information: A certified copy of the death certificate, social security number of the deceased, social security number of spouse/dependents, birth certificates for spouse and dependent children, approximate earnings of the deceased in past year/last employer. Social Security's phone number is: 1-800-772-1213. Their website is www.ssa.gov.

19. If monthly benefits were being paid from Social Security via direct deposit, notify the bank or other financial institution of the beneficiary's death. Request that any funds received for the month of death and later be returned to Social Security as soon as possible.

20. If benefits were being paid by check, **DO NOT** cash or deposit any checks received for the month in which the beneficiary died or thereafter. Return any such checks to Social Security as soon as possible. Call Social Security to determine where to return the benefit and the exact amount needing to be repaid. Their phone number is 1-800-772-1213. Their website is www.ssa.gov.

21. A one-time payment of $255 is payable to the surviving spouse if he or she was living with the beneficiary at the time of death, OR if living apart, was eligible for Social Security benefits on the beneficiary's earnings record for the month of death. If there is no surviving spouse, the payment is made to a child who was eligible for benefits on the beneficiary's earnings record in the month of death.

22. Notify any other organization paying retirement, pension, or paying a monthly annuity of the death. Verify whether the survivor is entitled to continue receiving the payments subsequent to the decedent's death, and whether they are full or partial payments.

23. Contact Civil Service Office of Personnel Management if the deceased was an active or retired employee of the Civil Service.

24. Contact the holder of home/real estate loans for possible mortgage insurance coverage. Notify all creditors of the deceased's estate of the death. Check on credit life insurance.

25. Contact any fraternal organizations, unions, or associations the deceased may have been a member of for assistance and to determine benefits.

26. Review financial paperwork for other details (check stubs, canceled checks, stocks and bonds, real estate, safe deposit boxes, etc.) **Caution**: Do not open any safe deposit boxes without first consulting with an attorney.

27. Consider contacting the "abandoned property" division of any state in which the deceased has lived to see if there were any assets that have escheated to the state. In Florida, the site is https://www.fltreasurehunt.org. To find the links to the appropriate agency in other states, see: http://www.unclaimed.org.
28. If you are a spouse of the deceased, you should review your own life insurance policies to ensure that ownership and beneficiary designations are still current. If your spouse was the named beneficiary of your policy, you may want to name new beneficiaries to avoid the assets from possibly going through probate upon your death. Also, be sure to review your own present type of insurance and amount of coverage with a financial professional.
29. Similarly, if you were the joint tenant or beneficiary of any other accounts or assets in which the deceased had an interest, action should be taken to re-title the asset in your name alone, in your Trust, if any, or to name new beneficiaries.
30. Cancel voter's registration for the decedent.
31. Obtain booklet from Internal Revenue Service website (www.IRS.gov): Publication 559, "Information for Survivors."
32. The deceased's driver's license should be returned to the state that issued it. Contact local department of motor vehicles (DMV) for details regarding where to send it.

After You Have Received the Death Certificates

1. Process life insurance claims
2. Notify Social Security of the death, and if appropriate, apply for survivor Social Security Benefits at (800) 772-1213 (and/or the Veteran's office at (916) 731-7300, if applicable) and inform them of the death of the individual. Otherwise you will be required to pay back any monies that are overpaid to the deceased. The funeral home will often notify Social Security. But be sure to confirm with them whether they have done this for you.
3. Close credit card accounts and destroy credit cards.
4. Notify banks and brokerage firms and remove the deceased's name from any joint accounts.
5. Meet with the deceased's financial planner or yours, as appropriate, to develop a long-term investment plan for the estate assets, including any life insurance benefits to be received.

Within the Next Few Weeks after Death

1. Gather and organize all legal and financial documents:
    a. Estate planning documents, such as Wills and Trusts
    b. Bank accounts owned by the deceased, individually or jointly
    c. Investment or brokerage accounts owned by deceased, individually or jointly
    d. Mutual funds owned by the deceased, individually or jointly
    e. Annuities and/or life insurance policies owned by the deceased
    f. Certificates of Deposit in the deceased's name, individually or jointly
    g. Stock certificates registered in the deceased's name, individually or jointly
    h. Any promissory notes under which the deceased was entitled to receive payment
    i. Titles to motor vehicles and/or mobile homes that are listed in the deceased's name

j. Deeds to real property, vacation homes, time shares, etc. in the deceased's name

k. Any appraisals of jewelry, artwork, coin collections, or other valuable personal property owned by the deceased

2. Gather all current and/or past due bills, statements, claim forms, etc. Obtain the account balance on mortgages, loans, checking and savings accounts, and investment accounts as of the date of death.

3. Set up an initial meeting with the attorney, CPA, and financial planner to identify what needs to be done and coordinate who will do it.

4. If the decedent was over 70 ½ years of age at death and had an IRA or other retirement account, verify that the annual Required Minimum Distribution to the decedent has been made (There is a 50% IRS penalty if the RMD is not taken each year).

5. Gain access to and inventory any safe deposit box (Note: You may need the probate court's approval to do so).

6. Bring original Will, financial document balances, death certificates, and inventory of safe deposit box to meeting with attorney.

7. If there is a provision in the Will or a separate writing leaving the decedent's motor vehicle to a named individual, locate the registration (i.e. Certificate of Title) to the vehicle and have the title changed to the person named to receive it. Remember, it may be an electronic ("paperless") certificate of title as opposed to a paper Certificate of Title.

8. A final income tax return will need to be filed for the decedent (there is a place on the form to mark "Final Return.")

9. If there is a Revocable Living Trust in the decedent's name alone, locate the successor Trustee and arrange for a new tax ID number to be issued, as the trust is now, most likely, irrevocable. The new trustee will need to arrange for the filing of annual fiduciary income tax returns for the trust (IRS Form 1041).

10. If there is a joint Revocable Living Trust in the decedent's name along with the decedent's surviving spouse, review with your estate-planning attorney and/or financial advisor whether the tax identification number of the trust needs to be changed into the social security number of the surviving spouse.

11. Some of the tasks that will need to be addressed include the following:

    a. File the original will with the Clerk of the Circuit Court in the County of his/her domicile (legal residence). Florida requires this to be done within 10 days.

    b. See an attorney to determine whether a petition for probate of the Last Will and Testament must be filed.

    c. Begin to prepare for filing the estate tax return (Form 706). Some of the forms and documents you have been collecting will be needed by your CPA or attorney to document date of death calculations for that return.

    d. Your attorney or CPA can assist you with finalizing and understanding any legal documents and/or forms that you have received.

    e. The financial planner and estate attorney can also assist you with funding the trusts (if applicable) and with making distributions to any beneficiaries.

    f. The financial planner and CPA can help you make IRA and pension plan election decisions.

Within Two to Six Months

1. If automobiles are held in joint tenancy, change motor vehicle titles to reflect ownership only by the surviving joint tenant. Notify insurance company and lender of the change.
2. If individual stocks or bonds, brokerage accounts, bank accounts, etc., are held in joint tenancy, or have a named beneficiary, contact stockbroker and/or bank to change their records to reflect ownership only by the surviving joint tenant or beneficiary.
3. If you are a surviving spouse and owned your home jointly with the decedent, contact your local property appraiser's office to see if they offer an additional real estate tax exemption for surviving widows/widowers.

Some Final Things to Consider

1. When you are ready, taking charge of the financial affairs can help the healing process. It gives people focus and empowerment when they may need it the most.
2. If applicable, contact a human resources (HR) representative of the deceased's employer for help with retirement plans. A surviving spouse will usually be able to roll over money from the deceased spouse's retirement plan into his or her own IRA. In most cases, doing so will make sense, but if you are considerably younger than your spouse you may want to keep the assets in your spouse's retirement plan. That may allow you to tap into those assets at a younger age without penalty. Discuss this with your financial advisor before making any irrevocable decisions as the tax consequences can be substantial.
3. Make sure you have sufficient cash on hand. One of the biggest concerns immediately following a death in the family is making sure the survivors have enough cash to meet their current expenses as well as funeral costs. You may want to take part of your life insurance proceeds or other death benefits and increase your cash reserves. Try to have at least six months' worth of living expenses covered in a money market or other very accessible account. This will help ensure that you are not too rushed into making other major financial decisions right away.
4. Consider creating a lasting memorial. One of the most healing experiences for survivors is to find a way to honor the people they have lost. Whether it's through a brick paver in a memorial walkway, a scholarship in the name of your loved one at his or her alma mater, or a donation to a favorite charity, creating a tangible remembrance is an important part of paying tribute to those who have blessed our lives.
5. If you wonder if you could benefit from any type of bereavement counseling or other support, you probably could. Please feel free to ask your financial professional for a list of community resources. Don't overlook the vital role your church, synagogue, or mosque may play in providing spiritual and social support for you and the family involved.
6. For many, particularly those who are not the chief financial decision makers in the household, professional financial counseling may be a comfort. Be sure to carefully screen financial advisers before you agree to work with them.
7. After having gone through all this, if you have not already done so, you may want to treat this as your wake-up call to create your own estate plan, and take whatever action may be needed to make your own passing easier on your heirs and loved ones. Be sure to encourage your friends and family members to do the same.

Helpful Phone Numbers and Websites

The following is a list of phone numbers and websites that you may find useful:

1. Social Security: 1-800-772-1213

www.ssa.gov

2. Internal Revenue Service: 1-800-829-1040
   www.irs.gov

3. Veterans Administration 1-800-827-1000
   www.va.gov/

4. Civil Service Personnel Management Office 1-888-767-6738
   www.opm.gov/retirement-services/contact-retirement/

5. Military Benefits - DFAS Casualty Assistance Office (Cleveland) 1-800-269-5170
   www.military.com/benefits/

6. Office of Service Members Life Insurance 1-800-419-14736.
   www.insurance.va.gov/sglisite/miscellaneous/contact.htm

7. U.S. Vital Statistics - a site that provides a listing of every state's Department of Vital Statistics (a good resource for information on ordering certified copies of death certificates).
   www.cdc.gov/nchs/w2w.htm

8. Dept. of Public Debt, U.S. Treasury, for information on the transfer of ownership of U.S. Treasury bills, notes, and bonds.
   www.treasurydirect.gov/

9. Unclaimed property – Every state has its own department for helping you to locate abandoned or lost assets, such as from a safe deposit box or unclaimed insurance policy. This link will help you locate your state's unclaimed property division. (Remember to search ALL states in which the decedent has resided)
   www.unclaimed.org.

Supplement "A"

Additional Checklist Specifically for a Surviving Spouse

As a surviving spouse, it is important for you to take whatever action is necessary to protect yourself and your loved ones. For example, if you and your spouse were joint owners of bank accounts, your house, or other assets, you should consider speaking to your attorney about retitling the assets, putting them into a trust, or naming new beneficiaries to avoid the assets from going through probate or being inherited by someone whom you didn't want upon your death. Or, if you have minor children, your legal documents may need to be updated to name new guardians to take care of them in case something happens to you.

Many of the items in this checklist are included in the preceding Survivor's Checklist, but this checklist contains additional matters of importance to be considered by a surviving spouse.

IMMEDIATE CONCERNS

___ Have you contacted family members, friends, and your spouse's employer and informed of his/her death?
___ Have you reviewed your spouse's written wishes as to details regarding his/her funeral, burial, cremation, celebration of life, and other matters?
___ Have you engaged a funeral home and funeral director?
___ Have you organized the funeral service (memorial and/or celebration of life)?
___ Have you arranged for burial, interment, cremation, or donation of body?
___ Have you drafted and sent the obituary to the appropriate newspapers/publishers?
___ Are arrangements for payment of funeral expenses complete?
___ If your spouse was a business owner, have provisions been made for the short-term continuation of the business, if any?
___ If your spouse was an active investor in the financial markets (particularly if he/she used limit orders to buy or sell securities, stop loss orders, or invested in options or futures) has the financial advisor been notified of his or her death?

DOCUMENTS THAT WILL BE NEEDED

___ Birth certificate
___ Marriage certificate
___ Divorce decree / Property settlement agreement
___ Premarital (prenuptial) or post-marital (postnuptial) agreement
___ Military service documents
___ Death certificate
___ Life insurance policies
___ Investment statements (bank accounts, investment accounts, annuities, mutual funds, individual stocks, individual bonds, etc.)
___ Last Will and Testament
___ Trust agreement
___ Tax returns
___ Employee benefits statements
___ Deeds to real estate
___ Titles to vehicles, boats, etc.

ADVISORS TO BE NOTIFIED

___ Attorney
___ CPA / Accountant / Tax Advisor
___ Investment Advisor / Financial Planner
___ Insurance Agent
___ Clergy
___ Other

INSURANCE AND BENEFICIARY CONSIDERATIONS

Have you filed claims for potential death benefits from these sources?

___ Individual life insurance policies
___ Group life insurance policies
___ Employer-sponsored life insurance policies (don't forget previous employers)
___ Accidental death and dismemberment policies
___ Travel insurance policies (if death occurred on vacation or on trip)
___ Mortgage life insurance policies
___ Credit life insurance policies
___ Social Security (survivor's benefits)
___ Military (survivor benefits)
___ Federal employee benefits
___ State employee benefits
___ Civil service benefits
___ Union benefits
___ Fraternal, religious, or other organization benefits (some offer life insurance benefits)
___ Investment account assets of which you were named as a beneficiary
___ Investment account assets owned with your spouse as joint tenants with rights of survivorship (JTWROS) or Tenants by the Entireties
___ Retirement accounts on which you are named a beneficiary
___ Pension benefits (survivor benefits)
___ Qualified retirement plan / IRA benefits

SETTLING THE ESTATE

___ Have the executor (Personal Representative) of your spouse's will, trustee of any Trust, Guardians for minor children, and heirs and other beneficiaries been contacted?
___ Have an attorney and/or other advisor(s) been contacted?
___ Have you accumulated all the documents required to administer his or her estate?
___ Will a probate estate be necessary (consult with your attorney)?
___ Has a Taxpayer Identification Number (TIN or EIN) been obtained for the estate (this will probably be done by or through your attorney)?
___ If your spouse had a Trust, either individually or jointly with you, will the tax ID or social security number need to be changed on the Trust?
___ Have creditors been notified?
___ Have other institutions been notified?
___ Have assets been distributed to heirs/beneficiaries?
___ Have appropriate estate and income tax returns been filed for the estate?

TAX PLANNING CONCERNS

___ Has a tax advisor been contacted to see how your tax situation may have changed?
___ Has a final tax return been filed for the decedent?
___ Has a change in your tax-filing status been evaluated?
___ Have tax consequences of previous gifts been considered?
___ Have tax consequences of inherited assets been considered?
___ Has a portability election for preservation of estate tax exemption been filed?

RETIREMENT PLAN AND RETIREMENT PLANNING CONCERNS:

___ If your spouse was 70 ½ years of age or older, has the annual required minimum distribution (RMD) been taken from his/her retirement account?
___ Have you had your own retirement planning needs re-evaluated?
___ Have you updated beneficiary designations on your own existing IRAs and retirement plans?

IMPORTANT THINGS YOU SHOULD BE CERTAIN TO REMEMBER TO DO

___ Update your Last Will and Testament (if needed), including the named representatives
___ Update your Trust (if needed), including the named successor trustees
___ Change tax ID number to any joint Trust you may have had with your spouse
___ If your spouse had his/her own Trust, apply for a new tax ID number (EIN) with IRS for the Trust
___ Update your medical directives, if needed, including the named representatives
___ Update your Living Will, if needed, including the named representatives
___ Update your durable power of attorney, if needed, including the named representatives
___ Update beneficiary designations and/or joint ownership (title) to **ALL** assets with your banker, investment advisor, and insurance agent

  ___ Real estate
  ___ Vehicles
  ___ Investment accounts
  ___ Retirement accounts
  ___ Bank accounts
  ___ Safe deposit box
  ___ Individual stocks and bonds
  ___ Stock ownership plans directly at company (DRIP plan) or transfer agent (e.g. Computershare)

___ Review your tax filing status with your tax-preparer/advisor;
___ Make arrangements with your county tax collector to preserve your homestead deduction for real estate taxes, if needed
___ If you owned your home jointly with the decedent, check with your local property appraiser's office to see if they offer an additional real estate tax exemption for surviving widows or widowers
___ Review and reevaluate your:

  ___ Budget
  ___ Tax situation
  ___ Retirement situation
  ___ Income sources
  ___ Expenses (fixed and variable)
  ___ Credit situation (do you need to establish your own credit?)

___ If you have minor children, name Guardians for them, and provide for their educational and other needs, etc.

Chapter 12
Your Family Legacy

I was a young adult when I lost the last of my grandparents, so I know a bit about them. I know nothing about my great-grandparents except their names, and if I hadn't asked my parents what their names were while writing this book, I wouldn't have known their names, either. And I know absolutely nothing about their parents or generations before them. What were their lives like? What did they do for a living? How long did they live? How did they fall in love? What was happening in the world around them? What were their passions, their interests, their challenges? How would they have wanted to be remembered?

Wouldn't it be nice for future generations to know about you and what your life was like? Maybe you've had an exciting life, maybe not. But the details you may deem to be too mundane to share with future generations may just be full of incidental details they find fascinating!

You may have heard the expression, "It's all about the dash." This refers to the dates on your tombstone with the hyphen separating your year of birth and your year of death. The hyphen (i.e. the dash), refers to everything that happened in your life between the two dates. I don't know about you, but I'd like my life to be remembered as more than a date-dash-date in a footnote of history (Jerrold E. Slutzky [1952 – 20??]).

At the time of writing this book, my father just celebrated his 100th birthday and is the last surviving member of his entire generation on his side of my family, which is an enormous family. When he's gone, all his knowledge of our ancestors, our family's history, and family stories will go with him, lost forever.

So, we've been collecting as many of those memories as possible to keep them in perpetuity. One of my personal favorites was him describing his very first job, which would have been sometime in the early 1930s. His job was dipping bananas in chocolate before they were frozen, for which he would be paid $1.00 per day, plus all the frozen bananas he could eat! And boy, did he eat a lot of them!

He says, to this day, he can't even **look** at a frozen banana!!!

He also told us the story of his mother, my grandmother, taking a ship from Russia to America by herself at the age of 16, not knowing a single word of English. She got off the boat and immediately started learning English by pointing at things and asking people, *"Vas is das?"* ("What is that?") And when my father went away to war, rather than rely on others to write letters for her to her son, she went to school in her 40s to learn how to read and write to him by herself in English!

And then there was the time he was stationed with the army on Kodiak Island in Alaska and was on maneuvers. Thinking he was capturing a member of the enemy rustling in the deep grass, he threw down his rifle, yelled "Gotcha!" and grabbed the perpetrator, only to discover he had grabbed a handful of fur belonging to a young Kodiak bear! He grinned broadly as he admitted he was very thankful that the bear went running off in one direction, while he ran off in the opposite direction!

My mother, now 96, has her share of family stories, too, such as her mother warning her to stop being so picky about whom she wanted as a husband. After all, she was 21 years old! Did she want to be an old maid?

Everyone has fond memories of their lives and those of their parents, grandparents, and if they are lucky, other ancestors. And whether it is a matter of creating a family tree, or just writing down a narrative history of the family, wouldn't it be a wonderful legacy to share with future generations?

I can barely imagine my parents' lives as children, before television, air conditioning, and air travel. And it is even harder to comprehend the lives of my grandparents, when families had 8 to 12 children, no indoor plumbing, automobiles, or electricity.

I'd like to think some future generations will find it interesting that I can remember when a first-class postage stamp cost four cents and is now 49 cents. My father said he remembers when gasoline cost seven cents a gallon, while I remember when a gallon of gasoline cost 33 cents. If I wanted to borrow the car to go out on a date, my father would insist I fill half the tank, which cost about $2.00. In 2017, gasoline is currently $2.25 per gallon (although a couple years ago, it had spiked up to $4.50 per gallon.) Growing up, we had three channels on television (ABC, NBC, CBS), and later a public channel, and eventually, a Spanish-language channel was added.

McDonald's (and fast-food restaurants in general) was a brand-new concept, and you could buy a hamburger for a dime, French fries for 12 cents, and a milkshake for 20 cents. If we'd only had the foresight to buy 100 shares of McDonald's stock (I believe 100 shares cost about $1,200), Walmart stock, or later, Apple stock, we'd be mega-millionaires now.

When I first became an attorney in 1977, my law office had no computers, cloud storage, Internet, smartphones, fax machines, or even plain paper copy machines. They didn't exist yet. Copy machines were loaded with a huge roll of paper, which self-cut to the desired legal or letter length. A red stripe in the paper was the warning that you were running out of paper.

It cost over a thousand dollars to buy an IBM Selectric© typewriter with what was then a high-tech moveable typeball, and your choice of fonts was limited to either pica or elite. Your secretary, not known yet as a personal assistant, would type on legal size paper (8-1/2" x 14"). If extra copies were needed, onion skin paper was used with carbon paper in between each sheet of paper, because if a mistake was made, there was no auto-correct feature or spell-check function; you had to erase the mistake on each and every copy and re-type it. "White-out" liquid was a brand-new invention and was hailed a "miracle" that saved secretaries countless hours of time correcting typing errors.

I anticipate that future generations will probably be astounded that we had a mere 1,000 channels to watch on television, that we used carbon-based gasoline instead of nuclear fusion to power our old-fashioned automobiles, that we used antique smartphones instead of mental telepathy to communicate one another, that we needed airplanes to fly instead of anti-gravity belts, and took ships to transport us to a far-off Caribbean vacation, rather than taking a spaceship shuttle through a wormhole to the new Club Med on far-away galaxies!

Wouldn't it have been wonderful for your great-great grandparents to have taken the initiative to describe what their lives had been like? What their hopes, dreams, likes, and dislikes had been? Stories of how they met their loved ones?

I remember many stories that my parents shared with me about their lives, but I can probably only speak for about 10 minutes about my grandparents' stories. And as I mentioned at the beginning of the chapter, I didn't even know the names of my great-grandparents before writing this book, let alone any insights as to what their lives were like or my ancestors before them.

Think about it: We are a direct link between all our ancestors that have come before us since the beginning of the human race to all future generations until the end of our bloodline, possibly even until the end of the human race!

Wouldn't it be nice to share at least a few snippets of your family history and your favorite memories with those future generations?

There are many ways to accomplish this, the most basic of which is to start a diary, writing down a description of your current life, and commenting on what you are doing, who you have seen recently, and as the memories of your early life or family stories come to you, writing them down, too.

Since many people aren't fast typists or writers, using a word-to-text computer program such as Nuance Dragon® NaturallySpeaking can be of great help to you. You simply tell the stories out loud, and as you speak, the program converts your words to text. The accuracy of these programs has improved greatly over the years, but be sure to review what you have said to make sure the transcription is correct.

Similarly, you can simply start telling your memories or family stories, and record them as audio or video files. Future generations will be able to hear your own stories, told by you, in your own voice.

How about an interview type of recording? Put together a list of questions to jog memories, and record the stories as the memories start flowing. A section in the attached questionnaire has a list of questions to get you started on creating your own family legacy.

This year, during holidays and family events, I intend to go around the dinner table and ask everyone to tell at least one favorite family memory or story.

What about taking out a family photo album and, starting on the first page, telling the story about the pictures? It is said that a picture is worth a thousand words, so each picture should trigger a memory that can be transposed to paper. Talk about the people in the picture, the approximate date it was taken, what was the occasion, what was happening behind the scenes not shown in the picture, what you were feeling, what was happening in your life at the time the moment was captured on film. You've kept the picture because at one point in time, it was a moment that was important enough for you to snap a picture and put it into a memory album.

How often have you looked at your parents' photo albums and had no idea who was in the pictures or why they were an important memory to your parents? If you don't tell the story behind each picture, that particular story (or at least your personal slant on the events in the picture) will be lost.

Or, you can hire a professional videographer to prepare a legacy video for you. The videographer will usually provide you with a list of questions that you will be asked during a several-hour interview. They will create a video of the entire interview and scan in favorite family pictures, certificates, and other memorabilia. They will then edit everything down to a reasonable-length legacy video that can be made immediately available to your family, or saved to be given to family members at a future date, perhaps after your passing.

Whether you decide to use a video, audio, or written format, here are some of the topics that may jog some fond memories that future generations may find of interest:

1. Your family history, going as far back in time as you know
2. Your early childhood and upbringing
3. Your adolescent and early adulthood years
4. Your educational history (what schools you attended; what degrees and honors; what you learned about yourself)
5. Your work history (jobs, titles, awards, honors, what were you paid, who were your bosses, who were your mentors, who were your work friends, what you learned from these experiences)
6. Your proudest family moments
7. Your favorite life memories
8. Your favorite inspirational and quotes that were meaningful to you
9. Your heroes and inspirational individuals, and how they inspired you
10. Your proudest career and civic accomplishments and involvements

11. Your special personal achievements, awards, offices held
12. Life lessons learned that you want to share with others
13. Your life motto
14. How would you like friends, family, and future generations to remember you
15. Special thoughts you would like to share with your family.

You can share fun personal memories, such as telling the story of how you met your spouse, and the circumstances leading up to the proposal of marriage and wedding.

Or, you can share painful personal events that may have shaped your life, such as going to war, having a debilitating disease, learning impediment, or losing a loved one at an early age.

In addition, you can talk about your favorites, such as:
1. Your favorite books
2. Your favorite movies
3. Your favorite jokes
4. Your favorite stories
5. Your favorite recipes
6. Your favorite teachers in school
7. Your favorite friends growing up
8. Your favorite pictures and the stories behind them
9. Your favorite *tchotchkes* (Yiddish for "keepsakes kept on shelves") and the stories behind them; and
10. Pretty much anything else you think future generations may find interesting, funny, or memorable

Start the legacy by writing down or otherwise sharing all the family stories you can remember, before they are gone forever. Talk about your parents, grandparents, and relatives. Encourage other family members to share their memories, too. And then do the same about your life and your children, and encourage them to keep adding to it as circumstances warrant.

If you have favorite photographs, consider including them in your family legacy and telling future generations who the people are in the pictures, and the stories behind the pictures. Bring the pictures to life with your rendition of the tale.

And, of course, make a point of sharing your final words of love to those who are in your heart. If this was your last moment alive, what would you have wanted to say to each person you love, telling them about what they have meant to you and how they have impacted your life? What a wonderful legacy of love!

Take some time and start writing those letters now. Keep them readily available so they can be found when you are gone. As future life events inspire you, on the same letter, add appropriate new thoughts and comments, dating each entry as a point of reference.

My "Everything" File®

Everything my Loved Ones Need to Know about Me

Created by

Jerrold E. Slutzky, J.D., CFP®
Attorney at Law
Slutzky Law Firm

853 Main Street, Suite A
Safety Harbor, FL 34695
(727) 475-6200 Phone
(727) 474-0157 Fax

20719 Sterlington Drive, Suite 103
Land O' Lakes, FL 34638
(813) 909-1515 Phone
(813) 949-1105 Fax

www.SlutzkyLawFirm.com

CAUTION

Some of the information you provide in this questionnaire could help someone steal your identity and/or your assets. Keep all copies of this questionnaire in a locked and secure location which is only accessible by people you completely trust. Provide copies of this questionnaire only to persons who you believe can be trusted to honor the precautions needed to protect and maintain the secrecy of your information!

MY "EVERYTHING" FILE

Dear Reader:

You may have heard the expression, "It's all about the 'dash!'" The "dash" refers to the mark placed on your tombstone; that hyphen placed between the year you were born and the year you die! Your entire life is represented in that "dash!"

In preparing this questionnaire, it occurred to me that, while each of the seemingly-endless details contained in the following pages may be an important fact for others to know about you to enable them to handle your affairs on your behalf, it reveals little or nothing about you as a person: your life, your passions, your joys, your life experiences and memories, and the family stories you may want to share with future generations.

How much do you know about your great-grandparents? Do you even know their names, let alone any stories about them that may have been passed down through your grandparents and parents? Perhaps I'm sentimental, but in addition to the financial and other factual details contained here, wouldn't it be fun to take a moment to relive the memories, and then to share some of the memorable stories about you and your life with your descendants?

Therefore, I have tried to provide a small reminder in most of the sections to take a moment to tell the story behind each of the factual details of information you will be providing. The space provided isn't large enough to tell the entire story, so, as you complete each section, I recommend taking a moment to write down the memories each entry may have triggered. Write each story on a separate sheet of paper, in a notebook, or in a digital file, and keep them with this questionnaire. For example, when you write down the date of your marriage, why not share the story of how you met, why you fell in love with your spouse, describe the proposal, the wedding, the honeymoon, and share the emotions with future generations? When you talk about your parents and grandparents, take time to write down their stories, too, such as how they met, how they came to America, where they lived, what struggles they endured, what memories do you have of them, etc. This could be the start of a multi-generational legacy your family can enjoy.

Completing this questionnaire may seem a burden, and my wife has lovingly suggested to me that nobody is going to want to complete over 300 pages of questions! But I hope you will find it to be a more enjoyable process by taking a moment to relish the memories and retell the stories behind the factual details provided.

I also hope that this questionnaire will serve as an inspiration for you to share your life story, your life legacy, with your loved ones, far beyond the mere "stuff" you have accumulated over the years.

I hope you remember many happy memories while completing this questionnaire!

Sincerely,

/s/ Jerrold E. Slutzky

Jerrold E. Slutzky, J.D., CFP®

General Comments from Your Author

Obviously, this questionnaire doesn't really cover **everything**! There is far too vast an array of information about different people's lives to cover everything! But it **has** been designed to include **most** of the details your loved ones will need or want to know about you. The questionnaire contains details which will help guide you to let your loved ones know:

1. Vital information in case of an emergency
2. What you own
3. What you owe
4. Your family and employment history
5. Where your legal, tax, financial, insurance, and other important documents are located
6. Your medical history, health care providers, and prescriptions
7. Your digital data, including websites and passwords
8. Your life lessons and final wishes; and
9. So much other information, you'll wonder how your head didn't explode from keeping it all inside your brain!

My "Everything" File® is intended to help you create a comprehensive document containing almost everything you would want someone to know about you, for them to be able to take care of you or handle your affairs if you become unable to do so yourself, whether due to infirmity, illness, disability, dementia, stroke, incapacity, extended absence, or death.

For example, if you have a medical emergency, at the very moment some critical information about your medical history is needed, you will want your loved ones to have that information **immediately** available, particularly since they will be acting under a high degree of stress. In addition to having access to this information, at least one of your loved ones should have the **legal authority** to make important decisions regarding your care (and you should make them aware that they have the documents showing their legal authority to do so on your behalf).

Similarly, if you are incapacitated, whether temporarily or permanently, someone needs to be able to take care of you and your children, handle your financial matters, run your business, and basically step into your shoes to keep all the balls that you currently juggle by yourself in the air.

Upon your death, someone needs to know how to, and have the legal authority to, make your final arrangements, collect your assets, pay your bills, arrange for the disposition of your business interests and property, arrange for the care of your children, and do everything needed to finalize your personal and financial responsibilities and affairs. In today's world, in which your financial statements and your other critical information are sent to you via email and the Internet, would they even know where to begin to find what they need to know?

During your lifetime, you have accumulated a **vast** amount of information about yourself. If something happens to you, who else knows this information?

Would they know where all your important documents are located? Would they know who needs to be contacted if something happens to you and how to contact them? Would they know your account numbers? Would they know what bills need to be paid and to whom? Would they know passwords to gain access to your emails, social media, and password-protected computer and Internet-based programs? Would they know your medical history, what medications you are taking, the dosage, and where to obtain them? And would they have the written authority to act on your behalf without the necessity of being appointed as guardians by the court to be able to handle your affairs?

My spouse knows this information
If you are married or in a long-term committed relationship, perhaps your spouse or partner knows much of this information. But do they know it all? And if something happens to your spouse or partner, too, **who else** knows all this information?

If you are married, although some of the information requested applies both of you (such as children, advisors, assets, etc.), I have designed this questionnaire to be answered by only one person. I do **not** recommend creating a joint questionnaire with your spouse. Instead, I recommend creating a separate **My "Everything" File®** for each person. You can always make a copy of those few sections that contain information about joint assets, liabilities, common family details, and other matters that apply to both of you.

Are there any missing categories that may apply to you?
This questionnaire is meant to help jog your memory about additional information your loved ones and representatives should know. Just because I haven't included a category regarding a topic that is relevant to you, doesn't mean you shouldn't include it. Insert additional pages to include whatever information of importance you want your loved ones to know. If you believe I've missed an important category or question that you believe should be added to the list for the benefit of readers of future versions of this questionnaire, please send me a suggestion at **Info@MyEverythingFile.com.**

It is okay to make extra copies of some sections, if needed
This list is quite comprehensive, and I've tried to include extra sets of questions regarding topics for which you may need more than one set, but feel free to make extra copies of some of the pages, if needed. For example, I've provided sections for information about three children. If you have more than three children, you'll want to make extra copies of that section. This also applies to certain categories of assets, such as investment real estate, if you own more than one investment property.

Don't ignore sections that don't apply to you
You will find that many of the topics won't apply to you at all. I do not recommend removing the pages asking about those topics, as they may become applicable to you at some time in the future. Just make a notation that the section is not immediately applicable to you.

Knowing that the answer to a question or subject is "no" can be just as helpful to your loved ones as knowing that the answer is "yes." Knowing these answers may save them a lot of wasted effort searching for assets you don't own and for information that doesn't apply to you (e.g. "I don't have a safe deposit box" will save them a lot of worry about whether you have one or not, let alone where it might be!).

This questionnaire will also provide them with the answers to many important questions they may not have even thought to ask you (e.g. "What medications are you currently taking, what dosage, and what medical condition is it treating?")

Take your time in completing the questionnaire
Don't try to complete this questionnaire at a single sitting, or even over a weekend. Take your time, doing a few pages at a time, and enjoy (yes, enjoy!) what an interesting and varied life you have, the experiences you've had in accumulating everything you own, and all the people who have impacted your life in some way. There is probably a story behind your answer to each question.

Writing answers in this book versus typing in a fillable PDF version of the questionnaire
If you are writing down the answers to the questionnaire in this book, you may want to consider using a pencil, as much of the information will change from time to time.

If you prefer to type this information, a fillable PDF version of this questionnaire is available for purchase at a nominal expense online at **www.MyEverythingFile.com**. The PDF version will provide more space to include more details and useful information to your loved ones.

Security versus convenience

Carefully consider whether you will want to store this sensitive information on your computer. If your computer crashes, do you really want to answer all these questions a second time? And if your computer is stolen or hacked, do you want potential thieves to have access to this information, much of which may be sensitive or confidential?

If you are comfortable storing such sensitive information on your computer or in the cloud, please make sure it is a secure file or storage site with high-level encryption. Perhaps due to my age, I am not comfortable in doing so. If identify thieves can hack into government and multi-national corporation data bases, I don't believe anything is truly safe on your computer or in the cloud! If you are going to do this, do so at your own risk. You have been warned!

Instead of storing the completed questionnaire on your computer or in the cloud, you may want to consider keeping a printed copy of your completed **My "Everything" File®** in your safe deposit box with your other important documents. But you may also want to keep the master document on a thumb drive or other storage device (preferably encrypted) in your safe deposit box (but make sure someone whom you trust knows the encryption code). This way, you can make modifications to the digital form, re-print it, and then return it to the security of the safe deposit box.

Update, update, update

Remember to review and update your **My "Everything" File®** at least once a year. Consider doing your annual update shortly after you have completed filing your income tax returns, since much of your financial information will be up to date and at your fingertips.

Much of your information will change from time to time, such as when you buy or sell assets, change your bank or investment accounts, change doctors, update contact information, etc. Keeping this information current and up to date will be vital to the person who will be taking care of you and handling your affairs for you.

Do I really have to complete every detail of every section that applies to me?

It is not mandatory for you to complete every section of this questionnaire, even if the section applies to you. I wanted to provide you with a resource to be as all-inclusive as you'd like, and to be a guide to jog your memory as to details you may not have considered. You decide how much information you want to provide. If you merely want to provide the address to some real estate you own, but not provide details on the mortgage, insurance, tenants, etc., that is your choice. You could address the areas of interest you believe are most important to you and what you feel your representative and loved ones would need or want to know about you (and save them the time and hassle of tracking down the information you did not provide to them). Later, if you decide you want to expand into some of the other areas, you can do so at your leisure.

This is not a project you will be able to complete in a single sitting, and probably not in one weekend. It has taken you a lifetime to accumulate all this information, so take your time, do a little bit at a time, and reward yourself each step along the way.

Your loved ones will appreciate your forethought and efforts in providing them with this information.

IMPORTANT SECURITY AND PRIVACY REMINDERS
Identity thieves are everywhere! While this **My "Everything" File®** document contains information that will provide your loved ones with important personal, financial, and other details about you and your financial dealings, much of this information would also be helpful to **thieves** who want to steal your identity and money. So be **VERY CAREFUL** about who will have access to a copy of this document. It should be kept in a place accessible only by those whom you **completely** trust, not only to have access to this sensitive info, but also to take the necessary security precautions to protect your privacy.

Remember, while you will be very careful with this information, the ones to whom you provide a copy of this document may not be quite as careful as you, so the information may still become, inadvertently, available to thieves.

Consider completing the questionnaire in two separate versions First, create a **fully-completed** version to be kept in a secure place, such as a bank safe deposit box. Second, make an extra copy of the fully-completed version, but delete the personal identifying information you wouldn't want a thief to know (e.g. your social security number, account numbers, passwords, etc.), and keep this second version in a convenient place, so you can keep updating it, and your loved ones or representatives can find it. Include a note on the home copy as to where the all-inclusive original can be located. Or consider providing this copy to the ones you want to handle your affairs, and let them know where the original, fully-completed document is located.

If you maintain a digital copy of the **My "Everything" File®** on your computer, in the cloud, on an external hard drive, etc., consider encrypting it, and provide the encryption code only to the persons you want to have access to the document. But remember, if they lose the encryption code, all your time and effort will have been wasted, so be careful. Provide access to the full version **only** to those you completely trust.

DISCLAIMERS
The contents in this book and questionnaire are not intended to give you legal, tax, insurance, or investment advice. The laws of every state differ, and your own personal circumstances are unique to you and your family. Everything discussed in this book and questionnaire is merely intended to alert you to questions and issues regarding your own circumstances that you may want to discuss with your legal, tax, insurance, or investment advisors.

In addition, any references to websites or services mentioned throughout this book are for informational purposes only. **My Everything File, LLC**, and its author, **Jerrold E. Slutzky**, do not endorse, recommend, or validate the accuracy of the contents contained in said websites, and do not make any representations or warranties about said websites' safety and freedom from viruses, malware, cookies, etc.

I respectfully request that any reader and/or user of the contents of this questionnaire please respect my copyright. I have invested hundreds of hours in collecting, collating, organizing, and preparing the content contained in this questionnaire, so if you think others would benefit from their own copy, please tell them about it, but let them purchase their own copy of **My "Everything" File®.**

Sincerely,

/s/ Jerrold E. Slutzky

Jerrold E. Slutzky, J.D., CFP®

My "Everything" File®
Table of Contents

§1-A: General Recommendations to Make Things Easier for Your Survivors

These are some random reminders of things to do to make things easier for your survivors and representatives to find whatever is needed to take care of you and to locate all the things they will need to know.

Have an emergency grab-and-run kit:	Prepare a grab-and-run kit containing your "MUST HAVE" information and documents to take with you in case there is a fire or other emergency requiring you to flee from your home. If one could take just one thing with them from their house in an emergency, many people would want their family picture albums, so consider including a flash drive containing all your favorite digital pictures.
Consider adding copies of the following documents and to My "Everything" File®:	1. End-of-year financial statements (update at end of every year) 2. Life & other insurance policies 3. Pre-planned or pre-paid funeral policies 4. Copy of deeds to real estate and title to vehicles 5. Other documents you know your loved ones will need. Indicate where the original documents can be found
Make a checklist of important recurring dates:	Include personal info, such as birthdates, income tax filing deadlines, required distribution (RMD) dates from IRAs, annual physical check-ups, Medicare filing dates, etc. Be sure to include an annual date to review how all your assets are titled and any beneficiary designations. Consider doing this right after filing your income tax return, so all your account details are already available to you.
Beneficiary and contingent beneficiary designations:	Consider having a beneficiary designated on all financial assets, as well as a contingent beneficiary designation. Review them every year or two.
Make a home video of everything in your house (don't forget your basement, attic, storage locker, garage, and office or business):	Narrate it as you film, describing the item(s) you see, and sharing any details of importance about them. Update it every few years, and store it away from your home, so you won't lose the contents in case of a fire. Keep it safe for insurance purposes, too.
Update frequently:	Monitor your emails, credit card statements, bank statements, and incoming correspondence to keep track of what comes to you in paper format versus digital format in emails or over the internet. In addition, keep track of any account or bills that are automatically renewed, paid, and/or charged to your checking account or credit card, so your representative will know to turn off the auto-pay function.
For spare keys to everything:	Consider adding an envelope or key slot organizer so there is a single place where a second set of keys can be located (house, investment properties, storage locker, shed, vehicles, safe deposit box, etc.)
As you discover information you are missing for this questionnaire:	Use the next few pages to help you to jot down information, supplies, and equipment you discovered that you need to complete this document.
After you have prepared your estate planning documents:	Tell your loved ones not only **whether** you have prepared estate-planning documents, but if so, **where** the originals are located!
After you have finished filling out this copy of **My "Everything" File®**	The same applies to your completed **My "Everything" File®**! Why go through all that effort if they can't find it? Show them where it is!

§1-B: Your Follow-Up and To-Do List for Preparation of your "Everything" File®

*In working your way through **My "Everything" File®**, you will realize you don't have all the information, documents, or equipment you may need to complete it. So here is a place for you to list the information, supplies, and equipment you discovered that you need to complete this document.*

Information I need to obtain (and from whom): **Completed?**

1. ______ ☐
2. ______ ☐
3. ______ ☐
4. ______ ☐
5. ______ ☐
6. ______ ☐
7. ______ ☐
8. ______ ☐
9. ______ ☐
10. ______ ☐
11. ______ ☐
12. ______ ☐
13. ______ ☐
14. ______ ☐
15. ______ ☐
16. ______ ☐
17. ______ ☐
18. ______ ☐

People I need to contact (and what information is needed from them): **Completed?**

1. ______ ☐
2. ______ ☐
3. ______ ☐
4. ______ ☐
5. ______ ☐
6. ______ ☐
7. ______ ☐
8. ______ ☐
9. ______ ☐
10. ______ ☐
11. ______ ☐
12. ______ ☐
13. ______ ☐
14. ______ ☐
15. ______ ☐
16. ______ ☐

Documents I need to locate: **Completed?**

1. ______ ☐
2. ______ ☐
3. ______ ☐
4. ______ ☐
5. ______ ☐
6. ______ ☐
7. ______ ☐
8. ______ ☐
9. ______ ☐
10. ______ ☐
11. ______ ☐
12. ______ ☐
13. ______ ☐
14. ______ ☐
15. ______ ☐
16. ______ ☐
17. ______ ☐
18. ______ ☐
19. ______ ☐
20. ______ ☐
21. ______ ☐

Equipment and supplies I need to purchase: **Completed?**

1. ______ ☐
2. ______ ☐
3. ______ ☐
4. ______ ☐
5. ______ ☐
6. ______ ☐
7. ______ ☐
8. ______ ☐
9. ______ ☐
10. ______ ☐
11. ______ ☐
12. ______ ☐
13. ______ ☐
14. ______ ☐
15. ______ ☐
16. ______ ☐
17. ______ ☐
18. ______ ☐
19. ______ ☐
20. ______ ☐

Miscellaneous other things I need to do: **Completed?**

1. ______________________________ ☐
2. ______________________________ ☐
3. ______________________________ ☐
4. ______________________________ ☐
5. ______________________________ ☐
6. ______________________________ ☐
7. ______________________________ ☐
8. ______________________________ ☐
9. ______________________________ ☐
10. ______________________________ ☐
11. ______________________________ ☐
12. ______________________________ ☐
13. ______________________________ ☐
14. ______________________________ ☐
15. ______________________________ ☐
16. ______________________________ ☐
17. ______________________________ ☐
18. ______________________________ ☐
19. ______________________________ ☐
20. ______________________________ ☐
21. ______________________________ ☐
22. ______________________________ ☐
23. ______________________________ ☐
24. ______________________________ ☐
25. ______________________________ ☐
26. ______________________________ ☐
27. ______________________________ ☐
28. ______________________________ ☐
29. ______________________________ ☐
30. ______________________________ ☐
31. ______________________________ ☐
32. ______________________________ ☐
33. ______________________________ ☐
34. ______________________________ ☐
35. ______________________________ ☐
36. ______________________________ ☐
37. ______________________________ ☐
38. ______________________________ ☐
39. ______________________________ ☐
40. ______________________________ ☐
41. ______________________________ ☐
42. ______________________________ ☐

My "Everything" File®

____

(Print your name on line)

To the Person Reading this Document:

This information is being provided to you so that, in the event of my death, infirmity, incapacity, or extended absence, you will have some basic information about the important people in my life, my assets, my debts, my financial affairs, my health, and other details you may find to be of importance.

Please honor my privacy and confidentiality, and do whatever is necessary to take care of me and my loved ones. I greatly appreciate all that you will be doing on my behalf.

Sincerely,

x____ (Your Signature)

§2-A: IMMEDIATE ACTIONS TO BE TAKEN UPON MY DEATH OR INCAPACITY

*This is emergency **MUST-KNOW** information about me, and specifies the very first people who should **immediately** be notified if something happens to me.*

Version of My "Everything" File®

This copy of My "Everything" File®:	☐ The **complete** version, including personal & confidential information (e.g. social security numbers, account numbers, passwords, etc.), ☐ A **partial** version with **confidential information removed**. Where is the **complete** version located (e.g. home safe, safe deposit box, etc? Location: ______________________________
When was this questionnaire last updated (date)?	

My Basic Information

My legal (birth certificate) name:	
My nickname:	
My street address:	
City, state & zip code:	
My birthdate:	
My social security number:	
My health insurance company:	
Health insurance company phone:	
My spouse's name	
My spouse's cell phone:	
Location of spare key to house:	
Location of alarm box:	
Alarm activation/deactivation code:	
Alarm company security password:	
My cell phone number:	

Emergency Contact Information

Name of my **1st emergency contact**:	
Relationship to me:	
Telephone number:	
Email address:	
Name of **2nd emergency contact**:	
Relationship to me:	
Telephone number:	
Email address:	
Name of **3rd emergency contact**:	
Relationship to me:	
Telephone number:	
Email address:	

Final Emergency Instructions, if any

In addition to this questionnaire, I have prepared a list of instructions to be followed in the event of my death or incapacity.	☐ Yes ☐ No
If yes, where is the list located, or who has the list?	

Other Emergency Phone numbers

Ambulance phone number:	
Fire Department phone number:	
Police Department phone number:	
Local hospital name:	
Hospital address:	
Hospital city, state, and zip code:	
Hospital phone number:	
My primary care physician's name:	
Physician's telephone number:	
Crucial medical information the doctors need to know about me:	
My blood type (if known)	A+ A- B+ B- AB+ AB- O+ O-

Clergy/Spiritual advisor

My religion, if any (specify):	
Name of my clergy/spiritual advisor:	
Phone number:	
Email address:	

Allergies

I have the following **allergies**, if any:	☐ **I HAVE NO ALLERGIES (More listed in the medical info section)**
Local anesthetics	☐ Yes ☐ No
Aspirin	☐ Yes ☐ No
Penicillin or other antibiotics	☐ Yes ☐ No
Barbiturates	☐ Yes ☐ No
Sedatives, sleeping pills	☐ Yes ☐ No
Sulfa drugs	☐ Yes ☐ No
Codeine or other narcotics	☐ Yes ☐ No
Metals	☐ Yes ☐ No
Latex (rubber)	☐ Yes ☐ No
Adhesive tape	☐ Yes ☐ No
Iodine	☐ Yes ☐ No
Hay fever/other seasonal	☐ Yes ☐ No
Animals	☐ Yes ☐ No
Food	☐ Yes ☐ No
Other (specify)	☐ Yes ☐ No

Vaccination history

I've had the following vaccinations	Most recent vaccination date:
Tetanus, diphtheria, pertussis (Td/Tdap)	☐ Yes ☐ No If yes, when?
PPSV (Pneumococcal Polysaccharide Vaccine)	☐ Yes ☐ No If yes, when?
Hepatitis A Vaccine	☐ Yes ☐ No If yes, when?
Hepatitis B Vaccine	☐ Yes ☐ No If yes, when?
HPV (Human Papillomavirus) Vaccine	☐ Yes ☐ No If yes, when?
MMR (Measles, Mumps, Rubella) Vaccine	☐ Yes ☐ No If yes, when?
Varicella (Chickenpox) Vaccine	☐ Yes ☐ No If yes, when?
Meningococcal Vaccine	☐ Yes ☐ No If yes, when?
Shingles (Zoster) Vaccine	☐ Yes ☐ No If yes, when?
Flu	☐ Yes ☐ No If yes, when?
Polio	☐ Yes ☐ No If yes, when?
Smallpox	☐ Yes ☐ No If yes, when?
Typhoid	☐ Yes ☐ No If yes, when?

People to IMMEDIATELY contact upon my death

Name of person to contact:	
Phone:	
Email address:	
Relationship to me:	
Name of person to contact:	
Phone:	
Email address:	
Relationship to me:	
Name of person to contact:	
Phone:	
Email address:	
Relationship to me:	
Name of person to contact:	
Phone:	
Email address:	
Relationship to me:	
Name of person to contact:	
Phone:	
Email address:	
Relationship to me:	
Name of person to contact:	
Phone:	
Email address:	
Relationship to me:	
Name of person to contact:	
Phone:	
Email address:	
Relationship to me:	

In the event of my death

I have donated my body to science:	☐ Yes ☐ No
If yes, name of organization:	
Phone number:	
Website:	
Location of documents:	
I have a pre-paid or pre-arranged funeral or cremation plan:	☐ Yes ☐ No Which do you prefer: ☐ Funeral ☐ Cremation
If yes, name of organization:	
Phone number:	
Website address:	
Location of documents:	
I own a cemetery plot (or vault):	☐ Yes ☐ No
If yes, name of the cemetery:	
Cemetery address:	
City, state, and zip code:	
Telephone number:	
Location of the deed:	
Burial plot in name of:	
Section:	
Plot or vault number:	
Block:	
Have you left any special instructions regarding your burial?	☐ Yes ☐ No
If yes, where are they located?	
If **no,** where you would like to be buried?	
If you wish to be buried next to a deceased spouse, parent, or child, provide details on their location, and whether you own the plot:	
My **Last Will and Testament** location, if any:	
If it is in a safe, lockbox, or safe deposit box, who else has the key or combination?	

Additional people to contact

In addition, as quickly as possible, **please contact these individuals.** Their contact information is contained elsewhere in this document:	☐ My employer or business associates ☐ My assistant at work ☐ My clergy ☐ My successor trustee (if a Trust) ☐ My Personal Representative ☐ My landlord ☐ My financial advisor ☐ Social Security Admin. (800) 772-1213 or www.socialsecurity.gov ☐ Veteran's Administration re: pension and monument ☐ Life insurance agent (if death) ☐ My attorney ☐ My accountant ☐ Other (specify):

Guardian for children

Name of my **children's Guardian**:	
Guardian's phone number:	
Guardian's email address:	
Location of Guardianship documents	

Caregiver for pet(s)

Name **of caregiver for my pet(s):**	
Phone number:	
Email address:	

Miscellaneous instructions

If I die or am incapacitated, you should **immediately** take the following actions: **Add additional pages of instructions, if needed**	☐ Stop automatic payments from checking account (but only if I die) ☐ Make arrangements for care of my children (see above) ☐ Make arrangements for care of my pets (see above) ☐ Other: ☐ Other: ☐ Other:

My Estate-Planning Documents

ESTATE-PLANNING DOCUMENTS	Have you prepared the following estate-planning documents?
Location of my estate-planning documents (if they are in a safe or safe deposit box, who has the key or knows the combination?):	
Revocable Living Trust	☐ Yes ☐ No
Name of my successor trustee:	
His/her phone number:	
His/her email address:	
Durable Power of Attorney	☐ Yes ☐ No
Name of my attorney-in-fact:	
His/her phone number:	
His/her email address:	
Health Care Surrogate	☐ Yes ☐ No
Name of my health care surrogate:	
His/her phone number:	
His/her email address:	
Living Will	☐ Yes ☐ No
Name of my surrogate:	
His/her phone number:	
His/her email address:	
Pre-Need Guardian Designation	☐ Yes ☐ No
Name of Guardian of my person:	
His/her phone number:	
His/her email address:	
Pre-Need Guardian Designation	☐ Yes ☐ No
Name of Guardian of my assets:	
His/her phone number:	
His/her email address:	
I have a **Do Not Resuscitate (DNR)** order with my doctor or hospital :	☐ Yes ☐ No
If yes, name of my doctor:	
Doctor's phone number:	

Safe and Safe Deposit Box

Location of my **safe deposit box**:	
Bank name and address:	
Box number:	
Who is authorized to enter the box?	
Who has access to the key (or know where the key is located)?	
Documents of importance kept in the safe deposit box:	
Location of **home safe** or **lockbox**	
If a **key,** name and phone of person who has or knows where key is	
If a **combination lock**, name and phone of person who knows it	
OR - What is the combination?	
What documents of **immediate** importance kept in safe or lockbox?	

Family emergency meeting places

Local neighborhood emergency family meeting place (e.g. landmark, school, etc.):	
Out-of-town emergency family meeting place (e.g. landmark, name of building, school, etc.):	
What is your family's secret password or code? (This is especially important for young children to know, so they can confirm someone getting a message from you to the child, or picking up the child, is truly doing so on your behalf):	

Guns & Firearms

I have a gun, rifle, or other firearms	☐ Yes ☐ No
Is there a registration permit?	☐ Yes ☐ No
If yes, registration number:	
Location of the gun:	
Combination to gun lock or safe:	
If a gun has a lock key, where is it?	
What is to be done with the gun?	

Property or Documents being held for someone else

I am holding onto the following property or documents **which belong to someone else**.	☐ Yes ☐ No
If yes, what is being held, for whom, and why are you holding it?	

Are you a caregiver for another person?

Are you a **caregiver, Guardian, health care surrogate, or attorney-in-fact under a power of attorney** for another person?	☐ Yes ☐ No
If yes, what is the person's name and relationship to you, if any?	
Who should be notified so that someone else can take over care?	
Name of person or agency:	
Phone number:	

Information stored on computer

Is any **immediately essential information** stored in your computer?	☐ Yes ☐ No
If yes, what is the essential info stored on the computer?	
Location of directory/folder/file:	
Name of folder/file:	
Password & other access info:	
Please list any additional immediate action(s) you want someone to take on your behalf or other emergency information someone will need to know:	

Additional notes:

____

____

____

____

Miscellaneous Useful, Need-to-Know Information

What is your home address:	
City, state, and zip code:	
Do you have a **personal P.O. Box?**	☐ Yes ☐ No
If yes, where is it located?	
What is the box number?	
Name of your employer:	
Your work address:	
City, state, and zip code:	
Do you have a **work P.O. Box?**	☐ Yes ☐ No
If yes, where is it located?	
What is the box number?	

Neighbors and Friends

Name of neighbor(s) to your left:	
Address, city, state, and zip code:	
Telephone:	
Name of neighbor(s) to your right:	
Address, city, state, and zip code:	
Telephone:	
Name of neighbor across the street	
Address, city, state, and zip code:	
Telephone:	
Name of good friend:	
Address, city, state, and zip code:	
Telephone:	
Name of good friend:	
Address, city, state, and zip code:	
Telephone:	

Miscellaneous

Where is your **circuit breaker box**?	
Where is your **security system box**?	
Where is your **water-main cut-off**?	
Where is your main **thermostat**?	
What days is **garbage picked up**?	Regular trash: Recycled trash pick-up:
Phone for **newspaper delivery**:	
Name of **yard-care / landscaper**: Phone number:	
Name of **house-cleaning service:**	
Phone number:	
Name of **pool-cleaning service**:	
Phone number:	
Other service provider:	
Phone number:	
Other service provider:	
Phone number:	
Other service provider:	
Phone number:	
Other service provider:	
Phone number:	
Other service provider:	
Phone number:	
Other service provider:	
Phone number:	
Other service provider:	
Phone number:	

§2-B: Video & Asset Inventory

Every year or two, it is important to make a video inventory of all the possessions you keep at home and work. This is important for insurance purposes, as it would be impossible for most people to remember a fraction of their possessions, let alone all them. Think of how many shirts, slacks, and pairs of shoes you own, not to mention all your underwear and how much it would cost to replace them all! While pictures may be helpful to jog one's memory, narrating a video, describing the items you see, and counting them, one at a time, as you go through your closet and drawers, will leave no doubt as to what and how many you owned.

Be sure to start the video with a front page of a newspaper, zooming-in on the date to establish the date of the video, and/or narrate the date you are taking the video. Be sure to keep the video in a safe place away from your home (such as a safe deposit box), so it doesn't get destroyed in the event of a fire at your home.

Don't forget about including the contents of your garage, attic, basement, closets, drawers, shelves, storage lockers, sheds, contents of boxes, trunk of car, safe and safe deposit box, hiding places, etc. Remember to include the contents kept at your place of employment.

Finally, many of your possessions should trigger many fond memories and stories of how you came to acquire them. These are the stories that will make your possessions more meaningful to the people who will inherit them from you. Savor (and share) the memories.

Do you have an **insurance video inventory** of all possessions you keep in your home and office/workplace?	☐ Yes ☐ No	
Date when it was taken:		
Who was the videographer?		
Who else was present during video?		
Where is it stored (**Not at home!)?**		
If you do not have an insurance video, it is recommended that you prepare a **detailed** written inventory of all the possessions you keep in your home and workplace, including a description of the furnishings and contents for all your possessions contained in the following locations:	☐ Living Room ☐ Family Room ☐ Dining Room ☐ Breakfast Room ☐ Den/Study ☐ Bedroom #1 ☐ Bedroom #2 ☐ Bedroom #3 ☐ Bedroom #4 ☐ Bedroom #5	☐ Bathrooms ☐ Utility Room ☐ Show/Workroom ☐ Garage/Basement ☐ Attic ☐ Yard storage and furnishings ☐ Separate storage unit ☐ Artwork and statuary ☐ Work/office ☐ Other:

FUN MEMORIES AND STORIES	Share some memories and stories for future generations to enjoy!
How did you acquire the possession i.e. Did you buy it? Was it a gift?	
Was it for a special occasion?	
Is it valuable (e.g. antique, limited edition, signed by artist, etc.)?	

§3-A: Mini-Version of My "Everything" File®

Since few people will want to complete over 300 pages of information, this "mini-version" of ***My "Everything" File®*** *can be used as a smaller, more-condensed version of the full document to help you identify which sections apply to you, and should be completed in greater detail in the comprehensive version.*

About me and my family (complete appropriate section in questionnaire) **Section**

			Section
Your full legal name:			5-A
Your current address:			5-A
Your birthdate:			5-A
Your place of birth:			5-A
Your social security number:			5-A
You are:	☐ Single ☐ Married ☐ Divorced ☐ Widowed ☐ Legally Separated		5-A
If married, name of spouse:			5-B
Date & place of marriage:			5-B
Name of your previous spouse, if any:			5-B
How marriage ended:	☐ Death ☐ Divorce Date: ______________		5-B
Your children:	**Names**	**Birth dates**	5-C
Your grandchildren:	**Names**	**Birth dates**	5-C
Your great-grandchildren:	**Names**	**Birth dates**	5-C
Benefits available to your spouse and children:			5-D
Your mother's name:			5-E
Your father's name:			5-E
I am adopted:	☐ Yes ☐ No		5-E

If yes, the names of your biological parents are:	Mother: ______ Father: ______	5-E
Your grandparents:		5-E
Your great-grandparents:		5-E
Do you have any other persons who are dependent upon you?	☐ Yes ☐ No Name(s):	5-G
Your employment information:	☐ Yes ☐ No	5-H
Your education history:	☐ Yes ☐ No	5-I
Were you in the military?	☐ Yes ☐ No IF yes, which branch: ______	5-J
Any public service organization?	☐ Yes ☐ No Name: ______	5-K
Do you rent your home?	☐ Yes ☐ No	5-L
Do you have one or more pets?	☐ Yes ☐ No	5-M
Your religion:		5-A
I am a U.S. citizen:	☐ Yes ☐ No	5-A
If no, the date and place of your naturalization:		5-A
I am a citizen of the following country:		5-A
Where are all your important records stored?	Complete section to right:	4-A

Financial Information

		Section
What are all your sources of income?	☐ Salary ☐ Pension ☐ Social Security ☐ Property Settlement ☐ Alimony ☐ Child Support ☐ Royalties ☐ Dividends/Interest ☐ Other (specify): ______	6-A
Monthly income:	$	6-B
Monthly cash flow:	List your detailed monthly income and expenses	6-B
Have you made gifts of over $14,000 to anyone in a single year ($28,000 if jointly made with spouse)?	☐ Yes ☐ No If yes, to whom? ______ Year ______ Amount of gift: $______ If yes, did you file a gift tax return for that year? ☐ Yes ☐ No	6-D
Where are your income, gift, and estate tax records?	Complete section number to right:	6-D

Estate planning documents

		Section
Last Will and Testament	☐ Yes ☐ No If yes, complete section number to right:	6-E
Revocable Living Trust	☐ Yes ☐ No If yes, complete section number to right:	6-E
Durable Power of Attorney	☐ Yes ☐ No If yes, complete section number to right:	6-E
Health care surrogate/health care power of attorney	☐ Yes ☐ No If yes, complete section number to right:	6-E
Living Will/advanced directive	☐ Yes ☐ No If yes, complete section number to right:	6-E
Guardian Designation	☐ Yes ☐ No If yes, complete section number to right:	6-E

Your assets (What do you own?)

		Section
Do you own any real estate?	☐ Yes ☐ No If yes, fill out appropriate section for each property	7-A

Do you own your own home? What is the property address? What is the approx. value? Is there a mortgage? Approx. mortgage balance: Name of mortgage company: Account number: Phone number: Name of insurance agent: Insurance company: Insurance phone number: Policy number:	☐ Yes ☐ No If yes, complete section number to right: $ ☐ Yes ☐ No $	7-A1
Do you own your own second or vacation home? What is the property address? What is the approximate value? Is there a mortgage? Approximate mortgage balance: Name of mortgage company: Account number: Phone number: Name of insurance agent: Insurance company: Insurance phone number: Policy number:	☐ Yes ☐ No If yes, complete section number to right: $ ☐ Yes ☐ No $	7-A2
Do you own a time-share unit? What is the property address? What is the approximate value? Is there a mortgage? Approximate mortgage balance? Name of mortgage company: Account number: Phone number:	☐ Yes ☐ No If yes, complete section number to right: $ ☐ Yes ☐ No $	7-A3
Do you own investment real estate? What is the property address? What is the approximate value? Is there a mortgage? Approximate mortgage balance: Name of mortgage company: Account number: Phone number: Name of insurance agent: Insurance company: Insurance phone number: Policy number:	☐ Yes ☐ No If yes, complete section number to right: $ ☐ Yes ☐ No $	7-A4
Do you own your own business? Name of business:	☐ Yes ☐ No If yes, complete section number to right	7-B

What is the business address?		
What is the approximate value?	$	
Are there any business loans?	☐ Yes ☐ No	
Approximate amount of loans?	$	
Name of loan company:		
Loan account number:		
Mortgage phone number:		
Name of co-owners, if any:		
Bank name:		
Bank account number(s)		
Bank phone number:		
Name of insurance agent:		
Insurance company:		
Insurance phone number:		
Policy number:		
Name and phone of accountant:		
Name and phone of attorney:		
Do you own an automobile or other vehicle?	☐ Yes ☐ No If yes, complete section number to right	7-C
Year, manufacturer, and model?		
What is the approximate value?		
Is there a loan?	☐ Yes ☐ No	
Approximate amount of loan?	$	
Name of loan company:		
Loan account number:		
Loan company phone number:		
Name of insurance agent:		
Insurance company:		
Insurance phone number:		
Policy number:		
Do you own any equipment and/or machinery?	☐ Yes ☐ No If yes, complete section number to right	7-D
What type of machinery?		
Year, manufacturer, and model:		
What is the approximate value?	$	
Is there a loan on it?	☐ Yes ☐ No	
Approximate loan balance:	$	
Name of loan company:		
Loan account number:		
Loan company phone number:		
Name of insurance agent:		
Insurance company:		
Insurance phone number:		
Policy number:		
Do you have any bank accounts?	☐ Yes ☐ No If yes, complete section number to right	7-E
Types of accounts:	☐ Checking ☐ Money market ☐ Savings ☐ CDs	
Approximate balance:	$	

Name of bank: Account number(s): Bank phone number: Name and phone of banker: Name of account owner(s): Name of beneficiary: Name of contingent beneficiary:		
Do you have any investment accounts (non-retirement)? Types of accounts: Approximate balance: Name of investment company: Account number(s): Investment co. phone number: Name and phone of advisor: Name of account owner(s): Name of beneficiary: Name of contingent beneficiary:	☐ Yes ☐ No If yes, complete section number to right $	7-F
Do you have any retirement accounts? Types of accounts: Approximate balance: Name of investment company: Account number(s): Investment co. phone number: Name and phone of advisor: Name of account owner(s): Name of beneficiary: Name of contingent beneficiary:	☐ Yes ☐ No If yes, complete section number to right ☐ IRA ☐ Roth IRA ☐ SEP-IRA ☐ 401(k) ☐ 403(b) ☐ SIMPLE-IRA ☐ Profit-Sharing Plan ☐ Money Purchase Plan ☐ Pension ☐ Other $	7-G
Do you have any cash value life insurance policies? Types of insurance: Face value of policy: Cash value of policy: Name of insurance company: Policy contract number(s): Insurance co. phone number: Name/phone of insurance agent: Name of Policy owner(s): Name of insured person: Name of beneficiary: Name of contingent beneficiary:	☐ Yes ☐ No If yes, complete section number to right $ $	7-H
Do you have any annuities? Types of annuities: Is this qualified or non-qualified? Initial investment:	☐ Yes ☐ No If yes, complete section number to right ☐ Fixed ☐ Variable ☐ Index ☐ Immediate ☐ Qualified (IRA; 403(b), etc. ☐ Non-qualified $	7-I

Current value of policy: Name of insurance company: Policy contract number(s): Insurance co. phone number: Name/phone of insurance agent: Name of policy owner(s): Name of insured person: Name of beneficiary: Name of contingent beneficiary:	$	
Does anyone owe you money ? Name of person or company: Telephone number: Reason for loan: Original amount of loan: Approximate balance of loan: Other important loan details:	☐ Yes ☐ No If yes, complete section number to right $ $	7-J
Do you have a safe deposit box? Name of bank: Address: Telephone number: Box number: Where is the key located? Describe any valuable contents:	☐ Yes ☐ No If yes, complete section number to right	7-K
Do you own any computers, smartphones, and other electronics?	☐ Yes ☐ No If yes, complete section number to right	7-L
Do you store important data and information on digital devices?	☐ Yes ☐ No If yes, complete section number to right:	7-M
Do you have digital assets and online accounts?	☐ Yes ☐ No If yes, complete section number to right:	7-N
Do you use online backup and storage websites?	☐ Yes ☐ No If yes, complete section number to right:	7-O
Do you own other electronics, appliances, and equipment?	☐ Yes ☐ No If yes, complete section number to right:	7-P
Do you have any of these? Provide details about these often forgotten or overlooked items. Home safe or lockbox: Office safe or lockbox: Off-premise storage unit: Assets held outside the USA: Antiques: Season passes for sports/theater: Health savings account: Assets with hidden value to the untrained eye: Patents, trademarks, royalties:	☐ Yes ☐ No If yes, complete section number to right: ☐ Yes ☐ No Details: ☐ Yes ☐ No Details: ☐ Yes ☐ No Details: ☐ Yes ☐ No Details: ☐ Yes ☐ No Details: ☐ Yes ☐ No Details: ☐ Yes ☐ No Details: ☐ Yes ☐ No Details:	7-Q

Life insurance on someone else's life: Barter exchange dollars: Boat in dry dock: Fur in cold storage: Assets at pawn or consignment shop: Medical/biological specimen: Pending or anticipated lawsuits: Valuable artwork: Precious metals/gems/coins: Jewelry and furs: Rare books and collectibles: Coins, stamps, other collections: Mineral or forestry rights: Guns and firearms: Piano, organ, musical instruments: Horses, cattle, livestock: Hiding places:	☐ Yes ☐ No Details: ☐ Yes ☐ No Details: ☐ Yes ☐ No Details: ☐ Yes ☐ No Details: ☐ Yes ☐ No Details: ☐ Yes ☐ No Details: ☐ Yes ☐ No Details: ☐ Yes ☐ No Details: ☐ Yes ☐ No Details: ☐ Yes ☐ No Details: ☐ Yes ☐ No Details: ☐ Yes ☐ No Details: ☐ Yes ☐ No Details: ☐ Yes ☐ No Details: ☐ Yes ☐ No Details: ☐ Yes ☐ No Details: ☐ Yes ☐ No Details: ☐ Yes ☐ No Details:	
Do you expect to be the beneficiary of a Trust?	☐ Yes ☐ No If yes, complete section number to right:	7-Q
Do you expect to be the beneficiary of a bequest in a Will?	☐ Yes ☐ No If yes, complete section number to right:	7-Q
Do you expect to inherit income and/or assets?	☐ Yes ☐ No If yes, complete section number to right:	7-Q
Do you have any sentimental assets that you want to give to specific individuals? Describe each item in detail: Who is to receive the item?	☐ Yes ☐ No If yes, complete section number to right:	7-R
Assets you are holding for the benefit of others: Describe the item being held: Why are you are holding them? Name and phone number of the person for whom it is being held:	☐ Yes ☐ No If yes, complete section number to right: ☐ 529 Education Savings Plan ☐ Uniform Transfer to Minor's Account ☐ Other: ______ ☐ Assets to be delivered upon occurrence of event ☐ Collateral for a loan ☐ Other: ______	7-S

Your debts, liabilities, and obligations		**Section**
Do you have mortgages, 2nd mortgages, or equity lines of credit on your real estate?	☐ Yes ☐ No If yes, complete section number to right:	7-A
Do you have any business loans?	☐ Yes ☐ No If yes, complete section number to right:	7-B

Do you have any vehicle loans?	☐ Yes ☐ No If yes, complete section number to right:	7-C
Do you have any student loans?	☐ Yes ☐ No If yes, complete section number to right:	8-A
Do you have any home improvement loans (e.g., new roof, room extension, pool, etc.)?	☐ Yes ☐ No If yes, complete section number to right:	8-B
Do you have secured loans (e.g., item purchased is collateral, such as jewelry, furnishings, etc.	☐ Yes ☐ No If yes, complete section number to right:	8-C
Do you have credit cards?	☐ Yes ☐ No If yes, complete section number to right:	8-D
Do you have other unsecured personal loans (no collateral)?	☐ Yes ☐ No If yes, complete section number to right:	8-E
Do you have any legal obligations (e.g., under divorce decree)?	☐ Yes ☐ No If yes, complete section number to right:	8-F
Do have any charitable obligations (e.g. pledge or tithe)?	☐ Yes ☐ No If yes, complete section number to right:	8-F
Do you have any moral obligations (e.g., taking care of parents, friends, or neighbors)?	☐ Yes ☐ No If yes, complete section number to right:	8-F
Have you been named in someone else's Power of Attorney to act on their behalf?	☐ Yes ☐ No	8-F
If yes, provide the name and phone number of the person:	Name: Phone:	8-F
Who else needs to be notified if you are unable to do so:	Name: Phone:	8-F
Have you been named a health care surrogate to make medical decisions for someone else?	☐ Yes ☐ No	8-F
If yes, provide the name and phone number of the person:	Name: Phone:	8-F
Who else needs to be notified if you are unable to do so:	Name: Phone:	8-F
Are you a caregiver for someone else?	☐ Yes ☐ No	8-F
If yes, provide the name and phone number of the person:	Name: Phone:	8-F
Who else needs to be notified if you are unable to do so:	Name: Phone:	8-F

Your insurance policies

		Section
Do you have renter's insurance?	☐ Yes ☐ No If yes, complete section number to right:	5-L
Do you have homeowner's insurance?	☐ Yes ☐ No If yes, complete section number to right:	7-A
Do you have flood insurance?	☐ Yes ☐ No If yes, complete section number to right:	7-A
Do you have any type of business insurance?	☐ Yes ☐ No If yes, complete section number to right:	7-B
Do you have insurance for your vehicle(s)?	☐ Yes ☐ No If yes, complete section number to right:	7-C
Do you have insurance on equipment or machinery?	☐ Yes ☐ No If yes, complete section number to right:	7-D
Do you have term life insurance?	☐ Yes ☐ No If yes, complete section number to right:	9-A
Do you have accidental death and dismemberment insurance?	☐ Yes ☐ No If yes, complete section number to right:	9-B
Do you have an umbrella policy?	☐ Yes ☐ No If yes, complete section number to right:	9-C
Do you qualify for Medicare?	☐ Yes ☐ No If yes, complete section number to right:	9-D
Do you have a Medicare supplemental coverage policy?	☐ Yes ☐ No If yes, complete section number to right:	9-D
Do you have health insurance?	☐ Yes ☐ No If yes, complete section number to right:	9-E
Do you have dental insurance?	☐ Yes ☐ No If yes, complete section number to right:	9-F
Do you have vision insurance?	☐ Yes ☐ No If yes, complete section number to right:	9-G
Do you have prescription drug insurance?	☐ Yes ☐ No If yes, complete section number to right:	9-H
Do you have disability insurance?	☐ Yes ☐ No If yes, complete section number to right:	9-I
Do you have a supplemental health or short-term disability policy (e.g. Aflac)	☐ Yes ☐ No If yes, complete section number to right:	9-J
Do you have long-term care insurance?	☐ Yes ☐ No If yes, complete section number to right:	9-K
Do you have a personal articles insurance policy (e.g. jewelry, artwork, etc.)?	☐ Yes ☐ No If yes, complete section number to right:	9-L
Do you have any other types of insurance coverage?	☐ Yes ☐ No If yes, complete section number to right:	9-M

Your medical history and health information

		Section
Are you having medical issues or challenges?	☐ Yes ☐ No If yes, complete section number to right:	10-A
Do you wear the following:	☐ Yes ☐ No If yes, complete section number to right:	10-A
Hearing aids?	☐ Yes ☐ No	
Contact lenses?	☐ Yes ☐ No	
Artificial limbs?	☐ Yes ☐ No	
Pacemaker?	☐ Yes ☐ No	
Defibrillator?	☐ Yes ☐ No	
Automated insulin delivery device?	☐ Yes ☐ No	

Have you ever had surgery?	☐ Yes ☐ No If yes, complete section number to right:	10-B
Do you have doctors and/or other medical providers?	☐ Yes ☐ No If yes, complete section number to right:	10-C
Do you take prescription medications?	☐ Yes ☐ No If yes, complete section number to right:	10-D
Do you take non-prescription medications, vitamins, and supplements?	☐ Yes ☐ No If yes, complete section number to right:	10-E
Do you have allergies?	☐ Yes ☐ No If yes, complete section number to right:	10-F
Provide all of your medical history:	☐ Yes ☐ No If yes, complete section number to right:	10-G

Your burial/cremation/donation of body preferences		**Section**
What is your preference?	☐ Burial ☐ Cremation ☐ Donate body to science ☐ No preference	11-A
Do you have a prepaid burial/cremation plan?	☐ Yes ☐ No If yes, complete section number to right:	11-A
Do you want a military burial?	☐ Yes ☐ No If yes, complete section number to right:	11-A
Do you own a cemetery plot?	☐ Yes ☐ No If yes, complete section number to right:	11-A
Plan your own funeral:	Complete section number to right:	11-A
Have you created a video legacy?	☐ Yes ☐ No If yes, complete section number to right:	13-A
Do you want any of your usable organs donated?	☐ Yes ☐ No If yes, complete section number to right:	11-B

Miscellaneous information		**Section**
Do you have a list of your advisors, important contacts, organizations, and affiliations?	☐ Yes ☐ No If yes, complete section number to right:	12-A
Do you have certain bills automatically paid from your bank account?	☐ Yes ☐ No If yes, complete section number to right:	12-B
Do you have certain bills automatically charged to your credit card?	☐ Yes ☐ No If yes, complete section number to right:	12-C
Do you have certain subscriptions and services automatically renewed??	☐ Yes ☐ No If yes, complete section number to right:	12-D
Do you have a complete list of all your security codes	☐ Yes ☐ No If yes, complete section number to right:	12-E
Do you have a complete list of your email addresses, Internet accounts, websites, usernames, and passwords	☐ Yes ☐ No If yes, complete section number to right:	12-F
Do you want to share your investment strategies and preferences?	☐ Yes ☐ No If yes, complete section number to right:	12-G

Your life legacy

		Section
Do you want to share some of your life stories and interesting details about yourself?	☐ Yes ☐ No If yes, complete section number to right:	13-A
Do you have an "ethical" will?	☐ Yes ☐ No If yes, complete section number to right:	13-B
Provide your final words of love:	Attach them to your "Everything" file!	13-B

§4-A: Location of Important Documents & Records

Provide the location of any paper documents, such as home filing cabinet, safe deposit box, home safe, office safe, wallet, shelf, closet, home desk, work desk, hiding place, etc.

If they are saved in digital format, indicate the file name and where the file can be located. If someone is holding the document (e.g. your attorney, accountant, financial planner, etc.), indicate who has it.

If you have any of the following documents, place a checkmark or an "x" to the left of the item.	Saved in what format? Paper, digital, or both	Where is this document located (or who has it)? (e.g. home file cabinet, office safe, safe deposit box, wallet, etc.) If saved in digital format, where is it stored (e.g. computer, thumb drive, cloud, etc.), what is the file name, and what is the username and password to access it (use a separate sheet of paper, if needed)?

Personal Documents

☐ Certified copy of your birth certificate	☐ Paper ☐ Digital	
☐ Certified copy of your spouse's birth certificate	☐ Paper ☐ Digital	
☐ Certified copy of each of your children's birth certificate(s)	☐ Paper ☐ Digital	
☐ Passport and/or Visa	☐ Paper ☐ Digital	
☐ Naturalization and citizenship papers	☐ Paper ☐ Digital	
☐ Driver's license or state ID	☐ Paper ☐ Digital	
☐ Health insurance card	☐ Paper ☐ Digital	
☐ Marriage certificate	☐ Paper ☐ Digital	
☐ Death certificates	☐ Paper ☐ Digital	
☐ Professional licenses	☐ Paper ☐ Digital	
☐ Military records and discharge papers (DD214)	☐ Paper ☐ Digital	
☐ Bankruptcy documents	☐ Paper ☐ Digital	
☐ Medical documents	☐ Paper ☐ Digital	
☐ Funeral and final resting place details	☐ Paper ☐ Digital	
☐ Religious papers and certificates	☐ Paper ☐ Digital	
☐	☐ Paper ☐ Digital	
☐	☐ Paper ☐ Digital	
☐	☐ Paper ☐ Digital	
☐	☐ Paper ☐ Digital	
☐	☐ Paper ☐ Digital	
☐	☐ Paper ☐ Digital	
☐	☐ Paper ☐ Digital	
☐	☐ Paper ☐ Digital	
☐	☐ Paper ☐ Digital	

Legal Documents

☐ Adoption records	☐ Paper ☐ Digital	
☐ Divorce or separation decree (and any amending orders)	☐ Paper ☐ Digital	
☐ Property settlement agreement	☐ Paper ☐ Digital	
☐ Guardianship, child custody, support, visitation agreements	☐ Paper ☐ Digital	
☐ Prenuptial (Pre-marital) Agreement	☐ Paper ☐ Digital	
☐ Postnuptial (Post-marital) Agreement	☐ Paper ☐ Digital	
☐ Community Property Agreement	☐ Paper ☐ Digital	
☐ Domestic Partner Agreement	☐ Paper ☐ Digital	
☐ Cohabitation Agreement	☐ Paper ☐ Digital	
☐ Life Care Agreement	☐ Paper ☐ Digital	
☐ Other Inter-Spousal Agreements	☐ Paper ☐ Digital	
☐ Other Court Decrees or Orders	☐ Paper ☐ Digital	
☐	☐ Paper ☐ Digital	

Funeral Arrangements

☐ Deed to cemetery plot/vault	☐ Paper ☐ Digital	
☐ Contract with mausoleum	☐ Paper ☐ Digital	
☐ Prepaid burial/Cremation arrangements/agreements	☐ Paper ☐ Digital	
☐ Donation of body documents	☐ Paper ☐ Digital	
☐ My self-written obituary	☐ Paper ☐ Digital	
☐ My self-written eulogy	☐ Paper ☐ Digital	
☐	☐ Paper ☐ Digital	

Children's Records

☐ Birth Certificates	☐ Paper ☐ Digital	
☐ Adoption Records	☐ Paper ☐ Digital	
☐ Passport and/or Visa	☐ Paper ☐ Digital	
☐ Naturalization/Citizenship	☐ Paper ☐ Digital	
☐ Baptismal or Religious Records	☐ Paper ☐ Digital	
☐ Life insurance policies	☐ Paper ☐ Digital	
☐ Medical records	☐ Paper ☐ Digital	
☐ School Records	☐ Paper ☐ Digital	
☐ Prepaid State-sponsored Tuition plans	☐ Paper ☐ Digital	
☐ 529 Education Plans	☐ Paper ☐ Digital	
☐ UTMA/UGMA accounts	☐ Paper ☐ Digital	
☐	☐ Paper ☐ Digital	

Estate Planning Documents

☐ Revocable Living Trust, Amendments, and Restatements of Trust	☐ Paper ☐ Digital	
☐ Last Will and Testament and codicils	☐ Paper ☐ Digital	
☐ Durable Power of Attorney	☐ Paper ☐ Digital	
☐ Health Care Surrogate (Health Care Power of Attorney)	☐ Paper ☐ Digital	
☐ Guardian Designations	☐ Paper ☐ Digital	
☐ Living Will (Advanced Health Care Directive)	☐ Paper ☐ Digital	
☐ Body / Organ Donor Form	☐ Paper ☐ Digital	
☐ All filed Gift Tax Returns	☐ Paper ☐ Digital	
☐ Irrevocable Trust	☐ Paper ☐ Digital	
☐ Special Needs Trust	☐ Paper ☐ Digital	
☐ Qualified Personal Residence Trust (QPRT)	☐ Paper ☐ Digital	
☐ Family Limited Partnership (FLP)	☐ Paper ☐ Digital	
Less-Common types of Trusts ☐ Irrevocable Life Insurance Trust (ILIT) ☐ Qualified Terminal Interest Property Trust (QTIP) ☐ Qualified Domestic Trust (QDOT) ☐ Grantor Retained Annuity Trust (GRAT) ☐ Grantor Retained Income Trust (GRIT) ☐ Intentionally Defective Grantor Trust (IDGT) ☐ Charitable Remainder Trust (CRT) ☐ Charitable Lead Trust (CLT) ☐ Charitable Shelter Trust (CST) ☐ IRA Trust ☐ Gun Trust ☐ Pet Trust ☐ Charitable Remainder Annuity Trust (CRAT) ☐ Charitable Remainder Unit Trust (CRUT)	☐ Paper ☐ Digital ☐ Paper ☐ Digital ☐ Paper ☐ Digital ☐ Paper ☐ Digital ☐ Paper ☐ Digital ☐ Paper ☐ Digital ☐ Paper ☐ Digital ☐ Paper ☐ Digital ☐ Paper ☐ Digital ☐ Paper ☐ Digital ☐ Paper ☐ Digital ☐ Paper ☐ Digital ☐ Paper ☐ Digital ☐ Paper ☐ Digital ☐ Paper ☐ Digital	
☐ Other:	☐ Paper ☐ Digital	
☐ Other:	☐ Paper ☐ Digital	
☐ Other:	☐ Paper ☐ Digital	
☐ Other:	☐ Paper ☐ Digital	
☐ Other:	☐ Paper ☐ Digital	
☐ Other:	☐ Paper ☐ Digital	
☐ Other:	☐ Paper ☐ Digital	
☐ Other:	☐ Paper ☐ Digital	

Household Documents

☐ Lease to home or apartment	☐ Paper ☐ Digital	
☐ Renter's insurance policy	☐ Paper ☐ Digital	
☐ **Home Documents** ☐ Deed ☐ Closing statement ☐ Bill of sale, if applicable ☐ Mortgage ☐ 2nd Mortgage/Line of credit ☐ Mortgage releases ☐ Title insurance policy ☐ Survey ☐ Appraisal ☐ Property tax bills and special assessments ☐ Major improvement records and receipts	 ☐ Paper ☐ Digital ☐ Paper ☐ Digital ☐ Paper ☐ Digital ☐ Paper ☐ Digital ☐ Paper ☐ Digital ☐ Paper ☐ Digital ☐ Paper ☐ Digital ☐ Paper ☐ Digital ☐ Paper ☐ Digital ☐ Paper ☐ Digital ☐ Paper ☐ Digital	
☐ Household inventory, receipts, photographs, video tapes, misc. records.	☐ Paper ☐ Digital	
☐ Personal property, artwork, jewelry, furs, collectables, and other valuables: ☐ Receipts ☐ Appraisals ☐ Personal effects policies	 ☐ Paper ☐ Digital ☐ Paper ☐ Digital ☐ Paper ☐ Digital	
☐ Appliances, electronics, computers, and other home equipment: ☐ Receipts ☐ Warranties ☐ Owner's manuals ☐ Maintenance records	 ☐ Paper ☐ Digital ☐ Paper ☐ Digital ☐ Paper ☐ Digital ☐ Paper ☐ Digital	
☐	☐ Paper ☐ Digital	
☐	☐ Paper ☐ Digital	
☐	☐ Paper ☐ Digital	
☐	☐ Paper ☐ Digital	

Home Service & Maintenance

☐ Home Appliances	☐ Paper ☐ Digital	
☐ Computer and Electronics	☐ Paper ☐ Digital	
☐ Lawn & Garden / Landscaping	☐ Paper ☐ Digital	
☐ Alarm System	☐ Paper ☐ Digital	
☐ Home Service/Repair Contracts	☐ Paper ☐ Digital	
☐	☐ Paper ☐ Digital	
☐	☐ Paper ☐ Digital	
☐	☐ Paper ☐ Digital	
☐	☐ Paper ☐ Digital	

Other Real Estate

☐ Land Trust documents	☐ Paper ☐ Digital	
☐ **VACATION HOME (2ND HOME)** ☐ Deed ☐ Closing statement ☐ Bill of sale, if applicable ☐ Mortgage ☐ 2nd Mortgage/Line of credit ☐ Mortgage releases ☐ Title insurance policy ☐ Survey ☐ Appraisal ☐ Property tax bills and assessments ☐ Major improvement records/receipts	 ☐ Paper ☐ Digital ☐ Paper ☐ Digital ☐ Paper ☐ Digital ☐ Paper ☐ Digital ☐ Paper ☐ Digital ☐ Paper ☐ Digital ☐ Paper ☐ Digital ☐ Paper ☐ Digital ☐ Paper ☐ Digital ☐ Paper ☐ Digital ☐ Paper ☐ Digital	
☐ **TIMESHARE / VACATION CLUB** ☐ Deed ☐ Closing statement ☐ Bill of sale, if applicable ☐ Mortgage ☐ Mortgage releases ☐ Title insurance policy ☐ Property tax bills assessments	 ☐ Paper ☐ Digital ☐ Paper ☐ Digital ☐ Paper ☐ Digital ☐ Paper ☐ Digital ☐ Paper ☐ Digital ☐ Paper ☐ Digital ☐ Paper ☐ Digital	
☐ **INVESTMENT PROPERTY #1** ☐ Deed ☐ Closing statement ☐ Bill of sale, if applicable ☐ Mortgage ☐ 2nd Mortgage/Line of credit ☐ Mortgage releases ☐ Title insurance policy ☐ Survey ☐ Appraisal ☐ Property tax bills and assessments ☐ Major improvement records/receipts ☐ Management company agreement	 ☐ Paper ☐ Digital ☐ Paper ☐ Digital ☐ Paper ☐ Digital ☐ Paper ☐ Digital ☐ Paper ☐ Digital ☐ Paper ☐ Digital ☐ Paper ☐ Digital ☐ Paper ☐ Digital ☐ Paper ☐ Digital ☐ Paper ☐ Digital ☐ Paper ☐ Digital ☐ Paper ☐ Digital	
☐ **INVESTMENT PROPERTY #2** ☐ Deed ☐ Closing statement ☐ Bill of sale, if applicable ☐ Mortgage ☐ 2nd Mortgage/Line of credit ☐ Mortgage releases ☐ Title insurance policy ☐ Survey ☐ Appraisal ☐ Property tax bills and assessments ☐ Major improvement records/receipts ☐ Management company agreement	 ☐ Paper ☐ Digital ☐ Paper ☐ Digital ☐ Paper ☐ Digital ☐ Paper ☐ Digital ☐ Paper ☐ Digital ☐ Paper ☐ Digital ☐ Paper ☐ Digital ☐ Paper ☐ Digital ☐ Paper ☐ Digital ☐ Paper ☐ Digital ☐ Paper ☐ Digital ☐ Paper ☐ Digital	

Vehicles & Other Transportation

☐ Primary Automobile: ☐ Ownership registration ☐ Lender and payment contract ☐ Vehicle rental agreement ☐ License plate information ☐ Warranties, maintenance records, receipts	 ☐ Paper ☐ Digital ☐ Paper ☐ Digital ☐ Paper ☐ Digital ☐ Paper ☐ Digital ☐ Paper ☐ Digital	
☐ 2nd Automobile or Motorcycle ☐ Ownership registration ☐ Lender and payment contract ☐ Vehicle Rental agreement ☐ License plate information ☐ Warranties, maintenance records, and receipts	 ☐ Paper ☐ Digital ☐ Paper ☐ Digital ☐ Paper ☐ Digital ☐ Paper ☐ Digital ☐ Paper ☐ Digital	
☐ 3rd Automobile or Motorcycle ☐ Ownership registration ☐ Lender and payment contract ☐ Vehicle Rental agreement ☐ License plate information ☐ Warranties, maintenance Records, and receipts	 ☐ Paper ☐ Digital ☐ Paper ☐ Digital ☐ Paper ☐ Digital ☐ Paper ☐ Digital ☐ Paper ☐ Digital	
☐ Boat, Plane, Other Vehicles ☐ Ownership registration ☐ Lender and payment contract ☐ Vehicle Rental agreement ☐ License plate information ☐ Warranties, maintenance Records, and receipts	 ☐ Paper ☐ Digital ☐ Paper ☐ Digital ☐ Paper ☐ Digital ☐ Paper ☐ Digital ☐ Paper ☐ Digital	
☐ Boat, Plane, Other Vehicles ☐ Ownership registration ☐ Lender and payment contract ☐ Vehicle Rental agreement ☐ License plate information ☐ Warranties, maintenance records, and receipts	 ☐ Paper ☐ Digital ☐ Paper ☐ Digital ☐ Paper ☐ Digital ☐ Paper ☐ Digital ☐ Paper ☐ Digital	
☐ Boat, Plane, Other Vehicles ☐ Ownership registration ☐ Lender and payment contract ☐ Vehicle Rental agreement ☐ License plate information ☐ Warranties, maintenance records, and receipts	 ☐ Paper ☐ Digital ☐ Paper ☐ Digital ☐ Paper ☐ Digital ☐ Paper ☐ Digital ☐ Paper ☐ Digital	
☐	☐ Paper ☐ Digital	
☐	☐ Paper ☐ Digital	
☐	☐ Paper ☐ Digital	

Insurance Policies

☐ Life Insurance	☐ Paper ☐ Digital	
☐ Health and Medical Insurance	☐ Paper ☐ Digital	
☐ Medicare Supplemental Insurance	☐ Paper ☐ Digital	
☐ Disability Insurance	☐ Paper ☐ Digital	
☐ Accidental Death Insurance	☐ Paper ☐ Digital	
☐ Long-Term Care Insurance	☐ Paper ☐ Digital	
☐ Homeowner/Renter's Insurance	☐ Paper ☐ Digital	
☐ Personal property or personal effects (e.g. jewelry, art, etc.)	☐ Paper ☐ Digital	
☐ Automobile or Boat Insurance	☐ Paper ☐ Digital	
☐ Personal Liability Umbrella	☐ Paper ☐ Digital	
☐ General Liability Insurance	☐ Paper ☐ Digital	
☐ Professional Liability Insurance	☐ Paper ☐ Digital	
☐ Errors and Omissions Insurance	☐ Paper ☐ Digital	
☐ Mortgage Insurance	☐ Paper ☐ Digital	
☐ Credit and Credit Card Insurance	☐ Paper ☐ Digital	
☐ Travel Insurance	☐ Paper ☐ Digital	
☐ Annuities	☐ Paper ☐ Digital	
☐ Burial or Prepaid Funeral Insurance	☐ Paper ☐ Digital	
☐ Business Insurance	☐ Paper ☐ Digital	
☐ Liability Insurance	☐ Paper ☐ Digital	
☐ Key Man Insurance	☐ Paper ☐ Digital	
☐ Buy/Sell Funding insurance	☐ Paper ☐ Digital	
☐	☐ Paper ☐ Digital	
☐	☐ Paper ☐ Digital	
☐	☐ Paper ☐ Digital	
☐	☐ Paper ☐ Digital	
☐	☐ Paper ☐ Digital	
☐	☐ Paper ☐ Digital	
☐	☐ Paper ☐ Digital	
☐	☐ Paper ☐ Digital	
☐	☐ Paper ☐ Digital	
☐	☐ Paper ☐ Digital	
☐	☐ Paper ☐ Digital	
☐	☐ Paper ☐ Digital	
☐	☐ Paper ☐ Digital	
☐	☐ Paper ☐ Digital	
☐	☐ Paper ☐ Digital	
☐	☐ Paper ☐ Digital	
☐	☐ Paper ☐ Digital	

Business Owner's Records

☐ Corporate or LLC Minute Book	☐ Paper ☐ Digital	
☐ Articles of Incorporation	☐ Paper ☐ Digital	
☐ LLC Articles of Organization	☐ Paper ☐ Digital	
☐ LLC Operating agreement	☐ Paper ☐ Digital	
☐ Shareholder/Member Agmt	☐ Paper ☐ Digital	
☐ Partnership/Joint Venture Agmt	☐ Paper ☐ Digital	
☐ Other business agreements	☐ Paper ☐ Digital	
☐ Business Stock/LLC certificates	☐ Paper ☐ Digital	
☐ Real estate leases or deeds	☐ Paper ☐ Digital	
☐ Equipment leases or bills of sale	☐ Paper ☐ Digital	
☐ Buy/Sell Agreements	☐ Paper ☐ Digital	
☐ Business income tax returns and records	☐ Paper ☐ Digital	
☐ Employment tax returns and records	☐ Paper ☐ Digital	
☐ Business Real Estate Records	☐ Paper ☐ Digital	
☐ Business Vehicle Records	☐ Paper ☐ Digital	
☐ Business Employee Records	☐ Paper ☐ Digital	
☐ Business Equipment Records	☐ Paper ☐ Digital	
☐ Miscellaneous Contracts	☐ Paper ☐ Digital	
☐ Vendor/supplier list / contracts	☐ Paper ☐ Digital	
☐ Customer/Client List	☐ Paper ☐ Digital	
☐ List of important websites and passwords	☐ Paper ☐ Digital	
☐ Business-owned assets	☐ Paper ☐ Digital	
☐	☐ Paper ☐ Digital	
☐	☐ Paper ☐ Digital	
☐	☐ Paper ☐ Digital	
☐	☐ Paper ☐ Digital	
☐	☐ Paper ☐ Digital	
☐	☐ Paper ☐ Digital	
☐	☐ Paper ☐ Digital	
☐	☐ Paper ☐ Digital	
☐	☐ Paper ☐ Digital	
☐	☐ Paper ☐ Digital	
☐	☐ Paper ☐ Digital	
☐	☐ Paper ☐ Digital	
☐	☐ Paper ☐ Digital	
☐	☐ Paper ☐ Digital	
☐	☐ Paper ☐ Digital	
☐	☐ Paper ☐ Digital	
☐	☐ Paper ☐ Digital	

Employee Records and Benefits

☐ Salary & Wage Statements	☐ Paper ☐ Digital	
☐ Employment/Independent Contractor Agreements	☐ Paper ☐ Digital	
☐ Non-Compete/Non-Disclosure Confidentiality Agreement	☐ Paper ☐ Digital	
☐ Employee handbook	☐ Paper ☐ Digital	
☐ Employee benefit statement	☐ Paper ☐ Digital	
☐ Life Insurance ☐ Term ☐ Dependent Life ☐ Split-Dollar Life	☐ Paper ☐ Digital ☐ Paper ☐ Digital ☐ Paper ☐ Digital ☐ Paper ☐ Digital	
☐ Property/casualty insurance	☐ Paper ☐ Digital	
☐ Vehicle & equipment insurance	☐ Paper ☐ Digital	
☐ Cyber liability insurance	☐ Paper ☐ Digital	
☐ Long-Term Care Insurance	☐ Paper ☐ Digital	
☐ Disability Insurance	☐ Paper ☐ Digital	
☐ Health Insurance	☐ Paper ☐ Digital	
☐ Dental Insurance	☐ Paper ☐ Digital	
☐ Vision Insurance	☐ Paper ☐ Digital	
☐ Qualified pension plan	☐ Paper ☐ Digital	
☐ 401(k) or 403(b) plan	☐ Paper ☐ Digital	
☐ Profit-Sharing Plan	☐ Paper ☐ Digital	
☐ Defined Benefit Plan	☐ Paper ☐ Digital	
☐ Incentive/Bonus Stock Plan	☐ Paper ☐ Digital	
☐ Employee Stock Plan	☐ Paper ☐ Digital	
☐ Deferred Compensation Plan	☐ Paper ☐ Digital	
☐ Stock Option plan	☐ Paper ☐ Digital	
☐	☐ Paper ☐ Digital	
☐	☐ Paper ☐ Digital	
☐	☐ Paper ☐ Digital	
☐	☐ Paper ☐ Digital	
☐	☐ Paper ☐ Digital	
☐	☐ Paper ☐ Digital	
☐	☐ Paper ☐ Digital	
☐	☐ Paper ☐ Digital	
☐	☐ Paper ☐ Digital	
☐	☐ Paper ☐ Digital	
☐	☐ Paper ☐ Digital	
☐	☐ Paper ☐ Digital	
☐	☐ Paper ☐ Digital	

Assets and Investments

☐ Net worth statement	☐ Paper ☐ Digital	
☐ Bank Account Statements (Checking, Savings, Money Market, Certificates of Deposit)	☐ Paper ☐ Digital	
☐ Investment Account Statements	☐ Paper ☐ Digital	
☐ Insurance and Annuity Statements	☐ Paper ☐ Digital	
☐ Mutual Fund Statements	☐ Paper ☐ Digital	
☐ Stock or dividend reinvestment (DRIP) account statements (held directly at company or through Computershare or equivalent)	☐ Paper ☐ Digital	
☐ 401(k) and employer-sponsored retirement account(s)	☐ Paper ☐ Digital	
☐ Stock Option and Deferred Compensation	☐ Paper ☐ Digital	
☐ Retirement Account Statements	☐ Paper ☐ Digital	
☐ Health Savings Accounts (HSA)	☐ Paper ☐ Digital	
☐ UTMA/UGMA Accounts	☐ Paper ☐ Digital	
☐ Coverdale Educational Accounts	☐ Paper ☐ Digital	
☐ 529 Educational Accounts	☐ Paper ☐ Digital	
☐ Inventory of contents of safe deposit box	☐ Paper ☐ Digital	
☐ Inventory of contents of safe/lockbox	☐ Paper ☐ Digital	
☐ Savings bond inventory	☐ Paper ☐ Digital	
☐ Mortgages owed to me	☐ Paper ☐ Digital	
☐ Debts owed to me	☐ Paper ☐ Digital	
☐ List of assets being held for me	☐ Paper ☐ Digital	
☐ Social security statement of benefits	☐ Paper ☐ Digital	
☐ Assets owned outside the USA	☐ Paper ☐ Digital	
☐ Intellectual Property Rights ☐ Copyrights ☐ Patents ☐ Trademarks ☐ License Agreements ☐ Other related rights	 ☐ Paper ☐ Digital ☐ Paper ☐ Digital ☐ Paper ☐ Digital ☐ Paper ☐ Digital ☐ Paper ☐ Digital	
☐	☐ Paper ☐ Digital	
☐	☐ Paper ☐ Digital	
☐	☐ Paper ☐ Digital	
☐	☐ Paper ☐ Digital	
☐	☐ Paper ☐ Digital	
☐	☐ Paper ☐ Digital	

Liabilities and Debts

☐ Mortgage loans	☐ Paper ☐ Digital	
☐ Lines of credit	☐ Paper ☐ Digital	
☐ Home improvement loans	☐ Paper ☐ Digital	
☐ Other secured loans	☐ Paper ☐ Digital	
☐ Auto loan documents	☐ Paper ☐ Digital	
☐ Reverse Mortgages	☐ Paper ☐ Digital	
☐ Student loan documents	☐ Paper ☐ Digital	
☐ Credit cards and charge account statements	☐ Paper ☐ Digital	
☐ Pledged or pawned item list	☐ Paper ☐ Digital	
☐ Debts owed to others	☐ Paper ☐ Digital	
☐ Agreements to support others	☐ Paper ☐ Digital	
☐ Obligations for which you are co-signer or guarantor	☐ Paper ☐ Digital	
☐ Credit reports	☐ Paper ☐ Digital	
☐	☐ Paper ☐ Digital	
☐	☐ Paper ☐ Digital	

Tax Returns and Tax Information

☐ Personal Income Tax Returns	☐ Paper ☐ Digital	
☐ IRS Form 8606 Non-Deductible IRA Contributions	☐ Paper ☐ Digital	
☐ Gift Tax and Estate Tax Returns	☐ Paper ☐ Digital	
☐ Fiduciary income tax returns	☐ Paper ☐ Digital	
☐ Partnership Income Tax Returns	☐ Paper ☐ Digital	
☐ Tax-Deductible Bills and Receipts	☐ Paper ☐ Digital	
☐ Non-Deductible Bills and Receipts	☐ Paper ☐ Digital	
☐	☐ Paper ☐ Digital	
☐	☐ Paper ☐ Digital	

Medical Records

☐ Doctors and Medical Providers	☐ Paper ☐ Digital	
☐ Prescriptions	☐ Paper ☐ Digital	
☐	☐ Paper ☐ Digital	
☐	☐ Paper ☐ Digital	

School/Education Records

☐ Diplomas	☐ Paper ☐ Digital	
☐ Student Loan Information	☐ Paper ☐ Digital	
☐ Awards and Certificates	☐ Paper ☐ Digital	
☐ Transcripts	☐ Paper ☐ Digital	
☐	☐ Paper ☐ Digital	

Pet Records

☐ Veterinary history and insurance	☐ Paper ☐ Digital	
☐ License Tags	☐ Paper ☐ Digital	
☐ Microchip	☐ Paper ☐ Digital	
☐	☐ Paper ☐ Digital	
☐	☐ Paper ☐ Digital	
☐	☐ Paper ☐ Digital	

Hobbies

☐ Equipment Sales Receipts and Warranties	☐ Paper ☐ Digital	
☐	☐ Paper ☐ Digital	
☐	☐ Paper ☐ Digital	
☐	☐ Paper ☐ Digital	

Military Records

☐ DD214 Discharge Papers	☐ Paper ☐ Digital	
☐ Veteran's Benefits	☐ Paper ☐ Digital	
☐ Veteran's Widow Benefits	☐ Paper ☐ Digital	
☐ Awards, medals / achievements	☐ Paper ☐ Digital	
☐	☐ Paper ☐ Digital	
☐	☐ Paper ☐ Digital	
☐	☐ Paper ☐ Digital	

Miscellaneous Records

☐ Location of spare keys	☐ Paper ☐ Digital	
☐ Final love letters / videos to loved ones	☐ Paper ☐ Digital	
☐ Safe Deposit Box receipt & key	☐ Paper ☐ Digital	
☐ Trust in which you are named a beneficiary	☐ Paper ☐ Digital	
☐ Lawsuits involving you	☐ Paper ☐ Digital	
☐ Receipts, Warranties and instruction manuals	☐ Paper ☐ Digital	
☐ Storage Locker contract	☐ Paper ☐ Digital	
☐ Cold Storage Contract/Receipt	☐ Paper ☐ Digital	
☐ Boat Dry Dock Agreement	☐ Paper ☐ Digital	
☐ Guns and Firearms Registrations	☐ Paper ☐ Digital	
☐	☐ Paper ☐ Digital	
☐	☐ Paper ☐ Digital	
☐	☐ Paper ☐ Digital	
☐	☐ Paper ☐ Digital	
☐	☐ Paper ☐ Digital	
☐	☐ Paper ☐ Digital	
☐	☐ Paper ☐ Digital	

§5-A: Information about Me

Basic details and information about me.

Basic information about you

Your full legal name:	
Your home address:	
City, state, and zip code:	
Your home telephone number:	
Your cell phone number:	
Your work telephone number:	
Your personal email address:	
Your work email address:	
Your fax number:	
Your social security number:	
Your birthdate:	
Your place of birth (city and state):	
Your Medicare number:	
Were you adopted?	☐ Yes ☐ No
If yes, do you know the identities of your biological parents?	☐ Yes ☐ No
If yes, provide whatever details you know about them:	
What is your citizenship?	☐ U.S. Citizen ☐ Resident Alien ☐ Non-Resident Alien ☐ Citizen of (specify country):
Your **driver's license or State ID** #:	
State where issued:	
ID issue date:	
ID expiration date:	
Your **passport number**:	
Passport issue date:	
Passport expiration date:	
Where do you store your passport?	
If a naturalized citizen, what is your green card number?	
Your military service number, if any	
Other types of ID card & ID numbers (e.g. Medicare number, concealed weapons permit, professional IDs):	
List any other name(s) you have used (maiden name, prior married name, nickname, alias):	
Your marital status (check one):	☐ Single ☐ Married

	☐ Divorced ☐ Separated but not divorced ☐ Widowed
Have you ever been married?	☐ Yes ☐ No If yes, complete the section about your spouse and/or former spouse(s).
Do you have a child or children?	☐ Yes ☐ No If yes, complete the section about your children.
Do you have any grandchildren?	☐ Yes ☐ No If yes, complete the section about your grandchildren.
In what states have you resided?	
What are your **former addresses** (in reverse order in time)?	From: ______________ To: ______________
Address: From when and to when?	From: ______________ To: ______________
Address: From when and to when?	From: ______________ To: ______________
Address: From when and to when?	From: ______________ To: ______________
Address: From when and to when?	From: ______________ To: ______________
Address: From when and to when?	From: ______________ To: ______________
Have you resided in and/or owned property in any of these **Community Property** states?	☐ Arizona ☐ California ☐ Idaho ☐ Louisiana ☐ Nevada ☐ New Mexico ☐ Texas ☐ Washington ☐ Wisconsin
My religion, if any:	
I belong to the following fraternal or public service organizations:	
Other details about you (specify):	

Additional notes:

____

____

____

____

§5-B: Information about my Spouse (if any)

Basic details about my spouse (and previous spouse(s), if any.

Basic Information about my spouse(s)

Are you currently married?	☐ Yes ☐ No If yes, complete this section about your **current** spouse.
Date of marriage:	
Name of spouse:	
Spouse's telephone number:	
Spouse's email address:	
Spouse's birthdate:	
Spouse's social security number:	
Military Service Number, if any:	
What is my spouse's citizenship?	☐ U.S. Citizen ☐ Resident Alien ☐ Non-Resident Alien ☐ Citizen of (specify country):
Do you have a prenuptial agreement?	☐ Yes ☐ No If yes, where is a copy located?
Is your spouse employed?	☐ Yes ☐ No
If yes, what is the name and phone number of the employer?	
Are you separated, but not divorced?	☐ Yes ☐ No
If yes, what is your spouse's address and phone number?	
FUN MEMORIES AND STORIES	**Share some fun memories and stories for future generations to enjoy!**
How did you meet your spouse?	
When did you realize he/she was "The ONE?"	
Where and how did you propose or how did your spouse propose (on one knee, etc.)?	
Courtship/dating memories:	
Where did you get married?	
Where did you honeymoon?	
Favorite anniversary stories:	

Your previous spouse, if any

Have you previously been married?	☐ Yes ☐ No
More than once?	☐ Yes ☐ No If yes, how many times have you been married? ________
Name of previous spouse:	
Date of marriage:	
City and state of marriage:	
How did this marriage end?	☐ Divorce; ☐ Death; ☐ Annulment Date: ____________________
Names & birthdates of children born of this marriage:	
List any legal obligations to former spouse (e.g. child support, alimony, insurance, co-owned property):	
Location of property settlement and divorce decree (and court orders):	
FUN MEMORIES AND STORIES	**Be sure to share some stories, especially if there are children born of this marriage.**
How did you meet this spouse?	
When did you realize he/she was "The ONE?"	
How did you propose /How did your spouse propose (on one knee, etc.)?	
Courtship/dating memories:	
Where did you get married?	
Where did you honeymoon?	
Favorite anniversary stories:	

Is there another previous spouse?

Is there another previous spouse?	☐ Yes ☐ No
If yes, name of previous spouse:	
Date of marriage:	
City and state of marriage:	
How did this marriage end?	☐ Divorce; ☐ Death; ☐ Annulment Date: ____________________
Names and birthdates of children born of this marriage:	
List any legal obligations to former spouse (e.g. child support, alimony, insurance, co-owned property, etc.):	
Location of property settlement and divorce decree (and court orders):	
FUN MEMORIES AND STORIES	Be sure to share some stories, if there are children born of this marriage.

§5-C: Information about my Children

If someone is ever placed in the position of becoming caregiver to your children, they will need as many of the following details as you can provide to them.

For estate-planning purposes, also provide the basic information about any children that may have pre-deceased you (name, birthdate, and date of death), and if so, specify whether they left their own children surviving them, and provide information about them in the section for grandchildren.

I have provided enough 6-page questionnaires for three children. If you have more than three children, make as many extra copies as you need.

There should be no shortage of wonderful memories and stories to share about your children, so start writing them down for future generations to enjoy.

If you have never had any children, you may skip this section.	
Do you currently have any children?	☐ Yes ☐ No If yes, provide details on the following pages.
Do you have any children who predeceased you?	☐ Yes ☐ No If yes, provide details on the following pages.

FUN MEMORIES AND STORIES	Share some memories and stories for future generations to enjoy!
Were there issues or problems in getting pregnant?	
Share stories about the pregnancy from both the mother's point of view and father's point of view:	
Are there funny stories about the delivery of the baby?	

§5-C (1): Information about Your First Child

Name of First Child: ____

Full legal name of child:	
Nickname, maiden, or other name(s)?	
Address:	
City, state, and zip code:	
Mobile telephone number:	
Home telephone number, if any:	
Work telephone number:	
Email address:	
Child's birthdate:	
Place of birth (city and state):	
Social Security Number:	
Is this child alive?	☐ Yes ☐ No
Did this child have any children (your grandchildren)?	☐ Yes ☐ No If yes, complete information about this child's children on next page.
Was this child adopted?	☐ Yes ☐ No
Citizenship of this child:	☐ USA ☐ Other (specify):
Passport number:	
Issue date:	
Expiration date:	
Is this child married?	☐ Yes ☐ No
If yes, name of child's spouse:	
Telephone number of spouse:	
Date of marriage, if known:	
What is the name of this child's other parent (if not your current spouse)?	
If an adult, has this child named you as his or her agent in: Durable Power of Attorney? Health Care Surrogate? Living Will? Guardian for child or grandchildren?	 ☐ Yes ☐ No ☐ Yes ☐ No ☐ Yes ☐ No ☐ Yes ☐ No
Location of document(s):	

This child's children, if any (your grandchildren)

Does this child have any children (your grandchildren)?	☐ Yes ☐ No If yes, provide details below for each grandchild:

Legal name of **first child**, if any:	
Birthdate:	
Social Security Number:	
Name of this child's other parent:	
Name of this child's spouse, if any:	
FUN MEMORIES AND STORIES	**Share some memories and stories about this grandchild!**
What makes you smile when you think about this grandchild?	

Legal name of **second child**, if any:	
Birthdate:	
Social Security Number:	
Name of this child's other parent:	
Name of this child's spouse, if any:	
FUN MEMORIES AND STORIES	**Share some memories and stories about this grandchild!**
What makes you smile when you think about this grandchild?	

Legal name of **third child**, if any:	
Birthdate:	
Social Security Number:	
Name of this child's other parent:	
Name of this child's spouse, if any:	
FUN MEMORIES AND STORIES	**Share some memories and stories about this grandchild!**
What makes you smile when you think about this grandchild?	

Legal name of **fourth child**, if any:	
Birthdate:	
Social Security Number:	
Name of this child's other parent:	
Name of this child's spouse, if any:	
FUN MEMORIES AND STORIES	**Share some memories and stories about this grandchild!**
What makes you smile when you think about this grandchild?	

If this child is a minor (under 18 years of age) or dependent upon you, provide the following information:

Babysitter(s)

Name and Phone of Babysitter #1:	
Name and Phone of Babysitter #2:	

If this child attends a day care center

Name of day care center, if any:	
Address:	
City, state, and zip code:	
Phone number:	
Website address:	
Name of owner of day care center:	
On what days does the child attend:	☐ Mon. ☐ Tue. ☐ Wed. ☐ Thu. ☐ Fri. ☐ Sat. ☐ Sun.
Hours of attendance:	________ a.m./p.m. through ________ a.m./p.m.
What is the cost?	$

If this child has a nanny

Name of nanny service, if any:	
Address:	
City, state, and zip code:	
Phone number:	
Website address:	
Name of owner of the nanny service:	
On what days does the nanny work?	☐ Mon. ☐ Tue. ☐ Wed. ☐ Thu. ☐ Fri. ☐ Sat. ☐ Sun.
Hours of attendance:	________ a.m./p.m. through ________ a.m./p.m.
What is the cost?	$

What school does this child attend?

Name of child's school	
What type of school is this?	☐ Public ☐ Private ☐ Parochial ☐ Other:
Address:	
City, state, and zip code:	
Phone number:	
Website address:	www.
Username:	
Password:	
Name of teacher:	
Teacher's phone number:	
Teacher's email address:	
What grade is this child in?	
Combination to locker:	
What is annual tuition cost, if any?	$

If child has special needs or behavioral issues

Does this child have any special needs or behavioral issues?	☐ Yes ☐ No
If yes, describe or provide details:	
If yes, is there a special needs Ttrust?	☐ Yes ☐ No
Location of document:	

Vaccination history of child:

Vaccination history	Date of Most Recent Vaccination:
Hib (Haemophilus influenza type b)	☐ Yes ☐ No If yes, date of most recent vaccination:
Pneumonia	☐ Yes ☐ No If yes, date of most recent vaccination:
Tetanus, diphtheria, pertussis (Td/Tdap)	☐ Yes ☐ No If yes, date of most recent vaccination:
PPSV (Pneumococcal Polysaccharide Vaccine)	☐ Yes ☐ No If yes, date of most recent vaccination:
Hepatitis A Vaccine	☐ Yes ☐ No If yes, date of most recent vaccination:
Hepatitis B Vaccine	☐ Yes ☐ No If yes, date of most recent vaccination:
HPV (Human Papillomavirus) Vaccine	☐ Yes ☐ No If yes, date of most recent vaccination:
MMR (Measles, Mumps, Rubella) Vaccine	☐ Yes ☐ No If yes, date of most recent vaccination:
Varicella (Chickenpox) Vaccine	☐ Yes ☐ No If yes, date of most recent vaccination:
Meningococcal Vaccine	☐ Yes ☐ No If yes, date of most recent vaccination:
Shingles (Zoster) Vaccine	☐ Yes ☐ No If yes, date of most recent vaccination:
Flu (Influenza)	☐ Yes ☐ No If yes, date of most recent vaccination:
Polio	☐ Yes ☐ No If yes, date of most recent vaccination:
Smallpox	☐ Yes ☐ No If yes, date of most recent vaccination:
Typhoid	☐ Yes ☐ No If yes, date of most recent vaccination:
Other (specify):	
Are there any other medical, behavioral, and/or emotional issues or history a caregiver should know about this child?	☐ Yes ☐ No If yes, provide details:
Is this child taking any medications? If yes, what drugs and what dosage?	☐ Yes ☐ No

Allergies

This child has the following **allergies**:	☐ **THIS CHILD HAS NO ALLERGIES (See medical Information section)**
Local anesthetics	☐ Yes ☐ No
Aspirin	☐ Yes ☐ No
Penicillin or other antibiotics	☐ Yes ☐ No
Barbiturates, sedatives, sleeping pills	☐ Yes ☐ No
Sulfa drugs	☐ Yes ☐ No
Codeine or other narcotics	☐ Yes ☐ No
Metals	☐ Yes ☐ No
Latex (rubber)	☐ Yes ☐ No
Adhesive tape	☐ Yes ☐ No
Iodine	☐ Yes ☐ No
Hay fever/other seasonal	☐ Yes ☐ No
Animals	☐ Yes ☐ No
Food	☐ Yes ☐ No
Other (specify)	☐ Yes ☐ No

Miscellaneous Matters

Have you made any provisions for the education of this child (529 or state tuition plan, Uniform Transfer to Minor's Account (UTMA), scholarship, or other provisions in a Trust, etc.)?	☐ Yes ☐ No If yes, insert a brief summary of the details here, but complete the more-detailed applicable section later in this questionnaire.
Is this child named as a beneficiary for a life insurance policy or Trust?	☐ Yes ☐ No
If yes, provide details here. If this child is a minor, **please** talk to your estate-planning attorney about potential problems this may cause.	
If something were to happen to you which would prevent you from being able to care for your minor children, indicate your **preference** as to whom you would like to be the Guardian responsible for taking care of your children and their assets until they are adults. **(Note: This is merely a statement of your preference, and is <u>not</u> binding on a court of law).**	**<u>IMPORTANT</u>**: This questionnaire is **<u>not</u>** a legal document and is not binding on a court of law. A Guardianship designation should be made in your Last Will and Testament, or another legal document. **Discuss this with your attorney in detail!**

THIS CHILD'S HEALTH CARE PROVIDERS

Primary Physician or Pediatrician

Name of **Primary Physician** or **Pediatrician:**	
Name of medical practice:	
Address:	
City, state, and zip code:	
Work telephone number:	
Cell phone number:	
Email address:	
Website:	www.
Username:	
Password:	
Any additional information:	

Dentist

Name of **Dentist**:	
Name of dental practice:	
Address:	
City, state, and zip code:	
Work telephone number:	
Email address:	
Website:	www.
Any additional information:	

Orthodontist

Name of **Orthodontist:**	
Name of medical practice:	
Address:	
City, state, and zip code:	
Work telephone number:	
Email address:	
Website:	www.
Any additional information:	

Eye Doctor

Name of **Eye Doctor**:	
Name of medical practice:	
Address:	
City, state, and zip code:	
Work telephone number:	
Email address:	
Website:	www.
Any additional information:	

Psychologist or Psychiatrist

Name of **Psychologist** or **Psychiatrist**	
Name of medical practice:	
Address:	
City, state, and zip code:	
Work phone number:	
Mobile phone number	
Email address:	
Website:	www.
Any additional information:	

Counselor

Name of **Counselor**:	
Name of medical practice:	
Address:	
City, state, and zip code:	
Work phone number:	
Mobile phone number	
Email address:	
Website:	www.
Any additional information:	

Drugstore

Name of **Drugstore:**	
Address:	
City, state, and zip code:	
Work phone number:	
Fax number:	
Email address:	
Website:	www.
Username:	
Password:	
Medications purchased here:	
Any additional information:	

Home Health Care Service

Name of **home health care service**:	
Address:	
City, state, and zip code:	
Work phone number:	
Fax number:	
Email address:	
Website:	www.
Username:	
Password:	
Any additional information:	

Other Service Provider

Name of service provider:	
Type of service provided:	
Name of business:	
Address:	
City, state, and zip code:	
Work phone number:	
Fax number:	
Email address:	
Website:	www.
Username:	
Password:	
Any additional information:	

FUN MEMORIES AND STORIES	Share some memories and stories about this child for future generations to enjoy!

§5-C (2): Information about Your Second Child

Name of Second Child: ______________________________

Full legal name of child:	
Nickname, maiden, or other name(s)?	
Address:	
City, state, and zip code:	
Mobile telephone number:	
Home telephone number, if any:	
Work telephone number:	
Email address:	
Child's birthdate:	
Place of birth (city and state):	
Social Security Number:	
Is this child alive?	☐ Yes ☐ No
Did this child have any children (your grandchildren)?	☐ Yes ☐ No If yes, complete information about this child's children on next page.
Was this child adopted?	☐ Yes ☐ No
Citizenship of this child:	☐ USA ☐ Other (specify):
Passport number:	
Issue date:	
Expiration date:	
Is this child married?	☐ Yes ☐ No
If yes, name of child's spouse:	
Telephone number of spouse:	
Date of marriage, if known:	
What is the name of this child's other parent (if not your current spouse)?	
If an adult, has this child named you as his or her agent in: Durable Power of Attorney? Health Care Surrogate? Living Will? Guardian for child or grandchildren?	☐ Yes ☐ No ☐ Yes ☐ No ☐ Yes ☐ No ☐ Yes ☐ No
Location of document(s):	

This child's children, if any (your grandchildren)

Does this child have any children (your grandchildren)?	☐ Yes ☐ No If yes, provide details below for each grandchild:

Legal name of **first child**, if any:	
Birthdate:	
Social Security Number:	
Name of this child's other parent:	
Name of this child's spouse, if any:	
FUN MEMORIES AND STORIES	**Share some memories and stories about this grandchild!**
What makes you smile when you think about this grandchild?	

Legal name of **second child**, if any:	
Birthdate:	
Social Security Number:	
Name of this child's other parent:	
Name of this child's spouse, if any:	
FUN MEMORIES AND STORIES	**Share some memories and stories about this grandchild!**
What makes you smile when you think about this grandchild?	

Legal name of **third child**, if any:	
Birthdate:	
Social Security Number:	
Name of this child's other parent:	
Name of this child's spouse, if any:	
FUN MEMORIES AND STORIES	**Share some memories and stories about this grandchild!**
What makes you smile when you think about this grandchild?	

Legal name of **fourth child**, if any:	
Birthdate:	
Social Security Number:	
Name of this child's other parent:	
Name of this child's spouse, if any:	
FUN MEMORIES AND STORIES	**Share some memories and stories about this grandchild!**
What makes you smile when you think about this grandchild?	

If this child is a minor (under 18 years of age) or dependent upon you, provide the following information:

Babysitter(s)

Name and Phone of Babysitter #1:	
Name and Phone of Babysitter #2:	

If this child attends a day care center

Name of day care center, if any:	
Address:	
City, state, and zip code:	
Phone number:	
Website address:	
Name of owner of day care center:	
On what days does the child attend:	☐ Mon. ☐ Tue. ☐ Wed. ☐ Thu. ☐ Fri. ☐ Sat. ☐ Sun.
Hours of attendance:	__________ a.m./p.m. through _____________ a.m./p.m.
What is the cost?	$

If this child has a nanny

Name of nanny service, if any:	
Address:	
City, state, and zip code:	
Phone number	
Website address:	
Name of owner of nanny service:	
On what days does the nanny work?	☐ Mon. ☐ Tue. ☐ Wed. ☐ Thu. ☐ Fri. ☐ Sat. ☐ Sun.
Hours of attendance:	__________ a.m./p.m. through _____________ a.m./p.m.
What is the cost?	$

What school does this child attend?

Name of child's school	
What type of school is this?	☐ Public ☐ Private ☐ Parochial ☐ Other:
Address:	
City, state, and zip code:	
Phone number:	
Website address:	www.
Username:	
Password:	
Name of teacher:	
Teacher's phone number:	
Teacher's email address:	
What grade is this child in?	
Combination to locker:	
What is annual tuition cost, if any?	$

If child has special needs or behavioral issues

Does this child have any special needs or behavioral issues?	☐ Yes ☐ No
If yes, describe or provide details:	
If yes, is there a special needs Trust?	☐ Yes ☐ No
Location of document:	

Vaccination history of child

Vaccination history	Date of Most Recent Vaccination:
Hib (Haemophilus influenza type b)	☐ Yes ☐ No If yes, date of most recent vaccination:
Pneumonia	☐ Yes ☐ No If yes, date of most recent vaccination:
Tetanus, diphtheria, pertussis (Td/Tdap)	☐ Yes ☐ No If yes, date of most recent vaccination:
PPSV (Pneumococcal Polysaccharide Vaccine)	☐ Yes ☐ No If yes, date of most recent vaccination:
Hepatitis A Vaccine	☐ Yes ☐ No If yes, date of most recent vaccination:
Hepatitis B Vaccine	☐ Yes ☐ No If yes, date of most recent vaccination:
HPV (Human Papillomavirus) Vaccine	☐ Yes ☐ No If yes, date of most recent vaccination:
MMR (Measles, Mumps, Rubella) Vaccine	☐ Yes ☐ No If yes, date of most recent vaccination:
Varicella (Chickenpox) Vaccine	☐ Yes ☐ No If yes, date of most recent vaccination:
Meningococcal Vaccine	☐ Yes ☐ No If yes, date of most recent vaccination:
Shingles (Zoster) Vaccine	☐ Yes ☐ No If yes, date of most recent vaccination:
Flu (Influenza)	☐ Yes ☐ No If yes, date of most recent vaccination:
Polio	☐ Yes ☐ No If yes, date of most recent vaccination:
Smallpox	☐ Yes ☐ No If yes, date of most recent vaccination:
Typhoid	☐ Yes ☐ No If yes, date of most recent vaccination:
Other (specify):	
Are there any other medical, behavioral, and/or emotional issues or history a caregiver should know about this child?	☐ Yes ☐ No If yes, provide details:
Is this child taking any medications? If yes, what drugs & what dosage?	☐ Yes ☐ No

Allergies

This child has the following **allergies**:	☐ **THIS CHILD HAS NO ALLERGIES (See medical Information section)**
Local anesthetics	☐ Yes ☐ No
Aspirin	☐ Yes ☐ No
Penicillin or other antibiotics	☐ Yes ☐ No
Barbiturates, sedatives, sleeping pills	☐ Yes ☐ No
Sulfa drugs	☐ Yes ☐ No
Codeine or other narcotics	☐ Yes ☐ No
Metals	☐ Yes ☐ No
Latex (rubber)	☐ Yes ☐ No
Adhesive tape	☐ Yes ☐ No
Iodine	☐ Yes ☐ No
Hay fever/other seasonal	☐ Yes ☐ No
Animals	☐ Yes ☐ No
Food	☐ Yes ☐ No
Other (specify)	☐ Yes ☐ No

Miscellaneous Matters

Have you made any provisions for the education of this child (529 or state tuition plan, Uniform Transfer to Minor's Account (UTMA), scholarship, or other provisions in a Trust, etc.)?	☐ Yes ☐ No If yes, insert a brief summary of the details here, but complete the more-detailed applicable section later in this questionnaire.
Is this child named as a beneficiary for a life insurance policy or Trust?	☐ Yes ☐ No
If yes, provide details here. If this child is a minor, **please** talk to your estate-planning attorney about potential problems this may cause.	
If something were to happen to you which would prevent you from being able to care for your minor children, indicate your **preference** as to whom you would like to be the Guardian responsible for taking care of your children and their assets until they are adults. **(Note: This is merely a statement of your preference, and is not binding on a court of law).**	**IMPORTANT**: This questionnaire is **not** a legal document and is not binding on a court of law. A Guardianship designation should be made in your Last Will and Testament, or another legal document. **Discuss this with your attorney in detail!**

THIS CHILD'S HEALTH CARE PROVIDERS

Primary Physician or Pediatrician

Name of **Primary Physician** or **Pediatrician:**	
Name of medical practice:	
Address:	
City, state, and zip code:	
Work telephone number:	
Mobile phone number:	
Email address:	
Website:	www.
Username:	
Password:	
Any additional information:	

Dentist

Name of **Dentist**:	
Name of dental practice:	
Address:	
City, state, and zip code:	
Work telephone number:	
Email address:	
Website:	www.
Any additional information:	

Orthodontist

Name of **Orthodontist:**	
Name of medical practice:	
Address:	
City, state, and zip code:	
Work telephone number:	
Email address:	
Website:	www.
Any additional information:	

Eye Doctor

Name of **Eye Doctor**:	
Name of medical practice:	
Address:	
City, state, and zip code:	
Work telephone number:	
Email address:	
Website:	www.
Any additional information:	

Psychologist or Psychiatrist

Name of **Psychologist** or **Psychiatrist**	
Name of medical practice:	
Address:	
City, state, and zip code:	
Work phone number:	
Mobile phone number	
Email address:	
Website:	www.
Any additional information:	

Counselor

Name of **Counselor**:	
Name of medical practice:	
Address:	
City, state, and zip code:	
Work phone number:	
Mobile phone number	
Email address:	
Website:	www.
Any additional information:	

Drugstore

Name of **Drugstore:**	
Address:	
City, state, and zip code:	
Work phone number:	
Fax number:	
Email address:	
Website:	www.
Username:	
Password:	
Medications purchased here:	
Any additional information:	

Home Health Care Service

Name of **home health care service**:	
Address:	
City, state, and zip code:	
Work phone number:	
Fax number:	
Email address:	
Website:	www.
Username:	
Password:	
Any additional information:	

Other Service Provider

Name of service provider:	
Type of service provided:	
Name of business:	
Address:	
City, state, and zip code:	
Work phone number:	
Fax number:	
Email address:	
Website:	www.
Username:	
Password:	
Any additional information:	

FUN MEMORIES AND STORIES	Share some memories and stories about this child for future generations to enjoy!

§5-C (3): Information about Your Third Child

Name of Third Child: ______________________________

Full legal name of child:	
Nickname, maiden, or other name(s)?	
Address:	
City, state, and zip code:	
Mobile telephone number:	
Home telephone number, if any:	
Work telephone number:	
Email address:	
Child's birthdate:	
Place of birth (city and state):	
Social Security Number:	
Is this child alive?	☐ Yes ☐ No
Did this child have any children (your grandchildren)?	☐ Yes ☐ No If yes, complete information about this child's children on next page.
Was this child adopted?	☐ Yes ☐ No
Citizenship of this child:	☐ USA ☐ Other (specify):
Passport number:	
Issue date:	
Expiration date:	
Is this child married?	☐ Yes ☐ No
If yes, name of child's spouse:	
Telephone number of spouse:	
Date of marriage, if known:	
What is the name of this child's other parent (if not your current spouse)?	
If an adult, has this child named you as his or her agent in: Durable Power of Attorney? Health Care Surrogate? Living Will? Guardian for child or grandchildren?	☐ Yes ☐ No ☐ Yes ☐ No ☐ Yes ☐ No ☐ Yes ☐ No
Location of document(s):	

This child's children, if any (your grandchildren)

Does this child have any children (your grandchildren)?	☐ Yes ☐ No If yes, provide details below for each grandchild:

Legal name of **first child**, if any:	
Birthdate:	
Social Security Number:	
Name of this child's other parent:	
Name of this child's spouse, if any:	
FUN MEMORIES AND STORIES	**Share some memories and stories about this grandchild!**
What makes you smile when you think about this grandchild?	

Legal name of **second child**, if any:	
Birthdate:	
Social Security Number:	
Name of this child's other parent:	
Name of this child's spouse, if any:	
FUN MEMORIES AND STORIES	**Share some memories and stories about this grandchild!**
What makes you smile when you think about this grandchild?	

Legal name of **third child**, if any:	
Birthdate:	
Social Security Number:	
Name of this child's other parent:	
Name of this child's spouse, if any:	
FUN MEMORIES AND STORIES	**Share some memories and stories about this grandchild!**
What makes you smile when you think about this grandchild?	

Legal name of **fourth child**, if any:	
Birthdate:	
Social Security Number:	
Name of this child's other parent:	
Name of this child's spouse, if any:	
FUN MEMORIES AND STORIES	**Share some memories and stories about this grandchild!**
What makes you smile when you think about this grandchild?	

This child's children, if any (your grandchildren)

Does this child have any children (your grandchildren)?	☐ Yes ☐ No If yes, provide details below for each grandchild:

Legal name of **first child**, if any:	
Birthdate:	
Social Security Number:	
Name of this child's other parent:	
Name of this child's spouse, if any:	
FUN MEMORIES AND STORIES	**Share some memories and stories about this grandchild!**
What makes you smile when you think about this grandchild?	

Legal name of **second child**, if any:	
Birthdate:	
Social Security Number:	
Name of this child's other parent:	
Name of this child's spouse, if any:	
FUN MEMORIES AND STORIES	**Share some memories and stories about this grandchild!**
What makes you smile when you think about this grandchild?	

Legal name of **third child**, if any:	
Birthdate:	
Social Security Number:	
Name of this child's other parent:	
Name of this child's spouse, if any:	
FUN MEMORIES AND STORIES	**Share some memories and stories about this grandchild!**
What makes you smile when you think about this grandchild?	

Legal name of **fourth child**, if any:	
Birthdate:	
Social Security Number:	
Name of this child's other parent:	
Name of this child's spouse, if any:	
FUN MEMORIES AND STORIES	**Share some memories and stories about this grandchild!**
What makes you smile when you think about this grandchild?	

If this child is a minor (under 18 years of age) or dependent upon you, provide the following information:

Babysitter(s)

Name and Phone of Babysitter #1:	
Name and Phone of Babysitter #2:	

If this child attends a day care center

Name of day care center, if any:	
Address:	
City, state, and zip code:	
Phone number	
Website address:	
Name of owner of day care center:	
On what days does the child attend:	☐ Mon. ☐ Tue. ☐ Wed. ☐ Thu. ☐ Fri. ☐ Sat. ☐ Sun.
Hours of attendance:	________ a.m./p.m. through __________ a.m./p.m.
What is the cost?	$

If this child has a nanny

Name of nanny service, if any:	
Address:	
City, state, and zip code:	
Phone number	
Website address:	
Name of owner of the nanny service:	
On what days does the nanny work?	☐ Mon. ☐ Tue. ☐ Wed. ☐ Thu. ☐ Fri. ☐ Sat. ☐ Sun.
Hours of attendance:	________ a.m./p.m. through __________ a.m./p.m.
What is the cost?	$

What school does this child attend?

Name of child's school	
What type of school is this?	☐ Public ☐ Private ☐ Parochial ☐ Other:
Address:	
City, state, and zip code:	
Phone number:	
Website address:	www.
Username:	
Password:	
Name of teacher:	
Teacher's phone number:	
Teacher's email address:	
What grade is this child in?	
Combination to locker:	
What is annual tuition cost, if any?	$

If child has special needs or behavioral issues

Does this child have any special needs or behavioral issues?	☐ Yes ☐ No
If yes, describe or provide details:	
If yes, is there a special needs Trust?	☐ Yes ☐ No
Location of document:	

Vaccination history of child

Vaccination history	Date of Most Recent Vaccination:
Hib (Haemophilus influenza type b)	☐ Yes ☐ No If yes, date of most recent vaccination:
Pneumonia	☐ Yes ☐ No If yes, date of most recent vaccination:
Tetanus, diphtheria, pertussis (Td/Tdap)	☐ Yes ☐ No If yes, date of most recent vaccination:
PPSV (Pneumococcal Polysaccharide Vaccine)	☐ Yes ☐ No If yes, date of most recent vaccination:
Hepatitis A Vaccine	☐ Yes ☐ No If yes, date of most recent vaccination:
Hepatitis B Vaccine	☐ Yes ☐ No If yes, date of most recent vaccination:
HPV (Human Papillomavirus) Vaccine	☐ Yes ☐ No If yes, date of most recent vaccination:
MMR (Measles, Mumps, Rubella) Vaccine	☐ Yes ☐ No If yes, date of most recent vaccination:
Varicella (Chickenpox) Vaccine	☐ Yes ☐ No If yes, date of most recent vaccination:
Meningococcal Vaccine	☐ Yes ☐ No If yes, date of most recent vaccination:
Shingles (Zoster) Vaccine	☐ Yes ☐ No If yes, date of most recent vaccination:
Flu (Influenza)	☐ Yes ☐ No If yes, date of most recent vaccination:
Polio	☐ Yes ☐ No If yes, date of most recent vaccination:
Smallpox	☐ Yes ☐ No If yes, date of most recent vaccination:
Typhoid	☐ Yes ☐ No If yes, date of most recent vaccination:
Other (specify):	
Are there any other medical, behavioral, and/or emotional issues or history a caregiver should know about this child?	☐ Yes ☐ No If yes, provide details:
Is this child taking any medications? If yes, what drugs and what dosage?	☐ Yes ☐ No

Allergies

This child has the following **allergies**:	☐ **THIS CHILD HAS NO ALLERGIES (See medical Information section)**
Local anesthetics	☐ Yes ☐ No
Aspirin	☐ Yes ☐ No
Penicillin or other antibiotics	☐ Yes ☐ No
Barbiturates, sedatives, sleeping pills	☐ Yes ☐ No
Sulfa drugs	☐ Yes ☐ No
Codeine or other narcotics	☐ Yes ☐ No
Metals	☐ Yes ☐ No
Latex (rubber)	☐ Yes ☐ No
Adhesive tape	☐ Yes ☐ No
Iodine	☐ Yes ☐ No
Hay fever/other seasonal	☐ Yes ☐ No
Animals	☐ Yes ☐ No
Food	☐ Yes ☐ No
Other (specify)	☐ Yes ☐ No

Miscellaneous Matters

Have you made any provisions for the education of this child (529 or state tuition plan, Uniform Transfer to Minor's Account (UTMA), scholarship, or other provisions in a Trust, etc.)?	☐ Yes ☐ No If yes, insert a brief summary of the details here, but complete the more-detailed applicable section later in this questionnaire.
Is this child named as a beneficiary for a life insurance policy or Trust?	☐ Yes ☐ No
If yes, provide details here. If this child is a minor, **please** talk to your estate-planning attorney about potential problems this may cause.	
If something were to happen to you which would prevent you from being able to care for your minor children, indicate your **preference** as to whom you would like to be the Guardian responsible for taking care of your children and their assets until they are adults. **(Note: This is merely a statement of your preference, and is <u>not</u> binding on a court of law).**	**<u>IMPORTANT</u>**: This questionnaire is **<u>not</u>** a legal document and is not binding on a court of law. A Guardianship designation should be made in your Last Will and Testament, or another legal document. **Discuss this with your attorney in detail!**

THIS CHILD'S HEALTH CARE PROVIDERS

Primary Physician or Pediatrician

Name of **Primary Physician** or **Pediatrician:**	
Name of medical practice:	
Address:	
City, state, and zip code:	
Work telephone number:	
Cell phone number:	
Email address:	
Website:	www.
Username:	
Password:	
Any additional information:	

Dentist

Name of **Dentist**:	
Name of dental practice:	
Address:	
City, state, and zip code:	
Work telephone number:	
Cell phone number:	
Email address:	
Website:	www.
Any additional information:	

Orthodontist

Name of **Orthodontist:**	
Name of medical practice:	
Address:	
City, state, and zip code:	
Work telephone number:	
Cell phone number:	
Email address:	
Website:	www.
Any additional information:	

Eye Doctor

Name of **Eye Doctor**:	
Name of medical practice:	
Address:	
City, state, and zip code:	
Work telephone number:	
Cell phone number:	
Email address:	
Website:	www.
Any additional information:	

Psychologist or Psychiatrist:

Name of **Psychologist** or **Psychiatrist**	
Name of medical practice:	
Address:	
City, state, and zip code:	
Work phone number:	
Cell phone number:	
Email address:	
Website:	www.
Any additional information:	

Counselor:

Name of **Counselor**:	
Name of medical practice:	
Address:	
City, state, and zip code:	
Work phone number:	
Cell phone number	
Email address:	
Website:	www.
Any additional information:	

Drugstore

Name of **Drugstore:**	
Address:	
City, state, and zip code:	
Work phone number:	
Fax number:	
Email address:	
Website:	www.
Username:	
Password:	
Medications purchased here:	
Any additional information:	

Home Health Care Service

Name of **home health care service**:	
Address:	
City, state, and zip code:	
Work phone number:	
Fax number:	
Email address:	
Website:	www.
Username:	
Password:	
Any additional information:	

Other Service Provider

Name of service provider:	
Type of service provided:	
Name of business:	
Address:	
City, state, and zip code:	
Work phone number:	
Fax number:	
Email address:	
Website:	www.
Username:	
Password:	
Any additional information:	

FUN MEMORIES AND STORIES	Share some memories and stories about this child for future generations to enjoy!

§5-D: Benefits Available to Your Spouse and/or Your Children

If something happens to you, provide information regarding the benefits your spouse and/or your children are entitled to receive, and the source of those benefits.

If you die, what benefits will your spouse be entitled to receive?

From the federal government (e.g. social security):	
From military service (e.g. VA pension or benefits):	
From the State Government:	
From your employer:	
From insurance (Life, accidental death, etc.):	
From any other source (specify):	

If you die, what benefits will your children be entitled to receive?

From the federal government (e.g. social security):	
From military service (e.g. VA pension or benefits):	
From the State Government:	
From your employer:	
From insurance (Life, accidental death, etc.):	
From any other source (specify):	

If you are incapacitated or disabled, what benefits will your spouse be entitled to receive?

From the federal government (e.g. social security):	
From military service (e.g. VA pension or benefits):	
From the State Government:	
From your employer:	
From insurance (e.g. disability, long-term care, Aflac):	
From any other source (specify):	

If you are incapacitated or disabled, what benefits will your child(ren) be entitled to receive?

From the federal government (e.g. social security):	
From military service (e.g. VA pension or benefits):	
From the State Government:	
From your employer:	
From insurance (e.g. disability, long-term care, Aflac):	
From any other source (specify):	
From the federal government (e.g. social security):	

Education and other benefits available to your children

What, if any, educational benefits are available to your children due to your death or disability?	
What other benefits are available to your children?	

§5-E: Information about your Parents, Grandparents, Brothers, and Sisters

Details about your family that future generations may want to know:

My father

Name of my **father**:	
Birthdate:	
Place of birth (city and state):	
Is he still alive?	☐ Yes ☐ No
If deceased, date of death:	
Special memories and stories about your father:	

My father's father (my paternal grandfather)

Name of my **paternal grandfather**:	
Birthdate:	
Place of birth (city and state):	
Is he still alive?	☐ Yes ☐ No
If deceased, date of death:	
Special memories and stories about this grandfather:	

My father's mother (my paternal grandmother)

Name of my **paternal grandmother:**	
Birthdate:	
Place of birth (city and state):	
Is she still alive?	☐ Yes ☐ No
If deceased, date of death:	
Special memories and stories about this grandmother:	

My father's brothers and sisters (my paternal aunts and uncles)

Name and birthdate:	
Special memories and stories about this aunt or uncle:	
Name and birthdate:	
Special memories and stories about this aunt or uncle:	
Name and birthdate:	
Special memories and stories about this aunt or uncle:	
Name and birthdate:	
Special memories and stories about this aunt or uncle:	

Name of my mother

Name of my **mother**	
Birthdate:	
Place of birth (city and state):	
Is she still alive?	☐ Yes ☐ No
If deceased, date of death:	
Special memories and stories about my mother:	

Name of my mother's father (my maternal grandfather)

Name of my **maternal grandfather**	
Birthdate:	
Place of birth (city and state):	
Is he still alive?	☐ Yes ☐ No
If deceased, date of death:	
Special memories and stories about this grandfather:	

Name of my mother's mother (my maternal grandmother)

Name of my **maternal grandmother**	
Birthdate:	
Place of birth (city and state):	
Is she still alive?	☐ Yes ☐ No
If deceased, date of death:	
Special memories and stories about this grandmother:	

My mother's brothers and sisters (my maternal aunts and uncles)

Name and birthdate:	
Special memories and stories about this aunt or uncle:	
Name and birthdate:	
Special memories and stories about this aunt or uncle:	
Name and birthdate:	
Special memories and stories about this aunt or uncle:	
Name and birthdate:	
Special memories and stories about this aunt or uncle:	
Name and birthdate:	
Special memories and stories about this aunt or uncle:	

MY BROTHERS & SISTERS

Name of brother or sister (your siblings)

Name of sibling:	
Brother or sister?	☐ Brother ☐ Sister ☐ Half-Brother ☐ Half-Sister
If a half-sibling, name of mother: If a half-sibling, name of father:	
Birthdate:	
Is this sibling still alive?	☐ Yes ☐ No
If deceased, date of death:	
Address:	
City, state, and zip code:	
Mobile phone number:	
Email address:	
Name of spouse, if any:	
Spouse's cell phone number:	
Names and birthdates of children (your nieces & nephews):	1: 2: 3: 4:
Special memories and stories about this brother or sister:	

Name of brother or sister

Name of sibling:	
Brother or sister?	☐ Brother ☐ Sister ☐ Half-Brother ☐ Half-Sister
If a half-sibling, name of mother: If a half-sibling, name of father:	
Birthdate:	
Is this sibling still alive?	☐ Yes ☐ No
If deceased, date of death:	
Address:	
City, state, and zip code:	
Mobile phone number:	
Email address:	
Name of spouse, if any:	
Spouse's cell phone number:	
Names and birthdates of children (your nieces and nephews):	1: 2: 3: 4:
Special memories and stories about this brother or sister:	

Name of brother or sister

Name of sibling:	
Brother or sister?	☐ Brother ☐ Sister ☐ Half-Brother ☐ Half-Sister
If a half-sibling, name of mother: If a half-sibling, name of father:	
Birthdate:	
Is this sibling still alive?	☐ Yes ☐ No
If deceased, date of death:	
Address:	
City, state, and zip code:	
Mobile phone number:	
Email address:	
Name of spouse, if any:	
Spouse's cell phone number:	
Names and birthdates of children (your nieces and nephews):	1: 2: 3: 4:
Special memories and stories about this brother or sister:	

Name of brother or sister

Name of sibling:	
Brother or sister?	☐ Brother ☐ Sister ☐ Half-Brother ☐ Half-Sister
If a half-sibling, name of mother: If a half-sibling, name of father:	
Birthdate:	
Is this sibling still alive?	☐ Yes ☐ No
If deceased, date of death:	
Address:	
City, state, and zip code:	
Mobile phone number:	
Email address:	
Name of spouse, if any:	
Spouse's cell phone number:	
Names and birthdates of children (your nieces and nephews):	1: 2: 3: 4:
Special memories and stories about this brother or sister:	

If you know information about additional ancestors, be sure to name them, and on a separate sheet of paper, share as many of the stories you have heard about them. Future generations will appreciate your efforts.

§5-F: Your Family Tree

Creating your own family tree can be fun. Due to numerous circumstances which can affect one's family tree such as divorce, remarriage, children born of different parents, etc., a basic five-generation family tree for you to use is provided below as a starting point.

There are many family tree template program and applications available online (some for free), which will enable you to create a family tree which corresponds to your own unique lineage and family hierarchy.

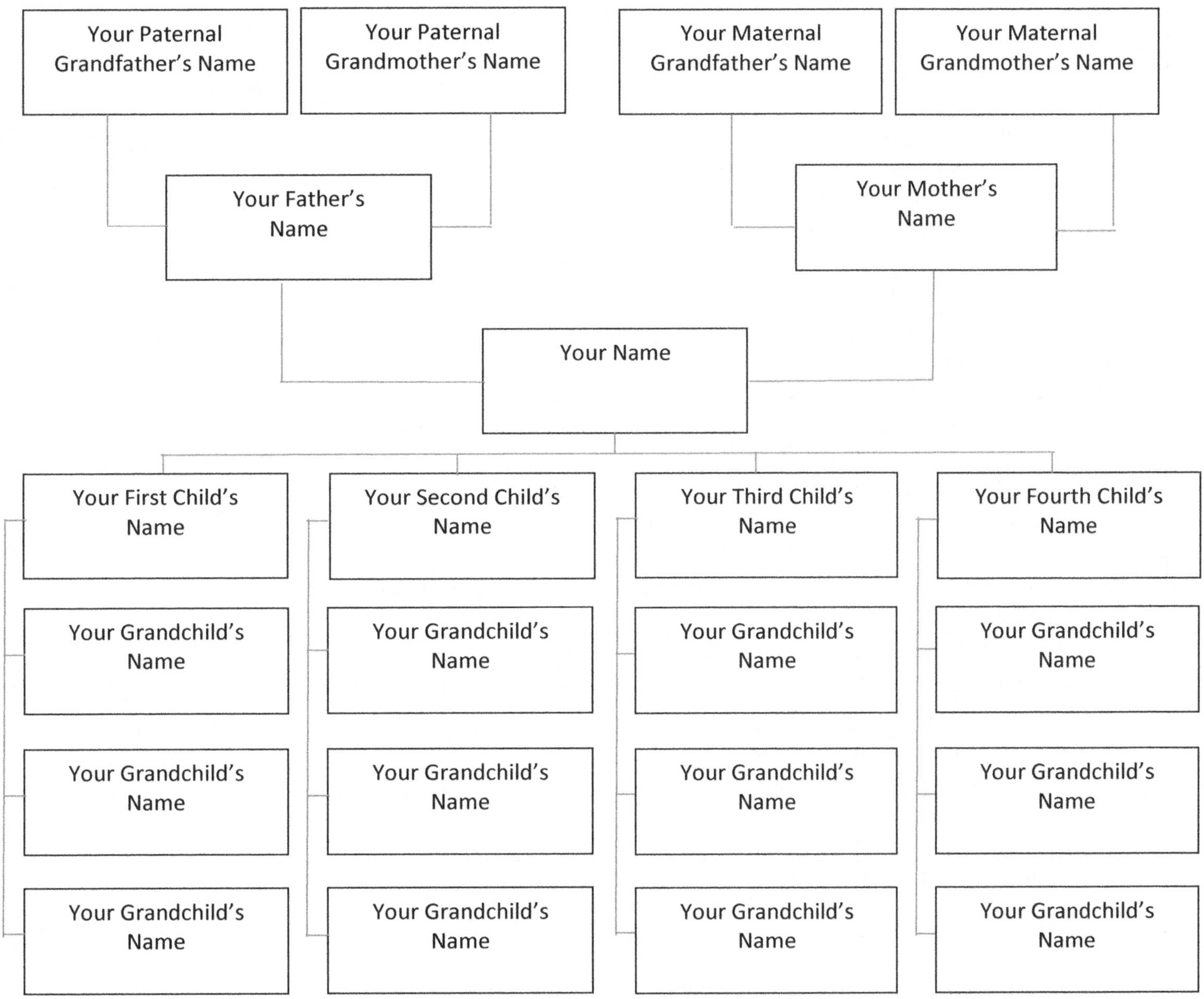

§5-G: Other Dependents, or Special Needs Dependents, if any

In this section, list any individuals (other than your own children) who are now, or may in the future, become dependent upon you for financial support. Include parents, siblings, relatives, friends, and neighbors who you help, even if you have no legal obligation to do so.

(Make an extra copy of this page for each dependent.)

Full name of individual:	
Address:	
City, state, and zip code:	
Telephone Number:	
Email address:	
Relationship to you, if any:	
Is this a person with a disability or special needs?	☐ Yes ☐ No
If yes, what is nature of disability or special need?	
What services does this person receive?	
Are you Court-appointed Guardian? If yes, location of documents:	☐ Yes ☐ No
Is this a legal or contractual obligation?	☐ Yes ☐ No
If yes, provide details:	
If not, why are you doing this for this person?	☐ Yes ☐ No
Is this a current obligation or a future obligation? Provide details:	☐ Current Obligation ☐ Future Obligation
Is there a written document or Trust outlining your obligations?	☐ Yes ☐ No
If yes, location of documents?	
What is the dollar amount of the obligation, if any? Provide details:	$
Location of bank accounts and other assets to be used for this person:	
Special memories and stories about this person:	

Additional notes:

____

____

____

§5-H: Information about my Employment

Provide information about your current place of employment.
If you have more than one employer, complete this information regarding each place of employment.

If you are not currently employed

Are you unemployed (but not retired)?	☐ Yes ☐ No If yes, provide details on a separate sheet of paper.
Are you retired?	☐ Yes ☐ No If no, provide employment information below.
Provide previous employer name and details:	
Are you receiving Social Security?	☐ Yes ☐ No If yes, how much per month? $
Are you disabled?	☐ Yes ☐ No If yes, provide details on a separate sheet of paper.
Are you receiving Social Security Disability (SSD)?	☐ Yes ☐ No If yes, how much per month? $

If you are currently employed

Name of current employer:	
Address:	
City, state, and zip code:	
Your work telephone number:	
Your work email address:	
Do you own this business?	☐ Yes ☐ No If yes, complete section on business ownerships
What is your occupation/job title?	
Name of your supervisor, if any:	
Supervisor's phone number:	
Supervisor's email address:	
Name of your assistant, if any:	
Assistant's phone number:	
Assistant's email address:	
Phone number and email address of human resources department:	
Hire date:	
What is your employee ID #?	
What is your salary?	$
Other compensation (e.g. bonus, commissions, overrides, etc.)?	
Do you have an employment contract?	
Location of documents:	
Special memories and stories about this job, your boss, and your co-workers:	

Benefits provided by this employer

Specify benefits you are entitled to receive through employer:	
☐ Life insurance benefits:	☐ Term Life Amount: $ ☐ Dependent Life Amount: $ ☐ Split-Dollar Life: $ ☐ Other (specify):
☐ Health insurance benefits:	☐ Major Medical / HMO ☐ Dental Care ☐ Vision Care ☐ Long-Term Care ☐ Disability benefits ☐ Other (specify):
☐ Retirement and Compensation benefits:	☐ 401(k) / 403(b) / 457 plan? (circle one, if applicable) ☐ Pension: Details: ☐ Profit Sharing / Money purchase plan / Keogh (circle one, if applicable ☐ Non-Qualified Deferred compensation plan ☐ Stock Bonus Plan ☐ Employee Stock purchase plan ☐ Stock Options ☐ Other (specify):
☐ Miscellaneous other benefits:	☐ Automobile ☐ Vacation/Holiday package ☐ Sick Pay ☐ Disability Income ☐ Child care ☐ Section 125 (cafeteria plan) ☐ Flexible spending account ☐ Tuition reimbursement plan for you or your children ☐ Other educational benefits for you or your children ☐ Other (specify):

Union information, if any

Do you belong to a union?	☐ Yes ☐ No If yes, provide details:
If yes, name of union:	
Union chapter or local number:	
Union contact name:	
Union contact telephone number:	

Possessions kept at work or office

What valuables or personal effects do you keep at work (e.g. personal computer, pictures, etc.)?	
Who needs to be contacted to be able to retrieve them (Name)?	
Contact phone number:	

Employee Benefits or Human Resources Department

Employee benefits or Human Resources contact name:	
Contact phone number:	
Website:	
Username:	
Password:	

Previous Employment History

Previous employer name:	
Start & finish dates:	From: ______________________ to ______________________
Are you entitled to retirement, death, insurance, or other benefits from this employer?	☐ Yes ☐ No
If yes, provide details:	
Employer contact person's name:	
This person's title or position:	
Phone and/or email address:	
Special memories and stories about this job, your boss, and your co-workers:	

Previous Employment History

Previous employer name:	
Start & finish dates:	From: ______________________ to ______________________
Are you entitled to retirement, death, insurance, or other benefits from this employer?	☐ Yes ☐ No
If yes, provide details:	
Employer contact person's name:	
This person's title or position:	
Phone and/or email address:	
Special memories and stories about this job, your boss, and your co-workers:	
What is the best job you ever had, and why was it the best?	
What is the worst job you ever had, and why was it the worst?	
What did you want to be when you grew up?	
Did you achieve your dream?	

§5-I: Information about my Education

Provide your educational history.

My Grade School

Name of grade school:	
Location (city and state):	
Year of graduation:	
Clubs, activities, etc.:	
Best friends:	
Favorite classes and activities:	
Favorite teachers (and what made them favorites):	
Special memories and stories about this school, your friends, your teachers, your activities, clubs, etc.:	

My Middle School

Name of middle/junior high school:	
Location (city and state):	
Year of graduation:	
Clubs, activities, etc.:	
Best friends:	
Favorite classes and activities:	
Favorite teachers (and what made them favorites):	
Special memories and stories about this school, your friends, your teachers, your activities, clubs, etc.:	

My High School

Name of high school:	
Location (city and state):	
Year of graduation:	
Honors and distinctions:	
Clubs, activities, etc.:	
Best friends	
Favorite classes and activities:	
Favorite teachers (and what made them favorites):	
Who was your first girl or boy friend?	
Special memories and stories about this school, your friends, your teachers, your activities, clubs, etc.:	

My Trade School, Learning Experience, or Other Certification

Name of school or certification:	
Location (city and state):	
Did you graduate?	☐ Yes ☐ No
If yes, year of graduation:	
Degree or certification earned:	
Honors and distinctions:	
Clubs, activities, etc.:	
Best friends:	
Favorite classes and activities:	
Favorite teachers (and what made them favorites):	
Special memories and stories about this school, your friends, your teachers, your activities, clubs, etc.:	

My First (or only) College or University

Name of college or university:	
Location (city and state):	
Did you graduate?	☐ Yes ☐ No
If yes, year of graduation:	
Degree or certification earned:	
Grade point average:	
Honors and distinctions:	
Special memories and stories about this school, your friends, your teachers, your activities, clubs, etc.:	

My Second College or University

Name of college or university:	
Location (city and state):	
Did you graduate?	☐ Yes ☐ No
If yes, year of graduation:	
Degree earned:	
Grade point average:	
Honors and distinctions:	
Clubs, activities, etc.:	
Best friends:	
Favorite classes and activities:	
Special memories and stories about this school, your friends, your	

teachers, your activities, clubs, etc.:	

My Master's Program

Name of college or university:	
Location (city and state):	
Did you graduate?	☐ Yes ☐ No
If yes, year of graduation:	
Degree earned:	
Grade point average:	
Honors and distinctions:	
Clubs, activities, etc.:	
Best friends	
Favorite classes and activities:	
Favorite teachers (and what made themfavorites):	
Special memories and stories about this school, your friends, your teachers, your activities, clubs, etc.:	

My Doctoral Program

Name of college or university:	
Location (city and state):	
Did you graduate?	☐ Yes ☐ No
If yes, year of graduation:	
Degree earned:	
Grade point average:	
Honors and distinctions:	
Clubs, activities, etc.:	
Best friends	
Favorite classes and activities:	
Favorite teachers (and what made them favorites):	
Special memories and stories about this school, your friends, your teachers, your activities, clubs, etc.:	

My Other Specialized Advanced Skills Programs

Name of school:	
Location (city and state):	
Did you graduate?	☐ Yes ☐ No
If yes, year of graduation:	
Degree or certification earned:	
Special memories and stories about this school, your friends, your teachers, your activities, clubs, etc.:	

§5-J: Military Service

*If you have served in the military service of the United States (or any other country), provide the details here. And **thank you** for serving!*

Basic military service details

Did you serve in the military service of the Unites States of America?	☐ Yes ☐ No
If yes, which branch?	☐ Marine Corps ☐ Marine Corps Reserves ☐ Army ☐ Army Reserves ☐ Army National Guard ☐ Navy ☐ Navy Reserves ☐ Navy Medical Corps ☐ Air Force ☐ Air Force Reserves ☐ Air National Guard ☐ Coast Guard ☐ Coast Guard Reserves
Did you ever serve in the military of another country?	☐ Yes ☐ No
If yes, which country and which branch?	
Highest grade/rank achieved:	
Military service serial number:	
Date of enlistment:	
Date of discharge, if applicable:	
Type of discharge:	☐ Honorable ☐ Other: ____________________
Location of DD214 form (Release and Discharge from active duty):	
What medals, honors, ribbons, and other distinctions have you received (e.g. Purple Heart, Silver Cross, etc.)	
List your special skills, certifications, and educational achievements:	
Names of veteran organizations to which you belong:	
Contact name and phone number:	
Location of your military service, pension, and other benefits records:	
Other information of importance:	
On a separate sheet of paper, consider sharing some interesting & meaningful stories about your time in the military, and the people with whom you served (non-classified details, of course):	

Military benefits available to you, your spouse, and your children (see www.ebenefits.va.com or www.militarybenefits.com)

Local benefits office address:	
City, state, and zip code:	
Military benefits contact person:	
Benefits contract phone number:	
Do you have a national service officer who helps you with your VA benefits?	☐ Yes ☐ No (A list of national service officers in your state can be found at www.purpleheart.com)
If yes, name and contact information:	
Contact information:	
Location of benefit documents:	
Other details of importance:	

Medical benefits

Are you entitled to **medical benefits**?	☐ Yes ☐ No
If yes, what is the name of your home VA hospital facility?	
Address	
City, state, and zip code:	
Telephone number:	
Are you receiving medical care there?	☐ Yes ☐ No
If yes, provide details:	
Location of document:	
Other details of importance:	

Pension benefits

Are you entitled to a **military pension**?	☐ Yes ☐ No
If yes, are you currently receiving it?	☐ Yes ☐ No
If not currently receiving it, when do you become entitled to receive it?	
If yes, what is your monthly benefit?	$
Is it paid directly to your bank acct?	☐ Yes ☐ No
If yes, what is the name of the bank?	
What is the account number?	
Location of pension documents:	
Other details of importance:	

Military disability benefits

Are you <u>entitled</u> to **military disability** or other compensation?	☐ Yes ☐ No
If yes, are you currently receiving it?	☐ Yes ☐ No
If no, when do you become entitled to receive it?	
If yes, what is your monthly benefit?	$
Type of disability:	
Disability percentage:	___________ %
Veterans Administration disability #:	
Location of pension documents:	
Other details of importance:	

Other veterans' benefits

Other military veterans' benefits you are **currently** receiving, if any:	
What other military veterans' benefits are you entitled to receive (specify)?	
Other details of importance:	

Survivor benefits to spouse

Do you have a survivor benefit plan for **your spouse**?	☐ Yes ☐ No
If yes, provide details:	
Do you have a serviceman's life insurance policy?	☐ Yes ☐ No
If yes, what is the plan name:	
Policy number:	
What other military benefits is your spouse entitled to receive, if any (specify):	

Survivor benefits to children

What military benefits are your children entitled to receive, if any (specify)?	

§5-K: Non-Military Service

If you served in any non-military or other public service organization, provide details below.
Thank you for your service!

Peace Corps or other non-military organization service

Did you serve in the Peace Corps or another non-military organization in lieu of military service?	☐ Yes ☐ No
If yes, provide name of organization:	
Contact information:	
What was your position?	
If you are entitled to any benefits from this organization, provide details:	
Share some of your interesting stories and experiences with this organization:	

Public service, charitable, or other not-for-profit organizations

Do you volunteer for any public service, charitable, or other not-for-profit organizations (e.g. Humane Society, Doctors without Borders, etc.)?	☐ Yes ☐ No If yes, provide details (add more pages as needed):
If yes, provide name of organization:	
Contact information:	
What was your position?	
If you are entitled to any benefits from this organization, provide details:	
Share some of your interesting stories and experiences with this organization:	

Any other public service, charitable, or other not-for-profit organizations

If yes, provide name of organization:	
Contact information:	
What was your position?	
If you are entitled to any benefits from this organization, provide details:	
Share some of your interesting stories and experiences with this organization:	

Additional notes:

§5-L: Information about My Rented Apartment, Condo, or Home

*If you **own** your primary residence, skip to the next section*

Basics

Rental property address:	
Apartment or unit number:	
City, state, and zip code:	
Type of rental unit	☐ Apartment ☐ Condominium ☐ Single Family Home ☐ Room ☐ Farm ☐ Other: ____________
Monthly Rent:	$
Security deposit:	$
Additional pet or other deposit:	$
Is there a written lease?	☐ Yes ☐ No
If yes, start and end date of lease:	Start: ____________ End: ____________
Location of Lease:	
If no lease, are you on a month-to-month basis?	☐ Yes ☐ No
Did anyone sign as a guarantor on your lease?	☐ Yes ☐ No
If yes, what is name of guarantor:	
Phone number of guarantor:	
Where do you store an extra set of spare keys, if any?	

Co-Tenants, Sub-Tenants, and Assignments

Co-Tenant	A **co-tenant** lives with you and is also obligated to pay his or her share of the rent to the landlord—you are both obligated to pay rent.
Do you have a **co-tenant**?	☐ Yes ☐ No
If yes, what is co-tenant's name?	
Did this person also sign the lease?	☐ Yes ☐ No
Co-tenant's telephone number:	
Co-tenant's email address:	

Sub-Tenant

Sub-Tenant	A **sub-tenant** pays rent to you (or to your landlord on your behalf). The sub-tenant may live with you, or may have taken over your rental unit, but you are the one who is still liable to the landlord for rent.
Do you have a **sub-tenant**?	☐ Yes ☐ No
If yes, what is sub-tenant's name?	
Telephone number:	
Email address:	
Has the landlord consented to this person living here as a sub-tenant?	☐ Yes ☐ No
If yes, is the consent in writing?	☐ Yes ☐ No

Assignment of Lease

Assignment	An **assignee** replaces you as the tenant on the lease. This person is now the one who is solely liable to pay rent to the landlord. You are no longer obligated on the lease.
Have you **assigned** the lease to another person?	☐ Yes ☐ No
If yes, provide the assignee's name:	
Telephone number:	
Email address:	
Has the landlord consented to this assignment **(in writing)**?	☐ Yes ☐ No

Owner/Landlord Information

Name of Owner/Landlord:	
Address:	
City, state, and zip code:	
Phone number:	
Email address:	

Property Manager Information

Is there a property manager?	☐ Yes ☐ No
Management company name:	
Contact name:	
Address:	
City, state, and zip code:	
Phone number:	
Email address:	
Website:	
Username & password:	

Renter's Insurance Information

Do you have renter's insurance?	☐ Yes ☐ No
If yes, what is the policy number?	
Amount of Premium:	$______________ Paid: ☐ Annually ☐ Quarterly ☐ Monthly
Is there replacement cost coverage?	☐ Yes ☐ No
Name of Insurance Company:	
Address of Insurance Company:	
City, state, and zip code:	
Telephone number of company:	
Website address:	www.
Name of your insurance agent:	
Name of insurance agency:	
Phone number of insurance agent:	
Location of policy and documents:	

§5-M: Information about My Pets (Pet #1)

If you do not have a pet, you may disregard this section.
If you have more than one pet, make an extra copy of this section for each additional pet.

Type of Pet: ______________________________

Name of Pet: ______________________________

Basic Information

Type of pet:	☐ Dog ☐ Bird ☐ Cat ☐ Horse ☐ Other (specify): ______________________
Name of pet:	
Pet's birthdate:	
Approximate financial value of pet:	$
Preferred food and serving size:	
Important or special instructions regarding dietary, behavioral, or other issues about this pet:	

Breed and Breeder

Breed:	
Is this pet purebred?	☐ Yes ☐ No
If yes, where are the pedigree or lineage papers located?	
Name of breeder:	
Address of breeder:	
City, state, and zip code:	
Phone number of breeder:	
Website:	www.
Other details of importance:	

Microchip, tag, or brand

Does this pet have a microchip?	☐ Yes ☐ No
Location of chip on pet:	
If yes, what is the chip number?	
Chip company name:	
Chip company phone number:	
Website for additional information:	
Does this pet have a tag?	☐ Yes ☐ No
Location of tag on pet:	
Does this pet have a brand or other identifying marking?	☐ Yes ☐ No
Location of brand or marking:	

Pet Insurance

Do you have a pet insurance policy?	☐ Yes ☐ No
If yes, pet insurance company name:	
Policy number:	
Telephone number:	
Website:	www.
Location of policy:	

Veterinarian Information

Veterinarian's name:	
Veterinarian's hospital name:	
Veterinarian's address:	
City, state, and zip code:	
Veterinarian's Telephone Number:	
Email address:	
Website:	www.

Health-Related Matters

Does this pet have medical allergies or other health-related issues?	☐ Yes ☐ No
If yes, provide details:	
Medications and dosage:	

Groomer Information

Groomer's Name:	
Groomer's Address:	
City, state, and zip code:	
Groomer's Telephone Number:	
Groomer's email address:	

Kennel or Stable

Name of kennel (for a dog) or stable (for a horse):	
Address:	
City, state, and zip code:	
Phone number:	
Email address:	
Kennel or stable fees:	$____________ per ☐ month ☐ week ☐ other: ______________

Who Will Care for Pet in your Absence?

Name of person to take care of this pet if you die or are incapacitated:	
Is this person to be paid?	☐ Yes ☐ No If yes, how much? $______________________ ***(Note: this is <u>not</u> a binding legal document. It is better to provide for payment in a Pet Trust or in your Will or Revocable Living Trust)***

Pet Trust

Have you created a Pet Trust?	☐ Yes ☐ No
If yes, location of document?	
Other details of importance:	

Awards, Prizes, or Other Distinctions

Describe awards, prizes, or other distinctions won by this pet:	

Special Tricks, Behaviors, or Talents

If this pet has any special tricks, behaviors, or talents, list them here:	

Favorite Stories and Memories

How did you come to acquire this pet?	
What sorts of mischief did this pet get into?	
Did this pet ever escape or run away?	
Favorite stories or memories about this pet:	

Additional notes:

____

____

____

____

§5-M: Information about my Pets (Pet #2)

If you do not have a pet, you may disregard this section.
If you have more than one pet, make an extra copy of this section for each additional pet.

Type of Pet: ______________________________

Name of Pet: ______________________________

Basic Information

Type of pet:	☐ Dog ☐ Bird ☐ Cat ☐ Horse ☐ Other (specify): ______________________
Name of pet:	
Pet's birthdate:	
Approximate financial value of pet:	$
Preferred food and serving size:	
Important or special instructions regarding dietary, behavioral, or other issues about this pet:	

Breed and Breeder

Breed:	
Is this pet purebred?	☐ Yes ☐ No
If yes, where are the pedigree or lineage papers located?	
Name of breeder:	
Address of breeder:	
City, state, and zip code:	
Phone number of breeder:	
Website:	www.
Other details of importance:	

Microchip, tag, or brand

Does this pet have a microchip?	☐ Yes ☐ No
Location of chip on pet:	
If yes, what is the chip number:	
Chip company name:	
Chip company phone number:	
Website for additional information:	
Does this pet have a tag?	☐ Yes ☐ No
Location of tag on pet:	
Does this pet have a brand or other identifying marking?	☐ Yes ☐ No
Location of brand or marking:	

Pet Insurance

Do you have a pet insurance policy?	☐ Yes ☐ No
If yes, pet insurance company name:	
Policy number:	
Telephone number:	
Website:	www.
Location of policy:	

Veterinarian Information

Veterinarian's name:	
Veterinarian's hospital name:	
Veterinarian's Address:	
City, state, and zip code:	
Veterinarian's Telephone Number:	
Email address:	
Website:	www.

Health-Related Matters

Does this pet have medical allergies or other health-related issues?	☐ Yes ☐ No
If yes, provide details:	
Medications and dosage:	

Groomer Information

Groomer's Name:	
Groomer's Address:	
City, state, and zip code:	
Groomer's Telephone Number:	
Groomer's email address:	

Kennel or Stable

Name of kennel (for a dog) or stable (for a horse):	
Address:	
City, state, and zip code:	
Phone number:	
Email address:	
Kennel or stable fees:	$_____________ per ☐ month ☐ week ☐ other: _______________

Who Will Care for Pet in your Absence?

Name of person to take care of this pet if you die or are incapacitated?	
Is this person to be paid?	☐ Yes ☐ No If yes, how much? $________________________ ***(Note: this is <u>not</u> a binding legal document. It is better to provide for payment in a Pet Trust or in your Will or Revocable Living Trust)***

Pet Trust

Have you created a Pet Trust?	☐ Yes ☐ No
If yes, location of document?	
Other details of importance:	

Awards, Prizes, or Other Distinctions

Describe awards, prizes, or other distinctions won by this pet:	

Special Tricks, Behaviors, or Talents

If this pet has any special tricks, behaviors, or talents, list them here:	

Favorite Stories and Memories

How did you come to acquire this pet?	
What sorts of mischief did this pet get into?	
Did this pet ever escape or run away?	
Favorite stories or memories about this pet:	

Additional notes:

§5-N: Miscellaneous Information about Me

If you have other details and information your loved ones may need to know about you that have not been covered above, please include them here:

§6-A: Sources of Income & Other Revenues

For each, specify the source of revenues and the contact information for the person or organization that is making payments to you.

Specify where your payments are sent, and include when the payments are due to end.

Salary from job/employment

Do you receive **Salary from job**?	☐ Yes ☐ No Amount: $________ per pay period.
How often are payments received?	☐ weekly ☐ bi-weekly ☐ twice a month ☐ monthly ☐ annually
Name of payor:	
Contact person name and phone:	
How are payments made to you?	☐ Check mailed to you; or ☐ Direct deposit to: ______________
Other details:	
Special memories and stories about this employer and your experiences there:	

Commissions, bonuses, overrides

Commissions, bonuses, overrides:	☐ Yes ☐ No Amount: $________ per pay period.
How often are payments received?	☐ weekly ☐ bi-weekly ☐ twice a month ☐ monthly ☐ annually
Name of payor:	
Contact person name and phone:	
How are payments made to you?	☐ Check mailed to you; or ☐ Direct deposit to: ______________
Other details:	
What is the largest commission or bonus you ever received?	

Income from business ownership

Do you receive income from a **Business** you own?	☐ Yes ☐ No Amount: $________ per pay period.
How often are payments received?	☐ weekly ☐ bi-weekly ☐ twice a month ☐ monthly ☐ annually
Name of payor:	
Contact person name and phone:	
How are payments made to you?	☐ Check mailed to you; or ☐ Direct deposit to: ______________
Other details:	
Special memories and stories about this business:	

Social Security Income (SSI)

Do you receive **Social Security Income**?	☐ Yes ☐ No Amount: $________ per pay period.
If not yet, when do payments begin?	
How often are payments received?	☐ weekly ☐ bi-weekly ☐ twice a month ☐ monthly ☐ annually
Contact person name and phone:	
How are payments made to you?	☐ Check mailed to you; or ☐ Direct deposit to: ______________
Other details:	
Obtain your statement of benefits at	www.socialsecurity.gov/mystatement

Social Security Disability (SSD) Income

Do you receive **Social Security Disability Income**?	☐ Yes ☐ No Amount: $_________ per pay period.
How often are payments received?	☐ weekly ☐ bi-weekly ☐ twice a month ☐ monthly ☐ annually
What is your disability?	
Contact information:	
When do payments begin?	
How are payments made to you?	☐ Check mailed to you; or ☐ Direct deposit to: _______________
When do payments end?	
Other details:	
Special memories and stories about the disability qualifying you for benefits:	

Military Retirement Benefits

Do you receive **Military Retirement Benefits:** (Pension, Disability, or Survivor Benefit Plan)?	☐ Yes ☐ No Amount: $_________ per pay period.
How often are payments received?	☐ weekly ☐ bi-weekly ☐ twice a month ☐ monthly ☐ annually
Name of payor:	
Contact person name and phone:	
How are payments made to you?	☐ Check mailed to you; or ☐ Direct deposit to: _______________
When do payments end?	
Will payments continue to your spouse?	☐ Yes ☐ No Amount: $_________ per pay period.
Will payments continue to your children?	☐ Yes ☐ No Amount: $_________ per pay period.
Other details:	
Special memories and stories about your military experience:	

Employer Pension Plan Income

Do you receive income from an **employer pension plan**?	☐ Yes ☐ No Amount: $_________ per pay period.
How often are payments received?	☐ weekly ☐ bi-weekly ☐ twice a month ☐ monthly ☐ annually
Name of payor:	
Contact person name and phone:	
When do payments begin?	
How are payments made to you?	☐ Check mailed to you; or ☐ Direct deposit to: _______________
When do payments end?	
Will payments continue to your spouse?	☐ Yes ☐ No Amount: $_________ per pay period.
Will payments continue to your children?	☐ Yes ☐ No Amount: $_________ per pay period.
Other details:	
What did you do with your first pension plan payment:	

Deferred Compensation Payments

Do you receive payments from a **Deferred compensation plan**?	☐ Yes ☐ No Amount: $_________ per pay period.
How often are payments received?	☐ weekly ☐ bi-weekly ☐ twice a month ☐ monthly ☐ annually
Name of payor:	
Contact person name and phone:	
When do payments begin?	
How are payments made to you?	☐ Check mailed to you; or ☐ Direct deposit to: _______________
When do payments end?	
Will payments continue to your spouse?	☐ Yes ☐ No Amount: $_________ per pay period.
Will payments continue to your children?	☐ Yes ☐ No Amount: $_________ per pay period.
Other details:	
Special memories and stories about this source of income:	

Alimony and/or Child Support

Do you receive **Alimony and/or Child Support**?	☐ Yes ☐ No Amount: $_________ per pay period.
How often are payments received?	☐ weekly ☐ bi-weekly ☐ twice a month ☐ monthly ☐ annually
Name of payor:	
Contact person name and phone:	
When do payments begin?	
How are payments made to you?	☐ Check mailed to you; or ☐ Direct deposit to: _______________
When do payments end?	
Other details:	
Yes, there **CAN** be funny alimony stories!	

Property Settlement Agreement Payments

Do you receive **Property Settlement Agreement?**	☐ Yes ☐ No Amount: $_________ per pay period.
How often are payments received?	☐ weekly ☐ bi-weekly ☐ twice a month ☐ monthly ☐ annually
Name of payor:	
Contact person name and phone:	
When do payments begin?	
How are payments made to you?	☐ Check mailed to you; or ☐ Direct deposit to: _______________
When do payments end?	
Will payments continue to your children?	☐ Yes ☐ No Amount: $_________ per pay period.
Other details:	
Are other financial benefits owed to you under the property settlement?	
Special memories and stories about the disability qualifying you for benefits:	

Required Minimum Distributions (RMD) from IRA Account?

Do you receive **Required Minimum Distributions:** (RMD) from IRA account?	☐ Yes ☐ No Amount: $_________ per pay period.
How often are payments received?	☐ weekly ☐ bi-weekly ☐ twice a month ☐ monthly ☐ annually
Approx. when do you take your RMD?	
Is it paid automatically, or manually?	☐ Automatically ☐ No – I have to call & request payment
Do you have Federal taxes withheld?	☐ Yes ☐ No Amount: $_________ or ________%
Do you have state taxes withheld?	☐ Yes ☐ No Amount: $_________ or ________% State: ______
Name of payor:	
Contact person name and phone:	
When do payments begin?	
How are payments made to you?	☐ Check mailed to you; or ☐ Direct deposit to: _______________
When do payments end?	
Will payments continue to your spouse?	☐ Yes ☐ No Amount: $_________ per pay period.
Will payments continue to your children?	☐ Yes ☐ No Amount: $_________ per pay period.
Other details:	
Special memories and stories about your 70th birthday celebration:	

Payments from Annuities

Do you receive payments from an **Annuity Contract?**	☐ Yes ☐ No Amount: $_________ per pay period.
How often are payments received?	☐ weekly ☐ bi-weekly ☐ twice a month ☐ monthly ☐ annually
Name of insurance company:	
Contract / Policy number:	
When do payments begin?	
Website:	www.
Username:	
Password:	
Are all the payments taxable to you?	
If not, what is your cost basis in annuity?	$
How are payments made to you?	☐ Check mailed to you; or ☐ Direct deposit to: _______________
When do payments end?	
Will payments continue to your spouse?	☐ Yes ☐ No Amount: $_________ per pay period.
Will payments continue to your children?	☐ Yes ☐ No Amount: $_________ per pay period.
Other details:	
Memories and stories behind this source of revenue:	

Distributions from bank or investment accounts

Do you receive distribution payments from bank or investment account?	☐ Yes ☐ No Amount: $__________ per pay period.☐ Check mailed to you; or ☐ Direct deposit to: ____________________
How often are payments received?	☐ weekly ☐ bi-weekly ☐ twice a month ☐ monthly ☐ annually
Name of payor:	
Contact person name and phone:	
Website:	www.
Username:	
Password:	
When do payments begin?	
How are payments made to you?	☐ Check mailed to you; or ☐ Direct deposit to: ______________
When do payments end?	
Will payments continue to your spouse?	☐ Yes ☐ No Amount: $__________ per pay period.
Will payments continue to your children?	☐ Yes ☐ No Amount: $__________ per pay period.
Other details:	
Memories and stories behind the assets in this source of revenue:	

Rental Income from Real Estate you Own

Do you receive **Rental Income (e.g. real estate)?** investment income)	☐ Yes ☐ No Amount: $__________ per pay period.
How often are payments received?	☐ weekly ☐ bi-weekly ☐ twice a month ☐ monthly ☐ annually
Address of the real estate:	
Name of payor:	
Contact person name and phone:	
When do payments begin?	
How are payments made to you?	☐ Check mailed to you; or ☐ Direct deposit to: ______________
When do payments end?	
Will payments continue to your spouse?	☐ Yes ☐ No Amount: $__________ per pay period.
Will payments continue to your children?	☐ Yes ☐ No Amount: $__________ per pay period.
Other details:	
Memories and stories behind this source of revenue (e.g. how did you come to acquire this property, etc.?):	

Distributions from a Trust

Do you receive **Distributions from a Trust**?	☐ Yes ☐ No Amount: $__________ per pay period.
How often are payments received?	☐ weekly ☐ bi-weekly ☐ twice a month ☐ monthly ☐ annually
Name and date of Trust:	
Name of payor:	
Contact person name and phone:	
When do payments begin?	
How are payments made to you?	☐ Check mailed to you; or ☐ Direct deposit to: ______________
When do payments end?	

Will payments continue to your spouse?	☐ Yes ☐ No Amount: $_________ per pay period.
Will payments continue to your children?	☐ Yes ☐ No Amount: $_________ per pay period.
Other details:	
Memories and stories behind this Trust:	

Dividends from Individual Stocks or Bonds

Do you receive **dividends from individual stocks or Interest payments from bonds**?	☐ Yes ☐ No Amount: $_________ per pay period.
How often are payments received?	☐ weekly ☐ bi-weekly ☐ twice a month ☐ monthly ☐ annually
Provide detailed list of payors:	
Contact person name and phone:	
Where are the stock and bond certificates located (e.g. safe deposit box, drawer, digitally held at company, etc.)?	
When do payments begin?	
How are payments made to you?	☐ Check mailed to you; or ☐ Direct deposit to: _______________
When do payments end?	
Will payments continue to your spouse?	☐ Yes ☐ No Amount: $_________ per pay period.
Will payments continue to your children?	☐ Yes ☐ No Amount: $_________ per pay period.
Other details:	
Memories and stories behind these stocks and/or bonds (e.g. inherited from grandparent, good stock tip, etc.):	

Lottery Winning Payments Received

Do you receive **Lottery winning payments?**	☐ Yes ☐ No Amount: $_________ per pay period.
How often are payments received?	☐ weekly ☐ bi-weekly ☐ twice a month ☐ monthly ☐ annually
Name of payor:	
Contact person name and phone:	
When do payments begin?	
How are payments made to you?	☐ Check mailed to you; or ☐ Direct deposit to: _______________
When do payments end?	
Will payments continue to your spouse?	☐ Yes ☐ No Amount: $_________ per pay period.
Will payments continue to your children?	☐ Yes ☐ No Amount: $_________ per pay period.
Other details:	
What did you do with your first lottery check?	

Structured Settlements

Do you receive payments from a **Structured Settlement (e.g. Personal injury lawsuit settlement)?**	☐ Yes ☐ No Amount: $_________ per pay period.
How often are payments received?	☐ weekly ☐ bi-weekly ☐ twice a month ☐ monthly ☐ annually
Name of payor:	
Contact person name and phone:	
When do payments begin?	
How are payments made to you?	☐ Check mailed to you; or ☐ Direct deposit to: _______________
When do payments end?	
Will payments continue to your spouse?	☐ Yes ☐ No Amount: $_________ per pay period.
Will payments continue to your children?	☐ Yes ☐ No Amount: $_________ per pay period.
Other details:	
What is the story behind the reason you have a structured settlement (e.g. car crash, lawsuit, etc.)?	

Disability income

Do you receive income from a **Disability insurance or supplemental income policy** (e.g. AFLAC or employer provided plan)?	☐ Yes ☐ No Amount: $_________ per pay period.
How often are payments received?	☐ weekly ☐ bi-weekly ☐ twice a month ☐ monthly ☐ annually
Name of payor:	
Contact person name and phone:	
When do payments begin?	
How are payments made to you?	☐ Check mailed to you; or ☐ Direct deposit to: _______________
When do payments end?	
Will payments continue to your spouse?	☐ Yes ☐ No Amount: $_________ per pay period.
Will payments continue to your children?	☐ Yes ☐ No Amount: $_________ per pay period.
Other details:	
What happened to qualify you to receive this income?	

Farming Income

Do you receive income from **farming, crop sharing, property rights, etc.?**	☐ Yes ☐ No Amount: $_________ per pay period.
How often are payments received?	☐ weekly ☐ bi-weekly ☐ twice a month ☐ monthly ☐ annually
Location of farm:	
Name of payor:	
Contact person name and phone:	
When do payments begin?	
How are payments made to you?	☐ Check mailed to you; or ☐ Direct deposit to: _______________
When do payments end?	
Will payments continue to your spouse?	☐ Yes ☐ No Amount: $_________ per pay period.
Will payments continue to your children?	☐ Yes ☐ No Amount: $_________ per pay period.

Other details:	
Was this a family-owned farm? What are your farming stories?	

Annual Gifts Received

Do you receive **Annual gift(s) received?**	☐ Yes ☐ No Amount: $_________ per pay period.
How often are payments received?	☐ weekly ☐ bi-weekly ☐ twice a month ☐ monthly ☐ annually
Name of payor:	
Contact person name and phone:	
When do payments begin?	
How are payments made to you?	☐ Check mailed to you; or ☐ Direct deposit to: ________________
When do payments end?	
If gifts exceed $14,000 per year, are gift tax returns being filed by the payor?	☐ Yes ☐ No
Will payments continue to your spouse?	☐ Yes ☐ No Amount: $_________ per pay period.
Will payments continue to your children?	☐ Yes ☐ No Amount: $_________ per pay period.
Other details:	
Memories and stories behind this source of income:	

Royalties, Licensing, etc.

Do you receive **Royalties, Licensing Income?**	☐ Yes ☐ No Amount: $_________ per pay period. Source of royalties – book, timberland, oil rights,
How often are payments received?	☐ weekly ☐ bi-weekly ☐ twice a month ☐ monthly ☐ annually
What is the asset resulting in this income (e.g. oil rights, patents, licensing, etc.)?	
Name of payor:	
Contact person name and phone:	
When do payments begin?	
How are payments made to you?	☐ Check mailed to you; or ☐ Direct deposit to: ________________
When do payments end?	
Will payments continue to your spouse?	☐ Yes ☐ No Amount: $_________ per pay period.
Will payments continue to your children?	☐ Yes ☐ No Amount: $_________ per pay period.
Other details:	
Memories and stories behind this source of income:	

Limited Partnership Income

Do you receive income from a **Limited Partnership?**	☐ Yes ☐ No Amount: $_________ per pay period.
How often are payments received?	☐ weekly ☐ bi-weekly ☐ twice a month ☐ monthly ☐ annually
Name of Limited Partnership:	
Contact person name and phone:	
When do payments begin?	
How are payments made to you?	☐ Check mailed to you; or ☐ Direct deposit to: _______________
When do payments end?	
Will payments continue to your spouse?	☐ Yes ☐ No Amount: $_________ per pay period.
Will payments continue to your children?	☐ Yes ☐ No Amount: $_________ per pay period.
Other details:	
Memories and stories behind this source of income:	

Real Estate Investment Trust Income

Do you receive income from a **Real Estate Investment Trust (REITs)?**	☐ Yes ☐ No Amount: $_________ per pay period.
How often are payments received?	☐ weekly ☐ bi-weekly ☐ twice a month ☐ monthly ☐ annually
Name of payor:	
Contact person name and phone:	
When do payments begin?	
How are payments made to you?	☐ Check mailed to you; or ☐ Direct deposit to: _______________
When do payments end?	
Will payments continue to your spouse?	☐ Yes ☐ No Amount: $_________ per pay period.
Will payments continue to your children?	☐ Yes ☐ No Amount: $_________ per pay period.
Other details:	
Memories and stories behind this source of income:	

Public Assistance and Food Stamps

Do you receive **Public assistance?**	☐ Yes ☐ No Amount: $_________ per pay period.
How often are payments received?	☐ weekly ☐ bi-weekly ☐ twice a month ☐ monthly ☐ annually
Name of payor:	
Contact person name and phone:	
When do payments begin?	
How are payments made to you?	☐ Check mailed to you; or ☐ Direct deposit to: _______________
When do payments end?	
Will payments continue to your spouse?	☐ Yes ☐ No Amount: $_________ per pay period.
Will payments continue to your children?	☐ Yes ☐ No Amount: $_________ per pay period.
Other details:	
Memories and stories behind this source of revenue:	

Unemployment compensation

Do you receive **Unemployment compensation?**	☐ Yes ☐ No Amount: $_________ per pay period.
How often are payments received?	☐ weekly ☐ bi-weekly ☐ twice a month ☐ monthly ☐ annually
Name of payor:	
Contact person name and phone:	
When do payments begin?	
How are payments made to you?	☐ Check mailed to you; or ☐ Direct deposit to: _______________
When do payments end?	
Will payments continue to your spouse?	☐ Yes ☐ No Amount: $_________ per pay period.
Will payments continue to your children?	☐ Yes ☐ No Amount: $_________ per pay period.
Other details:	
Memories and stories behind this source of revenue:	

Other source of Income

Do you receive income from **another source (specify)?**	☐ Yes ☐ No Amount: $_________ per pay period.
How often are payments received?	☐ weekly ☐ bi-weekly ☐ twice a month ☐ monthly ☐ annually
Name of payor:	
Contact person name and phone:	
When do payments begin?	
What are these payments for?	
How are payments made to you?	☐ Check mailed to you; or ☐ Direct deposit to: _______________
When do payments end?	
Will payments continue to your spouse?	☐ Yes ☐ No Amount: $_________ per pay period.
Will payments continue to your children?	☐ Yes ☐ No Amount: $_________ per pay period.
Other details:	
Memories and stories behind this source of income:	

What is the highest income you ever earned, and what is the story behind it?	
What is the worst income you ever earned, and what is the story behind it?	
What is the wildest income opportunity you tried (e.g. get rich quick idea, etc.):	
What was the best income-related advice you ever received?	

§6-B: Cash Flow Statement

Specify each source of income and each expense and insert the amount in the appropriate column based upon whether it is paid monthly, quarterly, semi-annually, or annually. Convert this amount into an average monthly amount by dividing it by 3 (if quarterly), by 6 if semi-annually, and by 12 if annually. Post the result in the column on the right, entitled "Average Monthly Amount."

INCOME	How often do you receive these payments?	Average Monthly Amount
Salary/Wages	$________ per ☐ Month ☐ Quarter ☐ Twice/Year ☐ Year	$
Bonuses/Incentives/Commissions	$________ per ☐ Month ☐ Quarter ☐ Twice/Year ☐ Year	$
Business/Self-Employment draw	$________ per ☐ Month ☐ Quarter ☐ Twice/Year ☐ Year	$
Interest / Dividends	$________ per ☐ Month ☐ Quarter ☐ Twice/Year ☐ Year	$
Loan or note payments received	$________ per ☐ Month ☐ Quarter ☐ Twice/Year ☐ Year	$
Rents received	$________ per ☐ Month ☐ Quarter ☐ Twice/Year ☐ Year	$
Reverse mortgage	$________ per ☐ Month ☐ Quarter ☐ Twice/Year ☐ Year	$
Royalties / Licensing Fees	$________ per ☐ Month ☐ Quarter ☐ Twice/Year ☐ Year	$
Social Security benefits	$________ per ☐ Month ☐ Quarter ☐ Twice/Year ☐ Year	$
Social Security Disability benefits	$________ per ☐ Month ☐ Quarter ☐ Twice/Year ☐ Year	$
Unemployment compensation	$________ per ☐ Month ☐ Quarter ☐ Twice/Year ☐ Year	$
Alimony/Child Support	$________ per ☐ Month ☐ Quarter ☐ Twice/Year ☐ Year	$
Court structured settlement	$________ per ☐ Month ☐ Quarter ☐ Twice/Year ☐ Year	$
Disability insurance benefits	$________ per ☐ Month ☐ Quarter ☐ Twice/Year ☐ Year	$
Long-term care insurance benefits	$________ per ☐ Month ☐ Quarter ☐ Twice/Year ☐ Year	$
Workers' compensation	$________ per ☐ Month ☐ Quarter ☐ Twice/Year ☐ Year	$
Pension plan – work or military	$________ per ☐ Month ☐ Quarter ☐ Twice/Year ☐ Year	$
401(K) or 403(b) plan distributions	$________ per ☐ Month ☐ Quarter ☐ Twice/Year ☐ Year	$
Annuity payments	$________ per ☐ Month ☐ Quarter ☐ Twice/Year ☐ Year	$
Deferred compensation	$________ per ☐ Month ☐ Quarter ☐ Twice/Year ☐ Year	$
IRA/SEP/Keogh distributions	$________ per ☐ Month ☐ Quarter ☐ Twice/Year ☐ Year	$
Other (specify):	$________ per ☐ Month ☐ Quarter ☐ Twice/Year ☐ Year	$
	$________ per ☐ Month ☐ Quarter ☐ Twice/Year ☐ Year	$
	$________ per ☐ Month ☐ Quarter ☐ Twice/Year ☐ Year	$
	$________ per ☐ Month ☐ Quarter ☐ Twice/Year ☐ Year	$
	$________ per ☐ Month ☐ Quarter ☐ Twice/Year ☐ Year	$
	$________ per ☐ Month ☐ Quarter ☐ Twice/Year ☐ Year	$
	$________ per ☐ Month ☐ Quarter ☐ Twice/Year ☐ Year	$
	$________ per ☐ Month ☐ Quarter ☐ Twice/Year ☐ Year	$
	$________ per ☐ Month ☐ Quarter ☐ Twice/Year ☐ Year	$
TOTAL MONTHLY INCOME		$

EXPENSES	How often do you make these payments?	Average Monthly Amount
Residence		
Rent, if any	$________ per ☐ Month ☐ Quarter ☐ Twice/Year ☐ Year	$
Mortgage, 2nd mortgage, LOC	$________ per ☐ Month ☐ Quarter ☐ Twice/Year ☐ Year	$
Homeowner association fees	$________ per ☐ Month ☐ Quarter ☐ Twice/Year ☐ Year	$
Renter's/homeowner's insurance	$________ per ☐ Month ☐ Quarter ☐ Twice/Year ☐ Year	$
Real estate taxes	$________ per ☐ Month ☐ Quarter ☐ Twice/Year ☐ Year	$
Special assessments	$________ per ☐ Month ☐ Quarter ☐ Twice/Year ☐ Year	$
Home Utilities		
Electric	$________ per ☐ Month ☐ Quarter ☐ Twice/Year ☐ Year	$
Heating – Gas/oil/other	$________ per ☐ Month ☐ Quarter ☐ Twice/Year ☐ Year	$
Water/Sewer	$________ per ☐ Month ☐ Quarter ☐ Twice/Year ☐ Year	$
Cable/Satellite/Internet	$________ per ☐ Month ☐ Quarter ☐ Twice/Year ☐ Year	$
Garbage/Scavenger service	$________ per ☐ Month ☐ Quarter ☐ Twice/Year ☐ Year	$
Home telephone	$________ per ☐ Month ☐ Quarter ☐ Twice/Year ☐ Year	$
Other (specify)	$________ per ☐ Month ☐ Quarter ☐ Twice/Year ☐ Year	$
Household Miscellaneous		
Groceries/household supplies	$________ per ☐ Month ☐ Quarter ☐ Twice/Year ☐ Year	$
Child care/child education	$________ per ☐ Month ☐ Quarter ☐ Twice/Year ☐ Year	$
Mobile/Cellular telephone	$________ per ☐ Month ☐ Quarter ☐ Twice/Year ☐ Year	$
Medical/dental/optical care	$________ per ☐ Month ☐ Quarter ☐ Twice/Year ☐ Year	$
Clothing/personal care	$________ per ☐ Month ☐ Quarter ☐ Twice/Year ☐ Year	$
Laundry/dry cleaning	$________ per ☐ Month ☐ Quarter ☐ Twice/Year ☐ Year	$
Alarm monitoring/security	$________ per ☐ Month ☐ Quarter ☐ Twice/Year ☐ Year	$
Furnishings	$________ per ☐ Month ☐ Quarter ☐ Twice/Year ☐ Year	$
Maintenance and repairs	$________ per ☐ Month ☐ Quarter ☐ Twice/Year ☐ Year	$
House cleaning	$________ per ☐ Month ☐ Quarter ☐ Twice/Year ☐ Year	$
Lawn service	$________ per ☐ Month ☐ Quarter ☐ Twice/Year ☐ Year	$
Pool service	$________ per ☐ Month ☐ Quarter ☐ Twice/Year ☐ Year	$
Exterminator	$________ per ☐ Month ☐ Quarter ☐ Twice/Year ☐ Year	$
Other (specify)	$________ per ☐ Month ☐ Quarter ☐ Twice/Year ☐ Year	$
Automobile/Vehicle		
Auto loan or lease payments	$________ per ☐ Month ☐ Quarter ☐ Twice/Year ☐ Year	$
Fuel	$________ per ☐ Month ☐ Quarter ☐ Twice/Year ☐ Year	$
Maintenance/repairs	$________ per ☐ Month ☐ Quarter ☐ Twice/Year ☐ Year	$
Vehicle insurance	$________ per ☐ Month ☐ Quarter ☐ Twice/Year ☐ Year	$
Parking/tolls/commuting	$________ per ☐ Month ☐ Quarter ☐ Twice/Year ☐ Year	$
Insurance		
Health/Medicare insurance	$________ per ☐ Month ☐ Quarter ☐ Twice/Year ☐ Year	$
Life/Accident insurance	$________ per ☐ Month ☐ Quarter ☐ Twice/Year ☐ Year	$
Property/liability insurance	$________ per ☐ Month ☐ Quarter ☐ Twice/Year ☐ Year	$
Long-term/disability insurance	$________ per ☐ Month ☐ Quarter ☐ Twice/Year ☐ Year	$
Loan Payments		
Student loans	$________ per ☐ Month ☐ Quarter ☐ Twice/Year ☐ Year	$
Home improvement/furnishings	$________ per ☐ Month ☐ Quarter ☐ Twice/Year ☐ Year	$
Credit card payments	$________ per ☐ Month ☐ Quarter ☐ Twice/Year ☐ Year	$
Other debts (specify):	$________ per ☐ Month ☐ Quarter ☐ Twice/Year ☐ Year	$

Miscellaneous Categories		
Educational expenses for you	$________ per ☐ Month ☐ Quarter ☐ Twice/Year ☐ Year	$
Retirement plan contributions	$________ per ☐ Month ☐ Quarter ☐ Twice/Year ☐ Year	$
Savings/Investments	$________ per ☐ Month ☐ Quarter ☐ Twice/Year ☐ Year	$
Vacations/travel	$________ per ☐ Month ☐ Quarter ☐ Twice/Year ☐ Year	$
Entertainment/dining/hobbies	$________ per ☐ Month ☐ Quarter ☐ Twice/Year ☐ Year	$
Gifts/holidays	$________ per ☐ Month ☐ Quarter ☐ Twice/Year ☐ Year	$
Charitable donations/tithe	$________ per ☐ Month ☐ Quarter ☐ Twice/Year ☐ Year	$
Newspapers/magazines/books	$________ per ☐ Month ☐ Quarter ☐ Twice/Year ☐ Year	$
Pet food/pet care/veterinarian	$________ per ☐ Month ☐ Quarter ☐ Twice/Year ☐ Year	$
Taxes (Federal, State, Local)	$________ per ☐ Month ☐ Quarter ☐ Twice/Year ☐ Year	$
Other:	$________ per ☐ Month ☐ Quarter ☐ Twice/Year ☐ Year	$
Other:	$________ per ☐ Month ☐ Quarter ☐ Twice/Year ☐ Year	$
Other:	$________ per ☐ Month ☐ Quarter ☐ Twice/Year ☐ Year	$
Other:	$________ per ☐ Month ☐ Quarter ☐ Twice/Year ☐ Year	$
Other:	$________ per ☐ Month ☐ Quarter ☐ Twice/Year ☐ Year	$
TOTAL MONTHLY EXPENSES		$

§6-C: Net Worth Summary

Summarize all your assets and liabilities from the previous pages.

Assets minus Liabilities = Net Worth

ASSETS	Value	LIABILITIES	Amt Owed
Cash & Cash Equivalents		**Real Estate Loans**	
Checking, Savings, Money Market	$	Primary Residence Mortgage	$
Certificates of Deposit	$	2nd Mortgage	$
Cash value of Life Insurance	$	Home Equity Loan/ Line of Credit	$
Retirement Assets		**Automobile/Vehicle Loans**	
IRA/SEP/SIMPLE IRA	$	Vehicle Loan 1:	$
Vested Pension Lump Sum Value	$	Vehicle Loan 2:	$
401(k), 403(b), 457 Plan	$	Vehicle Loan 3:	$
Tax-Deferred Annuity	$	**Credit Cards**	
After-Tax Annuities	$	Credit Card 1:	$
Non-Qualified Annuities	$	Credit Card 1:	$
Other:	$	Credit Card 1:	$
Investment Assets		**Student Loan(s)**	
Investment Accounts	$	Education/Student Loan	$
Individual Stocks/Bonds	$	**Other Types of Loans**	
Rental Real Estate	$	Business Loan	$
Notes/Loans Receivable	$	Personal Loan/Note Payable	$
Business Ownership	$	Loan Against Insurance Policy	$
Other:	$	Other Debts or Liabilities (List Below):	$
Personal Assets			
Primary Residence	$		
Vacation home/2nd home	$		
Vacation Club/Time Share	$		
Automobiles/vehicles	$		
Boat, Airplane, RV, etc.	$		
Furnishing	$		
Art, jewelry, antique, collectibles	$		
Precious metals, furs, etc.	$		
Other	$		
TOTAL ASSETS	**$**	**TOTAL DEBTS & LIABILITIES**	**$**

NET WORTH (ASSETS - LIABILITES) = $__________

§6-D: Personal Income Taxes, Estate Taxes, and Gift Taxes

Information you may need to know about my taxes:

Income Taxes

Do you file a **federal** tax return every year?	☐ Yes ☐ No
Are you up-to-date with filing your taxes?	☐ Yes ☐ No
If no, what year is the last year you filed?	
Do you file a **state** tax return every year?	☐ Yes ☐ No
In which state(s) do you file (specify)?	
Who prepares your income tax returns?	☐ Myself ☐ My spouse ☐ Name: ____________
Name of tax preparation firm, if any:	
Name of individual tax preparer:	
Tax preparer address:	
City, state, and zip code:	
Tax preparer phone number:	
Tax preparer email address:	
What is your filing status?	☐ Single ☐ Married filing jointly ☐ Head of household ☐ Married filing separate
Do you pay estimated taxes quarterly?	☐ Yes ☐ No If yes, how much per quarter? $____________
Do you claim income tax exemptions for: Yourself? Your spouse? Your children (specify all names)? Age 65 or older? Being blind? Other dependents (e.g. parents)?	 ☐ Yes ☐ No ☐ Yes ☐ No ☐ Yes ☐ No Names: ____________ ☐ Yes ☐ No ☐ Yes ☐ No ☐ Yes ☐ No Names: ____________
Does somebody else claim you as a dependent on their tax return?	☐ Yes ☐ No
If yes, what is name of person who claims you:	☐ Yes ☐ No
Do you usually get a refund?	☐ Yes ☐ No If yes, approximately how much? $____________
Do you have capital loss carryforwards?	☐ Yes ☐ No If yes, provide details:
Do you have charitable deduction carryforwards?	☐ Yes ☐ No If yes, provide details:
If you are 70-1/2 years of age or older, are you taking required minimum distributions (RMDs) from your retirement account(s)?	☐ Yes ☐ No
Do you store copies of tax returns and records online (e.g. at Turbotax.com, etc.)?	☐ Yes ☐ No
If yes, what is URL of website:	www.
Username:	
Password:	
Location of your old income tax returns:	

Fiduciary Taxes (Partnerships, Trusts, Corporations, Etc.)

Do you file any of the following types of corporate or fiduciary income tax returns?	
1120 (Corporation):	☐ Yes ☐ No If yes, tax ID (EIN): ______________________
Form 1065 (Partnership):	☐ Yes ☐ No If yes, tax ID (EIN): ______________________
Form 1041 (Fiduciary – Trust/estate):	☐ Yes ☐ No If yes, tax ID (EIN): ______________________
If yes, name of tax preparer:	
Name of tax preparation firm:	
Tax firm address:	
City, state, and zip code:	
Phone number:	
Email address:	
Where do you keep copies of the tax returns?	

Gift Taxes

Have you made gifts to anyone exceeding $14,000 per year ($28,000 per year if gift was made jointly with spouse)?	
For **every** gift given exceeding $14,000, provide the following details:	
Name of donee (Who received the gift?):	
Date of gift:	☐ Yes ☐ No If yes, when? ______________________
What was the value on date of the gift?	$______________ Date: ______________________
Describe property given, if not paid by cash or check:	
The gift was given:	☐ Outright ☐ In Trust ☐ Conditional (specify): ______________________
Was the gift split with your spouse?	☐ Yes ☐ No If yes, you gave: $______; Spouse gave: $________
Was a gift tax return filed (even if no gift tax was due)?	☐ Yes ☐ No If yes, provide details:
Amount and date of gift tax paid, if any:	$______________ Date: ______________________
Was a generation-skipping gift tax paid?	☐ Yes ☐ No If yes, provide details:
Is your spouse a U.S. citizen?	☐ Yes ☐ No
Who prepared the tax return, if any?	
Location of gift documents and gift tax return(s):	
Special memories and share the story behind each of the gifts given:	

Federal Estate and State Income Taxes

Have you filed a federal estate tax return for a spouse, parent, or child?	☐ Yes ☐ No
If yes, for whom, and the year filed:	Name: Relation to you: Year filed: Tax due: Paid-in-full?
Does your state of residence have an estate or inheritance tax?	☐ Yes ☐ No
Have you filed a state estate or inheritance tax return for a spouse, parent, or child?	☐ Yes ☐ No
If yes, for whom, and the year filed:	State where filed: Name: Relation to you: Year filed: Tax due: Paid-in-full?
Location of estate and inheritance tax returns:	
If your spouse died before you, did his/her estate file an estate tax **portability election**?	☐ Yes ☐ No
If yes, when was this done?	
Who prepared the estate tax return?	

Past due taxes

Do you owe taxes for any previous years?	☐ Yes ☐ No
What type of tax is owed?	☐ Income tax ☐ Fiduciary tax ☐ Gift tax ☐ Estate tax
If yes, approximate amount owed to IRS:	$______ Tax year(s) for which taxes are owed: 20_______
If yes, what payment plan (if any) have your reached with the IRS? Provide details:	
Do you owe taxes to any state or other taxing authority?	☐ Yes ☐ No If yes, provide details as to which taxing authority and how much is owed:
Are you in any currently pending or are you anticipating any tax litigation?	☐ Yes ☐ No If yes, provide details:
What is the story behind the taxes liability?	

Additional notes:

____
____
____
____
____

§6-E: My Estate Planning Documents

List which estate-planning documents you have had prepared, if any, and basic information contained in them.

If you have more than one Trust, or if you have an individual Trust for some assets, and a joint Trust with your spouse for joint assets, make an extra copy of the Trust page(s).

Revocable Living Trust

Do you have a **Revocable Living Trust?**	☐ Yes ☐ No
What is the full name of Trust:	
Is this your Trust or a joint Trust with your spouse?	☐ Individual ☐ Joint with spouse
If yes, what is the date of the Trust?	
Have you made any amendments or restatements?	
If yes, how many amendments or restatements?	☐ Yes ☐ No
Date of most recent amendment or restatement?	
Trust tax ID Number or EIN:	
Name and Phone of 1st Trustee (if not you):	
Name and Phone of successor trustee:	
Name and Phone of 2nd successor trustee:	
What major assets are in the Trust?	
Location of original Trust document:	
<u>Reminder</u>: Confirm the following periodically: Are all real estate holdings owned by the Trust? Are any businesses you own in the name of the Trust? Are your investment accounts owned by the Trust? Are your bank accounts owned by the Trust?	☐ Yes ☐ No ☐ Yes ☐ No ☐ Yes ☐ No ☐ Yes ☐ No
For any assets you have kept in your own name individually (or jointly with your spouse), is the Trust named as **primary beneficiary** or **contingent beneficiary** on your: Bank accounts? Retirement accounts? Life insurance policies? Annuities? Other (Specify)?	☐ Yes ☐ No ☐ Beneficiary ☐ Contingent beneficiary ☐ Yes ☐ No ☐ Beneficiary ☐ Contingent beneficiary ☐ Yes ☐ No ☐ Beneficiary ☐ Contingent beneficiary ☐ Yes ☐ No ☐ Beneficiary ☐ Contingent beneficiary
Since people frequently buy or invest in new assets, it is important to periodically verify everything is owned by or titled in the name of the Trust, or has the Trust named as beneficiary or contingent beneficiary.	

Last Will And Testament

Do you have a **Last Will and Testament?**	☐ Yes ☐ No Date of Will:
Have you made any codicils to the Will?	☐ Yes ☐ No If yes, date of codicil:
Name of Personal Representative (Executor):	
Phone number of Personal Representative:	
Name of 1st Alternate Personal Representative	
Phone number of1st Alt. Personal Representative:	
Name of 2nd Alternate Personal Representative:	
Phone number of 2nd Alt. Personal Representative:	
Does your will name a Guardian for your child(ren)?	☐ Yes ☐ No
If yes, what is the name & phone number of Guardian:	
Name & phone number of alternate Guardian:	
Location of original Will:	

Durable Power of Attorney

Do you have a **Durable Power of Attorney?**	☐ Yes ☐ No
Name and phone number of 1st Attorney-in-Fact:	
Name and phone number of 2nd Attorney-in-fact:	
Name and phone number of 3rd Attorney-in-fact:	
Who else has copies of this document?	
Location of original document:	

Separate Writing Disposing of Tangible Personal Property

Do you have a **Separate Writing** disposing of tangible personal property? (This is a document, usually attached to your Will, which allows you to leave specified items of personal property to any specified individuals)	☐ Yes ☐ No If you're not sure, check with your attorney.
Location of original document:	

Advanced Health Care Directive

Do you have an **Advanced Health Care Directive** (Also called a Health Care Surrogate or Health Care Power of Attorney)	☐ Yes ☐ No
Name and phone number of 1st Surrogate:	
Name and phone number of 2nd Surrogate:	
Name and phone number of 3rd Surrogate:	
Location of original document:	
Who has copies of this document?	

Living Will

Do you have a **Living Will?**	☐ Yes ☐ No
Name and phone number of 1st Surrogate:	
Name and phone number of 2nd Surrogate:	
Name and phone number of 3rd Surrogate:	
Location of original document:	
Who has copies of this document?	

Ethical Will

Do you have an **Ethical Will** (a written expression of your values blessings, life's lessons, hopes and dreams for the future, love, and forgiveness)? It is **not** a binding legal document.	☐ Yes ☐ No If "no," there is a section in this questionnaire to help you create your own ethical will.
Location of document:	

Lady Bird Deed or Transfer-on-Death Deed

Lady Bird (Enhanced Life Estate) deed or Transfer-on-Death deed in those states that allow their use:	☐ Yes ☐ No
If yes, property address:	
Name(s) of Remainderman/Remaindermen:	

OTHER FREQUENTLY-USED TRUSTS

Marital Trust

Do you have a **Marital Trust (**also called an **"A" Trust)**?	☐ Yes ☐ No
Name of Trust:	
Date of Trust:	
Tax ID Number or EIN:	
Location of document:	

Credit Shelter Trust

Do you have a **Credit Shelter Trust (CST) (**also called a **"B" Trust, Family Trust,** and **By-Pass Trust)**?	☐ Yes ☐ No
Name of Trust:	
Date of Trust:	
Tax ID Number or EIN:	
Location of document:	

Irrevocable Trust

Do you have an **Irrevocable Trust** (e.g. asset protection Trust, life insurance Trust, etc.)?	☐ Yes ☐ No More Irrevocable Trusts are below.
Name of Trust:	
Date of Trust:	
Tax ID Number or EIN:	
Location of document:	

Qualified Personal Residence Trust (QPRT)

Do you have a **Qualified Personal Residence Trust** (Sometimes referred to as a **QPRT)?**	☐ Yes ☐ No
Name of Trust:	
Date of Trust:	
Address of property in the Trust:	
Tax ID Number or EIN:	
Location of document:	

Irrevocable Trust

Do you have an **Irrevocable Trust** (e.g. asset protection Trust, life insurance Trust, etc.)?	☐ Yes ☐ No More Irrevocable Trusts are below.
Name of Trust:	
Date of Trust:	
Tax ID Number or EIN:	
Location of document:	

Special Needs Trust

Do you have a **Special Needs Trust (Supplemental Needs Trust)**?	☐ Yes ☐ No
Name of Trust:	
Date of Trust:	
Name of person who is to benefit from this Trust?	
Relationship to you:	
Reason for the Trust:	
Tax ID Number or EIN:	
Location of document:	

LESS COMMONLY-USED ESTATE-PLANNING DOCUMENTS

Family Limited Partnership

Do you have a **Family Limited Partnership**?	☐ Yes ☐ No
Name of partnership:	
Date of Partnership:	
Name(s) of general partner(s) and ownership %:	
Name(s) of limited partners & ownership interest(s):	
Tax ID Number or EIN:	
Location of document:	

Irrevocable Life Insurance Trust

Do you have an **Irrevocable Life Insurance Trust**?	☐ Yes ☐ No
Name of Trust:	
Date of Trust:	
Face amount of life insurance policy in the Trust:	$
Life insurance company name:	
Policy number:	
Tax ID Number or EIN:	
Location of document:	

IRA Trust

Do you have an **IRA Trust**?	☐ Yes ☐ No
Name of Trust:	
Date of Trust:	
Tax ID Number or EIN:	
Location of document:	

Gun Trust

Do you have a **Gun Trust**?	☐ Yes ☐ No
Name of Trust:	
Date of Trust:	
Location of gun(s) or other firearm(s):	
Tax ID Number or EIN:	
Location of document:	

Pet Trust

Do you have a **Pet Trust**?	☐ Yes ☐ No
Name of Trust:	
Date of Trust:	
Name of pet(s):	
Tax ID Number or EIN:	
Location of document:	

Qualified Terminable Interest Property Trust (QTIP)

Do you have a **Qualified Terminable Interest Property Trust (QTIP)**?	☐ Yes ☐ No
Name of Trust:	
Date of Trust:	
Tax ID Number or EIN:	
Location of document:	

Qualifying Domestic Trust (QDOT)

Do you have a **Qualifying Domestic Trust (QDOT)**? (Used for Non-US Citizens)	☐ Yes ☐ No
Name of Trust:	
Date of Trust:	
Tax ID Number or EIN:	
Location of document:	

Grantor Retained Annuity or Income Trusts

Grantor Retained Annuity Trust (GRAT)? **Grantor Retained Income Trust (GRIT)**?	☐ Yes ☐ No ☐ Yes ☐ No
Name of Trust:	
Date of Trust:	
Tax ID Number or EIN:	
Location of document:	

Charitable Remainder Trusts

Do you have a **Charitable Remainder Trust (CRT)**? **Charitable Remainder Annuity Trust (CRAT)**? **Charitable Remainder Unitrust (CRUT)**?	☐ Yes ☐ No ☐ Yes ☐ No ☐ Yes ☐ No
Name of Trust:	
Date of Trust:	
Tax ID Number or EIN:	
Location of document:	

Charitable Lead Trust

Do you have a **Charitable Lead Trust**?	☐ Yes ☐ No
Name of Trust:	
Date of Trust:	
Tax ID Number or EIN:	
Location of document:	

Intentionally Defective Grantor Trust

Do you have an **Intentionally Defective Grantor Trust (IDGT)**?	☐ Yes ☐ No
Name of Trust:	
Date of Trust:	
Tax ID Number or EIN:	
Location of document:	

Generation Skipping Trust

Do you have a **Generation Skipping Trust**?	☐ Yes ☐ No
Name of Trust:	
Date of Trust:	
Tax ID Number or EIN:	
Location of document:	

Other Type of Trust

Other (specify document):	☐ Yes ☐ No
Name of Trust:	
Date of Trust:	
Tax ID Number or EIN:	

Other "Creative" Methods of Estate Planning (Not Recommended)

Have you used any other "creative" method of estate planning to try to get around the expense or hassle of preparing documents, such as:	
Naming a relative or friend as beneficiary or joint owner of a bank account or other asset, because that person will know "what to do" and "what needs to be done."	☐ Yes ☐ No If yes, you may want to reconsider this strategy by discussing it with your estate-planning attorney.
Adding a child's name to property that you already own (particularly if it has increased in value since you bought it)?	☐ Yes ☐ No If yes, you may want to reconsider this strategy by discussing it with your estate-planning attorney.
Signing a deed which is to be delivered to a child or another person **after** you die?	☐ Yes ☐ No If yes, you may want to reconsider this strategy by discussing it with your estate-planning attorney.
Telling someone where you have hidden assets to be retrieved by them after you die?	☐ Yes ☐ No If yes, you may want to reconsider this strategy by discussing it with your estate-planning attorney. And what if that person dies before you?

SECTION 7: ASSETS

Information about My Assets

This section is the place to list ***everything*** *you own. Be sure to include* ***all*** *assets, including those upon which you still owe a debt or other financial obligation. It includes not only assets with financial value, but also those with family or sentimental value. Remember, if you don't let your loved ones know what assets you own, as well as where they are located (such as hiding places), they may never find those assets.*

Items Which are often Forgotten or Neglected

Most categories of assets are included in this section, but only you know everything you own. To help you remember them all, check out the section on items that people often forget or neglect to include in their asset list. Please answer ***all*** *them, as a* ***"No"*** *answer is just as important as a* ***"Yes"*** *answer in helping your loved ones to know whether they need to bother searching for an asset.*

If you answer ***"Yes"*** *to any of these questions, be sure to attach a separate sheet of paper providing the details about the asset; what it is (describe it in detail); where it is located; whether there is an identifying account or receipt number and who has access to it; as well as any key or combination needed to gain access to it.*

Remember to include items that may be kept at a second home, at work, out of the country, or stored elsewhere.

With so many account statements being delivered electronically now, try to remember if there any accounts, insurance policies, or other assets for which you no longer receive paper statements. How will your loved ones know about them if you don't list them here, or in the appropriate sections in this book?

And don't forgot about digital assets. A separate section on this new category of assets is included.

Unclaimed (or Abandoned) Asset Search

When you agree to "go green" and receive your investment account statements digitally, instead receiving paper versions in the mail, it is easy to forget to notify the financial institution involved when you move. Eventually, if statements are continuously returned to the bank for a certain period of time, by law, the account goes "dormant," and the funds in that account escheat to the state in which they were located. This applies to safe deposit box assets, uncashed dividend checks, and even to old security deposit with public utility companies, etc.

Every state has an unclaimed property division which has a website, listing assets which have escheated to the state. When this happens, the state doesn't get to keep it; they hold it for you, although some assets can be auctioned-off under certain circumstances. It is amazing what you can find there, and there is no cost (at least in Florida). For fun, when I searched for assets under my name, I found a $200 deposit from the local gas company from 28 years ago. When I searched under my wife's name, I didn't find anything specifically for her, but did find items belonging to two of her brothers (with the same last name., both of whom now live in different states.

When you do your own search, don't only search for your first and last name, but also for just the last name. You may find more "hits" this way and discover some belonging to relatives with the same last name. If you have lived in more than one state, be sure to do a search for every state in which you have lived.

In ***Florida****, the website to check is* ***https://www.fltreasurehunt.org/*** *Yes, it is actually called "Florida Treasure Hunt!*

To search other states, you can go to the site hosted by the National Association of Unclaimed Property Administrators (NAUPA), which provides links to all 50 of the states (and most Canadian province's abandoned property websites. Their website is: ***https://www.unclaimed.org/***

§7-A: Real Estate

Real estate (also known as "real property") is a tangible asset you can touch. For purposes of this section, real estate includes a house, condominium, cooperative (co-op), apartment building, commercial or industrial land, vacant land, a farm, timeshare, timberland, and more. Just think of anything built on or attached to "dirt."

*If you **rent** (but don't own your home), complete the section on your rental home or apartment.*

*If you **own** any form of real estate, complete the appropriate real estate section for each property you own, whether it is your personal residence, an investment property, timeshare, or other type of property.*

If you live in someone else's home or apartment and pay no rent, this information is reported in the "All about You" section.

Do you rent your home (even if you aren't obligated to pay rent)?	☐ Yes ☐ No If yes, complete section 5-L in **"All about You" section**
Do you own your home?	☐ Yes ☐ No If yes, complete section 7-A in **"Assets – Real Estate"**
Do you own a second home?	☐ Yes ☐ No If yes, complete section 7-A in **"Assets – Real Estate"**
Do you own a timeshare unit or vacation club membership?	☐ Yes ☐ No If yes, complete section 7-A in **"Assets – Real Estate"**
Do you own investment real estate?	☐ Yes ☐ No If yes, complete section 7-A in **"Assets – Real Estate"**

§7-A (1): My Personal <u>Primary</u> Residence

*This refers to your primary home that you **own**; not a home that you rent.*

Property Address: ______________________________

City: ____________________ **State:** __________ **Zip:** __________

Basic Details

Do you **own** a personal residence?	☐ Yes ☐ No
Property address:	
City, county, state, and zip code:	
Property tax ID number:	PIN:
Do you consider this **state** to be your **primary domicile?**	☐ Yes ☐ No
If no, what state do you consider to be your **primary** residence?	
Purchase price and purchase date:	$__________ Date: __________
Approximate market value:	$__________ (**Disregard any mortgage balance**)
Have you made **capital improvements** (e.g. built an addition, new roof, new kitchen, deck, wood floors, etc.)?	☐ Yes ☐ No If yes, provide date, cost, and details regarding each improvement. Use additional paper, if necessary.
Location of documents and receipts?	
Property type:	☐ Single family dwelling ☐ Condominium ☐ Cooperative ☐ Farm ☐ Mobile home ☐ Townhouse ☐ Specify other: __________
How is the property owned/titled?	☐ In my name alone ☐ Jointly with my spouse as Tenants by the Entireties[2] ☐ Jointly with (name(s)): __________ ☐ as Joint Tenants with Right of Survivorship ☐ as Tenants in common (no rights of survivorship) ☐ In my Revocable Living Trust: __________ ☐ In a business name: __________ ☐ In an LLC, corporation or land Trust (circle one) and provide details ☐ Life Estate to (name(s)): __________ with remainder to (name(s)): __________ ☐ Other: __________
Is there a condo/homeowner's association?	☐ Yes ☐ No
If yes, contact name and phone:	
Dues:	$__________ paid ☐ Monthly; ☐ Annually; ☐ Other: __________
Location of title documents:	

1st Mortgage Information

Do you have a **<u>1st mortgage</u>?**	☐ Yes ☐ No
If yes, mortgage account number:	
Name of the mortgage lender:	
Address:	
City, state, and zip code:	
Telephone Number:	
Website:	www.
Username:	
Password:	
Date of loan and amount of loan:	Date: ____________ Initial loan amount: $____________
What is the approximate balance?	$____________ as of ____________(date)
Payment type:	☐ Principal and Interest ☐ Interest only
Monthly payments:	$________ Principal & interest (not including tax or insurance escrow)
Term of loan:	# of years: ________
Interest rate:	________%
Type of loan:	☐ Fixed rate ☐ Adjustable rate (details): ____________ ☐ Balloon (details): ____________
Do you have mortgage insurance to pay off this loan upon your death?	☐ Yes ☐ No
If yes, name of insurance company:	
Policy number:	
Phone number of company:	
Location of mortgage documents:	

2nd Mortgage, if any

Do you have a **2nd mortgage?**	☐ Yes ☐ No
If yes, mortgage account number:	
Name of the mortgage lender:	
Address:	
City, state, and zip code:	
Telephone Number:	
Website:	www.
Username:	
Password:	
Date of loan and amount of loan:	Date: ____________ Initial loan amount: $____________
What is the approximate balance?	$____________ as of ____________(date)
Payment type:	☐ Principal and Interest ☐ Interest only
Monthly payments:	$________ Principal & interest (not including tax or insurance escrow)
Term of loan:	# of years: ________
Interest rate:	________%
Type of loan:	☐ Fixed rate ☐ Adjustable rate (details): ____________ ☐ Balloon (details): ____________
Do you have mortgage insurance to pay off this loan upon your death?	☐ Yes ☐ No
If yes, name of insurance company:	
Policy number:	
Phone number of company:	
Location of mortgage documents:	

Equity Line of Credit, if any

Do you have an **equity line of credit?**	☐ Yes ☐ No
If yes, line of credit acct number:	
Name of the mortgage lender:	
Address:	
City, state, and zip code:	
Telephone Number:	
Website:	www.
Username:	
Password:	
Date of loan and amount of loan:	Date: ____________ Initial loan amount: $____________
What is the approximate balance?	$____________ as of ____________(date)
Payment type:	☐ Principal and Interest ☐ Interest only
Monthly payments:	$________ Principal & interest (not including tax or insurance escrow)
Term of loan:	# of years: ________
Interest rate:	________%
Type of loan:	☐ Fixed rate ☐ Adjustable rate (details): ____________ ☐ Balloon (details): ____________

Do you have mortgage insurance to pay off this loan upon your death?	☐ Yes ☐ No
If yes, name of insurance company:	
Policy number:	
Phone number of company:	
Location of mortgage documents:	

Reverse Mortgage

Do you have an **reverse mortgage?**	☐ Yes ☐ No
If yes, reverse mortgage acct #:	
Name of the mortgage lender:	
Address:	
City, state, and zip code:	
Telephone Number:	
Website:	www.
Username:	
Password:	
Date of loan and amount of loan:	Date: ____________ Initial loan amount: $____________
What is the approximate balance?	$____________ as of ____________(date)
How much are you receiving from the reverse mortgage?	$____________ flat amount $____________ per month or specify: ____________
Total loan amount available:	$
Do you have mortgage insurance to pay off this loan upon your death?	☐ Yes ☐ No
If yes, name of insurance company:	
Policy number:	
Phone number of company:	
Location of mortgage documents:	

Other liens

Are there any other **liens** of any type against this property?	☐ Yes ☐ No
What type of lien?	☐ Tax lien ☐ Mechanic lien ☐ Judgment lien ☐ Other: ____________
What is the reason for the lien?	
To whom is the lien owed:	
Amount of lien:	$
Location of lien documents:	

Insurance on this Property

Do you have a Homeowner's Insurance policy on this property?	☐ Yes ☐ No
If yes, what is the policy number?	
Name of insurance company:	
Address of insurance company:	
Telephone number of company:	
Username:	
Website address:	www.
Password:	
Name of your insurance agent:	
Name of insurance agency:	
Address of insurance agency:	
City, state, and zip code:	
Phone number of insurance agent:	
Location of policy and documents:	

Flood Insurance on this Property

Is this property on a flood plain?	☐ Yes ☐ No
If yes, are you **required** to maintain flood insurance on this property?	☐ Yes ☐ No ☐ Not required, but I maintain flood insurance anyway
If you have insurance, is it a private company or is it government-sponsored?	☐ Private company ☐ Government-sponsored ☐ No insurance
If yes, what is the policy number?	
Name of insurance company:	
Address of insurance company:	
Telephone number of company:	
Username:	
Website address:	www.
Password:	
Name of your insurance agent:	
Name of insurance agency:	
Address of insurance agency:	
City, state, and zip code:	
Phone number of insurance agent:	
Location of policy & documents:	

Location of documents

Location of the original deed, title insurance policy, mortgage, survey, and other documents relating to this property?	

How did you come to own this house?	
Talk about parties, barbeques, and special events you've hosted here:	
Special memories and stories about this home:	

Additional notes:

___

___

___

___

§7-A (2): My Second Home (or Vacation Home)

This refers to a home that you own; not a home that you rent.
If you have none, you may disregard the next two pages.

Property Address: ______________________________

City: ______________________ **State:** __________ **Zip:** __________

Basic Details

Do you own a 2nd home or vacation home? (Do not include a timeshare unit)	☐ Yes ☐ No
Property address:	
City, county, state, and zip code:	
Property tax ID number:	PIN:
Purchase price and purchase date:	$______________ Date: ______________
Approximate market value	$______________ (**Disregard any mortgage balance**)
Have you made **capital improvements** (e.g. built an addition, new roof, new kitchen, deck, wood floors, etc.)?	☐ Yes ☐ No If yes, provide date, cost, and details regarding each improvement. Use additional paper, if necessary.
Location of documents / receipts?	
Property type:	☐ Single family dwelling ☐ Condominium ☐ Cooperative ☐ Farm ☐ Mobile home ☐ Townhouse ☐ Specify other: __________
How is the property owned/titled?	☐ In my name alone ☐ Jointly with my spouse as Tenants by the Entireties[2] ☐ Jointly with (name(s)): __________ ☐ as Joint Tenants with Right of Survivorship ☐ as Tenants in common (no rights of survivorship) ☐ In my Revocable Living Trust: __________ ☐ In a business name: __________ ☐ In an LLC, corporation or land Trust (circle one) & provide details ☐ Life Estate to (name(s)): __________ with remainder to (name(s)): __________ ☐ Other: __________
Is there a condo/homeowner's association?	☐ Yes ☐ No
If yes, contact name and phone:	
Dues	$________ paid ☐ Monthly; ☐ Annually; ☐ Other: __________
Location of title documents	

1st Mortgage Information

Do you have a **1st mortgage?**	☐ Yes ☐ No
If yes, mortgage account number:	
Name of the mortgage lender:	
Address:	
City, state, and zip code:	
Telephone Number:	
Website:	www.
Username:	
Password:	
Date of loan and amount of loan:	Date: ____________________ Initial loan amount: $__________________
What is the approximate balance?	$___________________ as of _________________________________(date)
Payment type:	☐ Principal and Interest ☐ Interest only
Monthly payments:	$__________ Principal & interest (not including tax or insurance escrow)
Term of loan:	# of years: ___________
Interest rate:	___________%
Type of loan:	☐ Fixed rate ☐ Adjustable rate (details): __________________________ ☐ Balloon (details): ____
Do you have mortgage insurance to pay off this loan upon your death?	☐ Yes ☐ No
If yes, name of insurance company:	
Policy number:	
Phone number of company:	
Location of mortgage documents:	

2nd Mortgage, if any

Do you have a **2nd mortgage?**	☐ Yes ☐ No
If yes, mortgage account number:	
Name of the mortgage lender:	
Address:	
City, state, and zip code:	
Telephone Number:	
Website:	www.
Username:	
Password:	
Date of loan and amount of loan:	Date: ____________ Initial loan amount: $____________
What is the approximate balance?	$____________ as of ____________(date)
Payment type:	☐ Principal and Interest ☐ Interest only
Monthly payments:	$________ Principal & interest (not including tax or insurance escrow)
Term of loan:	# of years: ________
Interest rate:	________%
Type of loan:	☐ Fixed rate ☐ Adjustable rate (details): ____________ ☐ Balloon (details): ____________
Do you have mortgage insurance to pay off this loan upon your death?	☐ Yes ☐ No
If yes, name of insurance company:	
Policy number:	
Phone number of company:	
Location of mortgage documents:	

Equity Line of Credit, if any

Do you have an **equity line of credit?**	☐ Yes ☐ No
If yes, line of credit acct number:	
Name of the mortgage lender:	
Address:	
City, state, and zip code:	
Telephone Number:	
Website:	www.
Username:	
Password:	
Date of loan and amount of loan:	Date: ____________ Initial loan amount: $____________
What is the approximate balance?	$____________ as of ____________(date)
Payment type:	☐ Principal and Interest ☐ Interest only
Monthly payments:	$________ Principal & interest (not including tax or insurance escrow)
Term of loan:	# of years: ________
Interest rate:	________%
Type of loan:	☐ Fixed rate ☐ Adjustable rate (details): ____________ ☐ Balloon (details): ____________
Do you have mortgage insurance to pay off this loan upon your death?	☐ Yes ☐ No
If yes, name of insurance company:	
Policy number:	
Phone number of company:	
Location of mortgage documents:	

Other liens

Are there any other **liens** of any type against this property?	☐ Yes ☐ No
What type of lien?	☐ Tax lien ☐ Mechanic lien ☐ Judgment lien ☐ Other: ________
What is the reason for the lien?	
To whom is the lien owed?	
Amount of lien:	$
Location of lien documents:	

Insurance on this Property

Do you have a liability insurance policy on this property?	☐ Yes ☐ No
If yes, what is the policy number?	
Name of insurance company:	
Address of insurance company:	
Telephone number of company:	
Website address:	www.
Username:	
Password:	
Name of your insurance agent:	
Name of insurance agency:	
Address of insurance agency:	
City, state, and zip code:	
Phone number of insurance agent:	
Location of policy & documents:	

Flood Insurance on this Property

Is this property on a flood plain?	☐ Yes ☐ No
If yes, are you **required** to maintain flood insurance on this property?	☐ Yes ☐ No ☐ Not required, but I maintain flood insurance anyway
If you have insurance, is it a private company or is it government-sponsored?	☐ Private company ☐ Government-sponsored ☐ No insurance
If yes, what is the policy number?	
Name of insurance company:	
Address of insurance company:	
Telephone number of company:	
Username:	
Website address:	www.
Password:	
Name of your insurance agent:	
Name of insurance agency:	
Address of insurance agency:	
City, state, and zip code:	
Phone number of insurance agent:	
Location of policy & documents:	

Location of documents

Location of the original deed, title insurance policy, mortgage, survey, and other documents relating to this property?	

How did you come to own this property?	
Talk about parties, barbeques, and special events you've hosted here:	
Special memories and stories about this home:	

Additional notes:

§7-A (3): My Timeshare Unit (Vacation Club Ownership)

If none, you may disregard the next two pages.

Property Address: ____________________

City: ____________________ **State:** __________ **Zip:** __________

Basic Information

Do you own a timeshare or Vacation Club unit?	☐ Yes ☐ No
If yes: Specify whether it is a:	☐ Time Share ☐ Vacation Club
Property address and unit number:	
City, county, state, and zip code:	
Property tax ID number:	PIN:
Purchase price and purchase date:	$____________________ Date: ____________________
Approximate market value	$____________________ (Disregard any mortgage balance)
What is your owner member account # (or other identifying #)?	

Details about your Unit

Details of unit (e.g. 2 bedroom, 3 bedroom with a lock-off, etc.):	
Do you own the unit, or is it a lease for a period of years?	☐ Own (deeded) ☐ Lease for ______ years
How is the property owned/titled?	☐ in my name as sole owner ☐ Jointly with my spouse as Tenants by the Entireties ☐ Jointly with my spouse as Joint Tenants with Rights of Survivorship ☐ Jointly with (name(s)): ____________________ ☐ In my Revocable Living Trust: ____________________ ☐ In an LLC, corporation or land Trust ☐ Life Estate with remainder to: ____________________ ☐ Other (specify): ____________________
What type of usage do you have?	☐ Fixed week (specify the week): ☐ Floating week ☐ Points
Details of your usage rights:	
Where are details explaining how to use the timeshare unit?	

Timeshare / Vacation Club Information

Timeshare / Vacation Club Name (e.g. Westgate, Marriot, Disney, Hilton, etc.):	
Address:	
City, state, and zip code:	
Phone number of organization:	
Website:	www.
Username:	
Password:	

Resort Information

Resort name:	
Address of property:	
City, County, State, and Zip Code:	

Exchange Organization

Do you belong to an **exchange organization** (e.g. Interval International, RCI, etc.)?	☐ Yes ☐ No If yes,
Exchange organization name:	
Exchange organization address:	
City, state, and zip code:	
Your membership number:	
Exchange organization website:	www.
Username:	
Password:	

Mortgage

Is there a mortgage on this unit?	☐ Yes ☐ No
Mortgage lender name:	
Mortgage lender address:	
City, state, and zip code:	
Phone number:	
Mortgage account number:	
Initial mortgage balance and term:	$________________; Term: ____________# of years
Payment terms and interest rate:	$_______ per __________; Interest rate: _______%
Balance still owed:	$___________, as of ____________________ (date)
Lender website:	$
Username:	
Password:	
Do you have mortgage insurance to pay off the loan upon death?	☐ Yes ☐ No
If yes, name of insurance company:	
Insurance company address	

City, state, and zip code:	
Phone number:	
Policy number:	

Location of documents

Location of the original deed, title insurance policy, mortgage, survey, and other documents relating to this property?	

How did you come to own this time share or vacation club?	
If you have used your exchange privileges, what exciting places have you visited?	
Special memories and stories about time spent here or other at timeshare or vacation clubs:	

Additional notes:

§7-A (4): Investment Real Estate

This refers to property you have invested in for income and/or future profit. If you have more than one parcel of investment real estate, make an extra copy of this section for each parcel.

If you have no investment real estate, you may disregard the pages regarding investment real estate.

Property Address: ______________________________

City: ____________________ **State:** __________ **Zip:** __________

If you have more than one parcel of investment real estate, make extra copies of this section.

Basic Information

Do you own any investment real estate?	☐ Yes ☐ No
Type of investment real estate:	☐ Apartment Building ☐ House/Condominium/Coop ☐ Vacant Land ☐ Commercial ☐ Industrial ☐ Farmland ☐ Mobile Home ☐ Marina/Boat Slip ☐ Forestland ☐ Mineral/Oil Rights ☐ Other: ____________
Address of property:	
City, county, state, and zip code:	
Property tax ID number:	PIN:
Purchase price and date:	$____________ Date: ____________
Approximate market value	$____________ (Disregard any mortgage balance)
How is the property owned/titled?	☐ In my name as sole owner ☐ Jointly with my spouse as Tenants by the Entireties[2] ☐ Jointly with my spouse as Joint Tenants with Rights of Survivorship ☐ Jointly with (name(s)): ____________ ☐ As Joint Tenants with Rights of Survivorship (JTWROS) ☐ As Tenants in Common (no rights of survivorship) ☐ In my Revocable Living Trust: ____________ ☐ In an LLC, corporation or land trust (provide details): ____________ ____________ ☐ In the name of my business: ____________ ☐ Life Estate with remainder to: ____________ ☐ Other (specify): ____________
Have you made major capital improvements (e.g. new roof, new kitchen, etc.)?	☐ Yes ☐ No If yes, provide date, cost, and details regarding each improvement.
Location of receipts:	
Annual gross rental income: Annual costs and expenses: Net cash flow:	$ $ $
Do you claim a depreciation deduction on this property on your tax return?	☐ Yes ☐ No If yes, provide details:
Are there any environmental, zoning, or other serious issues affecting this property?	☐ Yes ☐ No

If yes, provide details:	
Location of documents & receipts?	

First Mortgage

Do you have a **1st mortgage?**	☐ Yes ☐ No
If yes, mortgage account number:	
Name of the mortgage lender:	
Address:	
City, county, state, and zip code:	
Lender's phone number:	
Website:	www.
Username:	
Password:	
Date of Loan and Amount of loan:	Date: ____________ Initial loan amount: $____________
What is the approximate balance?	$____________ as of ____________(date)
Payment type:	☐ Principal and Interest ☐ Interest only
Monthly payments	$________ Principal & interest (not including tax or insurance escrow)
Term of loan:	________ years / months (circle one)
Interest rate:	________%
Type of loan:	☐ Fixed rate ☐ Adjustable rate (details): ____________ ☐ Balloon (details): ____________
Do you have mortgage insurance to pay off this loan at your death?	☐ Yes ☐ No
If yes, name of insurance company	
Policy number:	
Address:	
City, state, and zip code:	
Phone number:	
Are there any co-obligors or guarantors on this mortgage?	☐ Yes ☐ No
If yes, name of person:	
Person's contact information:	
Location of mortgage documents:	

2nd Mortgage, if any

Do you have a **2nd mortgage?**	☐ Yes ☐ No
If yes, mortgage account number:	
Name of the mortgage lender:	
Address:	
City, state, and zip code:	
Telephone Number:	
Website:	www.
Username:	
Password:	
Date of loan and amount of loan:	Date: ___________________ Initial loan amount: $__________________
What is the approximate balance?	$__________________ as of ______________________________(date)
Payment type:	☐ Principal and Interest ☐ Interest only
Monthly payments:	$__________ Principal & interest (not including tax or insurance escrow)
Term of loan:	# of years: ___________
Interest rate:	___________%
Type of loan:	☐ Fixed rate ☐ Adjustable rate (details): __________________________ ☐ Balloon (details): ____
Do you have mortgage insurance to pay off this loan upon your death?	☐ Yes ☐ No
If yes, name of insurance company:	
Policy number:	
Phone number of company:	
Location of mortgage documents:	

Equity Line of Credit, if any

Do you have an **equity line of credit?**	☐ Yes ☐ No
If yes, line of credit acct number:	
Name of the mortgage lender:	
Address:	
City, state, and zip code:	
Telephone Number:	
Website:	www.
Username:	
Password:	
Date of loan and amount of loan:	Date: ____________ Initial loan amount: $____________
What is the approximate balance?	$____________ as of ____________(date)
Payment type:	☐ Principal and Interest ☐ Interest only
Monthly payments:	$________ Principal & interest (not including tax or insurance escrow)
Term of loan:	# of years: ________
Interest rate:	________%
Type of loan:	☐ Fixed rate ☐ Adjustable rate (details): ____________ ☐ Balloon (details): ____________
Do you have mortgage insurance to pay off this loan upon your death?	☐ Yes ☐ No
If yes, name of insurance company:	
Policy number:	
Phone number of company:	
Location of mortgage documents:	

Other liens

Are there any other <u>**liens**</u> of any type against this property?	☐ Yes ☐ No
What type of lien?	☐ Tax lien ☐ Mechanic lien ☐ Judgment lien ☐ Other: ________
What is the reason for the lien?	
To whom is the lien owed:	
Amount of lien:	$
Location of lien documents:	

Insurance on this Property

Do you have a liability insurance policy on this property?	☐ Yes ☐ No
If yes, what is the policy number?	
Name of insurance company:	
Address of insurance company:	
Telephone number of company:	
Website address:	www.
Username:	
Password:	
Name of your insurance agent:	
Name of insurance agency:	
Address of insurance agency:	
City, state, and zip code:	
Phone number of insurance agent:	
Location of policy & documents:	

Flood Insurance on this Property

Is this property on a flood plain?	☐ Yes ☐ No
If yes, are you **required** to maintain flood insurance on this property?	☐ Yes ☐ No ☐ Not required, but I maintain flood insurance anyway
If you have insurance, is it a private company, or is it government-sponsored?	☐ Private company ☐ Government-sponsored ☐ No insurance
If yes, what is the policy number?	
Name of insurance company:	
Address of insurance company:	
Telephone number of company:	
Username:	
Website address:	www.
Password:	
Name of your insurance agent:	
Name of insurance agency:	
Address of insurance agency:	
City, state, and zip code:	
Phone number of insurance agent:	
Location of policy and documents:	

Location of documents

Location of the original deed, title insurance policy, mortgage, survey, and other documents relating to this property?	

Property Management Company, if any

Is this a rental property?	☐ Yes ☐ No
If yes, location of leases:	
Location of property financial records:	
Do you use a property manager?	☐ Yes ☐ No If yes, provide details.
Name of management company:	
Management company address:	
City, state, and zip code:	
Company phone number:	
Company fax number:	
Company email address:	
Name of management agent:	
Agent's work phone number:	
Cell phone number:	
Email address:	
Is there a written contract with the management company?	☐ Yes ☐ No
If yes, location of contract?	

Tenant Information (Complete one for each tenant; make additional copies as needed)

Name of Tenant(s):	
Company name (if commercial lease):	
Address:	
Apartment or Unit Number:	
City, state, and zip code:	
Phone number:	
Cell Phone:	
Email address:	
Monthly Rent:	$____________ Security Deposit: $____________
Is there a written lease?	☐ Yes ☐ No
If yes, what is term of lease?	☐ Yes ☐ No If yes, attach a copy or specify location of lease Start: ____________ End: ____________
If there is no lease, is this property rented on a month-to-month basis?	☐ Yes ☐ No
Does Tenant have renter's insurance?	☐ Yes ☐ No
Does Tenant have liability insurance?	☐ Yes ☐ No If yes, are you covered (as owner)? ☐ Yes ☐ No
How many people are allowed to reside in the unit?:	______ (#)
Are pets allowed?	☐ Yes ☐ No If yes, additional kept deposit, if any: $____________

Tenant Information (Complete one for each tenant; make additional copies as needed)

Name of Tenant(s):	
Company name (if commercial lease):	
Address:	
Apartment or Unit Number:	
City, state, and zip code:	
Phone number:	
Cell Phone:	
Email address:	
Monthly Rent:	$____________ Security Deposit: $____________
Is there a written lease?	☐ Yes ☐ No
If yes, what is term of lease?	☐ Yes ☐ No If yes, attach a copy or specify location of lease Start: ____________ End: ____________
If there is no lease, is this property rented on a month-to-month basis?	☐ Yes ☐ No
Does Tenant have renter's insurance?	☐ Yes ☐ No
Does Tenant have liability insurance?	☐ Yes ☐ No If yes, are you covered (as owner)? ☐ Yes ☐ No
How many people are allowed to reside in the unit?:	______ (#)
Are pets allowed?	☐ Yes ☐ No If yes, additional kept deposit, if any: $____________

Tenant Information (Complete one for each tenant; make additional copies as needed)

Name of Tenant(s):	
Company name (if commercial lease):	
Address:	
Apartment or Unit Number:	
City, state, and zip code:	
Phone number:	
Cell Phone:	
Email address:	
Monthly Rent:	$____________ Security Deposit: $____________
Is there a written lease?	☐ Yes ☐ No
If yes, what is term of lease?	☐ Yes ☐ No If yes, attach a copy or specify location of lease Start: ____________ End: ____________
If there is no lease, is this property rented on a month-to-month basis?	☐ Yes ☐ No
Does Tenant have renter's insurance?	☐ Yes ☐ No
Does Tenant have liability insurance?	☐ Yes ☐ No If yes, are you covered (as owner)? ☐ Yes ☐ No
How many people are allowed to reside in the unit?:	______ (#)
Are pets allowed?	☐ Yes ☐ No If yes, additional kept deposit, if any: $____________

Tenant Information (Complete one for each tenant; make additional copies as needed)

Name of Tenant(s):	
Company name (if commercial lease):	
Address:	
Apartment or Unit Number:	
City, state, and zip code:	
Phone number:	
Cell Phone:	
Email address:	
Monthly Rent:	$_________________ Security Deposit: $_________________
Is there a written lease?	☐ Yes ☐ No
If yes, what is term of lease?	☐ Yes ☐ No If yes, attach a copy or specify location of lease Start: _____________________ End: ____________________
If there is no lease, is this property rented on a month-to-month basis?	☐ Yes ☐ No
Does Tenant have renter's insurance?	☐ Yes ☐ No
Does Tenant have liability insurance?	☐ Yes ☐ No If yes, are you covered (as owner)? ☐ Yes ☐ No
How many people are allowed to reside in the unit?:	_______ (#)
Are pets allowed?	☐ Yes ☐ No If yes, additional kept deposit, if any: $_____________

Tenant Information (Complete one for each tenant; make additional copies as needed)

Name of Tenant(s):	
Company name (if commercial lease):	
Address:	
Apartment or Unit Number:	
City, state, and zip code:	
Phone number:	
Cell Phone:	
Email address:	
Monthly Rent:	$_________________ Security Deposit: $_________________
Is there a written lease?	☐ Yes ☐ No
If yes, what is term of lease?	☐ Yes ☐ No If yes, attach a copy or specify location of lease Start: _____________________ End: ____________________
If there is no lease, is this property rented on a month-to-month basis?	☐ Yes ☐ No
Does Tenant have renter's insurance?	☐ Yes ☐ No
Does Tenant have liability insurance?	☐ Yes ☐ No If yes, are you covered (as owner)? ☐ Yes ☐ No
How many people are allowed to reside in the unit?:	_______ (#)
Are pets allowed?	☐ Yes ☐ No If yes, additional kept deposit, if any: $_____________

§7-B: Closely Held Business Ownership

*Provide this information for **every** business you own. There are enough details regarding business ownership to fill another entire book, so this section will focus on providing a list of important general categories to help you create your own list of important details to share with the person(s) who will be charged with continuing your business, should you become unable to do so. Since every business is different, it is impossible to list everything your successors will need to know about your company or industry, so be sure to add any additional categories you consider relevant or unique to your business.*

Basic Information

Do you own a business (including a partial ownership of a business)?	☐ Yes ☐ No If no, you may skip this entire section.
If yes, percentage your ownership:	☐ 100% ☐ Other (specify): ___________%
Legal name of business:	
If different, "Doing business as" name	
Purpose or nature of business:	
Address:	
City, state, and zip code:	
Other states of operation (specify):	
Main business phone number:	
Fax number:	
Website address:	www.
Username:	
Password:	
Do you have a trademark, tradename, or copyright on the business name?	☐ Yes ☐ No If yes, provide details:
Type of business entity (There are more questions below regarding each type of business entity)	☐ Sole Proprietorship; ☐ Partnership ☐ Corporation; ☐ Subchapter S Corporation ☐ Limited Liability Company (LLC); ☐ Professional Association (PA) ☐ Other: ___________________________

Tax and License Numbers

Federal Tax ID number (EIN)	
State sales tax ID number	
State unemployment tax number	
State in which business is organized?	
State license numbers, if any?	
Professional/occupational license #:	
List all states of business operations:	
Do you pay for a **county** business license and/or occupational tax?	☐ Yes ☐ No If yes, what county?
Do you pay for a **city** business license and/or occupational tax?	☐ Yes ☐ No If yes, what city?
Is business on a calendar or fiscal year	☐ Calendar ☐ Fiscal year ending: ___________________

Financial Information

Capitalization of business (i.e. What was the source of capital to get business started):	
Investment by owners/shareholders:	$____________ Name: ____________________ $____________ Name: ____________________ $____________ Name: ____________________
Loans to the business (from individuals, companies, banks, etc.):	$____________ Name: ____________________ $____________ Name: ____________________
For the past three years, list your	Last Year (20_____) Previous Year (20____) Two Years Ago (20____)
Approximate annual sales (gross)	$____________ $____________ $____________
Approximate net income (net)	$____________ $____________ $____________
Approximate profit (or loss)	$____________ $____________ $____________
Approximate business value:	$
How was this amount determined?	
Location of business appraisal, if any:	
Assets the business owns:	Attach detailed balance sheet
Debts and obligations owed:	Attach detailed list of debts
Location of financial documents:	

Union Information

Do your employees participate in a trade union?	☐ Yes ☐ No If yes, provide union details and contact info
If yes, name of union and local #:	
Name of union representative:	
Address of union:	
City, state, and zip code:	
Telephone number:	
Email address:	
Website information:	www.

Franchise Information, if any

Is this a Franchise?	☐ Yes ☐ No
If yes, name of franchisor:	
Address of franchisor:	
City, state, and zip code:	
Telephone number:	
Contact person:	
Phone and/or email address:	
Website:	www.
Username:	
Password:	
Location of franchise documents:	

Business Continuation, Succession Planning, or Sale of Business Plans

Will this business be able to continue to operate without you running it?	☐ Yes ☐ No
If no, what are your plans for winding down the business?	
What are your plans for this business when you retire?	
Who will continue the business in the event of your death or disability?	
Phone number of person:	
Email of person:	
Does this person have written, **legal** authority?	☐ Yes ☐ No
What is the source of the legal authority?	☐ Co-owner of business ☐ Officer of the business ☐ Written agreement ☐ Durable power of attorney ☐ Other (specify): ________________

Succession Plan, if any

Is there a written succession plan document (e.g. Buy-Sell Agreement)?	☐ Yes ☐ No If yes, provide details:
Type of buy-sell agreement, if known:	☐ Cross-purchase ☐ stock redemption ☐ combination ☐ Other: ________________
Is this plan funded by life insurance?	☐ Yes ☐ No
If yes, name of insurance company:	
Policy number:	
Policy owner:	
Whose life is being insured (name)?	
Name of primary beneficiary:	
Name of contingent beneficiary:	
Method for determining value:	☐ Book Value ☐ Earnings multiple ☐ Appraisal ☐ Agreed Value: $________________ ☐ Other: ________________
If there is no succession plan, provide a list of people (or companies) who might have an interest in buying this business (including competitors):	
If there is no succession plan, how will your spouse or survivor(s) receive your share of the business?	
Will your spouse or survivor assume any of the company's liabilities?	☐ Yes ☐ No
Will your spouse or survivor assume any responsibility for operating the business?	☐ Yes ☐ No
If yes, provide details:	

Is a License Required?

Is a government-issued license required to operate this business (e.g. lawyer, electrician, etc.):	☐ Yes ☐ No
Can the business be owned by a non-licensed person?	☐ Yes ☐ No

Who should be notified about your death or incapacity?

Who else should be notified about your death or incapacity?	Provide names, phone numbers, and their relation to the business
Landlord name and phone number:	
Attorney name and phone number:	
CPA/Accountant name and phone:	
Insurance agent name and phone:	
Key employee names and phone numbers:	
Key clients/customer names and phone numbers:	
Other:	
Other:	
Other:	

Business Continuation Plan

In the event of an emergency, does your company have a **written** business continuation/disaster plan?	☐ Yes ☐ No
If yes, do all employees know the details and operation of the plan?	☐ Yes ☐ No
What is the date of the most recent "trial run" of your disaster plan?	
Location of document(s)?	
Is there also a continuation/disaster plan for your **digital data**?	☐ Yes ☐ No
If yes, do all employees know the details and operation of the plan?	☐ Yes ☐ No
What is the date of the most recent "trial run" of your disaster plan?	
Location of document(s)?	

IF A SOLE PROPRIETORSHIP	
You are the **only** owner, correct?	☐ Yes ☐ No If no, this cannot be a sole proprietorship!
Have you filed for a Fictitious Name?	☐ Yes ☐ No
List the name(s) and phone number(s) of the first person(s) to be contacted if something happens?	
Name of person who has the **legal, written authority** to operate the business for you?	
Phone number:	
Email address:	
Location of document(s) granting this power (e.g. Power of Attorney):	

IF A PARTNERSHIP (BUT NOT LLC)		
Name of general partner(s)	Name of General Partner(s): ____________________ ____________________ ____________________	Ownership Percentage: ______% ______% ______%
Name of limited partner(s)	Name of Limited Partner(s): ____________________ ____________________ ____________________	Ownership Percentage: ______% ______% ______%
Have you filed for a Fictitious Name	☐ Yes ☐ No	
List the name(s) and phone number(s) of the first person(s) to be contacted if something happens?		
Name of person who has the **legal, written authority** to operate the business for you?		
Phone number:		
Email address:		
Location of document(s) granting this power (e.g. Power of Attorney):		
Is there a written partnership agreement?	☐ Yes ☐ No	
If yes, location of agreement?		

Additional notes:

____

____

____

IF A CORPORATION	
Location of Corporate minute book, records, and seal, if any?	
Is this a **Subchapter S** corporation?	☐ Yes ☐ No
Date of incorporation	
State of incorporation	
List other states in which business is registered as a foreign corporation:	
Total shares authorized:	
Total shares issued:	
Shareholder ownership (how is the business owned/titled, i.e. 100 shares or 100% ownership?)	# of Shares How owned and by whom? __________ in my name only (or in my Trust, if any) __________ in my spouse's name only (or in spouse's Trust, if any) __________ jointly between my spouse and me __________ Name: ______________________ __________ Name: ______________________ __________ Name: ______________________ __________ Name: ______________________
Are there any preferred shares?	
If yes, provide details:	
Is there a shareholder agreement between the shareholders?	☐ Yes ☐ No
If yes, location of document:	

OFFICERS AND DIRECTORS

President

Name of **President**:	
Address:	
City, state, and zip code:	
Phone number:	
Number of shares owned:	
Is this person also a director?	☐ Yes ☐ No

Vice-President

Name of **Vice-President**:	
Address:	
City, state, and zip code:	
Phone number:	
Number of shares owned:	
Is this person also a director?	☐ Yes ☐ No

Secretary

Name of **Secretary**:	
Address:	
City, state, and zip code:	
Phone number:	
Number of shares owned:	
Is this person also a director?	☐ Yes ☐ No

Treasurer

Name of **Treasurer**:	
Address:	
City, state, and zip code:	
Phone number:	
Number of shares owned:	
Is this person also a director?	☐ Yes ☐ No

Registered Agent

Name of **Registered Agent**:	
Address:	
City, state, and zip code:	
Phone number:	

Additional Director, if any

Name of additional Director:	
Address:	
City, state, and zip code:	
Phone number:	
Number of shares owned:	

Additional Director, if any

Name of additional Director:	
Address:	
City, state, and zip code:	
Phone number:	
Number of shares owned:	

Additional Director, if any

Name of additional Director:	
Address:	
City, state, and zip code:	
Phone number:	
Number of shares owned:	

IF AN LLC (LIMITED LIABILITY COMPANY)	
Who has the legal, written authority to continue operating the business?	
Location of LLC minute book, records, and seal, if any?	
Have you made a **Subchapter S** election?	☐ Yes ☐ No
Is there a written operating and/or membership agreement?	☐ Yes ☐ No
If yes, location of document:	
How is your share of LLC owned/titled?	# of Units or Percentage owned by: ☐ ________ or ________% in my name only ☐ ________ or ________% in the name of my Revocable Living Trust ☐ ________ or ________% in my spouse's name only ☐ ________ or ________% jointly between my spouse and me
Are you a Member or Managing Member?	☐ Member ☐ Managing Member

Names of Other Managers & Ownership

Name(s):	# of Units or Percentage
1. ____________________	☐ ________ or ________% ☐ Member ☐ Managing Member
2. ____________________	☐ ________ or ________% ☐ Member ☐ Managing Member
3. ____________________	☐ ________ or ________% ☐ Member ☐ Managing Member
4. ____________________	☐ ________ or ________% ☐ Member ☐ Managing Member
5. ____________________	☐ ________ or ________% ☐ Member ☐ Managing Member

Additional notes:

____

____

____

____

CATEGORIES OF TOPICS ***(Add any additional categories that may apply to your own business)***	CREATE A BINDER OR FILE WITH THE FOLLOWING CATEGORIES: *For each of the following items in each category, provide as many details as possible, including the name, location, and contact information, location of documents, and anything else someone will need to know to continue your business operating.*
Organization/operation documents:	Articles of Incorporation; Operating Agreements; Fictitious name filings, corporate minute book; notes; and resolutions of meetings of shareholders, directors, and/or members, etc.
Ownership Information:	Who are the owners, what is the percentage ownership owned by each, shareholder agreement, buy-sell agreements, etc.
Employee(s), Employment contracts:	Roster of all employees and contact information; employment applications; immigration department form (I-9); employee personnel file; employee earnings records; "COBRA" notifications; employment or independent contractor agreements; non-disclosure/confidentiality agreements; staffing agency; employee handbook, etc.; personnel manual; company policies and procedures; performance evaluations; disciplinary actions; promotions; termination, etc. Include outsourced human resources information.
Employee benefits:	Pension; 401(k); life insurance; medical insurance; disability insurance; deferred compensation plan; Employee Stock Option Plan (ESOP); etc.
Governmental Employment rules:	Unemployment compensation; worker's compensation; proof of citizenship, etc.
Client or customer list:	Names and contact information for your best clientele
Service & maintenance agreements:	Contracts and contact information about who services your equipment, maintains your property, etc.
Technology, internet, IT, digital, media:	All information about electronic and digital equipment; Internet; media; communications; digital storage (cloud, hard drive, external, etc.)
Vendors, providers, and suppliers:	From whom do you buy your inventory, equipment? Do you have any special arrangements with any of them (e.g. quantity discount, special return or consignment arrangements, etc.)?
Rental/lease Agreements:	Leases of property, leased vehicles, equipment, etc. See detailed rental section below.
Utilities:	Electric, Gas, Phone, Cable, Internet, WiFi, network, garbage/scavenger service, etc.
Warranties and manuals:	Warranties and manuals for all equipment owned and/or leased

Additional notes:

____

____

____

____

LEASES, LEASED ASSETS, AND LEASED EMPLOYEES

Leased Business Location

Do you rent your **business location**?	☐ Yes ☐ No
Details about each rented location:	
Account number:	
If yes, provide name of lessor:	
Address:	
City, state, and zip code:	
Website:	www.
Phone number:	
Email address:	
Term of lease:	Start: ______________ End: ______________
Rent:	$__________ per ☐ Month ☐ Year ☐ Other: ______________
Other details of importance:	
Location of documents:	

Leased Vehicles

Do you lease your vehicles?	☐ Yes ☐ No
Describe each leased vehicle:	
Account number:	
If yes, provide name of lessor:	
Address:	
City, state, and zip code:	
Website:	www.
Phone number:	
Email address:	
Term of lease:	Start: ______________ End: ______________
Rent:	$__________ per ☐ Month ☐ Year ☐ Other: ______________
Other details of importance:	
Location of documents:	

Leased Equipment

Do you lease equipment?	☐ Yes ☐ No
Describe each leased item:	
Account number:	
If yes, provide name of lessor:	
Address:	
City, state, and zip code:	
Website:	www.
Phone number:	
Email address:	

Term of lease:	Start: ______________________ End: ______________________
Rent:	$__________ per ☐ Month ☐ Year ☐ Other: __________________
Other details of importance:	
Location of documents:	

Leased Employees

Do you lease your employees?	☐ Yes ☐ No
Account number:	
If yes, name of leasing agent:	
Leasing agent phone number:	
Leasing agent phone number:	
Leasing agent email address:	
Name of leasing agency:	
If yes, provide name of lessor:	
Address:	
City, state, and zip code:	
Website:	www.
Other details of importance:	
Location of documents:	

Any other Leased Items

Do you lease anything else?	☐ Yes ☐ No
Describe each leased item:	
Account number:	
If yes, provide name of lessor:	
Address:	
City, state, and zip code:	
Website:	www.
Phone number:	
Email address:	
Term of lease:	Start: ______________________ End: ______________________
Rent:	$__________ per ☐ Month ☐ Year ☐ Other: __________________
Other details of importance:	
Location of documents:	

Additional notes:

____

____

____

____

BUSINESS ASSETS	Remember to include location of documents, names and contact information, account numbers, serial numbers, and website information, where applicable. For templates to use, see appropriate sections elsewhere in this questionnaire (such as real estate, vehicles, etc.).
Real estate:	Details and copies of documents regarding real estate owned in the name of the business (loan info is in the next section); capital improvements to the property; major permanent fixtures (e.g. HVAC, lighting, plumbing, etc.), etc.
Vehicles:	Truck, autos, tractors, airplanes, boats, and anything else used for moving people and things from one place to another.
Furnishings & equipment:	Furniture, copier, file cabinets, typewriters, computers, calculators, office equipment, telecommunications. **See equipment section below.**
Appliances:	Refrigeration, stoves, cold storage, microwave, etc.
Electronics and digital hardware:	Computers, television, telephone and communications, fax machine, servers, routers, digital storage, cellular phones, physical intranet, television, cable, etc.
Inventory:	Details on each item; the vendors (and contact information) from whom you buy each item; websites; catalog numbers; approximate pricing and frequency of purchase, etc.
Bank accounts:	Bank checking; savings; money market, etc. Remember to include the names of authorized signers; online access info; and auto payments coming in and going out of the accounts.
Investment accounts:	If the business makes other investments, list all pertinent details here.
Other types of investments:	Artwork, statuary, and creative assets, precious metals, etc.
Retirement plans:	Types, company, and contact persons who is entitled to participate and the amounts they may contribute?
Ownership of other businesses	Details of ownerships.
Debts or obligations owed to your company from other companies, individuals, and government.	Include whether the obligation is in writing, and whether there is security/collateral, and contact information for debtor.
Intellectual property rights:	Patents, copyrights, trademarks, logos, licensing agreements, digital code owned by business, etc.
Digital assets:	Website (who owns, expiration, management, etc.); blogs; domain names; online accounts; business social media accounts; email, servers; intranet; VoIP; phone numbers; digital storage (internal, external, online, cloud-based); online store owned; assets sold through your online store or through eBay, Amazon, etc.; mailing lists; client information, etc.

Additional notes:

____

____

____

____

BUSINESS LIABILITIES, DEBTS, & OTHER OBLIGATIONS	Provide names, address, phone numbers, website info, etc. for all companies to whom your business is indebted, or to whom there is a contractual obligation owed. Include copies of loan documents, if any. Copy and use the debt templates used in other sections of this questionnaire for your business debts.
Mortgages on business real estate:	
Secured loans and lines of credit:	
Other unsecured loans and unsecured lines of credit:	
Credit cards:	
Personal loans (including made from you to the business):	
Tax liabilities:	
Unfunded pension or other benefits:	
Does the business owe you money?	☐ Yes ☐ No
If yes, provide details:	
Do you owe money to the business?	☐ Yes ☐ No
If yes, provide details:	
Other contractual obligations:	
Are you up to date in paying **ALL** your business's financial obligations?	☐ Yes ☐ No
If no, provide details on any delinquencies and steps being taken to come current.	
Have you guaranteed, or are you personally obligated, for any of the business debts?	
If yes, provide details:	

Additional notes:

____

____

____

____

INSURANCE	For detailed insurance templates to follow, see the appropriate sections in other sections of this questionnaire.
Asset-related insurance:	Property insurance; premises liability; business equipment; commercial auto/fleet; commercial liability; commercial property; comprehensive; umbrella
Business-related insurance:	Business continuation/interruption; rental; business equipment, business overhead; business liability; buy-sell agreement funding (life and/or disability), etc.
Employment related insurance:	Worker's compensation, key-employee life, group term, split dollar
Health-related insurance:	Life, disability, health, long-term-care
Debt-related insurance:	Insurance that will pay off debts in event of death or disability of owner or other person
Surety/bonding-related:	Bonds to secure and guarantee work
Profession-related insurance:	Errors and omissions, professional liability, malpractice
Other types of insurance:	Cyber liability (digital theft, hacking, ransomware, etc.); inland marine, commercial umbrella; commercial crime; labor reimbursement; goods in transit; product liability
Business insurance **inventory video:**	Just as we recommended for your home possessions for insurance verification purposes, it would be wise to periodically make a video inventory of all furnishings, equipment, inventory, storage, remote locations, and contents of any office, storeroom, showroom, lockers, closets, vehicles, etc. in case of a disaster requiring you to file an insurance claim for items that were lost or destroyed. Keep this in a fireproof and waterproof place far away from the work location.

Additional notes:

____

____

____

____

FINANCIAL AND ACCOUNTING	
Financial Statements:	Balance sheet; income statement; statement of retained earnings or equity; cash flow statement and projections; income and expense budget; financial and operational policies; accounting system (including software), etc.
Journals:	Sales journal; cash receipts journal; check register; accounts payable journal; payroll journal; general journal
General ledger:	Assets, liabilities, equity, income, expense, accounts receivable, accounts payable, plant and equipment
Federal, State, County, & Local Taxes:	Income taxes returns and records; employment/payroll taxes (form 941, 940, W4, W3, W2); tax withholding; sales and use taxes; business taxes; personal property taxes, etc.; who prepares the returns; where are they filed; where are they stored; do you file monthly-quarterly-annually, in paper or electronically
Receipts:	All receipts and records regarding expenses for taxes, equipment, etc.
Other:	

LEGAL MATTERS	
Contractual obligations:	All forms of written agreements, etc.
Governmental:	Annual business filings with state and local governments, zoning, ordinances.
Licenses & Registrations:	Professional; occupational; specialty business licenses applicable to your particular business (e.g. liquor, food service, surveyor, health department).
Litigation & Disputes:	Actual and potential matters in dispute. Specify whether business is plaintiff (seeking money, damages, or other relief), or defendant (defending from someone else seeking money, damages, or other relief). Include collection status on judgments for or against business. Include administrative matters (e.g. worker's compensation, unemployment compensation); zoning matters; tax litigation; employment disputes; and matters on appeal.
Other:	

Additional notes:

____

____

____

____

Website Info

Who owns your **website** domain?	
Expiration/renewal date of domain?	
Website address to Admin access:	
Username:	
Password:	
Who manages your domain?	
Name of company:	
Contact person:	
Telephone number:	
Email address:	

Social Media and other Advertising and Marketing

What forms of **marketing** do you use to promote your business?	☐ Television ☐ Radio ☐ Direct Mail ☐ email ☐ Newspaper ☐ Magazine ☐ Specialty (specify): ____________ ☐ Social Media ☐ Website ☐ Digital (specify): ____________ ☐ Conventions ☐ Chambers of Commerce ☐ Networking ☐ Other: ____________
For <u>**each**</u> of the marketing methods listed above, provide these details:	
Name of person/company in charge:	
Contact Person, if any:	
Phone number:	
Email Address:	
Website:	www.
Username:	
Password:	
What do they do for you?	
Cost of their service?	
Key contract terms:	
Location of contract, if any:	
Other details about this marketing:	
Your marketing advisor:	
Your advertising advisor:	
Your social media advisor:	

Additional notes:

____

____

____

____

MISCELLANEOUS CATEGORIES	For detailed templates to follow, see the appropriate sections in other sections of this questionnaire.
Marketing:	Sales events; print advertising; digital marketing; social media, website; networking, etc.
Forms, stationery, and supplies:	Stationery and envelopes; business cards; filing supplies/system; sales invoices; purchase orders; checks, etc.
Memberships:	Associations, unions, societies, professional organizations.
Security:	Names, contact information, account numbers, etc. for the companies who provide security for your buildings, equipment, website, digital assets, employees, confidential information, etc. Discuss any security concerns you have.
Passwords, security codes, etc.:	Provide a list (where someone knows to find it) of all security matters, such as passwords to websites for company, vendors, important clients, etc.; security code for entry into a building; a list of people who have keys to premises, etc. If there is an office safe or safe deposit box, where is it; who has access to it; and who has key (if any), or knows the combination to a lock (if any)? Be sure to have an always-updated list of computer access codes used by ALL employees on ALL devices that they use.
Charitable:	Any funding provided with charitable or social causes.
Trusted employees:	Which employees can be trusted with important, confidential information?
Hiding places:	List them here (for the copy to be kept securely locked away).
Pending negotiations/contracts:	Are you currently in negotiations with another party regarding your business (e.g. purchase/sale/merger of business, assets, inventory, etc.)
Auto pay / Auto renewal:	Do you have payments sent to others **automatically** from your business checking account, or charges being automatically charged to your business credit card or line of credit? Provide details on each payment or charge, and provide instructions on who needs to be contacted in order to stop the automatic payments and charges from continuing. If there are any of these payments or charges that should **NOT** be stopped (e.g. mandatory obligations such as rent, insurance, etc.), be sure to identify them.
Deadbeats and habitual late-payers:	Do you have particular customers who owe you money, or are habitually late in paying? Are any collection actions being taken?
Other miscellaneous categories:	
Other miscellaneous categories:	

BUSINESS ADVISORS

Business Law Firm

Business Law Firm Name:	
Name of company:	
Address:	
City, state, and zip code:	
Name of contact person:	
Phone number:	
Email Address:	
Website:	www.
Other information of importance:	
Location of records regarding firm:	

CPA/Accounting Firm

Business CPA/Accounting Firm:	
Name of company:	
Address:	
City, state, and zip code:	
Name of contact person:	
Phone number:	
Email Address:	
Website:	www.
Other information of importance:	
Location of records regarding firm:	

Business Insurance Agency

Business Insurance Agency Name:	
Name of company:	
Address:	
City, state, and zip code:	
Name of contact person:	
Phone number:	
Email Address:	
Website:	www.
Other information of importance:	
Location of records regarding firm:	

Technology/IT Firm

Technology/IT Firm Name:	
Name of company:	
Address:	
City, state, and zip code:	
Name of contact person:	
Phone number:	
Email Address:	
Website:	www.
Other information of importance:	
Location of records regarding firm:	

Bank/Lender

Bank/Lender Name:	
Name of company:	
Address:	
City, state, and zip code:	
Name of contact person:	
Phone number:	
Email Address:	
Website:	www.
Other information of importance:	
Location of records regarding firm:	

Marketing/Advertising Firm

Marketing/Advertising Firm Name:	
Name of company:	
Address:	
City, state, and zip code:	
Name of contact person:	
Phone number:	
Email Address:	
Website:	www.
Other information of importance:	
Location of records regarding firm:	

Human Resources (HR) Firm)

Human Resources (HR) Firm Name:	
Name of company:	
Address:	
City, state, and zip code:	
Name of contact person:	
Phone number:	
Email Address:	
Website:	www.
Other information of importance:	
Location of records regarding firm:	

Social Media Firm

Social Media Firm Name:	
Name of company:	
Address:	
City, state, and zip code:	
Name of contact person:	
Phone number:	
Email Address:	
Website:	www.
Other information of importance:	
Location of records regarding firm:	

Security Firm

Security Firm Name:	
Name of company:	
Address:	
City, state, and zip code:	
Name of contact person:	
Phone number:	
Email Address:	
Website:	www.
Other information of importance:	
Location of records regarding firm:	

Other Business Advisor

Other: ______________________	
Name of company:	
Address:	
City, state, and zip code:	
Name of contact person:	
Phone number:	
Email Address:	
Website:	www.
Other information of importance:	
Location of records regarding firm:	

Other Business Advisor

Other: ______________________	
Name of company:	
Address:	
City, state, and zip code:	
Name of contact person:	
Phone number:	
Email Address:	
Website:	www.
Other information of importance:	
Location of records regarding firm:	

Other Business Advisor

Other: ______________________	
Name of company:	
Address:	
City, state, and zip code:	
Name of contact person:	
Phone number:	
Email Address:	
Website:	www.
Other information of importance:	
Location of records regarding firm:	

Additional notes:

____

____

____

____

§7-C: My Vehicles

*Provide this information for **every** automobile, Motorcycle, RV, Boat, Airplane, Snowmobile, Jet Ski, Mobile Home, and other motorized vehicle you own. If more than two vehicles, make additional copies of these pages.*

Vehicle #1 Description:

____

Provide short description of this vehicle (Year, Manufacturer, Model/Body Style & Color)

Vehicle Basics

Type of Vehicle:	☐ Automobile ☐ Van ☐ SUV ☐ Motorcycle ☐ Golf Cart ☐ Boat ☐ Snowmobile ☐ Mobile Home ☐ Recreational Vehicle ☐ Jet Ski ☐ Airplane ☐ Other (specify): ________________
Vehicle Identification Number (VIN):	
License plate number:	
City sticker number, if any:	
Where are spare keys located?	

Lease Information (if applicable)

Is this vehicle **leased**?	☐ Yes ☐ No
Lease contract or account number:	
Address of leasing company:	
City, state, and zip code:	
Phone number:	
Website address:	www.
Username:	
Password:	
Terms of lease:	$__________ per month for __________(#) of months.
Amount of security deposit, if any:	$
Term of lease:	Start date: ______________ End date: ______________
Name of co-signer or guarantor of the lease, if any:	
Location of documents:	

Ownership Information (if applicable)

Is this vehicle **owned?**	☐ Yes ☐ No
If yes, title to this vehicle is?	☐ In my name only ☐ Jointly owned with (name): ________________ ☐ In the name of my business (specify): ________________ ☐ Other: ________________
Location of Title Documents:	
Did you buy an extended warranty?	☐ Yes ☐ No
If yes, name of warranty company:	
Warranty contract number:	
Phone number:	
Website:	www.
When does warranty expire:	Ending date: ______________ or # of miles: ______________

Other details of importance:	
Location of warranty documents:	

Vehicle Loan Information

Do you have a loan on this vehicle?	☐ Yes ☐ No, it is paid-in-full
If yes, loan contract number:	
Name of loan company:	
Address of lender:	
City, state, and zip code:	
Phone number:	
Website address:	www.
Username:	
Password:	
Terms of loan:	$_________ per month for ________(#) of months.
Interest rate:	__________%
Name of cosigner or guarantor of your vehicle loan, if any?	
Contact Information:	
Do you have **credit insurance** to pay off this loan upon your death?	☐ Yes ☐ No
Location of documents:	
Where do you store this vehicle?	e.g. If **boat**: dry-dock; marina; boat slip info; If **airplane**, airport hanger info

Vehicle Insurance Information

Do you have insurance on vehicle?	☐ Yes ☐ No
If yes, name(s) of insured driver(s):	
Policy Number:	______________________ Insurance coverage amount: $____________
Additional coverage and riders:	☐ Uninsured Motorist ☐ Under-Insured Motorist Amount: $_______ ☐ Other: ____
Amount of Premium	$______________ Paid: ☐ Annually ☐ Quarterly ☐ Monthly
Name of insurance company:	
Address of insurance company:	
Telephone number of company:	
Website address:	
Name of insurance agent:	
Name of insurance agency:	
Address of insurance agency:	
Phone number of insurance agent:	
Email address:	

My Vehicles

*Provide this information for **every** automobile, Motorcycle, RV, Boat, Airplane, Snowmobile, Jet Ski, Mobile Home, and other motorized vehicle you own. If more than two vehicles, make additional copies of these pages.*

Vehicle #2 Description:

____

Provide short description of this vehicle (Year, Manufacturer, Model/Body Style & Color)

Vehicle Basics

Type of Vehicle:	☐ Automobile ☐ Van ☐ SUV ☐ Motorcycle ☐ Golf Cart ☐ Boat ☐ Snowmobile ☐ Mobile Home ☐ Recreational Vehicle ☐ Jet Ski ☐ Airplane ☐ Other (specify): ____________________
Vehicle Identification Number (VIN):	
License plate number:	
City sticker number, if any:	
Where are spare keys located?	

Lease Information (if applicable)

Is this vehicle **leased**?	☐ Yes ☐ No
Lease contract or account number:	
Address of leasing company:	
City, state, and zip code:	
Phone number:	
Website address:	www.
Username:	
Password:	
Terms of lease:	$__________ per month for __________(#) of months.
Amount of security deposit, if any:	$
Term of lease:	Start date: ______________ End date: ______________
Name of co-signer or guarantor of the lease, if any:	
Location of documents:	

Ownership Information (if applicable)

Is this vehicle **owned?**	☐ Yes ☐ No
If yes, title to this vehicle is?	☐ In my name only ☐ Jointly owned with (name): ____________________ ☐ In the name of my business (specify): ____________________ ☐ Other: ____________________
Location of Title Documents:	
Did you buy an extended warranty?	☐ Yes ☐ No
If yes, name of warranty company:	
Warranty contract number:	
Phone number:	
Website:	www.
When does warranty expire:	Ending date: ______________ or # of miles: __________

Other details of importance:	
Location of warranty documents:	

Vehicle Loan Information

Do you have a loan on this vehicle?	☐ Yes ☐ No, it is paid-in-full
If yes, loan contract number:	
Name of loan company:	
Address of lender:	
City, state, and zip code:	
Phone number:	
Website address:	www.
Username:	
Password:	
Terms of loan:	$__________ per month for ________(#) of months.
Interest rate:	__________%
Name of cosigner or guarantor of your vehicle loan, if any?	
Contact Information:	
Do you have **credit insurance** to pay-off this loan upon your death?	☐ Yes ☐ No
Location of documents:	
Where do you store this vehicle (e.g. If **boat**: dry-dock; marina; boat slip info. If **airplane**, airport hangar info)	

Vehicle Insurance Information

Do you have insurance on vehicle?	☐ Yes ☐ No
If yes, name(s) of insured driver(s):	
Policy Number:	______________________ Insurance coverage amount: $_____________
Additional coverage and riders:	☐ Uninsured Motorist ☐ Under-Insured Motorist Amount: $_______ ☐ Other: ____
Amount of Premium	$______________ Paid: ☐ Annually ☐ Quarterly ☐ Monthly
Name of insurance company:	
Address of insurance company:	
Telephone number of company:	
Website address:	
Name of insurance agent:	
Name of insurance agency:	
Address of insurance agency:	
Phone number of insurance agent:	
Email address:	

§7-D: Equipment & Machinery

*Provide this information for **every** sizeable or expensive piece of equipment you own. If it is owned by a business you own, list it in the business assets section, not here. Make additional copies of this page, as needed*

Equipment Type:

____

Provide short description of this equipment or machinery (Year, Manufacturer, Model)

Type of Equipment:	
Brand Name:	
Model Number, if any:	
Serial Number, if any:	
Do you own or lease this item?	☐ Own ☐ Lease
If **leased**, term of lease:	Start date: ____________________ End date: ___________________
Rental amount:	$_____________ per month for ___________(#) of months.
Lessor or leasing company name:	
Address:	
City, state, and zip code:	
Website:	www.
Name of contact person, if any:	
Phone number & email address:	
If **owned**, purchase price & date:	$_________________ Date: ________________________
How is title held to this equipment?	☐ Individually owned by (name): ______________________________ ☐ Owned jointly with: ______________________________________ ☐ Owned by other: ____
Is there a loan on this equipment?	☐ Yes ☐ No
If yes, name of lender:	
Contact Information:	
Is there insurance on this equipment?	☐ Yes ☐ No
If yes, name of insurance company:	
Contact Information:	
Is there a maintenance contract?	☐ Yes ☐ No
If yes, maintenance company name:	
Contact Information:	
Provide details about this equipment:	
Location of documents:	

Additional notes:

____

____

____

§7-D: Equipment & Machinery

*Provide this information for **every** sizeable or expensive piece of equipment you own. If it is owned by a business you own, list it there, not here. Make additional copies of this page, as needed*

Equipment Type:

____

Provide short description of this equipment or machinery (Year, Manufacturer, Model)

Type of Equipment:	
Brand Name:	
Model Number, if any:	
Serial Number, if any:	
Do you own or lease this item?	☐ Own ☐ Lease
If **leased**, term of lease:	Start date: ______________ End date: ______________
Rental amount:	$__________ per month for ________(#) of months.
Lessor or leasing company name:	
Address:	
City, state, and zip code:	
Website:	www.
Name of contact person, if any:	
Phone number and email address:	
If **owned**, purchase price and date:	$____________ Date: ________________
How is title held to this equipment?	☐ Individually owned by (name): ________________ ☐ Owned jointly with: ____________________ ☐ Owned by other: ______________________
Is there a loan on this equipment?	☐ Yes ☐ No
If yes, name of lender:	
Contact Information:	
Is there insurance on this equipment?	☐ Yes ☐ No
If yes, name of insurance company:	
Contact Information:	
Is there a maintenance contract?	☐ Yes ☐ No
If yes, maintenance company name:	
Contact Information:	
Provide details about this equipment:	
Location of documents:	

Additional notes:

____

____

____

§7-E: Bank Accounts - Cash Assets & Equivalents

*Use this section to list your **Cash assets** and equivalents, including bank and credit union savings accounts, money market accounts, checking accounts, certificates of deposit, and other liquid asset accounts.*

Don't forget online bank accounts, if any.

Use the other sections of this questionnaire designed for investment accounts, retirement accounts, etc.

Complete one page for each type of account. Make photocopies for each additional account, as needed.

***Important Note:** In many states, if you die owning a bank account **in your own name only**, without a designated beneficiary, such an account will be required to go through probate. While some states may allow your beneficiaries to use a small estate affidavit to gain access to such accounts, other states (such as Florida) do not.*

Therefore, I recommend that my clients consider naming one or more beneficiaries and contingent beneficiaries on their accounts, so that, in the event or your death, probate will not be required on the account. Also discuss this with your estate-planning attorney, as you will want to have sufficient liquid assets on hand to pay your funeral, debts, and last expenses, and you don't want to accidentally override other aspects of the estate plan your attorney may have designed for you, such as through use of a Revocable Living Trust.

*In addition, be sure to confirm that, if you become incapacitated, your bank will honor your **durable power of attorney**. Comply with their requirements to make sure they will honor your attorney-in-fact's instructions, and make sure they are provided with a copy of it.*

Even with a durable power of attorney, some banks require their own forms to be used to enable someone else to sign checks on your account. Be careful, as they may require you to make the other a person a co-owner on the account, which may create other potential problems (see the "Assets" section elsewhere in this book).

So, be sure to double check with your banker to find out what they require to enable someone to sign checks on your behalf, should you become incapacitated. And be sure to discuss this with your estate-planning attorney, too.

Do you have one or more accounts at a bank or credit union?	☐ Yes ☐ No If yes, complete the **bank account** section. **(NOTE: Use the Retirement Account section for bank IRA accounts.)**
Do you have investment accounts?	☐ Yes ☐ No If yes, complete the **investment account** section.
Do you have retirement accounts?	☐ Yes ☐ No If yes, complete the **retirement account** section.

Bank Account Type: ☐ **Checking** ☐ **Savings** ☐ **Money Market** ☐ **Certificate of Deposit**

Bank Name: ______________________________

Account Number: ______________________________

Financial Institution

Name of financial institution:	
Address:	
City, state, and zip code:	
Telephone number:	
Website address:	www.
Username:	
Password:	

Account details

Account or CD account number:	
If not a CD, what is typical balance:	$
If a CD, amount of investment:	$
Interest rate:	____________%
Date of investment:	
Maturity/renewal date:	
Name(s) of owner(s) of account:	
How is this account owned?	☐ In my name only ☐ In my Trust ☐ Jointly with: ______________
Name of primary beneficiary or beneficiaries, if any:	
Name of contingent beneficiary or beneficiaries, if any:	
Do you use this account for online banking (payment of bills, etc.)?	☐ Yes ☐ No
Does this account receive **automatic deposits** from outside sources?	☐ Yes ☐ No
If yes, from whom?	☐ Employer ☐ Pension ☐ Social Security ☐ Annuity/settlement ☐ Other: ______________________________
Are any of your **bills paid** **automatically** from this account?	☐ Yes ☐ No If yes, see section on **Automatic Payments Section 12-B**
Is anyone else authorized to use the assets in, or sign on this account? If yes, name and phone number:	☐ Yes ☐ No
Location of passbook, check register, statements, and other documents regarding this account	

Additional notes:

____

____

Bank Account Type: ☐ **Checking** ☐ **Savings** ☐ **Money Market** ☐ **Certificate of Deposit**

Bank Name: ______________________________

Account Number: ______________________________

Financial Institution

Name of financial institution:	
Address:	
City, state, and zip code:	
Telephone number:	
Website address:	www.
Username:	
Password:	

Account details

Account or CD account number:	
If not a CD, what is typical balance:	$
If a CD, amount of investment:	$
Interest rate:	____________%
Date of investment:	
Maturity/renewal date:	
Name(s) of owner(s) of account:	
How is this account owned?	☐ In my name only ☐ In my Trust ☐ Jointly with: ____________
Name of primary beneficiary or beneficiaries, if any:	
Name of contingent beneficiary or beneficiaries, if any:	
Do you use this account for online banking (payment of bills, etc.)?	☐ Yes ☐ No
Does this account receive **automatic deposits** from outside sources?	☐ Yes ☐ No
If yes, from whom?	☐ Employer ☐ Pension ☐ Social Security ☐ Annuity/settlement ☐ Other: ______________________
Are any of your **bills paid <u>automatically</u>** from this account?	☐ Yes ☐ No If yes, see section on **Automatic Payments Section 12-B**
Is anyone else authorized to use the assets in, or sign on this account? If yes, name and phone number:	☐ Yes ☐ No
Location of passbook, check register, statements, and other documents regarding this account	

Additional notes:

____

____

Bank Account Type: ☐ **Checking** ☐ **Savings** ☐ **Money Market** ☐ **Certificate of Deposit**

Bank Name: ________________________________

Account Number: ________________________________

Financial Institution

Name of financial institution:	
Address:	
City, state, and zip code:	
Telephone number:	
Website address:	www.
Username:	
Password:	

Account details

Account or CD account number:	
If not a CD, what is typical balance:	$
If a CD, amount of investment:	$
Interest rate:	_____________%
Date of investment:	
Maturity/renewal date:	
Name(s) of owner(s) of account:	
How is this account owned?	☐ In my name only ☐ In my Trust ☐ Jointly with: ________________
Name of primary beneficiary or beneficiaries, if any:	
Name of contingent beneficiary or beneficiaries, if any:	
Do you use this account for online banking (payment of bills, etc.)?	☐ Yes ☐ No
Does this account receive **automatic deposits** from outside sources?	☐ Yes ☐ No
If yes, from whom?	☐ Employer ☐ Pension ☐ Social Security ☐ Annuity/settlement ☐ Other: ________________________________
Are any of your **bills paid automatically** from this account?	☐ Yes ☐ No If yes, see section on **Automatic Payments Section 12-B**
Is anyone else authorized to use the assets in, or sign on this account? If yes, name and phone number:	☐ Yes ☐ No
Location of passbook, check register, statements, and other documents regarding this account	

Additional notes:

____

____

§7-F: Taxable Investments and Investment Accounts – (Not Retirement Accounts)

*Use this section to list your **taxable** investment accounts (stocks, bonds, mutual funds, options, futures, real estate investment Trusts, etc.). There is a different section in this questionnaire for retirement accounts, annuities, etc.*

These will include brokerage accounts, mutual fund accounts, dividend reinvestment (DRIP) accounts, wherever they may be held (e.g. at a full-service brokerage firm; a discount brokerage firm; directly at a mutual fund company; in an individual company's dividend reinvestment plan, etc.) There will be other sections in which to report any annuities and retirement assets, as well as other types of investments.

Complete one page for each type of investment account. Make photocopies for additional accounts, as needed.

If you buy or sell options, futures, use limit orders, stop-loss orders, or use other "hands-on" types of investment strategies, it is important for the representative you name to understand how you use them, how they work, and know how to close out your positions in them to avoid such strategies from potentially hurting your investment portfolio when you aren't there to make the necessary day-to-day decisions regarding their use. Take the time to explain or teach them what they need to do regarding these types of investments.

***Author's Comments:** As in the previous section regarding bank accounts, in many states, if you die owning an investment account **in your own name only**, without a designated beneficiary, such an account will be required to go through probate. While some states may allow your beneficiaries to use a small estate affidavit to gain access to such accounts, other states (such as Florida) do not.*

Therefore, I recommend that my clients consider naming one or more beneficiaries and contingent beneficiaries on their accounts, so that in the event or your death, probate will not be required on the account. Also, discuss this with your estate-planning attorney, as you will want to have sufficient assets on hand to pay your funeral, debts and last expenses, and you don't want to accidentally override other aspects of the estate plan your attorney may have designed for you, such as through use of a Revocable Living Trust.

*In addition, be sure to confirm that, if you become incapacitated, the financial institution will honor your **durable power of attorney**. Comply with their requirements to make sure they will honor your attorney-in-fact's instructions, and make sure they are provided with a copy of it.*

*Even with a durable power of attorney, some investment firms and/or mutual fund companies require their own forms to be used to enable them even to **discuss** the account with someone else as well as to grant them authority to direct the investments in your account.*

*Many investment firms require use of their own **Limited Trading Authorization** form, to enable the person to buy or sell assets in your account (but not withdraw money), or a **Full Trading Authorization** form, if you also want the person to be able to withdraw money from the account on your behalf.*

In a rapidly declining market, having to wait for a court to grant someone authority to control your account can result in substantial losses. Verify in advance, whether the investment firm's own forms will be required in conjunction with, or in place of, the durable power of attorney, and other estate-planning documents, your attorney as prepared for you. This may enable your named representative the ability to sell some or all our investment account assets to reduce those losses, or the ability to take advantage of market opportunities to buy assets after a market sell-off is a useful tool.

So, please be sure to double check with each of your investment companies to find out what they require to enable someone to make decisions on your account on your behalf, should you become incapacitated. And be sure to discuss this with your estate-planning attorney, too.

Types & Locations of Investment Accounts

Before you list your investment accounts, let's list the type of investment accounts you have, or where you keep some of your investments. Some people keep their securities with full service brokerage firms, others in self-directed online accounts. Some prefer individual securities, others prefer mutual funds. Some people keep their securities in their safe deposit box, others in a company dividend reinvestment plans, Computershare, etc.

If you are receiving dividends directly from the company for which you own shares, it may be held at a transfer agent (e.g. Computershare, etc.). It is important to identify ***where*** *these assets are held and* ***how*** *to gain access.*

Where Do You Keep Your Investments?

Do you have one or more investment accounts at a **full-service brokerage firm** (e.g. Morgan Stanley, Merrill Lynch, Edward Jones, etc.)?	☐ Yes ☐ No If yes, complete an **Investment Account sheet** for each account below. (Note: There is a separate section for retirement accounts).
Do you have one or more **self-directed online investment accounts** (e.g. Scottrade, TD Ameritrade, etc.)?	☐ Yes ☐ No If yes, complete an **Investment Account sheet** for each account below. (There is a separate section for retirement accounts).
Do you have accounts at a **mutual fund company**?	☐ Yes ☐ No If yes, complete the Mutual Fund section below.
Do you have individual corporate or municipal bond certificates (at home, office, safe, or safe deposit box?)	☐ Yes ☐ No If yes, where are they located?
Do you have individual stock certificates at your home, office, safe, or safe deposit box)?	☐ Yes ☐ No If yes, where are they located?

Individual Stocks Held at Transfer Agent

Do you hold individual stocks directly at a **transfer agent** for publicly traded companies (e.g. Computershare)?	☐ Yes ☐ No If yes, for each stock, provide details below:
If yes, name of stock:	
Name of transfer agent company:	
Account number:	
Phone number:	
Website:	
Username:	
Password:	
Are dividends reinvested or sent to you?	☐ Reinvested ☐ Sent to me ☐ Sent directly to my checking account ☐ Other: ____________________
Other details of importance:	

Bonds owned through the Federal Reserve

Do you own **government bonds** through the **U.S. Federal Reserve**?	☐ Yes ☐ No
If yes, what is the account number?	
Name of owner(s) of this account	
How is this account owned?	☐ Individually by me ☐ In my Trust ☐ Jointly with: ______________
Primary beneficiary name(s)	
Contingent beneficiary name(s)	
Name of contact person:	
Telephone number:	
Website:	
Username:	
Location of your bonds:	

Mutual Funds Held at Mutual Fund Company

Do you own mutual funds directly at a mutual fund company (e.g. Fidelity, Vanguard, American Funds, etc.)?	☐ Yes ☐ No
Name of Mutual Fund Company:	
Account number:	
Address:	
City, state, and zip code:	
Telephone Number:	
Name(s) of owner(s) of account:	
How is this account owned?	☐ In my name only ☐ In my Trust ☐ Jointly with: ______________
Name of primary beneficiary or beneficiaries, if any:	
Name of contingent beneficiary or beneficiaries, if any:	
Are you on a systematic accumulation plan (monthly payments automatically deducted from checking account)?	
If yes, how much per month?	$
Which checking account is used?	
Where are the statement located?	

Investment Account (Not Including Retirement Accounts)

Financial Institution Name: ______________________________

Account Number: ______________________________

Financial Institution

Name of financial institution:	
Is this a full-service brokerage firm or self-directed online account?	☐ Full Service ☐ Self-directed ☐ Other:
Address:	
City, state, and zip code:	
Telephone Number:	
Website address:	www.
Username:	
Password:	
Other details of importance:	

Financial Advisor

Name of financial advisor, if any:	
Direct telephone number:	
Email address:	
Name and phone of assistant:	
How is your financial advisor compensated (if you use an investment advisor)?	☐ Brokerage (commission-based) ☐ Advisory (fee-based – percentage of assets). Annual fee: __________% ☐ Hourly fee: $__________ per hour ☐ Flat fee: $__________ per month / year / other: ______________
Does your advisor have **discretion** to buy and sell securities without speaking to you first?	☐ Yes ☐ No ☐ Not applicable

Account Basics

Name of owner(s) of this account:	
How is this account owned?	☐ Individually by me ☐ In my Trust ☐ Jointly with: ______________
Primary beneficiary name(s):	
Contingent beneficiary name(s):	
Typical average balance:	$______________ as of ______________________(date)
Who else is authorized to discuss this account with your advisor and direct its investments, if anyone?	
Does this person have legal authority to withdraw money from this account?	☐ Yes ☐ No
What is the source of authority?	☐ Durable Power of Attorney ☐ Trading authorization form (limited or full) ☐ Co-owner of account ☐ Other: ______________________

Distributions from Account

Do you receive income or other distributions from this account?	☐ Yes ☐ No
If yes, what is the source of payments?	☐ Dividends / Income ☐ Money market ☐ Sale of securities in account ☐ Whatever income and dividends are received into the account each month
If yes, how much and how often?	☐ A consistent monthly amount: $____________ per month ☐ Whenever funds are requested by me)
If yes, how do you receive your payments?	☐ Checks are mailed directly to me ☐ Deposited in my bank account ☐ Other: ________________________

Automatic Deposits into Account

Does this account <u>**receive**</u> **automatic deposits** from outside source?	☐ Yes ☐ No
If yes, from whom?	☐ Employer ☐ Pension ☐ Social Security ☐ Annuity/settlement ☐ IRA RMD Distribution ☐ My checking account ☐ Other: ________________________

Investment Strategies

In <u>this</u> account, do you:	
Actively trade (buy / sell) stocks?	☐ Yes ☐ No If yes, provide details:
Use Stop-Loss Orders?	☐ Yes ☐ No If yes, provide details:
Use limit orders?	☐ Yes ☐ No If yes, provide details:
Use margin?	☐ Yes ☐ No If yes, provide details:
Buy or sell options or use option	☐ Yes ☐ No If yes, provide details:
strategies?	☐ Yes ☐ No If yes, provide details:
Do you trade futures?	☐ Yes ☐ No If yes, provide details:
Invest in illiquid assets?	☐ Yes ☐ No If yes, provide details:
If you answered **"Yes"** above, what else should your representative know about your investments in, and investment philosophies about, this account?	See my answers in **My Investment Strategies section 12-G**
Location of investment account statements and documents:	

What is the best investment you have ever made?	
What is the worst investment you have ever made?	
Share other memories or stories about your investments:	

Additional notes:

____

____

Investment Account (Not Including Retirement Accounts)

Financial Institution Name: ____________________

Account Number: ____________________

Financial Institution

Name of financial institution:	
Is this a full-service brokerage firm or self-directed online account?	☐ Full Service ☐ Self-directed ☐ Other:
Address:	
City, state, and zip code:	
Telephone Number:	
Website address:	www.
Username:	
Password:	
Other details of importance:	

Financial Advisor

Name of financial advisor, if any:	
Direct telephone number:	
Email address:	
Name and phone of assistant:	
How is your financial advisor compensated (if you use an investment advisor)?	☐ Brokerage (commission-based) ☐ Advisory (fee-based – percentage of assets). Annual fee: ________% ☐ Hourly fee: $________ per hour ☐ Flat fee: $________ per month / year / other: ____________
Does your advisor have **discretion** to buy and sell securities without speaking to you first?	☐ Yes ☐ No ☐ Not applicable

Account Basics

Name of owner(s) of this account:	
How is this account owned?	☐ Individually by me ☐ In my Trust ☐ Jointly with: ____________
Primary beneficiary name(s):	
Contingent beneficiary name(s):	
Typical average balance:	$____________ as of ____________________(date)
Who else is authorized to discuss this account with your advisor and direct its investments, if anyone?	
Does this person have legal authority to withdraw money from this account?	☐ Yes ☐ No
What is the source of authority?	☐ Durable Power of Attorney ☐ Trading authorization form (limited or full) ☐ Co-owner of account ☐ Other: ____________________

Distributions from Account

Do you receive income or other	

distributions from this account?	☐ Yes ☐ No
If yes, what is the source of payments?	☐ Dividends / Income ☐ Money market ☐ Sale of securities in account ☐ Whatever income & dividends are received into the account each month
If yes, how much and how often?	☐ A consistent monthly amount: $____________ per month ☐ Whenever funds are requested by me)
If yes, how do you receive your payments?	☐ Checks are mailed directly to me ☐ Deposited in my bank account ☐ Other: ______________________________

Automatic Deposits into Account

Does this account **receive automatic deposits** from outside source?	☐ Yes ☐ No
If yes, from whom?	☐ Employer ☐ Pension ☐ Social Security ☐ Annuity/settlement ☐ IRA RMD Distribution ☐ My checking account ☐ Other: ______________________________

Investment Strategies

In this account, do you:	
Actively trade (buy / sell) stocks?	☐ Yes ☐ No If yes, provide details:
Use Stop-Loss Orders?	☐ Yes ☐ No If yes, provide details:
Use limit orders?	☐ Yes ☐ No If yes, provide details:
Use margin?	☐ Yes ☐ No If yes, provide details:
Buy or sell options or use option	☐ Yes ☐ No If yes, provide details:
strategies?	☐ Yes ☐ No If yes, provide details:
Do you trade futures?	☐ Yes ☐ No If yes, provide details:
Invest in illiquid assets?	☐ Yes ☐ No If yes, provide details:
If you answered **"Yes"** above, what else should your representative know about your investments in, and investment philosophies about, this account?	See my answers in **My Investment Strategies section 12-G**
Location of investment account statements and documents:	

What is the best investment you have ever made?	
What is the worst investment you have ever made?	
Share other memories or stories about your investments:	

Additional notes:

____

____

§7-G: Retirement Accounts

List your various retirement plans here, whether they are provided by your employer, or whether you created the plan yourself. Don't forget about plans that may exist at previous places of employment, and old IRA accounts you may have previously created and forgotten about. As with my author's comments in the previous sections about bank and investment accounts, make sure the financial institution that is acting as custodian of your retirement accounts will honor your representative's instructions through a Durable Power of Attorney. If not, complete whatever forms may be required by the financial institution to ensure it follows his or her instructions on your behalf.

There are numerous types of retirement plans, and you may have more than one, so be sure to complete one of these forms for each retirement account. Retirement plans include an IRA, Roth IRA, SEP, Profit Sharing, Money Purchase Plan, 401(k), 403(b), 457 plan, Pension, SIMPLE IRA, and many others.

Retirement Account Basics

Type of retirement plan:	☐ Traditional IRA ☐ Rollover IRA ☐ Roth IRA ☐ SIMPLE IRA ☐ SAR-SEP ☐ Spousal IRA ☐ SEP-IRA ☐ 401(k) ☐ 403(b) ☐ 457 ☐ Pension Plan ☐ Profit-sharing plan ☐ Money purchase plan ☐ Defined contribution ☐ Beneficiary IRA inherited from: ____________________ ☐ Other: ____________________
Is this retirement account from a **previous** employer?	☐ Yes ☐ No
If yes, name of previous employer:	
If no, name of current employer:	
Name of Plan, if any:	
Account Number:	
Approximate value:	$ as of ______________ (date)
Plan Sponsor (Usually employer)	

Financial Institution

Name of financial institution:	
Is this a full-service brokerage firm or self-directed online account?	☐ Full Service ☐ Self-directed ☐ Other: ______________
Address:	
City, state, and zip code:	
Telephone Number:	
Website address:	www.
Username:	
Password:	
Other details of importance:	

Financial Advisor

Name of financial advisor, if any:	
Direct telephone number:	
Email address:	
Name of assistant:	
Phone number of assistant:	
How is your financial advisor compensated (if you use an investment advisor)?	☐ Brokerage (commission-based) ☐ Advisory (fee-based – percentage of assets). Annual fee: ________% ☐ Hourly fee: $__________ per hour ☐ Flat fee: $__________ per month / year / other: ______________
Does your advisor have **discretion** to buy and sell securities without speaking to you first?	☐ Yes ☐ No ☐ Not applicable

Account Basics

Name of owner(s) of this account:	
Primary beneficiary name(s):	
Contingent beneficiary name(s):	
Typical average balance:	$_______________ as of ______________________________(date)
If this is an IRA, what is the amount of **non-deductible contributions**, if any:	$_______________ as of ______________________________(date)
Who else is authorized to discuss this account with your advisor and direct its investments, if anyone?	
Does this person have legal authority to withdraw money from this account?	☐ Yes ☐ No
What is the source of authority?	☐ Durable Power of Attorney ☐ Co-owner of account ☐ Trading authorization form (limited or full) ☐ Other: ______________________________

Required Minimum Distributions (RMD)

If you are 70 ½ or older, have you started taking your Required Minimum Distributions (RMDs) from this retirement account?	☐ Yes ☐ No
If yes, do they get sent to you automatically?	☐ Yes ☐ No
If yes, when do you receive them?	☐ Monthly ☐ Quarterly ☐ Annually in (specify month): __________
How and where do you receive them?	☐ Check mailed to my house ☐ Sent to my bank ☐ Sent to my bank Bank name: ____________________ Account # __________
Do you have taxes withheld?	☐ Yes ☐ No If yes, percentage: ☐ IRS ________% ☐ State ________%

Distributions from Account

Do you receive income or other distributions from this account?	☐ Yes ☐ No
If yes, what is source of payments?	☐ Dividends / Income ☐ Money market ☐ Sale of securities in account ☐ Whatever income & dividends are received into the account each month
If yes, how much and how often?	☐ A consistent monthly amount: $____________ per month ☐ Whenever funds are requested by me).
If yes, how do you receive your payments?	☐ Checks are mailed directly to me ☐ Deposited in my bank account ☐ Other: ______________________________

401(k) Loans, if any

If this is a 401(k) plan (or other retirement plan that allows loans, have you taken a loan?	☐ Yes ☐ No
If yes, how much you borrow?	$
How much is still owed?	$_______________ as of _______________________ (date)

Automatic Deposits into Account

Does this account <u>**receive**</u> **auto deposits** from outside source?	☐ Yes ☐ No
If yes, from whom?	☐ Employer ☐ Pension ☐ Social Security ☐ Annuity/settlement ☐ IRA RMD Distribution ☐ My checking account ☐ Other: ______________________________

Investment Strategies

In <u>this</u> account, do you:	
Actively trade (buy / sell) stocks?	☐ Yes ☐ No If yes, provide details:
Use Stop-Loss Orders?	☐ Yes ☐ No If yes, provide details:
Use limit orders?	☐ Yes ☐ No If yes, provide details:
Use margin?	☐ Yes ☐ No If yes, provide details:
Buy or sell options or use option	☐ Yes ☐ No If yes, provide details:
strategies?	☐ Yes ☐ No If yes, provide details:
Do you trade futures?	☐ Yes ☐ No If yes, provide details:
Invest in illiquid assets?	☐ Yes ☐ No If yes, provide details:
If you answered **"Yes"** above, what else should your representative know about your investments in, and investment philosophies about, this account?	See my answers in **My Investment Strategies section 12-G**.
Location of investment account statements and documents:	

What is the best investment you have ever made?	
What is the worst investment you have ever made?	

§7-H: Life Insurance with Cash Surrender Value

*In this section, list **only** life insurance policies that have a current cash value (e.g. whole life insurance). Include life insurance policies you may own on the life of someone else, if any. Term life insurance policies should be listed in the Insurance section of this questionnaire.*

Policy Basics

Do you have a life insurance policy with a cash surrender value?	☐ Yes ☐ No If no, skip this section
If yes, what is the policy number?	
Face amount of policy:	$
Cash value:	$
Issue date of policy:	
Type of policy	☐ Whole life ☐ Universal life ☐ Variable life ☐ Indexed life ☐ Other: ______
Name of insurance policy owner:	☐ Me ☐ My Trust ☐ Jointly with: ______ ☐ Other: ______
Name of insured person:	☐ Me ☐ Other: ______
Name of beneficiary(ies):	
Contingent beneficiary(ies):	
Is this a fully paid-up policy?	☐ Yes ☐ No If no, when will it be fully paid (if ever)? ______
If no, how much is your premium?	$______ per ☐ Month ☐ Year
How are premiums paid?	☐ By check ☐ Auto bank draft ☐ Other: ______
Is there a loan against this policy	☐ Yes ☐ No If yes, amount of loan: $______
Is this policy intended to fund a business purchase agreement or satisfy a loan or other obligation?	☐ Yes ☐ No
Policy endorsements, if any?	☐ Long-term care ☐ Accelerated death benefit ☐ Premium waiver ☐ Other: ______

Insurance Company & Agent

Name of Insurance Company:	
Address of Insurance Company:	
City, state, and zip code:	
Phone number of company:	
Website address:	
Username:	
Password:	
Name of insurance agent:	
Name of insurance agency:	
Address of insurance agency:	
City, state, and zip code:	
Phone number of insurance agent:	
Location of policy and statements:	

§7-I: Annuities

Include details about all fixed, variable, indexed, and immediate annuities

Annuity Basic Details

Type of annuity:	☐ Immediate ☐ Fixed ☐ Variable ☐ Index ☐ Other: ______________________________
Qualified or non-qualified:	☐ Qualified (funded with pre-tax money. e.g. IRA annuity) ☐ Non-qualified (funded with after-tax money)
Product name:	
Account number:	
Name of owner:	
Name of annuitant (if not owner):	
Name(s) of primary beneficiary or beneficiaries, if any:	
Name(s) of contingent beneficiary or beneficiaries, if any:	
Date of policy:	
Initial investment:	$
Additional investments added:	$
Approximate value of contract:	$______________ as of _________________________ (date)

Name of Insurance Company

Name of Annuity Company:	
Address:	
City, state, and zip code:	
Telephone number:	
Website:	
Username:	
Password:	
Name of agent, if any:	
Agent's company name:	
Address:	
City, state, and zip code:	
Telephone number:	
Email address:	

Miscellaneous Details

Was your initial investment an exchange from another annuity?	☐ Yes ☐ No
If yes, what was the cost basis from the previous annuity (your original investment plus any additions to it)?	$
Are you taking distributions?	☐ Yes ☐ No
If yes, have you **annuitized** the annuity (if you know)?	
Are you taking a periodic income?	
Value of the current death benefit:	$_______________ as of ______________________ (date)
Value of the current living benefit (if any):	$_______________ as of ______________________ (date)
Other special features:	
Location of policy, statements, etc.:	

Additional notes:

____

____

____

____

§7-J: Debts Owed by Others to You (e.g. Loans, Mortgages, and Notes Receivable)

If a person or business owes you money, list all the important details about the debt here.
Prepare a separate page for each debt owed to you.

Information about Debt Owed to You

Does anyone owe you money?	☐ Yes ☐ No
If yes, who owes this debt to you?	
If yes, how much is owed to you?	$
Interest rate, if any?	________%
Is this a personal or business loan?	☐ Personal ☐ Business
Have you filed a lawsuit to collect on this debt?	☐ Yes ☐ No
If yes, provide the state, county, and court division:	
What is the case or file number?	
Title of lawsuit:	
Name of your attorney:	
Name of defendant(s):	
Law Firm:	
Phone number:	
Email address:	
Has a money judgment been entered?	☐ Yes ☐ No
If yes, amount of judgment?	$
Details and story behind the debt:	

Loan details

Loan details (e.g. reason for loan, special provisions, etc.):	
Date of loan:	
Initial amount of loan:	$_____________
Current balance:	$_____________ as of ___________________________________ (date)
Interest rate:	________% ☐ Fixed-rate ☐ Floating ☐ Other: ___________________
Number of payments (or loan term):	_______ Number of: ☐ Months ☐ Years
Frequency of payments:	☐ Monthly ☐ Yearly ☐ In full at end ☐ Other: ___________________
Payment type:	☐ Principal & Interest ☐ Yearly ☐ In full at end ☐ Interest only ☐ Other: ____________
Is there a balloon payment?	☐ Yes ☐ No If yes, when is balloon payment due? ________________
Is debtor current with payments?	☐ Yes ☐ No As of (date): ___________________________________
Is this loan in writing? If yes, location of documents?	☐ Yes ☐ No
Is there collateral securing this loan?	☐ Yes ☐ No
If yes, what is the collateral (e.g. real estate, car, jewelry, etc.)?	

Is this debt to be forgiven upon your death?	☐ Yes ☐ No
Other loan details:	

If a Personal Loan

If personal loan, name of debtor(s):	
Address:	
City, state and zip code:	
Telephone number:	
Email address:	

If a Business Loan

If business loan, name of company:	
Name of contact person:	
Address:	
City, state and zip code:	
Telephone number:	
Email address:	

Co-Signer or Guarantor, if any

Is there a co-signer or guarantor?	☐ Yes ☐ No
If yes, name of co-signer/guarantor:	
Address:	
City, State, Zip:	
Telephone number:	
Email address:	

Is there an interesting story regarding this loan?	

Additional notes:

____

____

____

____

§7-K: Safe Deposit Box

If you keep cash, precious metals (e.g. gold coins), jewelry, or other valuables in the box, you will want to include proof of purchase (More than $10,000 in cash without an explanation as to the source of the money is particularly problematic. Were income taxes ever paid on whatever happened to result in the cash being in the box? Was it obtained legally? If no purchase receipt is available, consider writing (and signing) a letter of explanation as to the source of the cash).

For anything having a financial value, be sure to include the purchase receipt (or other proof of purchase), and a copy of any appraisal.

If you have more than one safe deposit box, make an extra copy of this page and provide the same information for each safe deposit box.

Safe Deposit Box Information

Name of bank:	
Address:	
City, state, zip code:	
Phone number:	
Safe deposit box number:	
Names and phone numbers of all authorized signers:	
Location of safe deposit box key(s):	
Who else has a key?	

LIST THE CONTENTS OF THE SAFE DEPOSIT BOX	Description, estimated purchase price, estimated value. If there an appraisal, where is it?
Special memories and stories regarding the assets in your safe deposit box.	
How did you come to acquire them?	
Are any of the items family heirlooms or other treasures?	

§7-L: Computers, Smartphones, Digital Hardware, Devices & Equipment

*This section is for the physical asset, such as computers, laptops, external hard drives, smartphones, etc. We used to store our important documents and information in a drawer, cabinet, or box. But now, as we store more and more essential data on our computers, it becomes equally essential for those who will need this information to know not only **where** it is stored, but also **how** to access it. Think about how many photographs are stored on your smartphone and computer. So, while this section lists varying types of equipment and storage devices on which the information is located, it is incumbent on you to provide sufficient directions so the digital files can be found and used. This is essential information that you **know** your loved ones and representatives will need or want!*

*Make a copy of this section for **each** digital hardware asset you have.*

Electronic Assets And Equipment

What type of device is this?	☐ Computer ☐ Laptop ☐ Tablet ☐ Smartphone ☐ Thumb drives ☐ External hard drives ☐ Other: ________________
Where is this device located?	☐ Home ☐ Work ☐ Other: ________________
Who is manufacturer (e.g. Dell)?	
What is the model number?	
What is the serial number?	
Name of device, if any:	
How do you log onto this device?	☐ Encryption Code: ________________ ☐ Log-in or Username: ________________ ☐ PIN: ________________ ☐ Fingerprint Sensor: ☐ Left Hand ☐ Right Hand Which finger? ________________ ☐ Optical Scanner ☐ Left eye ☐ Right eye ☐ Other: ________________
Security question, if any:	
Answer to security question:	
Is there a warranty on this device?	☐ Yes ☐ No
If yes, specify with whom:	
Location of warranty documents:	
Do you have a service contract?	☐ Yes ☐ No
If yes, name of service contract company?	
Service company contact name and phone number:	
When does the service contract expire?	
For essential records or files stored on this device, complete the information on the next page.	**See next page**

§7-M: Essential Information Stored on This Device:

*For **every** essential record, identify important folder names, file names, encryption codes & passwords. Provide detailed information describing the information stored, and the names of the folders and files located on this device (e.g. legal documents, tax records, family photos, financial statements, etc.)*

Make additional copies of this page, if needed.

Description of stored information:	
Folder name:	
File name:	
Encryption Code or password, if any:	
Other useful details:	

Description of stored information:	
Folder name:	
File name:	
Encryption Code or password, if any:	
Other useful details:	

Description of stored information:	
Folder name:	
File name:	
Encryption Code or password, if any:	
Other useful details:	

Description of stored information:	
Folder name:	
File name:	
Encryption Code or password, if any:	
Other useful details:	

Description of stored information:	
Folder name:	
File name:	
Encryption Code or password, if any:	
Other useful details:	

§7-N: Digital Assets and Online Accounts

This section includes digital assets such as online-only bank accounts, Bitcoin; online stores (e.g. eBay & PayPal), online sites for music/book archives, photographs and videos, etc.

If you have any of these types of assets or online accounts, be sure to include account numbers, websites, usernames, and passwords, and any other information that can help your representatives identify these assets and gain access to them.

Master Password Program, Application or Database

Do you use a master password program, application, or database?	☐ Yes ☐ No
If yes, name of program or file name:	☐ Program ☐ Application ☐ Database ☐ Written format
Name of program, app, or database:	
Where is it located/how to access?	
Website:	
Username:	
Password:	

Online Bank Accounts

Do you have an online bank account (other than accounts listed in the section about bank accounts)?	☐ Yes ☐ No
If yes, name of bank:	
Account number:	
Approximate value:	$______________ as of ________________________________ (date)
Website:	www.
Username:	
Password:	
Phone number:	
Other useful information and details:	

Digital Currency (e.g. Bitcoin)

Do you have a digital currency account?	☐ Yes ☐ No
If yes, name of company:	
Account number:	
Approximate value:	$______________ as of ________________________________ (date)
Website:	www.
Username:	
Password:	
Phone number:	
Other useful information and details:	
Memories, experiences, and stories to share about this asset:	

Online Business Ownership

Do you have an online business that you own and/or operate?	☐ Yes ☐ No
If yes, name of company:	
Name of domain:	
Account number, if any:	
Approximate value:	$______________ as of ________________________________ (date)
Website:	www.
Username:	
Password:	
Phone number:	
Other useful information and details:	
Memories, experiences, and stories to share about this asset:	

Hosted Website for Others

Do you host websites for others for which you receive revenues?	☐ Yes ☐ No
If yes, name of your company:	
Name of domain(s) hosted:	
Name of client(s):	
Contact information for client(s):	
Website:	www.
Username:	
Password:	
Revenues generated by site:	$______________ per ☐ Month ☐ Year ☐ Other: ______________
Other useful information and details:	
Memories, experiences, and stories to share about this business:	

Domain Name Owned for Sale or License to Others

Do you own website domain names for sale or license to others?	☐ Yes ☐ No
If yes, name of your company:	
Name of domain(s) owned:	
Price for sale of domain name:	
License fee charged for domain:	
Contact information for client(s):	
Website:	www.
Username & password:	
Other useful information and details:	
Memories, experiences, and stories to share about this business:	

Advertising or Referral Revenues

Do you receive advertising or referral revenues through your site?	☐ Yes ☐ No
If yes, name of your company:	
Describe how you receive revenues:	
Name of client(s):	
Contact information for client(s):	
Website:	www.
Username:	
Password:	
Revenues received:	$______________ per ☐ Month ☐ Year ☐ Other: ______________
Other useful information and details:	
Memories, experiences, and stories to share about this business:	

Online Music Account(s)

Do you have an online music account (e.g. iTunes)?	☐ Yes ☐ No
If yes, name of music website:	
Account number:	
Website:	www.
Username:	
Password:	
Phone number:	
Approximate value of account:	$______________ per ☐ Month ☐ Year ☐ Other: ______________
Other useful information and details:	
Memories , experiences, and stories to share about this account:	

Online Book/Movie Account(s)

Do you have any online books/movies account (e.g. Amazon)?	☐ Yes ☐ No
If yes, name of book/movie website:	
Account number:	
Website:	www.
Username:	
Password:	
Phone number:	
Approximate value of account:	$______________ per ☐ Month ☐ Year ☐ Other: ______________
Other useful information and details:	
Memories, experiences, and stories to share about this account:	

Frequent Flyer Mileage Program

Do you participate in a frequent flyer mileage program?	☐ Yes ☐ No
If yes, name of airline:	
Frequent flyer account number:	
Name of credit card company:	
Approximate miles earned:	______________ as of ______________________________ (date)
Website:	www.
Username:	
Password:	
Contact phone number:	
Approximate value of account:	$__________ per ☐ Month ☐ Year ☐ Other: _______________
Other useful information and details:	
Have you used your mileage points to take a memorable trip or vacation, or do something special?	
Memories, experiences, and stories to share about this account:	

Reward or Loyalty Points Program:

Do you participate in a reward or loyalty points program?	☐ Yes ☐ No
If yes, name of bank or store:	
Account number:	
Name of credit card company:	
Approximate points earned:	______________ as of ______________________________ (date)
Website:	www.
Username:	
Password:	
Contact phone number:	
Approximate value of account:	$__________ per ☐ Month ☐ Year ☐ Other: _______________
Other useful information and details:	
Have you used your mileage points to take a memorable trip or vacation, or do something special?	
Memories, experiences, and stories to share about this account:	

Additional notes:

____

____

____

____

§7-O: Other Online Digital Storage, Backup, Entertainment, and Information Sites

Identify other online storage, backup, and information sites at which you store anything saved in a digital format. Complete the detail for every item that applies. Add additional pages as needed:

1. *Email addresses*
2. *Online storage and backup sites for pictures, videos, and documents, such as Google Photos, YouTube, One Drive, Carbonite, Flickr, etc.*
3. *Social networking sites such as Facebook, LinkedIn, YouTube, Twitter*
4. *Personal or business blog site*
5. *Remote digital storage and backup facility or business*
6. *Personal or business website domain that you own*
7. *Tax return and financial storage sites such as TurboTax and Quicken*
8. *Genealogy sites (e.g. Ancestry.com, FamilySearch.org, etc.)*
9. *Password management software, storage & encryption site*
10. *Online gaming site*
11. *Online gambling site*
12. *Other digital sites*

Email accounts (e.g. Gmail, Yahoo, AOL, Verizon, Comcast, etc.)

Email address:		Password:	
Email address:		Password:	
Email address:		Password:	
Email address:		Password:	

Your personal websites, blogs, and copyrighted material

Do you own your own website?	☐ Yes ☐ No
If yes, website domain:	www.
Hosting company:	
Do you have a blog?	☐ Yes ☐ No
Provide details of blog:	
Username & password:	

Here is a short reminder of some common digital or cloud-based websites you may use (check any that apply)

Social Media		Shopping & Payment		Storage	
Facebook:	☐ Yes ☐ No	Amazon:	☐ Yes ☐ No	Box:	☐ Yes ☐ No
Instagram:	☐ Yes ☐ No	PayPal:	☐ Yes ☐ No	Dropbox:	☐ Yes ☐ No
Snapchat:	☐ Yes ☐ No	Bitcoin:	☐ Yes ☐ No	Apple iCloud Drive:	☐ Yes ☐ No
Twitter:	☐ Yes ☐ No	eBay:	☐ Yes ☐ No	Microsoft OneDrive:	☐ Yes ☐ No
Tumblr	☐ Yes ☐ No	Yahoo:	☐ Yes ☐ No	Google Drive:	☐ Yes ☐ No

Music / Books		Streaming Video		Backup	
iTunes:	☐ Yes ☐ No	Netflix:	☐ Yes ☐ No	Carbonite:	☐ Yes ☐ No
Kindle:	☐ Yes ☐ No	Hulu:	☐ Yes ☐ No	Zip Cloud:	☐ Yes ☐ No
Nook:	☐ Yes ☐ No	Amazon Video:	☐ Yes ☐ No	CrashPlan:	☐ Yes ☐ No
Pandora:	☐ Yes ☐ No	DirecTV Now:	☐ Yes ☐ No	SOS Online Backup	☐ Yes ☐ No

Provide the following details for <u>every</u> website, online account, cloud-based storage account, etc.

Type of digital asset or account:	Specify: ___________________________
Domain name:	
Value of digital asset, if any:	$____________ as of ___________________________date
Website address:	www.
Username:	
Password:	
Account number, if any:	
What is stored on this site:	
Other useful information and details:	
Memories and stories to share about this account:	

Type of digital asset or account:	Specify: ___________________________
Domain name:	
Value of digital asset, if any:	$____________ as of ___________________________date
Website address:	www.
Username:	
Password:	
Account number, if any:	
What is stored on this site:	
Other useful information and details:	
Memories and stories to share about this account:	

Type of digital asset or account:	Specify: ___________________________
Domain name:	
Value of digital asset, if any:	$____________ as of ___________________________date
Website address:	www.
Username:	
Password:	
Account number, if any:	
What is stored on this site:	
Other useful information and details:	
Memories and stories to share about this account:	

Type of digital asset or account:	Specify: ____________________
Domain name:	
Value of digital asset, if any:	$__________ as of ____________________date
Website address:	www.
Username:	
Password:	
Account number, if any:	
What is stored on this site:	
Other useful information and details:	
Memories and stories to share about this account:	

Type of digital asset or account:	Specify: ____________________
Domain name:	
Value of digital asset, if any:	$__________ as of ____________________date
Website address:	www.
Username:	
Password:	
Account number, if any:	
What is stored on this site:	
Other useful information and details:	
Memories and stories to share about this account:	

Type of digital asset or account:	Specify: ____________________
Domain name:	
Value of digital asset, if any:	$__________ as of ____________________date
Website address:	www.
Username:	
Password:	
Account number, if any:	
What is stored on this site:	
Other useful information and details:	
Memories and stories to share about this account:	

Type of digital asset or account:	Specify: ___________________________________
Domain name:	
Value of digital asset, if any:	$__________ as of ________________________date
Website address:	www.
Username:	
Password:	
Account number, if any:	
What is stored on this site:	
Other useful information and details:	
Memories and stories to share about this account:	

Type of digital asset or account:	Specify: ___________________________________
Domain name:	
Value of digital asset, if any:	$__________ as of ________________________date
Website address:	www.
Username:	
Password:	
Account number, if any:	
What is stored on this site:	
Other useful information and details:	
Memories and stories to share about this account:	

Type of digital asset or account:	Specify: ___________________________________
Domain name:	
Value of digital asset, if any:	$__________ as of ________________________date
Website address:	www.
Username:	
Password:	
Account number, if any:	
What is stored on this site:	
Other useful information and details:	
Memories and stories to share about this account:	

Type of digital asset or account:	Specify: ______________________________
Domain name:	
Value of digital asset, if any:	$____________ as of ______________________________ date
Website address:	www.
Username:	
Password:	
Account number, if any:	
What is stored on this site:	
Other useful information and details:	
Memories and stories to share about this account:	

Type of digital asset or account:	Specify: ______________________________
Domain name:	
Value of digital asset, if any:	$____________ as of ______________________________ date
Website address:	www.
Username:	
Password:	
Account number, if any:	
What is stored on this site:	
Other useful information and details:	
Memories and stories to share about this account:	

Type of digital asset or account:	Specify: ______________________________
Domain name:	
Value of digital asset, if any:	$____________ as of ______________________________ date
Website address:	www.
Username:	
Password:	
Account number, if any:	
What is stored on this site:	
Other useful information and details:	
Memories and stories to share about this account:	

§7-P: Other Electronic Devices, Appliances, and Equipment

This section is for electronic equipment, appliances, and miscellaneous equipment.

*Make additional copies of this section for **each** electronic asset you have.*

Electronic Equipment - Big Screen Television

Brand name and model number:	
Serial number:	
Approximate value & purchase date:	$
When does warranty expire:	☐ Out of warranty ☐ Date: ____________
Other details regarding this asset:	

Electronic Equipment - Home theater system

Brand name and model number:	
Serial number:	
Approximate value & purchase date:	$
When does warranty expire:	☐ Out of warranty ☐ Date: ____________
Other details regarding this asset:	

Electronic Equipment - DVD player/receiver

Brand name and model number:	
Serial number:	
Approximate value & purchase date:	$
When does warranty expire:	☐ Out of warranty ☐ Date: ____________
Other details regarding this asset:	

Electronic Equipment - Video game player

Brand name and model number:	
Serial number:	
Approximate value & purchase date:	$
When does warranty expire:	☐ Out of warranty ☐ Date: ____________
Other details regarding this asset:	

Electronic Equipment - Big Screen Television

Brand name and model number:	
Serial number:	
Approximate value & purchase date:	$
When does warranty expire:	☐ Out of warranty ☐ Date: ____________
Other details regarding this asset:	

Electronic Equipment - Stereo equipment

Brand name and model number:	
Serial number:	
Approximate value & purchase date:	$
When does warranty expire:	☐ Out of warranty ☐ Date: ______
Other details regarding this asset:	

Electronic Equipment – Other

Brand name and model number:	
Serial number:	
Approximate value & purchase date:	$
When does warranty expire:	☐ Out of warranty ☐ Date: ______
Other details regarding this asset:	

Electronic Equipment – Other

Brand name and model number:	
Serial number:	
Approximate value & purchase date:	$
When does warranty expire:	☐ Out of warranty ☐ Date: ______
Other details regarding this asset:	

Kitchen appliances – Refrigerator/freezer

Brand name and model number:	
Serial number:	
Approximate value & purchase date:	$
When does warranty expire:	☐ Out of warranty ☐ Date: ______
Other details regarding this asset:	

Kitchen appliances – Stove/range

Brand name and model number:	
Serial number:	
Approximate value & purchase date:	$
When does warranty expire:	☐ Out of warranty ☐ Date: ______
Other details regarding this asset:	

Kitchen appliances – Microwave oven

Brand name and model number:	
Serial number:	
Approximate value & purchase date:	$
When does warranty expire:	☐ Out of warranty ☐ Date: ______
Other details regarding this asset:	

Kitchen appliances – Dishwasher

Brand name and model number:	
Serial number:	
Approximate value & purchase date:	$
When does warranty expire:	☐ Out of warranty ☐ Date: ______________________
Other details regarding this asset:	

Kitchen appliances – Stand-alone freezer

Brand name and model number:	
Serial number:	
Approximate value & purchase date:	$
When does warranty expire:	☐ Out of warranty ☐ Date: ______________________
Other details regarding this asset:	

Kitchen appliances – Other

Brand name and model number:	
Serial number:	
Approximate value & purchase date:	$
When does warranty expire:	☐ Out of warranty ☐ Date: ______________________
Other details regarding this asset:	

Kitchen appliances – Other

Brand name and model number:	
Serial number:	
Approximate value & purchase date:	$
When does warranty expire:	☐ Out of warranty ☐ Date: ______________________
Other details regarding this asset:	

Other appliances – Washing machine

Brand name and model number:	
Serial number:	
Approximate value & purchase date:	$
When does warranty expire:	☐ Out of warranty ☐ Date: ______________________
Other details regarding this asset:	

Other appliances - Dryer

Brand name and model number:	
Serial number:	
Approximate value & purchase date:	$
When does warranty expire:	☐ Out of warranty ☐ Date: ______________________
Other details regarding this asset:	

Other equipment – Spa/Hot tub

Brand name and model number:	
Serial number:	
Approximate value & purchase date:	$
When does warranty expire:	☐ Out of warranty ☐ Date: ______________________
Other details regarding this asset:	

Other equipment – Heating system

Brand name and model number:	
Serial number:	
Approximate value & purchase date:	$
When does warranty expire:	☐ Out of warranty ☐ Date: ______________________
Other details regarding this asset:	

Other equipment – Air conditioner

Brand name and model number:	
Serial number:	
Approximate value & purchase date:	$
When does warranty expire:	☐ Out of warranty ☐ Date: ______________________
Other details regarding this asset:	

Other equipment – Water heater

Brand name and model number:	
Serial number:	
Approximate value & purchase date:	$
When does warranty expire:	☐ Out of warranty ☐ Date: ______________________
Other details regarding this asset:	

Other equipment – Water softener

Brand name and model number:	
Serial number:	
Approximate value & purchase date:	$
When does warranty expire:	☐ Out of warranty ☐ Date: ______________________
Other details regarding this asset:	

Other equipment – Grill

Brand name and model number:	
Serial number:	
Approximate value & purchase date:	$
When does warranty expire:	☐ Out of warranty ☐ Date: ______________________
Other details regarding this asset:	

Other equipment – Exercise machinery

Brand name and model number:	
Serial number:	
Approximate value & purchase date:	$
When does warranty expire:	☐ Out of warranty ☐ Date: ______________
Other details regarding this asset:	

Other equipment – Tractor/riding lawnmower

Brand name and model number:	
Serial number:	
Approximate value & purchase date:	$
When does warranty expire:	☐ Out of warranty ☐ Date: ______________
Other details regarding this asset:	

Other equipment – Piano/Organ

Brand name and model number:	
Serial number:	
Approximate value & purchase date:	$
When does warranty expire:	☐ Out of warranty ☐ Date: ______________
Other details regarding this asset:	

Other equipment

Brand name and model number:	
Serial number:	
Approximate value & purchase date:	$
When does warranty expire:	☐ Out of warranty ☐ Date: ______________
Other details regarding this asset:	

Other equipment

Brand name and model number:	
Serial number:	
Approximate value & purchase date:	$
When does warranty expire:	☐ Out of warranty ☐ Date: ______________
Other details regarding this asset:	

Other equipment

Brand name and model number:	
Serial number:	
Approximate value & purchase date:	$
When does warranty expire:	☐ Out of warranty ☐ Date: ______________
Other details regarding this asset:	

§7-Q: Miscellaneous Assets which are often Forgotten or Overlooked

This section contains numerous miscellaneous assets that are frequently forgotten or overlooked. There are so many different types of assets to remember! It also contains reminders of other places where your assets may be located, stored, or situations that might entitle you to receive assets.

The key is for you to provide as much information as possible, to help your representative locate these assets when you are unable to tell them about it. For example, does an asset have a hidden value that would not be obviously apparent to the untrained eye, such as a limited-edition print? Do you have a hiding place, such as a carved-out section of a book, secret compartment in a drawer, a toilet tank, in the backyard under a paver block, in an oatmeal box in the pantry, etc.? Does it have a special significance or sentimental value to you or your family?

Be sure to make a point of making a note about assets that others may think you still own, but which you have since disposed of, so they won't think someone took them, or waste time searching for them. For example, if you gave your mother's engagement ring to one daughter when another was expecting it, that is a future argument waiting to happen. Similarly, if you own jewelry but have replaced the valuable gems with imitation gems (e.g. due to financial need), provide details as to the circumstances, so nobody will think the jeweler stole them.

Please be sure to read the chapter in the book about assets. There are numerous types of assets beyond the obvious major categories such as real estate, bank and investment accounts, business ownership, jewelry, etc. So, if this questionnaire helps you remember an asset that should be added to the list, be sure to jot it down before it disappears from your mind again. Remember to list all miscellaneous assets here, and include all the details that are needed for your loved ones to find and identify them.

REMINDERS AS TO WHERE ASSETS MAY BE STORED

Attic

Do you have an **attic**?	☐ Yes ☐ No
If yes, what important items are stored in it?	

Basement

Do you have a **basement**?	☐ Yes ☐ No
If yes, what important items are stored in it?	

Garage

Do you have a **garage**?	☐ Yes ☐ No
If yes, what important items are stored in it?	

On-premises storage unit

Do you have an on-premises **storage unit** where you live?	☐ Yes ☐ No
What is the unit number, if any?	
What important items are stored in it?	
If there is a key, who has it?	
What is the combination, if any?	

Safe deposit box

Safe deposit box at your bank?	☐ Yes ☐ No If yes, **complete "Safe Deposit Box" section above**.
Name of bank:	
Location of bank:	
Phone number of bank:	
Safe deposit box number:	

Home safe or lockbox

Home safe or lockbox	☐ Yes ☐ No
Where is it located (or hidden)?	
If a key lock, who has a copy or where is it located?	
If a combination lock, what is the combination, or who knows it?	
What important items are in it?	

Office safe or lockbox

Office safe or lockbox:	☐ Yes ☐ No
Where is it located (or hidden)?	
If a key lock, who has a copy or where is it located?	
If a combination lock, what is the combination, or who knows it?	
What important items are in it?	

External storage locker or facility

External (off-premises) storage locker or facility:	☐ Yes ☐ No
Storage unit number:	
Name of storage facility:	
Address of facility:	
City, state , and zip code:	
Phone:	
Name of contact person:	
Access code to enter facility:	
Account number, if any:	
Website:	www.
Monthly rent:	$
If a key lock, who has a copy of the key or where is it located?	
If a combination lock, what is the combination, or who knows it?	
What important items are stored in it?	

MISCELLANEOUS ASSETS AND THE STORIES BEHIND THEM

Season Passes

Do you own **season passes** to sporting, theatrical, ballet, opera, or other events?	☐ Yes ☐ No
If yes, are they season passes for:	☐ Sport team ☐ Performing arts ☐ Museums ☐ Other (specify): ________
Name of venue:	
Address:	
City, state, and zip code:	
Phone number:	
Section and seat number:	
Where to you keep the passes?	
Other details:	
Memories and stories behind about these season passes:	

Assets held outside of USA

Do you own any **assets held <u>outside</u> of the continental United States?**	☐ Yes ☐ No
Where are the assets located?	
Describe the assets:	
Explain why the assets are being kept outside of the United States:	
Who else knows the details about these assets?	
Location of documents:	
Memories and stories behind about these assets:	

Hiding Places

Do you keep valuables in **Hiding Place(s)** (e.g. a tin can buried in back yard, taped behind a picture, jewelry in a Quaker Oats box, etc.)	☐ Yes ☐ No
Where is it located?	
What is in it?	
What is the value of the contents?	
How to access it?	
Who else knows about it?	
Memories and stories behind about these hidden assets:	

Hidden Compartments in Furniture

Hidden compartment in furniture:	☐ Yes ☐ No
Where is the hidden compartment located (e.g. secret drawer, etc.)?	
If a key lock, who has a copy or where is it located?	
If a combination lock, what is the combination, or who knows it?	
What is in it?	
What is the value of the contents?	
Who else knows about it?	
Memories and stories behind about these hidden assets:	

Assets Kept at Your Place of Employment

Do you keep **assets at your place of employment** (e.g. computers and electronics that belong to you, personally)?	☐ Yes ☐ No If yes, provide details:
Description of assets:	
Value of assets:	
Location of assets:	
Name of person to contact to retrieve the assets:	
Contact phone and email address:	
Other details of importance:	
Memories and stories behind about these hidden assets:	

Health Savings Account (HSA)

Do you have a **Health Savings Account (HSA)?**	☐ Yes ☐ No
Account number:	
Current approximate value:	$______________ as of ______________________________ (date)
If yes, name of institution where it is maintained:	
Website:	www.
Username:	
Password:	
Contact phone number:	
Who is named as beneficiary?	

Refunds Due to You

Are you owed any sizeable **refunds?** (e.g. income taxes)?	☐ Yes ☐ No If yes, details:

Security Deposits Due to You

Are you entitled to a refunds of **security deposit(s)**?	☐ Yes ☐ No If yes, provide details for each (e.g. name & contact information for who owes you the refund, and when, etc.)
Apartment:	$____________ Details:
Office:	$____________ Details:
Vehicle:	$____________ Details:
Equipment:	$____________ Details:
Other (specify):	$____________ Details:

Miscellaneous Items Stored Elsewhere

Miscellaneous items kept in other locations (see examples below):	For each item below, provide a description of the item, location, financial value, whom to contact to retrieve the item, and other pertinent details.
Furs kept in cold storage:	☐ Yes ☐ No If yes, provide details below:
Auto or motorcycle at a garage:	☐ Yes ☐ No If yes, provide details below:
Boats in a slip or dry dock:	☐ Yes ☐ No If yes, provide details below:
Airplane at airport:	☐ Yes ☐ No If yes, provide details below:
Horse at a stable:	☐ Yes ☐ No If yes, provide details below:
Precious metals stored elsewhere:	☐ Yes ☐ No If yes, provide details below:
Description and details:	
Description and details:	
Memories and stories behind about these assets:	

Your assets held by someone else

Do you have any of your **assets being held by another person?**	☐ Yes ☐ No
Description of asset(s) being held:	
Value of asset(s) being held:	
Name of person holding asset(s):	
Contact info for this person:	
Location of asset(s) being held:	
What is reason the asset(s) is/are being held by this person?	
Is/Are the asset(s) intended as collateral for a loan?	☐ Yes ☐ No
If yes, what are the details of loan?	
Is there written documentation?	☐ Yes ☐ No
If yes, location of document(s):	
Memories and stories behind about any of these assets:	

Assets you are holding for someone else

Are you holding **assets that belong to another person?**	☐ Yes ☐ No Complete section on "**Assets Held for Others**"
Description of asset(s) being held not discussed in section on Assets Held for Others:	
Value of asset(s) being held:	
Name of person holding asset(s):	
Contact info for this person:	
Location of asset(s) being held:	
What is reason the asset(s) is/are being held by this person?	
Is/Are the asset(s) intended as collateral for a loan?	☐ Yes ☐ No
If yes, what are the details of loan?	
Is there written documentation?	☐ Yes ☐ No
If yes, location of document(s):	
Memories and stories behind about any of these assets:	

Assets with a Hidden Value

Assets with a hidden value, not apparent to the untrained eye, (e.g. jewelry, collectibles, coinage, artwork, antiques, limited editions, rare books, autographed, etc.)	☐ Yes ☐ No **If yes, attach a picture and appraisal, if available.**
Description of asset:	
What makes this asset valuable?	
Value of asset:	
Location of asset:	
Name of person to contact to retrieve the asset:	
Contact phone and email address:	
Location of documents establishing value or authenticity:	
Other details of importance:	
Memories and stories behind about these hidden assets:	

Individual Stocks or Bonds

Do you keep any individual stocks or bonds at home or at work?	☐ Yes ☐ No
If yes, list the securities:	
Approximate value:	$
Where are they located (if hidden, specify where):	
Other details of importance:	
Memories and stories behind about these assets:	

Are you Beneficiary of Someone Else's Trust

Are you named as beneficiary of someone else's Trust?	☐ Yes ☐ No
Who created the Trust?	
What is relationship of person to you?	
Are you <u>currently</u> entitled to benefits?	☐ Yes ☐ No
If no, what has to occur for you to be entitled to receive benefits?	
Are you entitled to income only?	☐ Yes ☐ No
If yes, how much income are you entitled to receive, if known?	$
Are you <u>currently</u> entitled to principal distributions?	☐ Yes ☐ No
If no, what has to occur for you to receive your distribution of principal?	

Approximate value and timing of your principal distribution(s):	$__________ When: __________ $__________ When: __________
Is the trustee a person or institution?	☐ Person ☐ Institution
If an individual, name of the trustee:	
If an institution, name of institution:	
Contact person at institution:	
Phone number of contact person:	
Email address of contact person:	
Other details about the Trust:	
Memories and stories behind about these assets and the person who created the Trust:	

Inherited assets

Are you entitled to inherit assets from someone who has already died?	☐ Yes ☐ No
Name of person:	
Relationship to you:	
If yes, amount you expect to receive:	$
Are you named as beneficiary on a bank account, investment account, retirement plan, or insurance policy?	☐ Yes ☐ No
If yes, identify assets and details:	☐ Yes ☐ No
If not a beneficiary, has a probate estate been filed?	☐ Yes ☐ No
If yes, court case # and where filed:	
Name of Personal Representative (PR):	
PR phone number:	
PR email address:	
Name of attorney handling estate:	
Name of law firm:	
Phone number of attorney:	
Email address of attorney:	
Other details of importance:	
Memories and stories behind about these assets and the person who created the Trust:	

Anticipation of Inheritance

Do you anticipate inheriting assets from someone who has not yet died?	☐ Yes ☐ No
Name of person:	
Relationship to you:	
If yes, amount you expect to receive:	$
If you know, are you named as beneficiary on this person's bank account, investment account, retirement plan, or insurance policy?	☐ Yes ☐ No
If yes, identify assets and details:	☐ Yes ☐ No
Are you named as beneficiary in this person's Last Will and Testament?	
Memories and stories behind about these assets and this person:	

Former Investment Accounts or Insurance Policies

Think back: Are there any old bank or investment accounts, or insurance policies which you have forgotten?	☐ Yes ☐ No
If yes, name of company:	
Type of account:	
Account or policy number:	
Name of contact person:	
Contact information:	
Other details of importance:	

Previous Employer Retirement Accounts

Think back: Did any of your previous employers have retirement accounts, insurance, or other benefits which you have forgotten?	☐ Yes ☐ No
If yes, name of company:	
Type of account:	
Account or policy number:	
Name of contact person:	
Contact information:	
Other details of importance:	

Patents, Trademarks, Licensing, Royalties, etc.

Do you own patents, trademarks, copyrights, licensing rights, and other royalty rights?	☐ Yes ☐ No
Description of item:	
Owner's name and Contact Info:	
Registration ID number:	
Are rights licensed to another person or business?	☐ Yes ☐ No
If yes, provide name and contact info:	
Royalties payable to you:	$__________ per ☐ Month ☐ Year ☐ Other: ________________
When are payments due?	
Duration of royalties:	
If benefits are to continue being paid to your survivors, provide details:	
Location of documents:	
Other details of importance:	
Memories and stories behind about this asset:	

Life Insurance on Someone Else's Life

Do you own a life insurance policy on someone else's life?	☐ Yes ☐ No
If yes, who is the named insured?	
Policy number:	
Amount of policy:	$
Name of insurance company:	
Phone number:	
Website:	www.
Username:	
Password:	
Name of beneficiary:	
Location of insurance policy:	
What is the reason for the insurance?	
Other details of importance:	
Memories and stories behind about this asset:	

Barter Exchange Dollars

Barter exchange dollars (e.g. ITEX, NuBarter, Barter Network, etc.)	☐ Yes ☐ No
Name of barter organization:	
Account number:	
Approx. balance available	$____________ as of ________________________________(date)
Contact Person:	
Phone number:	
Website:	www.
Username:	
Password:	
Other details of importance:	
Memories and stories of how barter exchange dollars were used:	

Assets Being Sold on Consignment

Assets on **consignment:**	☐ Yes ☐ No
Description of asset(s):	
Value of asset(s):	
Name of consignment shop:	
Name of contact person:	
Address:	
City, state, and zip code:	
Phone number:	
Account or item number:	
Memories and stories behind about these assets:	

Assets Held at Pawn Shop

Assets at pawn shop	☐ Yes ☐ No
Description of asset(s) pledged:	
Value of asset(s):	
Redemption amount of loan:	$
Name of consignment shop:	
Name of contact person:	
Address:	
City, state, and zip code:	
Phone number:	
Location of claim ticket:	

Medical/Biological specimens

Medical or Biological specimens kept in storage:	☐ Yes ☐ No
Type of specimens:	☐ Sperm ☐ Embryo ☐ Stem cells ☐ Blood ☐ Eggs ☐ Plasma ☐ DNA ☐ Other: ______
Name of storage facility:	
Address of facility:	
City, state, and zip code:	
Name of contact person:	
Website address:	
Username:	
Password:	
Account or ID number:	
Other details of importance:	
Memories and stories behind about these hidden assets:	

Lawsuits or arbitrations currently pending

Are you currently involved in any **lawsuits** or **arbitrations**?	☐ Yes ☐ No
Are you Plaintiff (the one who filed the lawsuit) or Defendant (the one being sued)?	☐ Plaintiff ☐ Petitioner ☐ Claimant ☐ Defendant ☐ Respondent
Name(s) of other litigants:	
State & county where filed:	
Case number:	
Reason for lawsuit:	
Amount involved:	$
Name of law firm representing you:	
Name of your individual attorney:	
Law firm address:	
City, state, and zip code:	
Your lawyer's telephone number:	
Your lawyer's email address:	
Name and phone number of every potential witness:	
Location of any evidence or documents the attorney might require:	
What are the details behind the lawsuit?	

Lawsuits or arbitrations – Not yet filed

Do you anticipate a lawsuit or arbitration being filed **against you** in the future?	☐ Yes ☐ No
Do you believe you have a valid basis for a lawsuit **against a person, company, or government agency** not yet filed?	☐ Yes ☐ No **IMPORTANT: Beware of strict statute of limitation time limits by which litigation must begin! Review this with your attorney.**
Name(s) of other litigants:	
State and county where filed:	
Case number:	
Reason for lawsuit:	
Amount involved:	$
Name of law firm which would represent you:	
Name of your individual attorney:	
Law firm address:	
City, state, and zip code:	
Your lawyer's telephone number:	
Your lawyer's email address:	
Name and phone number of every potential witness:	
Location of any evidence or documents the attorney might require:	
What are the details behind the unfiled lawsuit or arbitration?	

Your Dry Cleaner

Name of your **dry cleaner** (so that your clothing can be retrieved)?	
Address:	
City, state, and zip code:	
Phone number:	
Where do you usually keep your claim check?	
Other details of importance:	

MISCELLANEOUS CATEGORIES	**On a separate sheet of paper, describe the asset, location of the asset, approximate value, and the story behind how you came to own the asset.** *Provide date acquired, purchase price, current value, location of appraisal, who owns it (i.e. you individually, or with someone else, etc.)*
Artwork:	☐ Yes ☐ No
Coin/stamp/other collections:	☐ Yes ☐ No
Precious metals/gems/gold coins:	☐ Yes ☐ No
Jewelry and furs:	☐ Yes ☐ No
Antiques, vintage clothing:	☐ Yes ☐ No
Rare books, first editions, and/or limited editions:	☐ Yes ☐ No
Other collectibles (specify):	☐ Yes ☐ No
Silverware, china, or crystal:	☐ Yes ☐ No
Mineral or forestry rights	☐ Yes ☐ No
Leasehold and mineral rights:	☐ Yes ☐ No
Licensing rights:	☐ Yes ☐ No
Food crops and forestry rights:	☐ Yes ☐ No
Guns and firearms:	☐ Yes ☐ No
Piano, organ, or other musical instruments:	☐ Yes ☐ No
Railroad cars, machinery & other types of equipment:	☐ Yes ☐ No
Horses, cattle, livestock:	☐ Yes ☐ No
Limited partnership interests:	☐ Yes ☐ No
Inheritances due to you:	☐ Yes ☐ No
Undistributed entitlements from estates or Trusts due to you:	☐ Yes ☐ No
Pending lawsuits or Claims:	☐ Yes ☐ No
Mortgages owed to you:	☐ Yes ☐ No
Debts Owed to You:	☐ Yes ☐ No See section on Notes receivable
Uncollected judgments against a person or business:	☐ Yes ☐ No
Life Insurance on Life of Another:	☐ Yes ☐ No
Tax refund due to you:	☐ Yes ☐ No
Unpaid judgment (against others):	☐ Yes ☐ No
Vintage automobiles:	☐ Yes ☐ No
Boats, aircraft, and other vehicles:	☐ Yes ☐ No
Computers, printers, scanners:	☐ Yes ☐ No See **Computer & Electronics Section 7-L**
Electronics and Appliances:	☐ Yes ☐ No
Cemetery plots:	☐ Yes ☐ No
Remember to share any memories and stories behind about any of these assets:	

§7-R: Sentimental Assets

This section includes special items that are of particular importance to you, or to your family, whether they have a financial value. For example, there may be silverware owned by your great-grandmother, your mother's wedding gown, your baseball card collection, and any other photographs, memorabilia, love letters, and anything else you believe would be treasured by your family.

If, in addition to the sentimental value, the asset also has a financial value, place an approximate value on it. The location of an appraisal, if any, and/or other documentation would be useful, too.

For fun, write down the story behind each item, so future generations can appreciate the significance of the item.

Do you own any item(s) having **sentimental value** to you or your family?	☐ Yes ☐ No If yes, describe each item in the appropriate place below, and the financial value, if any.

Furnishings having sentimental value

Furnishings (include antiques and art)?	☐ Yes ☐ No ☐ Check here if there is a story behind the item(s)
Describe the item(s):	
Estimated financial value, if any:	$
Location of the asset(s):	
Location of documents and appraisals:	
What is the sentimental significance of each item? What is the story behind it, and how did it come into your possession?	

Jewelry & clothing having sentimental value

Do you have any **jewelry & clothing?**	☐ Yes ☐ No ☐ Check here if there is a story behind the item(s)
Describe the item(s):	
Estimated financial value, if any:	$
Location of the asset(s):	
Location of documents and appraisals:	
What is the sentimental significance of each item? What is the story behind it, and how did it come into your possession?	

Collections and collectibles having sentimental value

Any **collections & collectibles?**	☐ Yes ☐ No ☐ Check here if there is a story behind the item(s)
Describe the item(s):	
Estimated financial value, if any:	$
Location of the asset(s):	
Location of documents and appraisals:	
What is the sentimental significance of each item? What is the story behind it, and how did it come into your possession?	

Pictures and photo albums

Do you have **family pictures & photo albums?**	☐ Yes ☐ No
Location of picture albums:	
Are there **digital** photo albums stored somewhere?	☐ Yes ☐ No
If yes, where are they stored (e.g. cloud storage, external hard drive, on computer, CD-ROM, etc.)?	
How to access the digital photos?	
What is the sentimental significance of each item? What is the story behind it, and how did it come into your possession?	

Family movies, videos, and recordings having sentimental value

Do you have **family movies, videos, recordings?**	☐ Yes ☐ No
Where are they located?	
Are there **digital** copies of these items stored somewhere?	☐ Yes ☐ No
IF yes, where are they stored (e.g. cloud storage, external hard drive, on computer, CD-ROM, etc.)?	
How to access the digital videos, etc.?	
What is the sentimental significance of each item? What is the story behind it, and how did it come into your possession?	

Family memorabilia

Do you have **family memorabilia?**	☐ Yes ☐ No
Describe the item(s):	
Estimated financial value, if any:	$
Location of the asset(s):	
Location of documents and appraisals:	
What is the sentimental significance of each item? What is the story behind it, and how did it come into your possession?	

Other items having sentimental value

Are there any other items having sentimental value?	☐ Yes ☐ No
Describe the item(s):	
Estimated financial value, if any:	$
Location of the asset(s):	
Location of documents and appraisals:	
What is the sentimental significance of each item? What is the story behind it, and how did it come into your possession?	

Other items having sentimental value

Are there any other items having sentimental value?	☐ Yes ☐ No
Describe the item(s):	
Estimated financial value, if any:	$
Location of the asset(s):	
Location of documents and appraisals:	
What is the sentimental significance of each item? What is the story behind it, and how did it come into your possession?	

Other items having sentimental value

Are there any other items having sentimental value?	☐ Yes ☐ No
Describe the item(s):	
Estimated financial value, if any:	$
Location of the asset(s):	
Location of documents and appraisals:	
What is the sentimental significance of each item? What is the story behind it, and how did it come into your possession?	

Additional notes:

§7-S: Assets Held for Benefit of Others

Are you the Custodian of an account for someone else, such as an educational account, or Uniform Transfer to Minor's (UTMA) account? Are you the Trustee for the benefit of someone else, such as under a Special Needs Trust?

Have you been entrusted with holding onto something to be delivered to someone at a time in the future or under certain circumstances, such as getting married, turning 18 years of age, graduating college, etc.?

Is something registered in your name, but really belongs to someone else? Make extra copies of this section if you are holding assets for the benefit of more than one person.

Trustee for someone else's benefit

Are you the **Trustee** of a Trust for someone else's benefit?	☐ Yes ☐ No
Is this a Special Needs Trust?	☐ Yes ☐ No
Who is the Grantor of the Trust (who created the Trust)?	
Name of Trust	
Tax ID (EIN) of Trust, if any:	
Name of beneficiary:	
Address:	
City, state, and zip code:	
Phone number:	
Email address:	
Name of bank/Trust company:	
Account number:	
Location of documents:	
Name of successor trustee, if any:	
Name of co-trustee, if any:	
Phone number of Successor Trustee:	
Details or reason(s) for the Trust:	
If there is a story to share regarding the beneficiary, provide the details:	

Custodian of 529 Educational Savings Plan

Are you the **Custodian** of a **529 Educational Savings Plan**?	☐ Yes ☐ No
Account number of plan:	
Name of beneficiary (the child):	
Child's address:	
City, state, and zip code:	
Birth date of child:	
Social security number of child:	
Plan name, if any:	
Name of institution where held:	
Telephone number:	
Website address:	www.
Name of financial representative:	
Company of financial representative:	
Phone number:	
Name of Successor Custodian, if any:	
Location of documents & statements	
If there is a story to share regarding the beneficiary, provide the details:	

Custodian of Coverdell Educational Savings Account (ESA)

Are you the Custodian of a **Coverdell Educational Savings Account (ESA)**?	☐ Yes ☐ No
Account number of plan:	
Name of beneficiary (the child):	
Child's address:	
City, state, and zip code:	
Birth date of child:	
Social security number of child:	
Plan name, if any:	
Name of institution where held:	
Telephone number:	
Website address:	www.
Name of financial representative:	
Company of financial representative:	
Phone number:	
Name of Successor Custodian, if any:	
Location of documents & statements	
If there is a story to share regarding the beneficiary, provide the details:	

Custodian of UTMA or UGMA

Are you the Custodian of a **UTMA or UGMA** account for a child (Uniform Transfer (or Gift) to Minor's Account)?	☐ Yes ☐ No
Account number of plan:	
Name of beneficiary (the child):	
State in which plan is organized:	
At what age does this child become entitled to the proceeds of the plan?	☐ 18 ☐ 21 ☐ Other (specify): ________
Child's address:	
City, state, and zip code:	
Birth date of child:	
Social security number of child:	
Plan name, if any:	
Name of institution where held:	
Telephone number:	
Website address:	www.
Name of financial representative:	
Company of financial representative:	
Phone number:	
Name of Successor Custodian, if any:	
Location of documents & statements	

Asset you are holding to be delivered to another person

Have you been entrusted with holding onto an asset or sum of money to be delivered to someone at a time in the future or under certain circumstances, such as getting married, turning 18 years of age, graduating college, etc.?	☐ Yes ☐ No
Name of person entitled to receive:	
Contact information for person:	
Asset or amount person is to receive:	
Location of asset(s) or money:	
What are the circumstances that must occur for the person to receive the asset or money?	
Are the terms of delivery in written document?	☐ Yes ☐ No
Location of documents:	
If there is a story to share regarding this matter, provide the details:	

Something titled in your name, but belonging to someone else

Is an asset titled in your name, but really belongs to someone else?	☐ Yes ☐ No
Provide details on why the asset is in your name, and the terms under which it is to be turned over to the other person:	
Name of person:	
Contact information	
Description of asset(s) being held:	
Location of asset(s) being held:	
Is there a written document regarding this matter?	☐ Yes ☐ No
Location of documents:	
If there is a story to share regarding this matter, provide the details:	

Assets being held as collateral for a loan

Are you holding an asset as collateral for a loan you have made to someone else?	☐ Yes ☐ No
Name of person owing the money:	
Contact information:	
Description of assets being held:	
Amount owed:	$
Repayment terms of loan:	
Interest rate of loan:	
Where are the payment records?	
Where are the assets located?	
Location of documents	
If there is a story to share regarding this matter, provide the details:	

Additional notes:

§7-T: Miscellaneous Other Assets – Did We Forget Anything?

List any other types of assets that may have been omitted from the previous pages. For each asset, provide as much of the following information as may be useful for your representatives and loved ones to know.

Make additional copies of this page, as needed.

Description of asset:	
Location of asset:	
Approximate value of asset, if any:	$
Account number, if any:	
Name of contact person:	
Name of company holding asset:	
Address:	
City, state, and zip code:	
Telephone number:	
Email address:	
Who is owner (or co-owner)?	
Location of documents, appraisals, proof of ownership, etc.:	
Other information about it:	
Is there a memorable or funny story about this asset?	

Description of asset:	
Location of asset:	
Approximate value of asset, if any:	$
Account number, if any:	
Name of contact person:	
Name of company holding asset:	
Address:	
City, state, and zip code:	
Telephone number:	
Email address:	
Who is owner (or co-owner)?	
Location of documents, appraisals, proof of ownership, etc.:	
Other information about it:	
Is there a memorable or funny story about this asset?	

§8: Mortgages, Loans & Other Debts

Use this section to list all your debts.

However, if the debt is owed for ***real estate, automobiles, or other vehicles,*** *for efficiency, these debts are included in the section for the asset for which the debt was incurred (e.g. If you have a personal residence, your mortgage, 2nd mortgage [if any], line of credit [if any] should be posted in the appropriate spaces for that specific property. Short-term loans affecting the real estate [e.g. home improvement loans], will be listed in this section).*

This will apply to automobile loans, too. The loan details will be found in the section for the appropriate vehicle. Loans affecting your business or its assets are in the section on your business.

Do you have any of the following types of mortgages, debts, or loans?

Do you have a **mortgage** or **line of credit** on your **personal residence**?	☐ Yes ☐ No If yes, answer the mortgage questions in the **personal residence section 7-A** relating to that specific property.
Do you have a **mortgage or other debt** on **investment property**?	☐ Yes ☐ No If yes, answer the mortgage questions in the **investment real estate section 7-A** relating to that specific property.
Do you have an **auto or vehicle loan**?	☐ Yes ☐ No If yes, answer the loan questions in the **automobile & other vehicle section 7-C** relating to that specific vehicle.
Do you have one or more **student loans**?	☐ Yes ☐ No If yes, answer the appropriate loan questions in the **student loan section 8-A** of this questionnaire.
Do you have a **home improvement** loan?	☐ Yes ☐ No If yes, answer the appropriate loan questions in the **home improvement loans section 8-B** of this questionnaire.
Do you have a **business loan**?	☐ Yes ☐ No If yes, answer the appropriate loan questions in the **business ownership section 7-B** relating to that business.
Do you have **secured loans**, in which the asset purchased is the collateral (e.g. jewelry, appliances, furniture)?	☐ Yes ☐ No If yes, answer the appropriate loan questions in the **secured loan section 8-C** of this questionnaire.
Do you have **credit card** debt?	☐ Yes ☐ No If yes, answer the appropriate questions in the **credit card section 8-D** of this questionnaire.
Do you have any **unsecured loans** (e.g. signature loans?	☐ Yes ☐ No If yes, answer the appropriate loan questions in the **unsecured loans section 8-E** of this questionnaire.
Are you a **co-signer or guarantor** of someone else's loan?	☐ Yes ☐ No If yes, answer the appropriate questions in the **other legal obligations section 8-f** of this questionnaire.
Do you **owe money to another person**?	☐ Yes ☐ No If yes, answer the appropriate questions in the **miscellaneous unsecured loan section 8-E** of this questionnaire.
Are you **required to make payments** to someone due to a court order (e.g. divorce decree, judgment)?	☐ Yes ☐ No If yes, answer the appropriate questions in the **other legal obligations section 8-F** of this questionnaire.
Do you **pay bills for another person**, even though you have no legal obligation to do so?	☐ Yes ☐ No If yes, answer the appropriate questions in the **other legal, charitable, or moral obligations section 8-F** of this questionnaire.
Do you owe other **miscellaneous** obligations?	☐ Yes ☐ No If yes, answer the appropriate questions in the **miscellaneous obligations section 8-F** of this questionnaire.

Additional notes:

____

____

____

____

§8-A: Student Loans

List all student loans here and details of any program which forgives or reduces your student loan debt.

Do you have a **student loan**?	☐ Yes ☐ No If yes, is this plan: ☐ Federal ☐ State ☐ Both
Name of lender/servicer:	
Lender/Servicer address:	
City, state, and zip code:	
Lender/servicer telephone number:	
Website:	www.
Username:	
Password:	
Account number:	
Balance owed:	$________________ as of ______________________ (date)
Loan terms:	Interest rate: _________%
Payment terms:	When must payments begin?
Is there a co-signer on this loan?	☐ Yes ☐ No
If yes, name of co-signer:	
Contact information for co-signer:	
Are you in any program under which this loan may be forgiven?	☐ Yes ☐ No
If yes, provide the terms and details of repayment of this program:	

Do you have another **student loan**?	☐ Yes ☐ No If yes, is this plan: ☐ Federal ☐ State ☐ Both
Name of lender/servicer:	
Lender/Servicer address:	
City, state, and zip code:	
Lender/servicer telephone number:	
Website:	www.
Username:	
Password:	
Account number:	
Balance owed:	$________________ as of ______________________ (date)
Loan terms:	Interest rate: _________%
Payment terms:	When must payments begin?
Is there a co-signer on this loan?	☐ Yes ☐ No
If yes, name of co-signer:	
Contact information for co-signer:	
Are you in any program under which this loan may be forgiven?	☐ Yes ☐ No
If yes, provide the terms and details of this program:	

§8-B: Home Improvement Loans

Provide details regarding any home improvement loans (e.g. new roof, swimming pool, room addition, etc.)

Do you have a **home improvement loan** (e.g. new roof, etc.)?	☐ Yes ☐ No
Name of lender:	
Lender address:	
City, state, and zip code:	
Lender telephone number:	
Website:	www.
Username:	
Password:	
Account number:	
Balance owed:	$_______________ as of _____________________ (date)
Loan terms:	Interest rate: ________%
Date of loan:	
Maturity date, if any:	
If payments are deferred, date when payments must begin:	
Is interest waived if paid-in-full by a certain date?	☐ Yes ☐ No If yes, what is that date? _________________________
Is there a co-signer on this loan? If yes, name and phone of co-signer:	☐ Yes ☐ No
Is there a lien against the house?	☐ Yes ☐ No
What was the reason for this loan?	
Is this someone else's loan, and you have co-signed or guaranteed payment?	
If yes, provide details:	

Additional notes:

____

____

____

____

§8-C: Secured Loans (loans with collateral)

Provide details on any secured loans here. A secured loan is one which has collateral pledged to guaranty payment of the debt, and which gives the creditor the power to repossess the property (such as jewelry, furniture, or appliances, etc.) if you fail to make payments. Space is provided for one secured loan.

If you have more than one such loan, make additional copies of this page as needed.

Secured loan for (identify the collateral for the loan):	
Account number, if any:	
Name of lender (person/company):	
Address:	
City, state, and zip code:	
Telephone number:	
Website:	www.
Username:	
Password:	
Initial amount of loan:	$
Balance owed on loan:	$__________ as of (date): ____________________
Terms of loan:	Interest rate: _____ % Number of monthly / yearly payments: _____
Who is co-signer or guarantor?	
Does this bill get paid automatically out of your bank account?	☐ Yes ☐ No
If yes, name of bank and account # from which payments are made:	
Do you have credit life insurance to pay-off this debt upon your death?	☐ Yes ☐ No
If yes, provide details:	
Location of loan documents, if any:	
Are there any memorable or funny stories regarding this loan or the collateral (e.g. engagement ring)?	

Additional notes:

____

____

____

____

§8-D: Credit Cards

Provide details on your various credit cards here. This includes major credit cards such as Visa, MasterCard, and American Express, as well as gas and department store credit cards.

Space is provided for four credit cards. If you have more than four credit cards, make additional copies of this page as needed.

Type of credit card:	☐ Visa ☐ MasterCard ☐ American Express ☐ Gas card ☐ Store ☐ Other (specify): ____________
Name of company issuing the card:	
Account number, if any:	
Does this card give you cash back, reward points, mileage points, etc.?	☐ Yes ☐ No
If yes, what type of rewards are given?	☐ Cash back ☐ Reward points ☐ Mileage points ☐ Other (specify): ____________
Approximate points earned:	
Name of lender (person/company):	
Address:	
City, state, and zip code:	
Telephone number:	
Website:	www.
Username:	
Password:	
Who is co-signer or guarantor?	
Does this bill get paid automatically out of your bank account?	☐ Yes ☐ No
If yes, name of bank and account # from which payments are made:	
Do you have credit life insurance to pay-off this debt upon your death?	☐ Yes ☐ No
If yes, provide details:	
Location of credit card documents and/or statements:	
If you used your reward points, describe the most fun item you used the points to purchase:	

Additional notes:

____

____

____

____

§8-D: Credit Cards

Provide details on your various credit cards here. This includes major credit cards such as Visa, MasterCard, and American Express, as well as gas and department store credit cards.

Space is provided for four credit cards. If you have more than four credit cards, make additional copies of this page as needed.

Type of credit card:	☐ Visa ☐ MasterCard ☐ American Express ☐ Gas card ☐ Store ☐ Other (specify): ____________
Name of company issuing the card:	
Account number, if any:	
Does this card give you cash back, reward or mileage points, etc.?	☐ Yes ☐ No
If yes, what type of rewards are given?	☐ Cash back ☐ Reward points ☐ Mileage points ☐ Other (specify): ____________
Approximate points earned:	
Name of lender (person/company):	
Address:	
City, state, and zip code:	
Telephone number:	
Website:	www.
Username:	
Password:	
Who is co-signer or guarantor?	
Does this bill get paid automatically out of your bank account?	☐ Yes ☐ No
If yes, name of bank and account # from which payments are made:	
Do you have credit life insurance to pay-off this debt upon your death?	☐ Yes ☐ No
If yes, provide details:	
Location of credit card documents and/or statements:	
If you used your reward points, describe the most fun item you used the points to purchase:	

Additional notes:

____

____

____

____

§8-D: Credit Cards

Provide details on your various credit cards here. This includes major credit cards such as Visa, MasterCard, and American Express, as well as gas and department store credit cards.

Space is provided for four credit cards. If you have more than four credit cards, make additional copies of this page as needed.

Type of credit card:	☐ Visa ☐ MasterCard ☐ American Express ☐ Gas card ☐ Store ☐ Other (specify): ____________
Name of company issuing the card:	
Account number, if any:	
Does this card give you cash back, reward or mileage points, etc.?	☐ Yes ☐ No
If yes, what type of rewards are given?	☐ Cash back ☐ Reward points ☐ Mileage points ☐ Other (specify): ____________
Approximate points earned:	
Name of lender (person/company):	
Address:	
City, state, and zip code:	
Telephone number:	
Website:	www.
Username:	
Password:	
Who is co-signer or guarantor?	
Does this bill get paid automatically out of your bank account?	☐ Yes ☐ No
If yes, name of bank and account # from which payments are made:	
Do you have credit life insurance to pay-off this debt upon your death?	☐ Yes ☐ No
If yes, provide details:	
Location of credit card documents and/or statements:	
If you used your reward points, describe the most fun item you used the points to purchase:	

Additional notes:

____

____

____

____

§8-D: Credit Cards

Provide details on your various credit cards here. This includes major credit cards such as Visa, MasterCard, and American Express, as well as gas and department store credit cards.

Space is provided for four credit cards. If you have more than four credit cards, make additional copies of this page as needed.

Type of credit card:	☐ Visa ☐ MasterCard ☐ American Express ☐ Gas card ☐ Store ☐ Other (specify): ____________
Name of company issuing the card:	
Account number, if any:	
Does this card give you cash back, reward or mileage points, etc.?	☐ Yes ☐ No
If yes, what type of rewards are given?	☐ Cash back ☐ Reward points ☐ Mileage points ☐ Other (specify): ____________
Approximate points earned:	
Name of lender (person/company):	
Address:	
City, state, and zip code:	
Telephone number:	
Website:	www.
Username:	
Password:	
Who is co-signer or guarantor?	
Does this bill get paid automatically out of your bank account?	☐ Yes ☐ No
If yes, name of bank and account # from which payments are made:	
Do you have credit life insurance to pay off this debt upon your death?	☐ Yes ☐ No
If yes, provide details:	
Location of credit card documents and/or statements:	
If you used your reward points, describe the most fun item you used your points to purchase:	

Additional notes:

____

____

____

____

§8-E: Miscellaneous Unsecured Loans

Provide details on any unsecured loans here. This would be money you have borrowed from a person or lender, but no collateral is provided to secure the loan.

Space is provided for two unsecured loans. If you have more than two unsecured loans, make additional copies of this page as needed.

Describe the unsecured loan:	
Name of lender (person/company):	
Account number, if any:	
Address:	
City, state, and zip code:	
Telephone number:	
Website:	www.
Username:	
Password:	
Initial amount of loan:	$
Balance owed on loan:	$_________________ as of ________________________ (date)
Terms of loan:	Interest rate: ______ %; Number of monthly/yearly payments: _______
Reason for loan:	
Who is co-signer or guarantor?	
Does this bill get paid automatically out of your bank account?	☐ Yes ☐ No
If yes, name of bank and account # from which payments are made:	
Do you have credit life insurance to pay off this debt upon your death?	☐ Yes ☐ No
If yes, provide details:	
Is there a written loan agreement?	☐ Yes ☐ No
Location of loan documents:	
Is there a memorable or funny story regarding the use of this loan (e.g. vacation in Bora Bora, etc.)?	

Additional notes:

___

___

___

___

§8-E: Miscellaneous Unsecured Loans

Provide details on any unsecured loans here. This would be money you have borrowed from a person or lender, but no collateral is provided to secure the loan.

Space is provided for two unsecured loans. If you have more than two unsecured loans, make additional copies of this page as needed.

Describe the unsecured loan:	
Name of lender (person/company):	
Account number, if any:	
Address:	
City, state, and zip code:	
Telephone number:	
Website:	www.
Username:	
Password:	
Initial amount of loan:	$
Balance owed on loan:	$__________________ as of ________________________ (date)
Terms of loan:	Interest rate: _____ %; Number of monthly/yearly payments: ________
Reason for loan:	
Who is co-signer or guarantor?	
Does this bill get paid automatically out of your bank account?	☐ Yes ☐ No
If yes, name of bank and account # from which payments are made:	
Do you have credit life insurance to pay-off this debt upon your death?	☐ Yes ☐ No
If yes, provide details:	
Is there a written loan agreement?	☐ Yes ☐ No
Location of loan documents:	
Is there a memorable or funny story regarding the use of this loan (e.g. vacation in Bora Bora, etc.)?	

Additional notes:

____

____

____

____

§8-F: Other Legal, Charitable, or Moral Obligations

Provide details on any other obligations you may have to others, such as acting as a co-signer or guarantor for someone else (e.g. co-signing for a child's car or lease). This may not be an obligation you currently owe, but if the primary debtor defaults in payments, you may be forced to pay the debt for him or her.

This section also includes legally enforceable obligations (e.g. being under court order to pay alimony or child support, or pay for a child's college). This section also includes any moral or voluntary obligations you have decided you are willing to pay, but have no legal obligation to do so (e.g. Taking care of an elderly neighbor; co-signing for a grandchild's car loan, etc.).

Co-signer or Guarantor for someone else's loan

Are you a **co-signer** or **Guarantor for someone else's loan or obligation?**	☐ Yes ☐ No
Loan Type (e.g. car loan, lease, etc.):	
Amount of loan:	$
Loan or account number:	
Name of **Primary obligor** (borrower):	
Name of creditor/lender:	
Lender address:	
City, state, and zip code:	
Telephone number:	
Email address:	
Purpose of loan obligation:	
Loan terms:	Interest rate: _____ %; Number of monthly/yearly payments: _______
Payment amount:	$____________ per ☐ Month ☐ Year ☐ Other
Balloon payment, if any:	Date: ___________________ Amount: $_______________
Security/collateral for loan, if any:	
Location of documents:	
Other details of importance:	
Stories or memories about this obligation:	

Obligations for your children

Do you have legal **obligations for the benefit of your children** (e.g. obligation under a divorce or settlement agreement)?	☐ Yes ☐ No If yes, provide details:
Is obligation voluntary or required?	☐ Required ☐ Voluntary
Amount of obligation:	$
When does this obligation end?	
Location of loan/debt documents:	
Other details of importance:	
Stories or memories about this obligation:	

Obligations for former spouse?

Do you have legal **obligations for the benefit of former spouse** (e.g. obligation under a divorce or settlement agreement)?	☐ Yes ☐ No If yes, provide details:
Is obligation voluntary or required?	☐ Required ☐ Voluntary
Amount of obligation:	$
When does this obligation end?	
Location of loan/debt documents:	
Other details of importance:	
Stories or memories about this obligation:	

Obligations for your parents

Do you have legal **obligations for the benefit of your parents** (e.g. nursing home, providing monthly or special income, medical care)	☐ Yes ☐ No If yes, provide details:
Is obligation voluntary or required?	☐ Required ☐ Voluntary
Amount of obligation:	$
When does this obligation end?	
Location of loan/debt documents:	
Other details of importance:	
Stories or memories about this obligation:	

Legal obligations for someone else?

Have you been named in someone else's Power of Attorney to act on their behalf?	☐ Yes ☐ No
If yes, provide the name and phone number of the person:	Name: Phone:
Who else needs to be notified if you are unable to do so?	Name: Phone:
Have you been named a health care surrogate to make medical decisions for someone else?	☐ Yes ☐ No
If yes, provide the name and phone number of the person:	Name: Phone:
Who else needs to be notified if you are unable to do so?	Name: Phone:
Are you providing care for someone?	☐ Yes ☐ No

If yes, provide the name and phone number of the person:	Name: Phone:
Who else needs to be notified if you are unable to do so?	Name: Phone:
Stories or memories about this person or obligation:	

Obligations to others

Do you have any other legal **obligations for any others** (whether required or voluntary)?	☐ Yes ☐ No If yes, provide details:
Is obligation voluntary or required?	☐ Required ☐ Voluntary
To whom is this obligation owed?	
Reason for the obligation:	
Amount of obligation:	$
When does this obligation end?	
Location of loan/debt documents:	
Other details of importance:	
Stories or memories about this obligation:	

Obligations that survive your death or disability

Do you have any **obligations that continue after your death or disability** (e.g. under a divorce decree, settlement agreement, prenuptial agreement, or private contract with others)?	☐ Yes ☐ No If yes, provide details:
Is obligation voluntary or required?	☐ Required ☐ Voluntary
Amount of obligation:	$
When does this obligation end?	
Location of documents:	
Other details of importance:	
Stories or memories about this obligation:	

Charitable Obligations

Do you have any **Charitable Obligations** (e.g. tithe, pledge, provision of charitable Trust, etc.)?	☐ Yes ☐ No If yes, provide details:
Name of charitable organization:	
Address of charitable organization:	
City, state, and zip code:	
Name of contact person:	
Telephone number and email address:	
Amount of obligation, tithe, or pledge:	$_______________ Frequency: ☐ One time ☐ Monthly ☐ Yearly
Source of funds for payments:	
Is obligation voluntary or required?	☐ Required ☐ Voluntary (contractual or charitable Trust obligation)
Is this obligation in writing and signed?	☐ Yes ☐ No
When does this obligation end?	
Do you want charitable payments to continue after your death?	☐ Yes ☐ No
Do you want charitable payments to continue after your incapacity?	☐ Yes ☐ No
Location of pledge documents:	
Other details of importance:	
Stories or memories about this obligation:	

Unpaid judgments against you?

Do you have any **unpaid judgments** against you?	☐ Yes ☐ No
If yes, what is the obligation?	
To whom is the obligation owed?	
Amount of the obligation?	$
Which court (county and state)?	
Case number:	
Name of lawyer for plaintiff:	
Law firm for plaintiff:	
Contact information for lawyer:	
Location of documents:	
Other details of importance:	
Stories or memories about this obligation:	

Unpaid tax, contractor, or tax liens

Do you have any **unpaid tax, contractor, or other liens against you or your assets?**	☐ Yes ☐ No
If yes, describe the reason for the lien:	
Amount and approximate date of lien:	$____________ Date: ______________________
To what entity is the obligation owed?	
Assets upon which lien has attached:	
Who needs to be contacted to satisfy this lien?	
Contact information (name/phone):	
Other details of importance:	
Stories or memories about this obligation:	

Voluntary Obligations

Do you make **voluntary payments** for the benefit of any person or organization, even though not legally required to do so?	☐ Yes ☐ No
If yes, describe the nature of the payments or obligation:	
Account number, if any:	
Amount of obligation/payments:	$
Frequency of payment(s):	☐ One time ☐ As needed ☐ Monthly ☐ Yearly
Name of person or organization to whom payments are being made:	
Who needs to be contacted regarding these payments?	
Address:	
City, state, and zip code:	
Contact information (phone/email):	
Do you want payments to continue if you become incapacitated?	☐ Yes ☐ No
Do you want payments to continue after your death)	☐ Yes ☐ No **Reminder: Your Will or Trust needs to have a provision for payments to continue.**
Other details of importance:	
Stories or memories about this obligation:	

Other obligations

Do you have any **other obligations not covered above?**	☐ Yes ☐ No
If yes, what is the obligation?	
Amount of obligation:	$
To whom is this obligation owed?	
Address:	
City, state, and zip code:	
Name of contact person:	
Telephone number and email address:	
Location of documents:	
Other details of importance:	
Stories or memories about this obligation:	

Other obligations

Do you have any **other obligations not covered above?**	☐ Yes ☐ No
If yes, what is the obligation?	
Amount of obligation:	$
To whom is this obligation owed?	
Address:	
City, state, and zip code:	
Name of contact person:	
Telephone number and email address:	
Location of documents:	
Other details of importance:	
Stories or memories about this obligation:	

§9: Miscellaneous Types of Insurance

NOTE: Insurance details for particular-types of assets (e.g. home, real estate, automobile, vehicles, boat, plane, and business-related insurance) are covered in the section for each of these particular assets. Life insurance policies with cash values are included under the "Assets" section.

Provide details on all other types of insurance policies and coverage you may have. If in doubt, list them here, even if you may have listed them elsewhere.

Do you have the following types of insurance

Do you have **Homeowner's/Property Owner's** Insurance?	☐ Yes ☐ No	If yes, go to the **Real estate section 7-A** regarding your ownership for each parcel of real estate
Do you have **Automobile** or other **Vehicle** Insurance (including boat, airplane, etc.)?	☐ Yes ☐ No	If yes, go to the **Vehicle section 7-C** regarding each particular automobile, boat, airplane, and any other type of vehicle you own.
Do you have **Umbrella** Insurance?	☐ Yes ☐ No	If yes, go to the **insurance section 9-C**
Do you have **Business Liability** Insurance?	☐ Yes ☐ No	If yes, go to the **business assets section 7-B insurance.**
Do you have **other Business** Insurance (e.g. business continuation, key-man, overhead expense, cyber security, etc.)?	☐ Yes ☐ No	If yes, go to the **business assets insurance section 7-B**
Do you have **Cash Value Life** Insurance?	☐ Yes ☐ No	If yes, go to previous assets **section 7-H** regarding life insurance with cash value.
Do you have **Term Life** Insurance?	☐ Yes ☐ No	If yes, go to the **Term life section 9-A**
Do you have **Accidental Death & Dismemberment (AD&D)** Insurance?	☐ Yes ☐ No	If yes, go to the **Accidental death & dismemberment section 9-B**
Do you have **Medicare** Insurance (including supplemental policies)?	☐ Yes ☐ No	If yes, go to the **Medicare section 9-D**
Do you have **Health** Insurance?	☐ Yes ☐ No	If yes, go to the **Health insurance section 9-E**
Do you have **Dental** Insurance?	☐ Yes ☐ No	If yes, go to the **Dental insurance section 9-F**
Do you have **Vision** Insurance?	☐ Yes ☐ No	If yes, go to the **Vision insurance section 9-G**
Do you have **Long-Term Care** Insurance?	☐ Yes ☐ No	If yes, go to the **Long-term care insurance section 9-K**
Do you have **Disability** Insurance?	☐ Yes ☐ No	If yes, go to the **Disability insurance section 9-I**
Do you have **Short-Term Disability** Insurance (e.g. Aflac, etc.)?	☐ Yes ☐ No	If yes, go to the **Supplemental health insurance section 9-J**
Do you have **Personal articles insurance** (e.g. for jewelry, etc.)?	☐ Yes ☐ No	If yes, go to the **Personal articles insurance section 9-L**
Other: ____________________		
Other: ____________________		

Additional notes:

____

____

____

____

§9-A: Term Life Insurance Policies

Term life insurance has no cash value. You are "renting" insurance for the period covered by the premium you pay. If you don't pay the premium, the insurance coverage lapses. Include all term life policies you own, including those your employer may provide for you through your place of employment. If you have more than one term life insurance policy, make extra copies of this section, as needed.

Do you have a term life policy?	☐ Yes ☐ No
Type of term life insurance policy:	☐ Term ☐ Level Term (_________ # of years before premiums increase) ☐ Other: ______________________________
If yes, what is the policy number?	
Face amount of policy:	$
Issue date of policy:	
Name of insurance policy owner:	☐ Me ☐ My Trust ☐ Jointly with: ____________________ ☐ Other: ______________________________
Name of insured person:	☐ Me ☐ Other: ______________________________
Name of beneficiary or beneficiaries and percentage:	Name 1: ______________________ ________% Name 2: ______________________ ________% Name 3: ______________________ ________%
Name of contingent beneficiary or beneficiaries & percentage:	Name 1: ______________________ ________% Name 2: ______________________ ________% Name 3: ______________________ ________%
Amount of premium:	$______________ per ☐ Month ☐ Year
How are premiums paid?	☐ By check ☐ Auto bank draft ☐ Other: ______________
Name of insurance company:	
Address of insurance company:	
City, state, and zip code:	
Telephone number of company	
Website:	
Username:	
Password:	
Name of insurance agent:	
Name of insurance agency:	
Address of insurance agency:	
City, state, and zip code:	
Telephone number of agent	
Is there a loan against this policy?	☐ Yes ☐ No If yes, amount of loan: $________________
Other details of importance:	

Additional notes:

____

____

____

§9-B: Accidental Death & Dismemberment (AD&D) Insurance Coverage

This type of insurance policy pays a specific dollar amount if death or loss of a limb or eyesight is caused by an accident. It is usually a stand-alone policy from your life insurance, but can sometimes be included as an additional benefit of your life insurance policy.

If yes, do you have an **Accidental Death & Dismemberment (AD&D)** insurance policy?	☐ Yes ☐ No
If yes, what is the policy number?	
If yes, what is the policy number?	
Insurance policy plan name:	
What benefits does it pay for:	Death: $__________ Loss of one arm: $________; Loss of both arms: $________ Loss of one leg: $ ________; Loss of both legs: $________ Loss of eyesight: $________ Other loss (specify): ____________ $________
Issue date of policy:	
Name of insurance policy owner:	☐ Me ☐ My Trust ☐ Jointly with: __________ ☐ Other: __________
Name of insured person:	☐ Me ☐ Other: __________
Amount of premium:	$________ per ☐ Month ☐ Year
How are premiums paid?	☐ By check ☐ Auto bank draft ☐ Other: __________
Name of insurance company:	
Address of insurance company:	
Telephone number of company:	
Website address:	
Username:	
Password:	
Name of insurance agent:	
Name of insurance agency:	
Address of insurance agency:	
City, state, and zip code:	
Phone number of agent:	
Location of policy and documents:	
Other details of importance:	

Additional notes:

____

____

____

____

§9-C: Umbrella Insurance Coverage

Umbrella insurance is an extra layer of liability insurance designed to help protect you from major claims which exceed the limits of your regular homeowners, auto, and boat insurance policies.

Do you have an **Umbrella** insurance policy?	☐ Yes ☐ No
If yes, what is the policy number?	
If yes, what is the policy number?	
Insurance policy plan name:	
Face amount of policy:	$
Issue date of policy:	
Name of insurance policy owner:	☐ Me ☐ My Trust ☐ Jointly with: ________ ☐ Other: ________
Name of insured person:	☐ Me ☐ Other: ________
Amount of premium:	$________ per ☐ Month ☐ Year
How are premiums paid?	☐ By check ☐ Auto bank draft ☐ Other: ________
Name of insurance company:	
Address of insurance company:	
Telephone number of company:	
Website address:	
Username:	
Password:	
Name of insurance agent:	
Name of insurance agency:	
Address of insurance agency:	
City, state, and zip code:	
Phone number of agent:	
Location of policy and documents:	
Other details of importance:	

Additional notes:

____

____

____

____

§9-D: Medicare

If you qualify for either or both Medicare and/or Medicaid, complete this section. For more information about Medicare, call (800) 633-4227 or visit their website at www.medicare.gov.

If you do not qualify and/or receive Medicare and/or Medicaid, you may disregard this page.

Basic Medicare information

Are you enrolled in Medicare?	☐ Yes ☐ No
If no, when will you qualify?	Date of your 65th birthday: ____________________ 20_____
If yes, what is the effective date of your Medicare enrollment:	
Medicare Insurance Number:	
Type of Medicare insurance:	☐ Part A ☐ Part B ☐ Part D
Monthly premium payment:	$
Are payments automatically deducted from your social security benefits?	☐ Yes ☐ No If yes, payments are for: ☐ Part A ☐ Part B ☐ Part D
Where is your Medicare card?	
Location of Medicare documents:	
Other information of importance:	

Medicare supplemental coverage

Do you have a Medicare supplemental policy (i.e. Medigap)?	☐ Yes ☐ No
If yes, what is the policy number?	
Monthly premium:	$
How paid:	☐ Auto-draft from bank acct ☐ Write check
Is this a Medicare Advantage Plan?	☐ Yes ☐ No If not, provide details on your Medicare supplement plan:
Insurance policy plan name:	
Was there a reason you chose this particular plan over other plans?	
Name of Insurance Company:	
Address of Insurance Company:	
Telephone number of company:	
Website address:	www.
Username:	
Password:	
Name of insurance agent:	
Name of insurance agency:	
Address of insurance agency:	
Phone number of insurance agent:	
Location of policy and documents:	
Other information of importance:	

Supplemental prescription drug plan

Do you have a supplemental **prescription drug** plan?	☐ Yes ☐ No
If yes, what is the policy number?	
Monthly premium:	$
How paid:	☐ Auto-draft from bank acct ☐ Write check
Insurance policy plan name:	
Was there a reason you chose this particular plan over other plans?	
Name of Insurance Company:	
Address of Insurance Company:	
Telephone number of company:	
Website address:	www.
Username:	
Password:	
Name of insurance agent:	
Name of insurance agency:	
Address of insurance agency:	
Phone number of insurance agent:	
Location of policy and documents:	
Other information of importance:	
What prescription drugs do you take that **ARE covered** by this plan?	
What prescription drugs do you take that are **NOT covered** by this plan?	

Medicaid

Do you qualify for **Medicaid** (This is a state-sponsored insurance program for the indigent)?	☐ Yes ☐ No **Note: Do not confuse this with Medicare!**
If yes, your Medicaid ID number:	
If yes, have you used Medicaid to cover your medical expenses?	☐ Yes ☐ No
Other information of importance:	

§9-E: Health or Medical Insurance

Provide details about any health or medical insurance coverage you currently have, and whether it is provided by your employer as a benefit, as a government-mandated program (e.g. "The Affordable Care Act"), or paid by you directly. In the event of your illness, injury, or incapacity, it will be important for your representatives to have complete information about your health insurance benefits, to enable them to better take care of you.

Do you have health insurance?	☐ Yes ☐ No
If yes, is it an employer group plan?	☐ Yes ☐ No
If yes, name of employer:	
Who is the group plan sponsor?	
Phone number of contact person:	
Type of plan:	☐ HMO ☐ PPO ☐ Other (specify):
What is group plan number, if any?	
What is the member policy number?	
Insurance policy plan name:	
Monthly premium:	$
How paid:	☐ Auto-draft from bank acct ☐ Write check
Amount of deductible:	$
Name of Insurance Company:	
Address of Insurance Company:	
Telephone number of company:	
Website address:	www.
Username:	
Password:	
Name of insurance agent:	
Name of insurance agency:	
Address of insurance agency:	
Phone number of insurance agent:	
Location of policy and documents:	
Does this policy cover your spouse?	☐ Yes ☐ No
Does this policy cover your children?	☐ Yes ☐ No
Do you have any supplemental health/medical insurance coverage?	☐ Yes ☐ No
If yes, provide details:	
Other information of importance:	

Additional notes:

§9-F: Dental Insurance

Provide details regarding any dental insurance coverage you may have, and whether it is provided by your employer as a benefit, or whether you pay for this insurance by yourself.

Do you have **dental** insurance?	☐ Yes ☐ No
If yes, is it an employer group plan?	☐ Yes ☐ No
If yes, name of employer:	
Phone number of contact person:	
If yes, what is the policy number?	
Insurance policy plan name:	
Monthly premium:	$
How paid:	☐ Auto-draft from bank acct ☐ Write check
Amount of deductible:	$
Name of Insurance Company:	
Address of Insurance Company:	
Telephone number of company:	
Website address:	www.
Username:	
Password:	
Name of insurance agent:	
Name of insurance agency:	
Address of insurance agency:	
Phone number of insurance agent:	
Location of policy and documents:	
Does this policy cover your spouse?	☐ Yes ☐ No
Does this policy cover your children?	☐ Yes ☐ No
Other information of importance:	

Additional notes:

___

___

___

___

§9-G: Vision Insurance

Provide details regarding any vision insurance coverage you may have, and whether it is provided by your employer as a benefit, or whether you pay for this insurance by yourself.

Do you have **vision** insurance coverage?	☐ Yes ☐ No
If yes, is it an employer group plan?	☐ Yes ☐ No
If yes, name of employer:	
Phone number of contact person:	
If yes, what is the policy number?	
Insurance policy plan name:	
Monthly premium:	$
How paid:	☐ Auto-draft from bank acct ☐ Write check
Amount of deductible:	$
Name of Insurance Company:	
Address of Insurance Company:	
Telephone number of company:	
Website address:	www.
Username:	
Password:	
Name of insurance agent:	
Name of insurance agency:	
Address of insurance agency:	
Phone number of insurance agent:	
Location of policy and documents:	
Does this policy cover your spouse?	☐ Yes ☐ No
Does this policy cover your children?	☐ Yes ☐ No
Other information of importance:	

Additional notes:

§9-H: Prescription Drug Insurance

Provide details regarding any prescription drug coverage you may have, and whether it is provided by your employer as a benefit, or whether you pay for this insurance by yourself.

Do you have **prescription drugs** insurance coverage?	☐ Yes ☐ No
If yes, is it an employer group plan?	☐ Yes ☐ No
If yes, name of employer:	
Phone number of contact person:	
If yes, what is the policy number?	
Insurance policy plan name:	
Monthly premium:	$
How paid:	☐ Auto-draft from bank acct ☐ Write check
Amount of deductible:	$
Name of Insurance Company:	
Address of Insurance Company:	
Telephone number of company:	
Website address:	www.
Username:	
Password:	
Name of insurance agent:	
Name of insurance agency:	
Address of insurance agency:	
Phone number of insurance agent:	
Location of policy and documents:	
Does this policy cover your spouse?	☐ Yes ☐ No
Does this policy cover your children?	☐ Yes ☐ No
Other information of importance:	

Additional notes:

§9-I: Disability Insurance

Provide details regarding any disability insurance coverage you may have, and whether it is provided by your employer as a benefit, or whether you pay for this insurance by yourself.

Do you have **disability** insurance?	☐ Yes ☐ No
If yes, is it an employer group plan?	☐ Yes ☐ No
If yes, name of employer:	
Phone number of contact person:	
What is the policy number?	
Insurance policy plan name:	
Premium:	$_______________ Paid: ☐ Annually ☐ Quarterly ☐ Monthly
How paid:	☐ Auto-draft from bank acct ☐ Write check
Amount of deductible:	$
Name of Insurance Company:	
Address of Insurance Company:	
Telephone number of company:	
Website address:	www.
Username:	
Password:	
Name of insurance agent:	
Name of insurance agency:	
Address of insurance agency:	
Phone number of insurance agent:	
Does this policy cover your spouse?	☐ Yes ☐ No
Does this policy cover your children?	☐ Yes ☐ No
Location of policy and documents:	

Details of disability plan

Coverage term:	☐ Long term ☐ Short term ☐ Other: _______________
Does coverage end at retirement?	☐ Yes ☐ No
Does coverage end if you lose job?	☐ Yes ☐ No
Does coverage end when your Medicare or Social Security begins?	☐ Yes ☐ No
Benefit type:	☐ Fixed Amount ☐ _____% Percentage of salary ☐ Oher: _________
Benefit amount:	$____________ per ☐ Day ☐ Week ☐ Month ☐ Quarter ☐ Year
Is your benefit amount reduced by social security disability payments?	☐ Yes ☐ No If yes, reduction calculation: _______________
Elimination (waiting) period, if any:	☐ ___________ # of days ☐ Other: _______________
Benefit period:	☐ For life ☐ Number of years: _______ ☐ Other: __________
Any cost-of-living (COLA) adjustment?	☐ Yes ☐ No
Is this an **own occupation** policy?	☐ Yes ☐ No

§9-J: Supplemental Health Insurance or Short-Term Disability Insurance

*Rather than pay your medical bills like other forms of health insurance, if you are sick or injured, this type of insurance pays cash benefits **to you**, so you can pay your other bills while unable to work. For example, a well-known provider of this type of insurance is Aflac®.*

Do you have **supplemental health** insurance (e.g. Aflac®)?	☐ Yes ☐ No
If yes, is it an employer group plan?	☐ Yes ☐ No
If yes, name of employer:	
Phone/email of contact person:	
What is the policy number?	
Insurance policy plan name:	
Amount of premium:	$______________ Paid: ☐ Annually ☐ Quarterly ☐ Monthly
How paid:	☐ Auto-draft from bank acct ☐ Write check
Amount of deductible:	$
Name of Insurance Company:	
Address of Insurance Company:	
Telephone number of company:	
Website address:	www.
Username:	
Password:	
Name of insurance agent:	
Name of insurance agency:	
Address of insurance agency:	
Phone number of insurance agent:	
Location of policy and documents:	
Does this policy cover your spouse?	☐ Yes ☐ No
Does the policy cover your children?	☐ Yes ☐ No

Details of short-term disability plan

Coverage term:	☐ Long-term ☐ Short-term ☐ Other: ______________________
Does coverage end at retirement?	☐ Yes ☐ No
Does coverage end if you lose job?	☐ Yes ☐ No
Does coverage end when your Medicare or Social Security begins?	☐ Yes ☐ No
Benefit type:	☐ Fixed Amount ☐ _____% Percentage of salary ☐ Oher: _________
Benefit amount:	$____________ per ☐ Day ☐ Week ☐ Month ☐ Quarter ☐ Year
Is your benefit amount reduced by social security disability payments?	☐ Yes ☐ No If yes, reduction calculation: ______________________________
Elimination (waiting) period, if any:	☐ ___________ # of days ☐ Other: ________________________
Benefit period:	☐ For life ☐ Number of years: _______ ☐ Other: ______________

§9-K: Long-Term Care Insurance

Provide details regarding any long-term care insurance coverage you may have, and whether it is provided by your employer as a benefit, or whether you pay for this insurance by yourself.

Do you have **Long-Term Care Insurance**?	☐ Yes ☐ No If yes, provide following details:
If yes, is it an employer group plan?	☐ Yes ☐ No
If yes, name of employer:	
Phone/email of contact person:	
What is the policy number?	
Insurance policy plan name:	
Amount of premium:	$______________ Paid: ☐ Annually ☐ Quarterly ☐ Monthly
How paid:	☐ Auto-draft from bank acct ☐ Write check
Amount of deductible:	$
Name of Insurance Company:	
Address of Insurance Company:	
Telephone number of company:	
Website address:	www.
Username:	
Password:	
Name of insurance agent:	
Name of insurance agency:	
Address of insurance agency:	
Phone number of insurance agent:	
Location of policy and documents:	
Does this policy cover your spouse?	☐ Yes ☐ No
Does the policy cover your children?	☐ Yes ☐ No

Details of Long-Term Care policy

Long-term care benefits value:	$
Inflation Rider, if any:	☐ None ☐ Fixed ____% ☐ Consumer Price Index ☐ Other: _______
How long must premium be paid:	☐ For life ☐ Number of years: _________ ☐ Other: _______________
Elimination (waiting) period, if any:	☐ ____________ # of days ☐ Other: ____________________
Benefit payout amount:	$____________ per ☐ Day ☐ Week ☐ Month ☐ Quarter ☐ Year
Benefit period:	☐ ____________ # of years ☐ For Life ☐ Other: _______________
Is this LTC coverage contained in a rider to a life insurance policy?	☐ Yes ☐ No
Is there a cash value?	☐ Yes ☐ No If yes, cash value: $____________ as of ______________
Is there a death benefit value?	☐ Yes ☐ No If yes, death value: $___________ as of ______________
Is home care covered?	☐ Yes ☐ No If yes, provide details:
Can any unused benefits be transferred to a surviving spouse?	☐ Yes ☐ No

§9-L: Personal Articles Insurance Coverage

This is either a stand-alone policy or a rider to an existing insurance policy which covers jewelry, artwork, computer equipment, and other personal effects that exceed the value covered by your typical homeowner's policy.

If yes, do you have a **Personal Articles** insurance policy?	☐ Yes ☐ No
If yes, what is the policy number?	
If yes, what is the policy number?	
Insurance policy plan name:	
What items are covered by policy	
Amount of coverage:	$
Issue date of policy:	
Name of insurance policy owner:	☐ Me ☐ My Trust ☐ Jointly with: ______________________________ ☐ Other: ____
Name of insured person:	☐ Me ☐ Other: ____
Amount of premium:	$______________ per ☐ Month ☐ Year
How are premiums paid?	☐ By check ☐ Auto bank draft ☐ Other: ______________________
Name of insurance company:	
Address of insurance company:	
Telephone number of company:	
Website address:	
Username:	
Password:	
Name of insurance agent:	
Name of insurance agency:	
Address of insurance agency:	
City, state, and zip code:	
Phone number of agent:	
Location of policy and documents:	
Other details of importance:	

Additional notes:

____

____

____

____

§9-M: Other Types of Insurance

There are too many other types of insurance coverage available, so it would be impractical to try to list them all. So, please provide information on any additional policies that have not already been discussed. A few examples, some of which are quite unique, would include:

Flood Insurance; Cancer Insurance; Personal Effects Policies (e.g. expensive jewelry, electronics, artwork, etc.); Earthquake Insurance; Body Part Insurance (e.g. a singer insuring her voice, an athlete insuring their legs, etc.), Kidnap, Extortion, and Ransom Insurance; and even ... are you ready for this? ...Alien Abduction Insurance!

So, for ***any*** *type of insurance policies not already covered, provide the following information:*

If yes, do you have **any other** insurance policies?	☐ Yes ☐ No
What type of insurance is it?	
What is covered by the insurance?	
What is the policy number?	
Insurance policy plan name:	
Amount of premium:	$_______________ Paid: ☐ Annually ☐ Quarterly ☐ Monthly
How paid:	☐ Auto-draft from bank acct ☐ Write check
Amount of deductible:	$
Name of Insurance Company:	
Address of Insurance Company:	
Telephone number of company:	
Website address:	www.
Username:	
Password:	
Name of insurance agent:	
Name of insurance agency:	
Address of insurance agency:	
Phone number of insurance agent:	
Location of policy and documents:	

Additional notes:

____

____

____

____

§10-A: General Medical Information

In the sections that follow, this is where you will provide information your caregiver needs to know about your medical history, surgeries, doctors, medications, etc.

Have you been dealing with any medical issues or challenges?	☐ Yes ☐ No
If yes, provide a brief description of your medical issues or challenges (e.g. arthritis, back issues, breathing, type of cancer, etc.):	
Do you wear or have the following?	
Hearing Aids:	☐ Yes ☐ No
Contact Lenses:	☐ Yes ☐ No
Artificial limbs:	☐ Yes ☐ No
Pacemaker:	☐ Yes ☐ No
Wearable defibrillator:	☐ Yes ☐ No
Automated insulin delivery device:	☐ Yes ☐ No
Other: ____________________	☐ Yes ☐ No
Other: ____________________	☐ Yes ☐ No
Other: ____________________	☐ Yes ☐ No

§10-B: Surgeries

In the sections that follow, provide information your caregiver needs to know about your medical history, surgeries, doctors, medications, etc. Attach additional copies of questions, if needed.

Surgeries

Have you had one or more surgeries?	☐ Yes ☐ No
If yes, for each surgery, specify the type, date, and details below:	

Type of surgery performed:	
Date of surgery:	
Was the surgery successful?	☐ Yes ☐ No
If no, what was not successful?	
Name of surgeon:	
Name of facility:	
Address:	
City, state, and zip code:	
Telephone number:	
Other details of importance:	
Memories and stories about this surgery, the circumstances leading up to it, and the recovery from it:	

Type of surgery performed:	
Date of surgery:	
Was the surgery successful?	☐ Yes ☐ No
If no, what was not successful?	
Name of surgeon:	
Name of facility:	
Address:	
City, state, and zip code:	
Telephone number:	
Other details of importance:	
Memories and stories about this surgery, the circumstances leading up to it, and the recovery from it:	

Type of surgery performed:	
Date of surgery:	
Was the surgery successful?	☐ Yes ☐ No
If no, what was not successful?	
Name of surgeon:	
Name of facility:	
Address:	
City, state, and zip code:	
Telephone number:	
Other details of importance:	
Memories and stories about this surgery, the circumstances leading up to it, and the recovery from it:	

Type of surgery performed:	
Date of surgery:	
Was the surgery successful?	☐ Yes ☐ No
If no, what was not successful?	
Name of surgeon:	
Name of facility:	
Address:	
City, state, and zip code:	
Telephone number:	
Other details of importance:	
Memories and stories about this surgery, the circumstances leading up to it, and the recovery from it:	

§10-C: Your Doctors & Medical Care Providers

In the following sections, list the doctors you are seeing, so your caregiver will know which doctors you consider to be important to you. Remember, these are the doctors that will know you, your circumstances, and your medical history. Use either the general "type" of doctor or specialty category, as applicable to provide information.

Most of us have numerous doctors, so make as many copies of the next pages as needed to list all your doctors.

Types of medical doctors	Specialties
Eyes:	Ophthalmologist, Optometrist, Optician,
Teeth & braces:	Dentist, Orthodontist, Endodontist (root canal), Other: ________________
Ears, Nose & Throat (ENT):	Otolaryngologist
Skin:	Dermatologist
Allergies:	Allergist
Mental Health:	Psychiatrist, Psychologist,
Heart:	Cardiologist,
Bones:	Orthopedist, Chiropractor,
Feet:	Podiatrist
Blood:	Hematologist
Kidneys & Urinary System:	Urologist
Lungs:	Pulmonologist
Kids:	Pediatrician
Women-related:	OB-GYN, obstetrician, gynecologist, Other: ___________________________
Old Age:	Geriatrician
Blood:	Endocrinologist
Cancer:	Oncologist
Nervous System:	Neurologist.
Digestive System:	Gastrologist
Hearing Disorders:	Audiologist
Physical medicine & rehabilitation	Physiatrist, Physical Therapist,
Oriental Medicine:	Acupuncturist,
Massage & Manipulation:	Chiropractor, Osteopath
Other:	Other: ____

Primary Care Physician

Type of doctor:	**Primary Care Physician**
Name of your doctor:	
Name of medical practice or facility:	
Address:	
City, state, and zip code:	
Telephone number:	
Email address:	
Website:	
Username:	
Password:	
Details regarding the services this doctor is providing to you:	

Dentist

Type of doctor:	**Dentist**
Name of your doctor:	
Name of medical practice or facility:	
Address:	
City, state, and zip code:	
Telephone number:	
Email address:	
Website:	
Username:	
Password:	
Details regarding the services this doctor is providing to you:	

Eye Doctor

Type of doctor:	**Eye Doctor**
Name of your doctor:	
Name of medical practice or facility:	
Address:	
City, state, and zip code:	
Telephone number:	
Email address:	
Website:	
Username:	
Password:	
Details regarding the services this doctor is providing to you:	

Type of doctor:	
Name of your doctor:	
Name of medical practice or facility:	
Address:	
City, state, and zip code:	
Telephone number:	
Email address:	
Website:	
Username:	
Password:	
Details regarding the services this doctor is providing to you:	

Type of doctor:	
Name of your doctor:	
Name of medical practice or facility:	
Address:	
City, state, and zip code:	
Telephone number:	
Email address:	
Website:	
Username:	
Password:	
Details regarding the services this doctor is providing to you:	

Type of doctor:	
Name of your doctor:	
Name of medical practice or facility:	
Address:	
City, state, and zip code:	
Telephone number:	
Email address:	
Website:	
Username:	
Password:	
Details regarding the services this doctor is providing to you:	

Type of doctor:	
Name of your doctor:	
Name of medical practice or facility:	
Address:	
City, state, and zip code:	
Telephone number:	
Email address:	
Website:	
Username:	
Password:	
Details regarding the services this doctor is providing to you:	

Type of doctor:	
Name of your doctor:	
Name of medical practice or facility:	
Address:	
City, state, and zip code:	
Telephone number:	
Email address:	
Website:	
Username:	
Password:	
Details regarding the services this doctor is providing to you:	

Type of doctor:	
Name of your doctor:	
Name of medical practice or facility:	
Address:	
City, state, and zip code:	
Telephone number:	
Email address:	
Website:	
Username:	
Password:	
Details regarding the services this doctor is providing to you:	

§10-D: Prescription Medications

Provide information for every prescription medication you are taking.

Name of drug:	
Is use of a generic version ok?	
Prescription number:	
Dosage:	
Frequency:	
What is the purpose of this drug (why are you taking the medication):	
Name of prescribing doctor:	
Name of pharmacy:	
Pharmacy telephone number:	
Insurance coverage and deductible:	$ Deductible: $
Other details or special instructions:	

Name of drug:	
Is use of a generic version okay?	
Prescription number:	
Dosage:	
Frequency:	
What is the purpose of this drug (why are you taking the medication)?	
Name of prescribing doctor:	
Name of pharmacy:	
Pharmacy telephone number:	
Insurance coverage and deductible:	$ Deductible: $
Other details or special instructions:	

Name of drug:	
Is use of a generic version ok?	
Prescription number:	
Dosage:	
Frequency:	
What is the purpose of this drug (why are you taking the medication)?	
Name of prescribing doctor:	
Name of pharmacy:	
Pharmacy telephone number:	
Insurance coverage and deductible:	$ Deductible: $
Other details or special instructions:	

Name of drug:	
Is use of a generic version okay?	
Prescription number:	
Dosage:	
Frequency:	
What is the purpose of this drug (why are you taking the medication)?	
Name of prescribing doctor:	
Name of pharmacy:	
Pharmacy telephone number:	
Insurance coverage and deductible:	$ Deductible: $
Other details or special instructions:	

Name of drug:	
Is use of a generic version okay?	
Prescription number:	
Dosage:	
Frequency:	
What is the purpose of this drug (why are you taking the medication)?	
Name of prescribing doctor:	
Name of pharmacy:	
Pharmacy telephone number:	
Insurance coverage and deductible:	$ Deductible: $
Other details or special instructions:	

Name of drug:	
Is use of a generic version okay?	
Prescription number:	
Dosage:	
Frequency:	
What is the purpose of this drug (why are you taking the medication)?	
Name of prescribing doctor:	
Name of pharmacy:	
Pharmacy telephone number:	
Insurance coverage and deductible:	$ Deductible: $
Other details or special instructions:	

§10-E: Non-Prescription Medications, Vitamins & Supplements

Provide information for each *non-prescription* *drug, vitamin, or supplement you are taking and your reason for using it.*

Name of product:	
Dosage:	
Frequency:	
What is the purpose of this product?	
Name of store where purchased:	
Website address, if purchased online:	
Store telephone number:	
Other details or special instructions:	

Name of product:	
Dosage:	
Frequency:	
What is the purpose of this product?	
Name of store where purchased:	
Website address, if purchased online:	
Store telephone number:	
Other details or special instructions:	

Name of product:	
Dosage:	
Frequency:	
What is the purpose of this product?	
Name of store where purchased:	
Website address, if purchased online:	
Store telephone number:	
Other details or special instructions:	

Name of product:	
Dosage:	
Frequency:	
What is the purpose of this product?	
Name of store where purchased:	
Website address, if purchased online:	
Store telephone number:	
Other details or special instructions:	

Name of product:	
Dosage:	
Frequency:	
What is the purpose of this product?	
Name of store where purchased:	
Website address, if purchased online:	
Store telephone number:	
Other details or special instructions:	

Name of product:	
Dosage:	
Frequency:	
What is the purpose of this product?	
Name of store where purchased:	
Website address, if purchased online:	
Store telephone number:	
Other details or special instructions:	

§10-F: Allergies

Provide as many details about your allergies as you can.

Allergies to medications

Are you allergic to any **medications?**	☐ Yes ☐ No	If yes, **specify which medications**:
Penicillin or other antibiotics:	☐ Yes ☐ No	
Local anesthetics:	☐ Yes ☐ No	
Barbiturates, sedatives, sleeping pills	☐ Yes ☐ No	
Sulfa drugs:	☐ Yes ☐ No	
Codeine or other narcotics:	☐ Yes ☐ No	
Ibuprofen:	☐ Yes ☐ No	
Aspirin:	☐ Yes ☐ No	
Sulfa drugs:	☐ Yes ☐ No	
Insulin:	☐ Yes ☐ No	
Other:	☐ Yes ☐ No	

Food allergies

Are you allergic to any **foods?**	☐ Yes ☐ No	If yes, **specify which foods**:
Milk:	☐ Yes ☐ No	
Eggs:	☐ Yes ☐ No	
Peanuts:	☐ Yes ☐ No	
Tree nuts:	☐ Yes ☐ No	
Soy:	☐ Yes ☐ No	
Wheat:	☐ Yes ☐ No	
Seeds:	☐ Yes ☐ No	
Shellfish:	☐ Yes ☐ No	
Other:	☐ Yes ☐ No	

Other allergies

Do you have any **other allergies?**	☐ Yes ☐ No	If yes, **specify which other allergies:**
Latex (rubber):	☐ Yes ☐ No	
Adhesive tape:	☐ Yes ☐ No	
Iodine:	☐ Yes ☐ No	
Pollen:	☐ Yes ☐ No	
Dust mites:	☐ Yes ☐ No	
Mold:	☐ Yes ☐ No	
Animals/animal dander:	☐ Yes ☐ No	
Insect bites/bee stings:	☐ Yes ☐ No	
Hay fever/other seasonal allergies:	☐ Yes ☐ No	
Metals:	☐ Yes ☐ No	
Other:	☐ Yes ☐ No	

§10-G: Your Medical History (Including Family Medical History)

If someone needs to make medical decisions on your behalf, it is important for them to know as much of your medical history as possible. Indicate whether you or an immediate family member have ever had, been told you had, or been treated for any of the following conditions (check all that apply, specify any immediate family member who has had it, and provide additional details about each on the next page.)

Attach an additional sheet of paper for further details, if needed.

Have you had any of the following childhood diseases?

Chicken Pox:	☐ Yes ☐ No
Measles:	☐ Yes ☐ No
Mumps:	☐ Yes ☐ No
German Measles:	☐ Yes ☐ No
Whooping Cough:	☐ Yes ☐ No
Asthma:	☐ Yes ☐ No
Childhood traumatic event or injury:	☐ Yes ☐ No
Other (specify):	
Other (specify):	

Which vaccinations have you received?	**If yes, when was your most recent vaccination?**
Influenza (Flu)	☐ Yes ☐ No If yes, when?
Tetanus, diphtheria, pertussis (Td/Tdap	☐ Yes ☐ No If yes, when?
PPSV (Pneumococcal Polysaccharide Vaccine)	☐ Yes ☐ No If yes, when?
Hepatitis A Vaccine	☐ Yes ☐ No If yes, when?
Hepatitis B Vaccine	☐ Yes ☐ No If yes, when?
HPV (Human Papillomavirus) Vaccine	☐ Yes ☐ No If yes, when?
MMR (Measles, Mumps, Rubella) Vaccine	☐ Yes ☐ No If yes, when?
Varicella (Chickenpox) Vaccine	☐ Yes ☐ No If yes, when?
Meningococcal Vaccine	☐ Yes ☐ No If yes, when?
Shingles (Zoster) Vaccine	☐ Yes ☐ No If yes, when?
Other (specify)____________________:	☐ Yes ☐ No If yes, when?
Other (specify) ____________________:	☐ Yes ☐ No If yes, when?
Other (specify) ____________________:	☐ Yes ☐ No If yes, when?

Additional notes:

____

____

____

____

Do you now have, or in the past, have you had, any of the following medical conditions?

ADD/ADHD	☐ Current ☐ In the Past
Addiction - drugs	☐ Current ☐ In the Past. To what?
Addiction - other	☐ Current ☐ In the Past. To what?
AIDS/HIV+	☐ Current ☐ In the Past ☐ Relative:
Alcohol abuse	☐ Current ☐ In the Past
Allergies - Medications	☐ Current ☐ In the Past **See previous section**
Allergies - Food	☐ Current ☐ In the Past **See previous section**
Allergies - Other	☐ Current ☐ In the Past **See previous section**
ALS (Lou Gehrig's disease)	☐ Current ☐ In the Past ☐ Relative:
Alzheimer's/dementia/cognitive impairment	☐ Current ☐ In the Pas
Anemia	☐ Current ☐ In the Past ☐ Relative:
Aneurysm	☐ Current ☐ In the Past
Angina	☐ Current ☐ In the Past
Anorexia	☐ Current ☐ In the Past
Arrhythmia (irregular heart rate)	☐ Current ☐ In the Past
Arthritis	☐ Current ☐ In the Past ☐ Relative:
Asthma	☐ Current ☐ In the Past ☐ Relative:
Artificial heart valve	☐ Current ☐ In the Past
Attempted suicide	☐ Current ☐ In the Past
Autism / Asperger syndrome	☐ Current ☐ In the Past ☐ Relative:
Automobile accident with injuries	☐ Current ☐ In the Past
Back / Spine problems	☐ Current ☐ In the Past.
Bipolar disorder	☐ Current ☐ In the Past
Bisphosphonate therapy	☐ Current ☐ In the Past
Bleeding problems	☐ Current ☐ In the Past
Blood diseases	☐ Current ☐ In the Past ☐ Relative:
Blood transfusion	☐ Current ☐ In the Past If yes, date:
Bloom's syndrome	☐ Current ☐ In the Past ☐ Relative:
Broken bones	☐ Current ☐ In the Past
Bulimia	☐ Current ☐ In the Past
Burns	☐ Current ☐ In the Past
Bronchitis	☐ Current ☐ In the Past
Cancer	☐ Current ☐ In the Past. Type: ☐ Relative:

Cataracts	☐ Current ☐ In the Past
Chemo-radiation therapy	☐ Current ☐ In the Past
COPD	☐ Current ☐ In the Past
Coronary artery or cerebrovascular disease	☐ Current ☐ In the Past
Crohn's disease	☐ Current ☐ In the Past ☐ Relative:
Celiac disease	☐ Current ☐ In the Past ☐ Relative:
Chicken Pox	☐ Current ☐ In the Past
Chronic fatigue syndrome	☐ Current ☐ In the Past
Cirrhosis	☐ Current ☐ In the Past
Colitis (ulcerative)	☐ Current ☐ In the Past
Concussion	☐ Current ☐ In the Past
Cosmetic surgery	☐ Current ☐ In the Past
Concussion	☐ Current ☐ In the Past
Cystic Fibrosis	☐ Current ☐ In the Past ☐ Relative:
Dementia / Alzheimer's disease	☐ Current ☐ In the Past ☐ Relative:
Depression	☐ Current ☐ In the Past
Diabetes (check one): ☐ Type I; ☐ Type II	☐ Current ☐ In the Past ☐ Relative:
Depression/anxiety	☐ Current ☐ In the Past ☐ Relative:
Dizzy spells	☐ Current ☐ In the Past
Down syndrome	☐ Current ☐ In the Past ☐ Relative:
Drug abuse	☐ Current ☐ In the Past
Eating disorder	☐ Current ☐ In the Past
Emphysema	☐ Current ☐ In the Past
Epilepsy	☐ Current ☐ In the Past ☐ Relative:
Fainting	☐ Current ☐ In the Past
Fibromyalgia	☐ Current ☐ In the Past ☐ Relative:
Gall bladder disease	☐ Current ☐ In the Past
Gastritis or peptic ulcer disease	☐ Current ☐ In the Past
GERD (reflux)	☐ Current ☐ In the Past
Glaucoma	☐ Current ☐ In the Past ☐ Relative:
Gout	☐ Current ☐ In the Past
Hashimoto or Graves	☐ Current ☐ In the Past
Headaches (severe)	☐ Current ☐ In the Past ☐ Relative:
Heart attack / surgery	☐ Current ☐ In the Past ☐ Relative:

Heart disease	☐ Current ☐ In the Past ☐ Relative:
Heart murmur, valve disorder, heart problems	☐ Current ☐ In the Past ☐ Relative:
Hepatitis & Type A / B / C (circle one)	☐ Current ☐ In the Past ☐ Relative:
High Blood Pressure	☐ Current ☐ In the Past ☐ Relative:
High cholesterol	☐ Current ☐ In the Past ☐ Relative:
Hodgkin's lymphoma (Hodgkin's disease)	☐ Current ☐ In the Past ☐ Relative:
Huntington's disease	☐ Current ☐ In the Past ☐ Relative:
Hypoglycemia	☐ Current ☐ In the Past ☐ Relative:
Hypothyroidism (low thyroid)	☐ Current ☐ In the Past
Hypothyroidism (overactive)	☐ Current ☐ In the Past
Immune dysfunction	☐ Current ☐ In the Past ☐ Relative:
Insulin resistance	☐ Current ☐ In the Past
Interstitial cystitis	☐ Current ☐ In the Past
Irregular heartbeat/palpitations	☐ Current ☐ In the Past
Irritable/inflammatory bowel syndrome	☐ Current ☐ In the Past
Jaundice	☐ Current ☐ In the Past
Joint replacement	☐ Current ☐ In the Past
Kidney disease	☐ Current ☐ In the Past
Kidney stones	☐ Current ☐ In the Past
Latex allergy	☐ Current ☐ In the Past
Liver problems	☐ Current ☐ In the Past
Low Blood Pressure	☐ Current ☐ In the Past
Lung disease	☐ Current ☐ In the Past ☐ Relative:
Lyme disease	☐ Current ☐ In the Past
Lupus SLE	☐ Current ☐ In the Past ☐ Relative:
Lymphoma-Non-Hodgkin's	☐ Current ☐ In the Past ☐ Relative:
Macular degeneration (eyes)	☐ Current ☐ In the Past ☐ Relative:
Malaria	☐ Current ☐ In the Past
Metabolic syndrome	☐ Current ☐ In the Past
Mental Illness	☐ Current ☐ In the Past ☐ Relative:
Measles	☐ Current ☐ In the Past
Meningitis	☐ Current ☐ In the Past ☐ Relative:
Migraine	☐ Current ☐ In the Past
Mononucleosis	☐ Current ☐ In the Past

Mumps	☐ Current ☐ In the Past
Multiple Sclerosis	☐ Current ☐ In the Past ☐ Relative:
Muscular Dystrophy	☐ Current ☐ In the Past ☐ Relative:
Neuropathy (numbness, tingling, pain, burning)	☐ Current ☐ In the Past
Neurological	☐ Current ☐ In the Past ☐ Relative:
Neuromuscular disease	☐ Current ☐ In the Past ☐ Relative:
Noonan syndrome	☐ Current ☐ In the Past ☐ Relative:
Osteoarthritis	☐ Current ☐ In the Past
Osteoporosis	☐ Current ☐ In the Past
Pacemaker	☐ Current ☐ In the Past
Pancreatitis	☐ Current ☐ In the Past ☐ Relative:
Paralysis	☐ Current ☐ In the Past
Parkinson's disease	☐ Current ☐ In the Past ☐ Relative:
Peripheral vascular disease	☐ Current ☐ In the Past.
Polio	☐ Current ☐ In the Past
Polycystic ovarian syndrome	☐ Current ☐ In the Past
Psychological care	☐ Current ☐ In the Past
Psychiatric care	☐ Current ☐ In the Past ☐ Relative:
Physical abuse	☐ Current ☐ In the Past
Rheumatic fever	☐ Current ☐ In the Past
Rheumatoid arthritis	☐ Current ☐ In the Past ☐ Relative:
Schizophrenia	☐ Current ☐ In the Past
Seizures	☐ Current ☐ In the Past ☐ Relative:
Sexual abuse	☐ Current ☐ In the Past
Sexually transmitted disease	☐ Current ☐ In the Past
Sickle cell anemia	☐ Current ☐ In the Past ☐ Relative:
Sinusitis	☐ Current ☐ In the Past
Sinus trouble	☐ Current ☐ In the Past
Sleep apnea	☐ Current ☐ In the Past. Details
Skin disease	☐ Current ☐ In the Past. Details:
Sleep disorder	☐ Current ☐ In the Past
Stroke	☐ Current ☐ In the Past ☐ Relative:
Suicide (attempted)	☐ Current ☐ In the Past
Surgeries	☐ Current ☐ In the Past **(See section above)**

Temporomandibular Joint Disorder (TMD/TMJ)	☐ Current ☐ In the Past
Thalassemia	☐ Current ☐ In the Past ☐ Relative:
Thyroid problems	☐ Current ☐ In the Past ☐ Relative:
Tobacco use	☐ Current ☐ In the Past
Tonsillitis	☐ Current ☐ In the Past
Tourette Syndrome	☐ Current ☐ In the Past ☐ Relative:
Trauma (head)	☐ Current ☐ In the Past
Tremors	☐ Current ☐ In the Past
Transfusions	☐ Current ☐ In the Past
Transplants	☐ Current ☐ In the Past
Tuberculosis	☐ Current ☐ In the Past
Vascular disease	☐ Current ☐ In the Past ☐ Relative:
Venereal disease	☐ Current ☐ In the Past ☐ Relative:
Other	☐ Current ☐ In the Past ☐ Relative:

Have you ever had any of the following

Cataract surgery	☐ Yes ☐ No
Lasik or other eye surgery	☐ Yes ☐ No
Implants (of any kind)	☐ Yes ☐ No
Joint replacement (specify)	☐ Yes ☐ No
Pacemaker	☐ Yes ☐ No
Heart surgery	☐ Yes ☐ No
Hearing aids/Cochlear implants	☐ Yes ☐ No
Pins or plates in bones	☐ Yes ☐ No
Vasectomy	☐ Yes ☐ No
Hysterectomy	☐ Yes ☐ No
Other surgeries (specify)	☐ Yes ☐ No

Additional notes:

____

____

____

____

For each medical condition checked on the previous pages, provide as much information as possible about it. Try to include dates, diagnosis, details, treatment, plus names, addresses, and phone numbers of all family members involved, and physicians and/or medical providers consulted. **This could be life and death information**, so attach as many pages as needed to provide details for each item.

List each medical condition that applies to you

List each medical condition identified above that applies to you	Assign each medical condition with a number, and continue your description of the condition, your symptoms, treatment, etc. on a separate sheet of paper, as needed.
	1.
	2.
	3.
	4.
	5.
	6.
	7.
	8.
Reminder to share the stories and memories behind each of the above medical conditions.	
Are any of these genetic conditions future generations should know about?	

§11-A: My Funeral, Cremation, or Body Donation Plans

Provide your preferences regarding your final resting place, and details regarding your funeral, cremation, or other disposition of your remains.

General information

Disposition of body:	☐ I want a funeral and my bodily remains should be buried (details below) ☐ My bodily remains should be cremated (details below) ☐ My body should be donated to science (details below)
What type of memorial service would you prefer?	☐ A **memorial** service with friends and family, but the body is not present ☐ A **funeral** service at the funeral home or cremation facility ☐ A **committal** service at the graveside or where your ashes are being interred ☐ A **celebration of life** or other life appreciation ceremony
Do you want a **celebration of life**? If yes, attach additional preferences and instructions.	☐ Yes ☐ No
If yes, should this be in addition to or in place of a memorial service?	☐ In addition to my memorial service. ☐ In place of a memorial service.

Prepaid or pre-arranged plans

Have you made any arrangements regarding your funeral, cremation, or disposition of your remains?	☐ Yes ☐ No
Have you **pre-paid** for these arrangements or have you pre-paid for a burial/cremation plan?	☐ Yes ☐ No
If yes, what is the name of the arrangement plan or plan provider:	
Telephone number:	
Plan or policy number:	
Location of document(s):	

People you specifically want informed or invited

Is there anyone that you specifically **<u>want</u>** to be notified of your death and/or invited to attend your funeral (other than the usual expected friends and relatives)?	☐ Yes ☐ No
If yes, provide name(s) and contact information for each person:	1 2 3

People you specifically do NOT want informed or invited

Is there anyone that you would prefer **NOT** to be notified of your death and/or **barred** from attending your funeral?	☐ Yes ☐ No
If yes, provide name(s):	1 2 3

Organizations to be notified

Are there any professional, educational, religious, fraternal, or other organizations, clubs, lodges, associations, or other groups, that should be notified of your death and provided with funeral details?	☐ Yes ☐ No
If yes, provide name and contact information for each:	1 2 3
Are there any fraternal organization services who will help with the planning or payment of your funeral?	☐ Yes ☐ No
If yes, name of organization:	
Contact person and information:	

Veteran's military burial & funeral benefits

Are you entitled to a military burial, honors, and/or memorial benefits (e.g. bugle, flag, rifle squad, etc.)?	☐ Yes ☐ No
If yes, would you like these benefits?	☐ Yes ☐ No **Reminder**: The funeral director needs to request military funeral honors on behalf of the veteran's family
Would you like a "Presidential Memorial Certificate?"	☐ Yes ☐ No **Reminder**: This may be requested in person at a VA regional office or by U.S. mail to the Veterans Administration.
To whom you would you like the American flag presented (Name)?	Name: **Reminder**: For an American flag, VA form 21-2008 must be submitted along with the veteran's discharge papers.
If you qualify, would you like your remains buried in a VA National Cemetery?	☐ Yes ☐ No

BURIAL AND FUNERAL PREFERENCES AND INFORMATION

Funeral home or mortuary

Name of funeral home or mortuary:	
Address:	
City, state, and zip code:	
Telephone number:	
Name of contact person:	
Other details of importance:	

Religious service preferences, if any

Do you have a preference as to having religious services?	☐ Yes ☐ No
If no, do you prefer:	☐ No service at all ☐ Specify: ________________
If yes, which religion:	
Name of officiating clergy:	
Cleric's phone number:	
Other details of importance:	

Miscellaneous funeral preferences

My viewing preference:	☐ Open casket ☐ Closed casket ☐ No Preference
Regarding cost, should your funeral arrangements be:	☐ Keep cost to a minimum ☐ moderate cost ☐ higher cost ☐ Premium – Pull out all the stops Other details:
Casket Preferences as to cost:	☐ Keep cost to a minimum ☐ moderate cost ☐ higher cost ☐ Premium – Pull out all the stops Other details:
Specify any apparel, jewelry, or other items that should accompany you in the casket or adorn your body for the viewing, if any:	
Specify any of the above items that are to be buried with you, if any:	
Music preferences, if any:	
Floral preferences, if any:	
If you have one or more preferred charity for memorial donations, provide each charity's name & address:	☐ Check this box if you prefer the donation is to be in lieu of flowers.
If you have a favorite song, poem,	

story, quote, Bible passage, etc. that you would like read or performed, provide details, where it can be located, and whom you would like to read or perform it:	
Who else would you like to make comments at your funeral, if anyone?	
If you have some comments, wishes, and/or other thoughts you would like shared with those attending your funeral, write them here:	

Your eulogy

Have you written or created your own eulogy?	☐ Yes ☐ No
If yes, what is the format:	☐ Written. I would prefer that it be read by the person named below. ☐ Audio recording to be played. ☐ Video recording to be played. ☐ Other (specify): ____________________
Where can the eulogy be found?	
Name and phone number of the person whom you would like to deliver your eulogy (or read the one you have written):	

Your obituary

Your legal name:	
Date of Birth:	
Birthplace:	
Name of surviving spouse:	
Name(s) of surviving parents:	
Names of surviving children:	
Names of surviving grandchildren:	
Provide a photograph for obituary?	☐ Yes ☐ No
How many years in current locale:	
Retired?	☐ Yes ☐ No If yes, when?
Profession or trade:	
Last employer:	
Schools, colleges, special training:	
Religious and civil affiliations:	
Military (branch, rank, war services, ribbons and awards):	
Other accomplishments:	

Pallbearer preferences

Name/Phone # - Pallbearer 1: Pallbearer 2: Pallbearer 3: Pallbearer 4: Pallbearer 5: Pallbearer 6:	
Name/Phone: Honorary Pallbearers Honorary Pallbearer 1: Honorary Pallbearer 2: Honorary Pallbearer 3: Honorary Pallbearer 4: Honorary Pallbearer 5: Honorary Pallbearer 6:	

Cemetery plot details, if any

Do you own a cemetery plot?	☐ Yes ☐ No
If no, where you would like to be buried?	
If yes, what is the cemetery name?	
Address:	
City, state, and zip code:	
Telephone:	
Location of the deed:	
Plot in name of:	
Section:	
Plot number:	
Block:	
Special instructions:	
If would like to be buried next to a deceased spouse, parent, or child, provide that person's name:	
Location of grave or urn:	
Other details of importance:	
Do you have a preference for the type or style of your gravestone, headstone, or monument?	
Do you have any preference for an epitaph on your tombstone?	☐ Yes ☐ No If yes, what is it?
Have you written your own obituary?	☐ Yes ☐ No
If yes, where can it be found?	
Have you arranged for eternal care of the grave?	☐ Yes ☐ No
If yes, what is the location of the information or documents?	

CREMATION PREFERENCES AND INFORMATION

Do you own a mausoleum vault?	☐ Yes ☐ No
If yes, where is the vault located?	
If no, do you have a preference as to the disposition of the ashes?	☐ Yes ☐ No
Location of documents:	
If yes, provide details (e.g. kept in an urn), and by whom or where (e.g. scattered by my wife in the Atlantic Ocean, made part of a barrier reef, compressed into a diamond, etc.):	
Do you want a memorial service?	☐ Yes ☐ No
If yes, complete the previous section for above funeral preferences, or provide details here:	

DONATION OF BODY PREFERENCES AND INFORMATION

Have you made arrangements for full body donation of your for science research or educational purposes?	☐ Yes ☐ No
If yes, who should be contacted to claim your remains?	
Telephone number:	
Address:	
City, state, and zip code:	
Website:	
Username:	
Password:	
Contract Number, if any:	
Name of organization (e.g. LifeQuest Anatomical, LLC) to receive your remains, if different from above:	
Location of documents:	
Other details of importance:	

Miscellaneous details

Do you want your children (or others) to be reimbursed for the cost of their travel (e.g. airfare, lodging, etc. if any) to and from your funeral?	☐ Yes ☐ No **(NOTE: Unless this provision is included in your Last Will and Testament and/or Trust documents, it will probably not be binding upon your Personal Representative or trustee)**
If yes, list their names, and be certain to let your Personal Representative and/or trustee know.	
Specify any limits to reimbursement per person:	$

Do you have any additional preferences?	☐ Yes ☐ No
If yes, what are your preferences? **Remember**, these are **your** final wishes, and yes, you can even be funny if you want (e.g. "I want a choir; I want an open bar for the guests to give me a final toast, etc.")	

A few additional thoughts and comments from your author

If you have some favorite family photographs or videos, why not consider putting together a video montage of them to be played at the funeral or celebration of life? Think of it as a video replay of your happiest moments in life.

If you don't want to prepare it yourself, or don't know how to do it, there are companies that will come into your house who will interview you about special memories, scan your favorite photographs or videos, and create a lasting video legacy for your family.

How about writing something about your life in your own words, to be read aloud? Or better yet, how about making an audio or video recording of yourself saying your own farewells? Read the chapter in my book about funerals for ideas.

If you do decide to leave a lasting written, spoken, or video legacy like the ones I've described, please keep it positive and loving. This is **not** the place or time to be mean, vindictive, or say something you've always wanted to say to that "no good son of a #&#%." In some states, spoken or written words, even after death, can be the basis for a defamation lawsuit. So, be sure to keep it pleasant, positive, and uplifting, so that people remember your last words as happy, uplifting, and loving ones. **JES**

Additional notes:

____

____

____

____

§11-B: Organ Donation

Vital organs quickly become unusable for transplantation after death, but tissues, such as bone, skin, heart valves, and corneas can be donated within the first 24 hours after death. So, it is not only important to complete these details, but to let your loved ones know about your preferences while you are still healthy enough to tell them.

Be sure to make the selection on your state's driver's license, so there is no doubt as to your preferences.

Do you want your organs donated to be used to help others:	☐ Yes ☐ No
Have you made a donor election on your state's driver's license?	☐ Yes ☐ No
Is this election made on any other document?	☐ Yes ☐ No
Location of document(s):	
If yes, specify organs and tissues to be donated, if any:	☐ Donate any of my organs or tissues that are usable. ☐ None of my organs or tissues are to be donated. ☐ Anything that is usable **EXCEPT** the following: ☐ Heart ☐ Intestine ☐ Kidneys ☐ Liver ☐ Lungs; ☐ Pancreas ☐ Bone ☐ Cartilage ☐ Corneas ☐ Fascia ☐ Heart Valves ☐ Ligaments ☐ Pericardium ☐ Skin ☐ Tendons ☐ Veins ☐ Others **(specify):** ☐ **ONLY** the following organs and tissues: ☐ Heart ☐ Intestine ☐ Kidneys ☐ Liver ☐ Lungs; ☐ Pancreas ☐ Bone ☐ Cartilage ☐ Corneas ☐ Fascia ☐ Heart Valves ☐ Ligaments ☐ Pericardium ☐ Skin ☐ Tendons ☐ Veins ☐ Others **(specify):**
Other details of importance:	

Additional notes:

____

____

____

§12-A: Advisors, Important Contacts, and Other Organizations and Affiliations

Provide contact information for those individuals who, or organizations which, may have information needed by your representatives to take care of your affairs on your behalf.

My personal attorney

My personal attorney's name:	
Name of law firm:	
Address:	
City, state, and zip code:	
Work telephone number:	
Mobile telephone number:	
Fax number:	
Email address:	
Other details of importance (e.g. documents being held for you, legal matters in process, etc.):	

My business attorney

My business attorney's name:	
Name of law firm:	
Address:	
City, state, and zip code:	
Work telephone number:	
Mobile telephone number:	
Fax number:	
Email address:	
Other details of importance (e.g. documents being held for you, legal matters in process, etc.):	

My CPA/accountant

My CPA/accountant's name:	
Name of accounting firm:	
Address:	
City, state, and zip code:	
Work telephone number:	
Mobile telephone number:	
Fax number:	
Email address:	
Other details of importance (e.g. documents being held for you, legal matters in process, etc.):	

My financial advisor

My primary financial advisor name:	
Name of investment firm:	
Address:	
City, state, and zip code:	
Work telephone number:	
Mobile telephone number:	
Fax number:	
Email address:	
Other details of importance (e.g. documents being held for you, legal matters in process, etc.):	

My 2nd financial advisor

My 2nd financial advisor name:	
Name of investment firm:	
Address:	
City, state, and zip code:	
Work telephone number:	
Mobile telephone number:	
Fax number:	
Email address:	
Other details of importance (e.g. documents being held for you, legal matters in process, etc.):	

My life insurance agent

My life insurance agent's name:	
Name of insurance agency:	
Address:	
City, state, and zip code:	
Work telephone number:	
Mobile telephone number:	
Fax number:	
Email address:	
Other details of importance:	

My health insurance agent

My health insurance agent name:	
Name of insurance agency:	
Address:	
City, state, and zip code:	
Work telephone number:	
Mobile telephone number:	
Fax number:	
Email address:	
Other details of importance:	

My auto/property insurance agent

My auto/property ins. agent name:	
Name of insurance agency:	
Address:	
City, state, and zip code:	
Work telephone number:	
Mobile telephone number:	
Fax number:	
Email address:	
Other details of importance:	

Other insurance agent (specify)

My other insurance agent's name:	
Type of Insurance:	
Name of insurance agency:	
Address:	
City, state, and zip code:	
Work telephone number:	
Mobile telephone number:	
Fax number:	
Email address:	
Other details of importance:	

Other insurance agent (specify)

My other insurance agent's name:	
Type of Insurance:	
Name of insurance agency:	
Address:	
City, state, and zip code:	
Work telephone number:	
Mobile telephone number:	
Fax number:	
Email address:	
Other details of importance:	

My banker

My banker's name:	
Name of bank:	
Address:	
City, state, and zip code:	
Work telephone number:	
Mobile telephone number:	
Fax number:	
Email address:	
Other details of importance:	

My Trust officer

My Trust officer's name:	
Name of bank or Trust company:	
Address:	
City, state, and zip code:	
Work telephone number:	
Mobile telephone number:	
Fax number:	
Email address:	
Other details of importance:	

My property manager

My property manager's name:	
Name of Property Mgmt Firm:	
Address:	
City, state, and zip code:	
Work telephone number:	
Mobile telephone number:	
Fax number:	
Email address:	
Other details of importance:	

My clergy/spiritual advisor

My clergy/spiritual advisor's name:	
Name of religious organization:	
Address:	
City, state, and zip code:	
Work telephone number:	
Mobile telephone number:	
Fax number:	
Email address:	
Other details of importance:	

My support group

Name of my support group:	
Contact person:	
Contact person phone number/email	
Name of group:	
Purpose of group:	
Address:	
City, state, and zip code:	
Work telephone number:	
Mobile telephone number:	
Fax number:	
Email address:	
Other details of importance:	

Professional, fraternal, union, or other organization

Name of Professional, Fraternal, Union or Other Organization:	
Membership number, if any:	
Individual contact person's name:	
Address:	
City, state, and zip code:	
Work telephone number:	
Mobile telephone number:	
Fax number:	
Email address:	
Website address:	www.
Username:	
Password:	
Specify any benefits you are entitled to receive from this organization, if (e.g. life insurance, pension, etc.):	
Other details of importance:	

Professional, fraternal, union, or other organization

Name of Professional, Fraternal, Union or Other Organization:	
Membership number, if any:	
Individual contact person's name:	
Address:	
City, state, and zip code:	
Work telephone number:	
Mobile telephone number:	
Fax number:	
Email address:	
Website address:	www.
Username:	
Password:	
Specify any benefits you are entitled to receive from this organization, if (e.g. life insurance, pension, etc.):	
Other details of importance:	

Other type of advisor (specify)

What type of advisor (specify)?	
Name of advisor:	
Name of business or group:	
Purpose of business or group:	
Address:	
City, state, and zip code:	
Work telephone number:	
Mobile telephone number:	
Fax number:	
Email address:	
Website:	www.
Username:	
Password:	
Other details of importance:	

Other type of advisor (specify)

What type of advisor (specify)?	
Name of advisor:	
Name of business or group:	
Purpose of business or group:	
Address:	
City, state, and zip code:	
Work telephone number:	
Mobile telephone number:	
Fax number:	
Email address:	
Website:	www.
Username:	
Password:	
Other details of importance:	

Additional notes:

§12-B: Automatic Payments from Your Bank Account

*If you have one or more bills that are automatically paid out of your bank checking or savings account, it is important to let your representative to know about each payment so it can be turned off, or the payments may continue being paid, whether you like it or not. Similarly, you may **not** want certain important payments stopped (e.g. health insurance premiums, utilities, mortgage payments, etc.)*

Your representative will need to know the name of the creditor or the bill being paid, the creditor's account number, and the bank name and checking or savings account number from which the bill is being paid, and how to turn the automatic payments off.

Do you have any bills or other payments being automatically paid from your bank account(s)?	☐ Yes ☐ No **If yes, for each payee, provide the following information below:**

Payee or creditor

Name of payee or creditor:	
Account number:	
Telephone number:	
Describe the bill being paid (e.g. mortgage payment, phone bill, etc.):	
Name of your bank:	
Account number:	
Website address:	www.
Username:	
Password:	
Should these automatic payments be stopped upon your death?	☐ Yes ☐ No
Should payments be stopped if you are incapacitated, but still alive?	☐ Yes ☐ No
What needs to be done to stop these automatic payments?	

Payee or creditor

Name of payee or creditor:	
Account number:	
Telephone number:	
Describe the bill being paid (e.g. mortgage payment, phone bill, etc.):	
Name of your bank:	
Account number:	
Website address:	www.
Username:	
Password:	
Should these automatic payments be stopped upon your death?	☐ Yes ☐ No

Should payments be stopped if you are incapacitated, but still alive?	☐ Yes ☐ No
What needs to be done to stop these automatic payments?	

Payee or creditor

Name of payee or creditor:	
Account number:	
Telephone number:	
Describe the bill being paid (e.g. mortgage payment, phone bill, etc.):	
Name of your bank:	
Account number:	
Website address:	www.
Username:	
Password:	
Should these automatic payments be stopped upon your death?	☐ Yes ☐ No
Should payments be stopped if you are incapacitated, but still alive?	☐ Yes ☐ No
What needs to be done to stop these automatic payments?	

Payee or creditor

Name of payee or creditor:	
Account number:	
Telephone number:	
Describe the bill being paid (e.g. mortgage payment, phone bill, etc.):	
Name of your bank:	
Account number:	
Website address:	www.
Username:	
Password:	
Should these automatic payments be stopped upon your death?	☐ Yes ☐ No
Should payments be stopped if you are incapacitated, but still alive?	☐ Yes ☐ No
What needs to be done to stop these automatic payments?	

Payee or creditor

Name of payee or creditor:	
Account number:	
Telephone number:	
Describe the bill being paid (e.g. mortgage payment, phone bill, etc.):	
Name of your bank:	
Account number:	
Website address:	www.
Username:	
Password:	
Should these automatic payments be stopped upon your death?	☐ Yes ☐ No
Should payments be stopped if you are incapacitated, but still alive?	☐ Yes ☐ No
What needs to be done to stop these automatic payments?	

Payee or creditor

Name of payee or creditor:	
Account number:	
Telephone number:	
Describe the bill being paid (e.g, mortgage payment, phone bill, etc.):	
Name of your bank:	
Account number:	
Website address:	www.
Username:	
Password:	
Should these automatic payments be stopped upon your death?	☐ Yes ☐ No
Should payments be stopped if you are incapacitated, but still alive?	☐ Yes ☐ No
What needs to be done to stop these automatic payments?	

§12-C: Automatic Charges to your Credit Card

*If you have any bills that are automatically charged to your credit card, it is important to let your representative to know about it so the charges can be stopped, or the charges may continue being charged to your account, whether you like it or not. Similarly, you may **not** want certain charges stopped (e.g. health insurance premiums, mortgage payments, etc.)*

Your representative will need to know the name of the creditor or the bill being charged, the creditor's account number, the charge card company and charge card number to which it is being charged, and what needs to be done to stop the automatic charges to your credit card.

Do you have any bills or other payments being automatically charged to your credit card?	☐ Yes ☐ No **If yes, for each payee, provide the following information below:**

Payee or creditor

Name of payee or creditor:	
Account number:	
Telephone number:	
Describe the bill being paid (e.g. mortgage payment, phone bill, etc.):	
Name of your credit card company:	☐ Visa ☐ Master Card ☐ American Express ☐ Other: ____________
Account number:	
Website address:	www.
Username:	
Password:	
Should these automatic charges be stopped upon your death?	☐ Yes ☐ No
Should charges be stopped if you are incapacitated, but still alive?	☐ Yes ☐ No
What needs to be done to stop these automatic charges?	

Payee or creditor

Name of payee or creditor:	
Account number:	
Telephone number:	
Describe the bill being paid (e.g. mortgage payment, phone bill, etc.):	
Name of your credit card company:	☐ Visa ☐ Master Card ☐ American Express ☐ Other: ____________
Account number:	
Website address:	www.
Username:	
Password:	
Should these automatic charges be stopped upon your death?	☐ Yes ☐ No

Should charges be stopped if you are incapacitated, but still alive?	☐ Yes ☐ No
What needs to be done to stop these automatic charges?	

Payee or creditor

Name of payee or creditor:	
Account number:	
Telephone number:	
Describe the bill being paid (e.g. mortgage payment, phone bill, etc.):	
Name of your credit card company:	☐ Visa ☐ Master Card ☐ American Express ☐ Other: ______________
Account number:	
Website address:	www.
Username:	
Password:	
Should these automatic charges be stopped upon your death?	☐ Yes ☐ No
Should charges be stopped if you are incapacitated, but still alive?	☐ Yes ☐ No
What needs to be done to stop these automatic charges?	

Payee or creditor

Name of payee or creditor:	
Account number:	
Telephone number:	
Describe the bill being paid (e.g. mortgage payment, phone bill, etc.):	
Name of your credit card company:	☐ Visa ☐ Master Card ☐ American Express ☐ Other: ______________
Account number:	
Website address:	www.
Username:	
Password:	
Should these automatic charges be stopped upon your death?	☐ Yes ☐ No
Should charges be stopped if you are incapacitated, but still alive?	☐ Yes ☐ No
What needs to be done to stop these automatic charges?	

Payee or creditor

Name of payee or creditor:	
Account number:	
Telephone number:	
Describe the bill being paid (e.g. mortgage payment, phone bill, etc.):	
Name of your credit card company:	☐ Visa ☐ Master Card ☐ American Express ☐ Other: ____________
Account number:	
Website address:	www.
Username:	
Password:	
Should these automatic charges be stopped upon your death?	☐ Yes ☐ No
Should charges be stopped if you are incapacitated, but still alive?	☐ Yes ☐ No
What needs to be done to stop these automatic charges?	

Payee or creditor

Name of payee or creditor:	
Account number:	
Telephone number:	
Describe the bill being paid (e.g. mortgage payment, phone bill, etc.):	
Name of your credit card company:	☐ Visa ☐ Master Card ☐ American Express ☐ Other: ____________
Account number:	
Website address:	www.
Username:	
Password:	
Should these automatic charges be stopped upon your death?	☐ Yes ☐ No
Should charges be stopped if you are incapacitated, but still alive?	☐ Yes ☐ No
What needs to be done to stop these automatic charges?	

§12-D: Subscriptions and Services on Automatic Renewal

If you have any subscriptions or services that are automatically renewed, it is important to let your representative to know about it so the auto-renewals can be stopped. Examples include software subscriptions, magazine subscriptions, gym memberships, and certain service providers (such as lawn care contracts).

Your representative will need to know the name of the company with whom the auto-renewal contract exists, and what needs to be done to stop the automatic renewals.

Do you have any subscriptions or services that are automatically renewed?	☐ Yes ☐ No **If yes, for <u>each</u> payee, provide the following information below:**

Payee or creditor

Name of company:	
Account number:	
Telephone number:	
Describe the service or subscription being automatically renewed:	
How is payment made?	☐ Check ☐ Auto debit from bank ☐ Auto charge to credit card
Specify bank account or charge card:	
Account number:	
Website address:	www.
Username:	
Password:	
Should these automatic renewals be stopped upon your death?	☐ Yes ☐ No
Should renewals be stopped if you are incapacitated, but still alive?	☐ Yes ☐ No
What needs to be done to stop these automatic renewals?	

Payee or creditor

Name of company:	
Account number:	
Telephone number:	
Describe the service or subscription being automatically renewed:	
How is payment made?	☐ Check ☐ Auto debit from bank ☐ Auto charge to credit card
Specify bank account or charge card:	
Account number:	
Website address:	www.
Username:	
Password:	
Should these automatic renewals be stopped upon your death?	☐ Yes ☐ No

Should renewals be stopped if you are incapacitated, but still alive?	☐ Yes ☐ No
What needs to be done to stop these automatic renewals?	

Payee or creditor

Name of company:	
Account number:	
Telephone number:	
Describe the service or subscription being automatically renewed:	
How is payment made?	☐ Check ☐ Auto debit from bank ☐ Auto charge to credit card
Specify bank account or charge card:	
Account number:	
Website address:	www.
Username:	
Password:	
Should these automatic renewals be stopped upon your death?	☐ Yes ☐ No
Should renewals be stopped if you are incapacitated, but still alive?	☐ Yes ☐ No
What needs to be done to stop these automatic renewals?	

Payee or creditor

Name of company:	
Account number:	
Telephone number:	
Describe the service or subscription being automatically renewed:	
How is payment made?	☐ Check ☐ Auto debit from bank ☐ Auto charge to credit card
Specify bank account or charge card:	
Account number:	
Website address:	www.
Username:	
Password:	
Should these automatic renewals be stopped upon your death?	☐ Yes ☐ No
Should renewals be stopped if you are incapacitated, but still alive?	☐ Yes ☐ No
What needs to be done to stop these automatic renewals?	

§12-E: Security Matters

For the numerous types of devices and techniques we use to keep our assets and information secure, if you are the only person to have access to the keys, combinations, codes, or other security techniques, if something happens to you, it will cost your representatives time, aggravation, and money, to try to gain access to the assets and information. They may need to pay a locksmith to drill open a safe, or a technology expert to try to get access to an important encrypted file. In some cases, they may be unsuccessful, and the information may be lost forever!

On the other hand, the reason for the security is to keep our assets and information safe. Therefore, remember to keep the codes, passwords, location of keys, etc. in a safe place, but let someone you trust know where to locate them.

Make an extra copy of this security section. Keep one with your important documents in a safe location such as a safe deposit box. This copy can have the full details including codes, passwords, etc. The second copy should still let your representatives know about the security devices and techniques you use, but omit the security codes, passwords, etc., but let them know how to access the fully-completed copy.

Above all else, use common sense. If you have a safe or lockbox, make sure it is both fire and water proof. If you have a list of passwords, don't leave them lying around the house or office or in a file on your computer that isn't password protected or encrypted. There are some smart thieves out there, but you don't need to make it easy for them to steal from you.

Spare keys

Do you have a set of spare keys for everything requiring a key to open (e.g. home, work, vehicles, storage locker, filing cabinet, wall safe, etc.)?	☐ Yes ☐ No
If yes, where are the keys located?	
Other details of importance:	

Home security

Do you have a home security system?	☐ Yes ☐ No
Location of security alarm panel:	
Name of Security/Alarm company:	
Telephone number:	
Password (for alarm company):	
Is your alarm registered with police?	☐ Yes ☐ No
What is police security code, if any?	

Home safe or lockbox?

Do you have a home safe or lockbox?	☐ Yes ☐ No
If yes, where is it located?	
If a combination lock, what is combination (or who else knows it)?	
If a key lock, where is the key (or who else has a copy of the key or knows where to find it?	

Do you have one or more guns, rifles, etc.?

Do you have weapons of any type?	☐ Yes ☐ No
If yes, for **each** weapon, describe the type of weapon:	
Where is the registration form, if any:	
Do you use a gun lock?	☐ Yes ☐ No
If yes, where is key located, or what is the combination?	
Do you have a gun safe or lockbox?	☐ Yes ☐ No If yes, ☐ Key lock ☐ Combination lock
If yes, where is key located, or what is the combination?	
Do you have a gun Trust (a legal document)?	☐ Yes ☐ No
If yes, where is it located?	
Other details of importance:	

Home computer encryption and/or password

Is your home computer encrypted?	☐ Yes ☐ No
If yes, what is the encryption code?	
What is computer password or code?	
Does your computer have a firewall?	☐ Yes ☐ No
If yes, provide details:	
Security software name:	☐ Kaspersky ☐ McAfee ☐ Avast ☐ Other: ____________
Website:	www.
Username:	
Password:	
Additional security software:	

Digital data storage security

Do you use an external hard drive or storage device for data and files?	☐ Yes ☐ No
If yes, where is it located?	
What is the password?	
Do you use cloud-based storage or backup services for your data and important documents?	☐ Yes ☐ No
If yes, what service to you use?	☐ iCloud ☐ Google ☐ One-Note ☐ Mozy ☐ Carbonite ☐ Other: ____________
If yes, website:	www.
Username:	
Password:	
Other security details:	

Work/Office security

Is there a workplace security system?	☐ Yes ☐ No
Location of home security panel:	
Name of security/alarm company:	
Telephone number:	
Alarm company password:	
If your alarm is registered with the police, what is the password?	
Card or code to get into garage/lot:	
Keyless door entry code:	
Swipe card location:	
Other details of importance:	

Security regarding digital and electronic equipment

Cell phone password or code:	
PIN number, if any:	
If finger scan, which finger?	
Alternate if swipe doesn't work?	
Is there an optical (eye) scanner?	☐ Yes ☐ No

Password storage

Do you store your passwords on a separate **password manager** app, site, digital file, device or paper file?	☐ Yes ☐ No
If yes, identify it and where it is located:	☐ Name of password manager app or program: ______________________ ☐ Spreadsheet ☐ Stored on my home computer ☐ Stored on my office computer ☐ Stored on an external device: ______________________ ☐ Written document ☐ Other: ______________________
Provide details on how to access your passwords:	

Miscellaneous security

Entry code to gated-community gate:	
Entry code to garage door, if any:	
Keyless front door entry code, if any:	
Keyless automobile door keycode:	
ATM debit card PIN code	
Family password or phrase used to confirm a message (e.g. to your child) is really coming from you, or that the person delivering it can be trusted:	

§12-F: Email addresses, Internet Accounts, Websites, and Passwords

*This information should be kept in a **safe place**, such as a safe deposit box. Just write a note on this page (without the passwords) indicting where this important information can be located. Much of this information is also included in the Digital Assets section, but having the location in both places will help to prevent your representatives from missing important sites.*

***Remember**, access to your online accounts by others may be **illegal** without your written authorization. Be sure that your estate-planning documents include language authorizing your representative in your Trust, Will, and/or Power of Attorney documents have the legal authority to access, modify, terminate, and/or distribute these assets.*

EMAIL ADDRESSES

Personal email address 1

Email address:	
Website:	www.
Username:	
Password:	
Security Question(s):	
Answer(s):	
Security picture, icon, or phrase:	
Other details of importance:	

Personal email address 2

Email address:	
Website:	www.
Username:	
Password:	
Security Question(s):	
Answer(s):	
Security picture, icon, or phrase:	
Other details of importance:	

Personal email address 3

Email address:	
Website:	www.
Username:	
Password:	
Security Question(s):	
Answer(s):	
Security picture, icon, or phrase:	
Other details of importance:	

Work email address 1

Email address:	
Name of employer:	
Is employer consent required?	☐ Yes ☐ No
If yes, name of contact person:	
Phone number of contact person:	
Website:	www.
Username:	
Password:	
Security Question(s):	
Answer(s):	
Security picture, icon, or phrase:	
Other details of importance:	

Work email address 2

Email address:	
Name of employer:	
Is employer consent required?	☐ Yes ☐ No
If yes, name of contact person:	
Phone number of contact person:	
Website:	www.
Username:	
Password:	
Security Question(s):	
Answer(s):	
Security picture, icon, or phrase:	
Other details of importance:	

Work email address 3

Email address:	
Name of employer:	
Is employer consent required?	☐ Yes ☐ No
If yes, name of contact person:	
Phone number of contact person:	
Website:	www.
Username:	
Password:	
Security Question(s):	
Answer(s):	
Security picture, icon, or phrase:	
Other details of importance:	

INTERNET ACCOUNTS AND WEBSITES

Internet account or website

Name of website:	
Type of website:	☐ Work ☐ Social Media ☐ Banking ☐ Investment ☐ Insurance ☐ Music ☐ Cloud storage ☐ Gaming ☐ Other: ________________
Website:	www.
Username:	
Password:	
Security Question(s):	
Answer(s):	
Security picture, icon, or phrase:	
What do you want done with the contents of this account/website?	☐ Terminate account ☐ Delete pictures ☐ Sell/Transfer site ☐ Other: ________________
Other details of importance:	

Internet account or website

Name of website:	
Type of website:	☐ Work ☐ Social Media ☐ Banking ☐ Investment ☐ Insurance ☐ Music ☐ Cloud storage ☐ Gaming ☐ Other: ________________
Website:	www.
Username:	
Password:	
Security Question(s):	
Answer(s):	
Security picture, icon, or phrase:	
What do you want done with the contents of this account/website?	☐ Terminate account ☐ Delete pictures ☐ Sell/Transfer site ☐ Other: ________________
Other details of importance:	

Internet account or website

Name of website:	
Type of website:	☐ Work ☐ Social Media ☐ Banking ☐ Investment ☐ Insurance ☐ Music ☐ Cloud storage ☐ Gaming ☐ Other: ________________
Website:	www.
Username:	
Password:	
Security Question(s):	
Answer(s):	
Security picture, icon, or phrase:	
What do you want done with the contents of this account/website?	☐ Terminate account ☐ Delete pictures ☐ Sell/Transfer site ☐ Other: ________________
Other details of importance:	

Internet account or website

Name of website:	
Type of website:	☐ Work ☐ Social Media ☐ Banking ☐ Investment ☐ Insurance ☐ Music ☐ Cloud storage ☐ Gaming ☐ Other: ________________
Website:	www.
Username:	
Password:	
Security Question(s):	
Answer(s):	
Security picture, icon, or phrase:	
What do you want done with the contents of this account/website?	☐ Terminate account ☐ Delete pictures ☐ Sell/Transfer site ☐ Other: ________________
Other details of importance:	

Internet account or website

Name of website:	
Type of website:	☐ Work ☐ Social Media ☐ Banking ☐ Investment ☐ Insurance ☐ Music ☐ Cloud storage ☐ Gaming ☐ Other: ________________
Website:	www.
Username:	
Password:	
Security Question(s):	
Answer(s):	
Security picture, icon, or phrase:	
What do you want done with the contents of this account/website?	☐ Terminate account ☐ Delete pictures ☐ Sell/Transfer site ☐ Other: ________________
Other details of importance:	

Internet account or website

Name of website:	
Type of website:	☐ Work ☐ Social Media ☐ Banking ☐ Investment ☐ Insurance ☐ Music ☐ Cloud storage ☐ Gaming ☐ Other: ________________
Website:	www.
Username:	
Password:	
Security Question(s):	
Answer(s):	
Security picture, icon, or phrase:	
What do you want done with the contents of this account/website?	☐ Terminate account ☐ Delete pictures ☐ Sell/Transfer site ☐ Other: ________________
Other details of importance:	

Internet account or website

Name of website:	
Type of website:	☐ Work ☐ Social Media ☐ Banking ☐ Investment ☐ Insurance ☐ Music ☐ Cloud storage ☐ Gaming ☐ Other: ________________
Website:	www.
Username:	
Password:	
Security Question(s):	
Answer(s):	
Security picture, icon, or phrase:	
What do you want done with the contents of this account/website?	☐ Terminate account ☐ Delete pictures ☐ Sell/Transfer site ☐ Other: ____
Other details of importance:	

Internet account or website

Name of website:	
Type of website:	☐ Work ☐ Social Media ☐ Banking ☐ Investment ☐ Insurance ☐ Music ☐ Cloud storage ☐ Gaming ☐ Other: ________________
Website:	www.
Username:	
Password:	
Security Question(s):	
Answer(s):	
Security picture, icon, or phrase:	
What do you want done with the contents of this account/website?	☐ Terminate account ☐ Delete pictures ☐ Sell/Transfer site ☐ Other: ____
Other details of importance:	

Internet account or website

Name of website:	
Type of website:	☐ Work ☐ Social Media ☐ Banking ☐ Investment ☐ Insurance ☐ Music ☐ Cloud storage ☐ Gaming ☐ Other: ________________
Website:	www.
Username:	
Password:	
Security Question(s):	
Answer(s):	
Security picture, icon, or phrase:	
What do you want done with the contents of this account/website?	☐ Terminate account ☐ Delete pictures ☐ Sell/Transfer site ☐ Other: ____
Other details of importance:	

Internet account or website

Name of website:	
Type of website:	☐ Work ☐ Social Media ☐ Banking ☐ Investment ☐ Insurance ☐ Music ☐ Cloud storage ☐ Gaming ☐ Other: ______________
Website:	www.
Username:	
Password:	
Security Question(s):	
Answer(s):	
Security picture, icon, or phrase:	
What do you want done with the contents of this account/website?	☐ Terminate account ☐ Delete pictures ☐ Sell/Transfer site ☐ Other: ______________
Other details of importance:	

Internet account or website

Name of website:	
Type of website:	☐ Work ☐ Social Media ☐ Banking ☐ Investment ☐ Insurance ☐ Music ☐ Cloud storage ☐ Gaming ☐ Other: ______________
Website:	www.
Username:	
Password:	
Security Question(s):	
Answer(s):	
Security picture, icon, or phrase:	
What do you want done with the contents of this account/website?	☐ Terminate account ☐ Delete pictures ☐ Sell/Transfer site ☐ Other: ______________
Other details of importance:	

Internet account or website

Name of website:	
Type of website:	☐ Work ☐ Social Media ☐ Banking ☐ Investment ☐ Insurance ☐ Music ☐ Cloud storage ☐ Gaming ☐ Other: ______________
Website:	www.
Username:	
Password:	
Security Question(s):	
Answer(s):	
Security picture, icon, or phrase:	
What do you want done with the contents of this account/website?	☐ Terminate account ☐ Delete pictures ☐ Sell/Transfer site ☐ Other: ______________
Other details of importance:	

COMMON WEBSITE SECURITY OR PASSWORD RESET CHALLENGE QUESTIONS	ANSWERS
Your mother's maiden name:	
Your father's middle name:	
What grade school did you attend?	
What high school did you attend?	
What was your high school mascot?	
What was the make of your first car?	
On what street did you live as a child?:	
Name of your first pet:	
In what city were you born?	
First name of your best friend:	
First name of your first boyfriend or girlfriend:	
What is your favorite movie?	
What is your favorite color?	
When is your anniversary?	
What is the name of your favorite pet?	
What was your favorite place to visit as a child:	
Which phone number do you remember most from your childhood?	
Who is your favorite actor, musician, or artist?	
What is the name of your first grade teacher?	
Oher security questions you use: 1. 2. 3. 4.	Answers: 1. 2. 3. 4.
Security icon (picture) you use:	Specify:
Security phrase you use:	Specify:

§12-G: My Investment Strategies

In the event I am unable to manage my own investments, I would like my decision-makers to utilize the following general approach to managing my investments (check all that apply, even if one investment strategy may seem to be inconsistent with another).

Risk tolerance

On a scale of 1 to 5, as an investor I am (check one):	☐ 1. I am ultra-conservative - I would lose sleep if I lost a penny. ☐ 2. Conservative – I am willing to risk a little to get a higher return. ☐ 3. Moderate – I believe in a balanced approach between stocks, bonds, mutual funds, cash, and other investments. ☐ 4. Aggressive – I am willing to take more risk to principal in return for the hope of a higher return (e.g. more in stocks than in bonds). ☐ 5. Speculative – I'm willing to take high risk with some, but not all, of my money, in the hopes of making a high return, but I'm not talking about gambling.

Preference for income-producing investments

I like **income-producing** investments (check all that you'd find acceptable, if any):	☐ Investment real estate (including real estate investment trusts (REIT)
	☐ Individual "Blue Chip" Stocks (e.g. S&P 500)
	☐ Individual utility stocks (e.g. electric, gas, water, oil)
	☐ Master limited partnerships (MLPs traded on stock exchange)
	☐ Stock Mutual Funds
	☐ Exchange-Traded Index Funds (ETFs traded on stock exchange)
	☐ Individual Bonds
	  ☐ U.S. Government Bonds (maximum maturity _____ years)
	  ☐ Corporate Bonds – AAA, AA, A, BBB (circle lowest rating)
	  ☐ Tax-Free Municipal Bonds – AAA, AA, A, BBB (circle lowest rating)
	  ☐ Other (specify): ______________________
	☐ Taxable Bond Mutual Funds
	  ☐ U.S. Government Bond Funds
	  ☐ Quality / Investment Grade Bond Funds
	  ☐ Hi-Yield (Junk) Bond Funds
	  ☐ Convertible Bond Funds
	  ☐ Developed Country Bond Funds
	  ☐ Emerging Market Bond Funds
	  ☐ Other (specify): ______________________
	☐ Tax-Free Municipal Bond Mutual Funds
	  ☐ AAA and/or Insured bond funds only
	  ☐ Quality / Investment-Grade Bond funds only
	  ☐ Hi-yield (Junk) bond funds
	  ☐ Other (specify): ______________________
	☐ Other: ______________________
	☐ Other: ______________________

My preferences and strategies

My investment preferences and strategies (check all that apply):	☐ I prefer growth in value to income, even if this means taking more risk; ☐ I prefer income over growth; ☐ I like growth and income ☐ I prefer tax-free and tax-advantaged investing, when possible ☐ I prefer paying lower capital gains tax rates over ordinary income tax rates, even though it requires me to hold an investment for over a year. ☐ I am a buy-and-hold investor, and I am willing to hold-on and ride-out market volatility ☐ I like tangible assets (e.g. real estate, gold, jewelry, antiques, art, etc.) ☐ I am a market timer, and prefer to get in and out of an investment to take quick profits (or losses), even though it results in higher taxes ☐ Other strategies: (Describe)

My investment time horizon

What is your investment time horizon (i.e. Other than an emergency, how long will you typically invest in an investment strategy)?	☐ 0-3 years ☐ 3-5 years ☐ 5-10 years ☐ 10-20 years ☐ 20+ years

Individual Securities

Do you have possession of individual stock or bond certificates?	☐ Yes ☐ No
If yes, where do you keep them?	
Do you own U.S. Govt **savings bonds**?	☐ Yes ☐ No
If yes, where do you store them?	

Dividend reinvestment (DRIP) plans

Do you participate in a publicly-traded company dividend reinvestment plan (also called DRIP plans)?	☐ Yes ☐ No If yes, provide the following details for each DRIP plan:
Name of company:	
Identify where shares are held:	
Telephone number:	
Account number:	
Website:	www.
Username:	
Password:	
Other details of importance:	

Stocks held at transfer agent (e.g. Computershare)

Do you have stocks held at a transfer agent (e.g. Computershare)?	☐ Yes ☐ No If yes, provide the following details for each stock and transfer agent:
Name of company stock:	
Name of transfer agent:	
Telephone number:	
Account number:	
Website:	www.
Username:	
Password:	
Other details of importance:	

Miscellaneous investments and investment strategies

Do you own illiquid, non-publicly-traded securities, such as individual limited partnerships, real estate investment Trusts (REITs), etc.?	☐ Yes ☐ No If yes, provide details:
Do you use stop-loss orders?	☐ Yes ☐ No If yes, provide details:
Do you use limit orders?	☐ Yes ☐ No If yes, provide details:
Do you use margin to leverage your investment accounts?	☐ Yes ☐ No If yes, provide details:
Do you buy or sell options or use option strategies?	☐ Yes ☐ No If yes, provide details:
Do you trade futures?	☐ Yes ☐ No If yes, provide details on types of futures:
Do you invest in commodities?	☐ Yes ☐ No If yes, provide details on types of commodities:
Do you invest in precious metals (gold, silver, gems, etc.)?	☐ Yes ☐ No If yes, provide details on types of investments, including where you store them:
Other types of investments:	

§13-A: My Life Story & Interesting & Fun Things I'd Like My Loved Ones to Know about Me

These are some fun topics (in random order) that future generations might like to know about you. There isn't enough room to respond to each, but you may want to consider responding to each on additional pages. Create a story about each including the people who were involved, when and where it took place, what memory is triggered when you think about it, why it is important to you, and anything else you can tell them to bring the memory alive for them. And, of course, be sure to add your own "special memory" categories.

Miscellaneous thoughts and memories (in no particular order of importance)

What is your life motto?	
What are your favorite inspirational quotes?	
What makes you happy?	
What was the best day of your life?	
What talents do you possess? (e.g. sing, dance, art, math, sports, gardening, photography, etc.):	
What do you consider to be the most significant accomplishments of your life and why?	
Discuss genetic or inherited medical conditions that run in your family:	
Discuss any records, genealogy information, or photographs that might be valuable to other family members:	
As a child, what is the worst thing you did, and you "got away" with it?	
Who is the first girl/boy you ever kissed, and whatever happened to him/her?	
What is your very first memory?	
Who were your best friends as a child?	
Who are your best friends as an adult?	
What is the best advice you have been given, and by whom?	
What life lessons have you learned that you want to share with future generations?	
What is in your "bucket" list (i.e.	

what did you want to do that you never got around to doing)?	
Reveal any fun secrets about yourself?	
What was your most embarrassing (funny or memorable) moment?	
Where did your family come from and when & how did they come to live in America?	
Do you recall any interesting, funny, awe-inspiring, heroic, or other fascinating stories about members of your family to share with future generations?	
How did you meet your spouse?	
How did you propose marriage or how did you spouse propose to you?	
What is your favorite form of relaxation?	
If you could have changed just one thing in your life, what would it be?	
Family secrets that need to be disclosed (but please don't destroy someone's life with this information):	
Are you especially grateful for someone or something extra special in your life?	
What is the nicest thing anyone ever did for you?	
What is the nicest thing you ever did for someone else?	
What happened that made you laugh so hard that you snorted?	

Your favorite memories

About your parents:	
About your brothers/sisters:	
About your children:	
About your grandchildren:	
About your spouse:	
About other family members:	

About yourself:	
About your pet(s):	
About your childhood:	
About your grade school:	
About your high school:	
About your college:	
About your religion:	
About your job(s):	
About previous relationships:	
About your hobbies:	
Other favorites:	

Miscellaneous favorites

Your favorite family pictures (and the stories behind them – be sure to attach the pictures):	
Your favorite family videos:	
Your favorite songs and musician:	
Your favorite music genre:	
Your least favorite music:	
Your favorite automobile:	
Your favorite poems:	
Your favorite movies and actors:	
Your favorite theatrical productions:	
Your favorite books and authors:	
Your favorite party:	
Your favorite foods:	
Your favorite "pig-out" food:	
Your favorite snack food:	
Your favorite recipes:	
Your favorite vacation memories:	
Your favorite friends:	
Your favorite teachers:	
Your favorite perfume/cologne:	
Your favorite charities:	
Other favorites:	

§13-B: Your Ethical Will, Your Final Thoughts, and Your Final Wishes

*An **Ethical Will** is **not** a formal estate-planning document. It is not legally binding, and will not override contrary provisions contained in your estate-planning documents. There are no special requirements, such as having it witnessed or notarized.*

It allows you to share your story; your morals; your values; your beliefs and opinions; your accomplishments; discuss principals which are important to you; lessons you have learned from your life experiences; lessons you have learned from other individuals (family, friends, employers, strangers); your hopes for the future; your final wishes; and it allows you to leave something meaningful behind so your family and future generations will have an insight as to what your life was all about.

In addition, while it is intended to be a message of love, it can be used to try to anticipate conflicts that may arise about your preferences and choices, and what your loved ones might argue about when you can no longer explain your intentions. It is designed to help reduce family conflict about your wishes. It can also be a tool to distribute sentimental assets, such as family photographs, recipes, and other items of personal, if not financial, value.

In addition to preparing your Living Will, consider having a family meeting to discuss the contents, and what your intentions are regarding various matters, such as why one child is getting more money than another, repayment (or forgiveness) of family loans, why one person is named as trustee and not another (and to confirm that person wants the responsibility. It is better to discuss as many potential sources of conflict while you are still alive and lucid, rather than risk having your family tear itself apart trying to guess what you really wanted, and your intentions behind what you have stated in your legal documents.

The suggestions provided below are intended to guide you through some of the topics you may want to include in your own ethical will. Add whatever additional topics you feel are appropriate.

There is no required or recommended format for an Ethical Will. It can be created as a formal written document, a diary, blog, audio or video recording, scrapbook, or any other method to share your thoughts.

*Since this document can be used to help resolve future conflict, and **not** to hurt someone or create additional conflict, be sure to try to keep your comments and thoughts positive and helpful.*

Potential topics to discuss in your ethical will

What are your final wishes (about ANYTHING)?	
Final words of love to your loved ones:	
Words of wisdom and life lessons learned that you would like to share with your loved ones and future generations:	
What do you consider to be your most important accomplishments in your life, and why?	
How would you like to be remembered by your friends & family?	
Your morals & principals that are important to you, and why:	
Discuss your values:	

Discuss the importance of religion in your life:	
What goals and dreams do you hope your loved ones will accomplish in their lives?	
What was your biggest surprise in life?	
Explanations and/or apologies to anyone whom you may have hurt or wronged:	
Words of forgiveness to anyone who may have hurt or wronged you:	
Discuss your feelings about other topics you anticipate your loved ones may argue about:	
Secrets you may not have disclosed to your family, which they **need** to know:	
What family stories from previous generations have been passed on to you that you would like to pass on to future generations?	
Discuss important decisions you have made regarding health, family, and others:	
Below, add any other matters you'd like to discuss or share:	

Your preferences

What are your preferences regarding burial vs. cremation vs. donating your body to science?	
If you have chosen cremation, do you have a preference on what is to happen to your ashes?	
If you are determined to be brain dead, what are your preferences about being kept alive by a machine? Should they "pull the plug?" Should they continue feeding and hydrating you, or should they just "let you go?"	
Explain unequal distributions of your estate between your children:	
Explain why you may have left nothing to a child in your Will or Trust:	
Explain why you may have chosen one person over another as your legal representative in your various estate-planning documents (e.g. one lives closer, one has more experience, etc.):	
Do you have a preference as to a nursing home or other facility?	
If you become incapacitated, what are your preferences about being kept at home versus residing in a facility (consider financial & emotional cost to your loved ones)?	
If, in the future, you are suffering from dementia, do you have a preference as to the medical care you are to receive and where you are to reside?	
If you have given anything of financial or sentimental value to one child, knowing that someone else wanted to receive it, specify the item, when you gave it, and why you did so:	
If you lent money to a child, have you forgiven that debt? Or do you expect it to be repaid?	
Add any other explanations, thoughts, and preferences you'd like to discuss or share:	

§14-A: Additional Space for More-Detailed Answers to Questions

Use this space to provide more comprehensive information and details about answers to questions asked in the questionnaire (or attach as many additional pages as necessary to provide details or answers).

Identify the section or page number and the topic or question you are answering. Add as many pages as needed to provide your loved ones and representatives the information they require to take care of you and your affairs.

Section Number: Page Number: Topic or Question:	
Section Number: Page Number: Topic or Question:	
Section Number: Page Number: Topic or Question:	
Section Number: Page Number: Topic or Question:	
Section Number: Page Number: Topic or Question	
Section Number: Page Number: Topic or Question:	

§14-B: Has Anything Been Missed?

Since we all have our own varied and unique lives, it is impossible to have included everything. So, if there are other details or information not listed elsewhere in this questionnaire, make notes of those details here.

If you believe these categories or subjects would benefit future readers of this questionnaire, please email your suggestions to Info@MyEverythingFile.com.

Thank you for taking the time to complete this questionnaire. Your loved ones will greatly appreciate your efforts on their behalf, and will enjoy any of the insights and stories about your life you may have shared!

Thank you for all your hard work in completing this questionnaire! Your loved ones will thank you for it!

Made in the USA
Middletown, DE
18 February 2024

49479388R00252